N

Key

Frontiers of Muscovy
at 1645

Maximum line of advance
at 1656

Tot'ma

ogda

Kostroma

Nizhnii Novgorod

Vladimir

enskoe

Kolomna

uga

a

rsk

Belgorod

COVY

Kazan

Arzamas

Simbirsk

R. Volga

BASHKIRS

R. Ural

SIBERIA

Saratov

R. Don

R. Volga

R. Emba

ARAL
SEA

Tsaritsyn

KALMYKS

DON
COSSACKS

Astrakhan

R. Don

Azov

Sea of Azov

CAUCASUS

CASPIAN SEA

a

PIRE

Miles

0   100   200

PERSIA

Alexis
Tsar of All the Russias

Alexis
Tsar of All the Russias

—◆—

PHILIP LONGWORTH

Franklin Watts
New York · 1984

ISBN 0-531-09770-6

Library of Congress Catalog Card
Number: 84-50633

Printed in Great Britain by
St Edmundsbury Press
Bury St Edmunds, Suffolk
and bound by
Mackay's of Chatham

Time in its irresistible and ceaseless flow carries along in its flood all created things, and drowns them in the depths of obscurity. . . . But the tale of history forms a very strong bulwark against the stream of time, and checks its irresistible flow to some extent. . . . It secures and binds together, and does not allow them to slip away into the abyss of oblivion.

– *Anna Comnena,* The Alexiad
(trans. E. R. A. Sewter)

To My Father and Mother
Leon and Cecilia

Contents

List of Illustrations

Preface

Soviet Russia today is still recognizably the descendant of Alexis's Russia, despite all the changes that have taken place over the last three centuries and more. Nonetheless many aspects of the world Alexis knew would seem strange to most contemporary Russians and even stranger to Westerners. Not only was it pre-industrial, but the organization of society, the pace of life, the modes of thought (or at least the expression of thought) were all dissimilar. Alexis reckoned time in a different way from the way we do; he spoke and wrote a language more obscure and less malleable than modern Russian; some of his beliefs and assumptions would seem impenetrable to most people today. His world therefore requires interpretation – and it is difficult to interpret without distortion. Inevitably I have had to make compromises.

Time presented the least of the problems. Muscovites reckoned the years from the supposed creation of the world and began them on 1st September. Days began at sunset and the clock was divided into hours of the day and night, the numbers of which varied according to the season. All this I have converted (though not the dates, which ran ten days behind the modern calendar). Thus the first hour of the day on 31st August 7168 becomes dawn on 31st August 1660; the first hour of the night on 2nd September 7169 becomes dusk on 1st September 1660.

Weights and measures sometimes proved trickier. I have generally converted them into their nearest English (imperial) equivalents, but Muscovites sometimes found measurements too rigid and tended to stretch them in order to fit circumstances and their sense of equity. Thus the unit of land known as the *chetvert'*, usually rendered as an acre and a third, might be four acres (if, in a three-field system, two-thirds of it lay fallow) or even five and a half acres (if applied to land which required extra labour or produced lower

xi

yields). Monetary values, of which Muscovites had several, I have converted into familiar rubles and kopeks, but I have not attempted to define exchange rates with other currencies, except occasionally with the imperial thaler.

Offices and ranks also posed problems. I have tried to explain my renderings the first time each is used, but some, like *voevoda* (which can mean 'military commander' or 'governor') and *strelets* (a military category which has no English parallel), I have translated differently according to the context or simply left in the original. I realize that some of my translations (e.g. 'sub-boyar' for *okol'nichii*) are clumsy, but I have been unable to think of more elegant expressions which would not mislead.

More daunting problems still derive from the fact that seventeenth-century Russian was not a standard or literary language. Alexis himself often had to grope for words and build up convoluted verbal constructions in attempts to convey what he had in mind when he found no vernacular phrase, bureaucratic expression or familiar quotation from the liturgy or Bible that would serve his purpose. A study of his use of language would have helped me, but so far as I know none has been written. As it is I have often found it difficult to distinguish between those of his expressions which are original and those which are not (sadly, some of his most vivid similes and metaphors turn out to be clichés). Furthermore one should not read Alexis and his contemporaries too literally. To 'weep' might only mean to be stirred emotionally or touched; to have a 'vision' or see an 'apparition' probably meant no more than to have an inspiration or to be struck by an idea. And since the overwhelming majority of books available to those few Muscovites who could read were church books, ideas which might nowadays be thought to be fundamentally secular tended to be expressed in religious terms.

But, beyond this, Russians at that time understood a language of imagery that had no need for words. Every saint stood for some quality or value; every icon had its message; and to make a public pilgrimage was to make a public declaration. Pomp and ceremony were also intended to convey messages, of course. When foreign envoys laughed at the fantastic protocol surrounding the Tsar's falcons they had simply failed to take the point.

There was a great deal of colour and music in Alexis's life, though most of the music sounded strange to Western ears, and I have tried to give some impression, however pale, of colour and atmosphere.

But historical imagination, essential though it is if one is to leap over such vast barriers of time and space, must be reined by evidence. Hence, if in this book bells are rung from time to time then it is on record that they rang at those times and in the ways I have described; and if a description of a confusing scene such as a riot or a battle should seem improbably detailed, those details are nevertheless wholly consistent with the surviving descriptions of eyewitnesses and contemporaries.

It remains for me to acknowledge my helpers, both institutions and individuals. The Phoenix Trust gave me support in a time of need; the British Academy and the USSR Academy of Sciences enabled me to visit the USSR in 1978; and the Delmas Foundation funded my research in Venice. I am also grateful to the staffs of the various archives and libraries where I worked: the Central State Archive of Ancient Acts and the Lenin Library in Moscow; the State Russian Museum in Leningrad (which helped me with Alexis's portraiture); the Bodleian and the British Library; the Library of the School of Slavonic Studies, the Skaryna Belorussian Library, the State Archive, Venice and the Oratory, Birmingham. I am indebted for advice, help and correction to members of the Moscow Institute of History (*sektor feodalizma*) and the Medieval and Eighteenth Century Study Groups of the British Universities' Association of Slavists, to J.G.S. Simmons and, above all, to Mme Liudmilla Aleksandrovna Nikitina and the late Professor Anne Pennington. I am grateful to Mark Hamilton and Tom Rosenthal for their quiet encouragement and great patience, and to those of my students at McGill University who asked penetrating questions. But my greatest debt is to my wife. She has borne with Alexis, and with me, through many vicissitudes and contributed much trenchant but constructive criticism.

P.L.

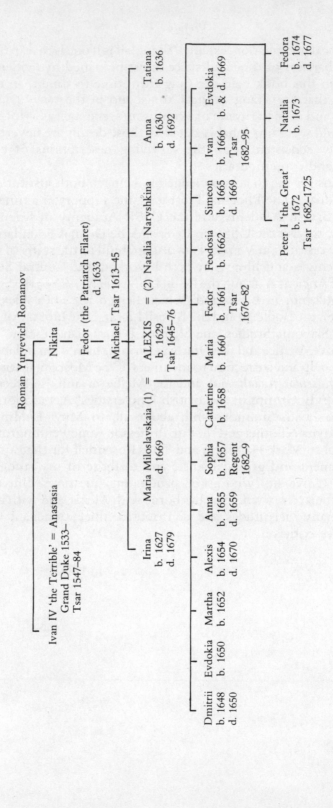

Roman Yuryevich Romanov

Ivan IV 'the Terrible' = Anastasia
Grand Duke 1533–
Tsar 1547–84

Nikita

Fedor (the Patriarch Filaret)
d. 1633

Michael, Tsar 1613–45

Irina
b. 1627
d. 1679

Tatiana
b. 1636

Anna
b. 1630
d. 1692

Maria Miloslavskaia (1)
d. 1669

ALEXIS = (2) Natalia Naryshkina
b. 1629
Tsar 1645–76

Dmitrii
b. 1648
d. 1650

Evdokia
b. 1650

Martha
b. 1652

Alexis
b. 1654
d. 1670

Anna
b. 1655
d. 1659

Sophia
b. 1657
Regent
1682–9

Catherine
b. 1658

Maria
b. 1660

Fedor
b. 1661
Tsar
1676–82

Feodosia
b. 1662

Simeon
b. 1665
d. 1669

Ivan
b. 1666
Tsar
1682–95

Evdokia
b. & d. 1669

Peter I 'the Great'
b. 1672
Tsar 1682–1725

Natalia
b. 1673

Fedora
b. 1674
d. 1677

Introduction

On 24th February 1710, shortly after winning his famous victory over the Swedes at Poltava, Peter the Great ordered a record to be made of all the surviving papers from his father's Private Office. It was a sudden gesture of filial piety towards a father who had died when Peter was only a child and whom he could barely have remembered. As a result a number of caskets, chests and boxes which had been gathering dust for more than thirty years in an obscure corner of the Moscow Printing Office were removed to Peter's Private Chancery and opened up. They revealed quantities of musty documents – the relics of a life, the detritus of a career.

There was a profusion of notebooks, letters and orders (some in draft), diaries, chronicles and reports. There were seemingly endless lists of payments, purchases and petitions (some with decisions scribbled in the margins), a whole boxful of foreign printed matter (much of it rotten or eaten away by mice), transcripts of trials and investigations, sheets of music, sketches, doodles, prayers, astrological forecasts, cipher books, some none-too-successful attempts at writing verse, and scores of maps. Three years passed before the register was complete.[1] The collection reflected its owner's interests, and these ranged widely – from sport and horticulture to medicine and drama; from religion and history to ballistics and the exploration of the world. The papers made it obvious that he had a keen visual sense and an ear for music; and some items in his own hand suggested that he may have had a subtle mind and a sensitive spirit. Together they indicated that as a Tsar he had not been devoid of energy, passion, and persistence. It was clear that Peter really was Alexis's son and not, as many believed, a changeling.

But although Peter himself was curious about his father, and tried to measure his own reputation against his (he once asked someone who had served them both which of them had done more for their

1

country – and received a predictably circumspect reply[2]), Alexis has been neglected by posterity, and still lacks a biography that does him justice.[3] It is ironic. The Tsar under whom Muscovy emerged as a power of European significance, and Russians traversed the icy wastes of Siberia to reach China and the Pacific; the Tsar in whose name the army was modernized and large parts of Ukraine and Belorussia were annexed; the Tsar who presided over the final enserfment of the peasantry and the great schism in the Church, who issued a Code of Laws that was to stand for almost two centuries, and who survived repeated assaults upon his throne, has attracted less serious attention than his associates and ministers. It is odd; but it is explicable.

One reason was the lack of material from which to reconstruct his life. Until the middle of the nineteenth century his archive was shielded from the prying eyes of historians, and the public records were insufficient for the purpose. Alexis had been a more august and exclusive person than Peter, and in his day the palace had been enveloped in secrecy. His public appearances had been mostly ceremonial and unrevealing, and the official acts of his reign contained scant indications of the extent to which he had personally directed policy. Beyond that there was little more than rumour – true or false, inspired or seditious, who could tell? So it was with justification that in 1854 one writer who attempted to assess his reign remarked that the paucity of sources made it impossible to write a full life of Alexis.[4] Shortly thereafter more of Alexis's letters were published (a few had appeared in an obscure journal some years before) and some of the Private Office papers too,[5] but it was not until the turn of the twentieth century that scholarly interest was revived. More of the Private Office papers were printed[6] and the first historical monographs based upon them appeared.[7] However, these tended to follow the current vogue for institutional history or concentrated on a single aspect of Alexis's activity at the expense of others. There was still no rounded picture of the man.

The other reason for the neglect of Alexis was the overwhelming reputation of Peter himself. If, as the westernizers believed, Peter had yanked Russia out of mediaeval torpor and launched it into the mainstream of European life; if Peter (in the words of the oration given at his funeral) had brought his country out of darkness into light, then Alexis must belong to the world of darkness. He might be given some credit for certain 'westernizing' tendencies, but otherwise he was abandoned to the obscurity of Peter's shadow.

The cult of Peter produced a reaction, of course. But the Slavophiles who believed that Russia had taken the wrong turning under Peter were content to hold Alexis up as a symbol of what they took to be the traditional Russian values. They pictured him in hagiographical fashion as a pious Tsar, sweet-natured but fundamentally passive. This image persisted. According to an historian of religion, Alexis 'was perhaps the only man worthy to wear the holy crown. Most quiet, most pious, almost a saint – he astounds us with the strength of his faith, his child-like purity of heart and his thirst for truth.' [8] Alexis has remained an icon for the nostalgic to this day; even Soviet Russia does not lack grown men whose eyes will fill with tears at the mention of his name.

There is evidence to support such a view of him (although Alexis also pursued his search for truth into the torture chamber, to interrogate suspects), and it was recognized by historians with less idealistic views of the past. Solov'ev describes Alexis as good-natured, soft – possibly the 'most attractive phenomenon' to occupy the throne of Russia. But then he makes his saintliness explicable by divesting him of all authority: 'Much of what seems pristine in his character,' he assures us, 'was actually weakness . . . [hence] the key to government rested not with him, but with a series of favourites.' Kliuchevskii follows suit, implying that Alexis was neglectful, a puppet of the boyars, surrounded by a crowd of worthless favourites; and Platonov, while paying lip-service to the icon, compiles an impressive list of denigrating adjectives – weak-willed, weak-spirited, lacking in energy, incapable of hard work and (of course) over-dependent on a succession of favourites.[9]

Liberal Russian historians of the late nineteenth and early twentieth centuries could hardly be said to have understood practical politics as well as they understood constitutional principles, least of all practical politics in times of revolutionary crisis (and Alexis's reign was a series of crises). Nevertheless Western historians have continued to parrot their views.[10] As for Soviet scholars, they have devoted attention to the events and developments of his reign (not only the rebellions and the conquests but cultural trends, the centralization of government and the re-establishment of autocratic rule), but paid little to Alexis himself. The reason is not simply ideological (even though Alexis was a sort of capitalist). Peter the Great, Ivan the Terrible and even Boris Godunov have all been the subjects of recent, and to a degree sympathetic, Soviet biographies.[11] More probably it is a consequence of historiographical inertia; and the fact that the Private Office papers have lately become the subject of a restoration programme holds out hope that interest in Alexis may be revived.

Meanwhile, however, we are left with a series of enigmas: Alexis the attractive weakling; Alexis the saintly nonentity; Alexis the paper autocrat. But what is the truth? Early in the nineteenth century a Scot who had lived in Russia and wrote a conscientious book about it suggested that Alexis's merits may have been 'too much overlooked by historians, and particularly by the adulators of Peter the Great'.[12]

So was Alexis really a puppet of the boyars, a figurehead hovering high above the turmoil of rebellions and wars – or could he have been a manipulative politician, a calculating strategist? Was he lazy, or determined? What aims and ambitions did he have? Could it be that he did as much as Peter to mould the fate of Russia? And was he truly as pious and as gentle as they say? Could it be that the ceremonial face he paraded in public was only a mask, and that a re-examination of the evidence might reveal the true, but hidden, Alexis? The reader with the patience to follow this story to the end may draw his own conclusions.

Chapter I

The Education of a Prince

In the small hours of Thursday, 10th March 1629, the Kremlin bells began to ring. One by one every church and monastery in Moscow took up the call until the atmosphere seemed heavy with their drone and the ground seemed to shake with their vibration; and in the days and weeks that followed, upon instruction from the highest authority, every belfry in the realm of Muscovy pealed out its signal for rejoicing.

The occasion was the birth of an infant prince. After five years of marriage the Tsaritsa Evdokia, Tsar Michael's second wife, had at last presented him with an heir. Romanov rule, established only sixteen years before, might now survive; the state of Muscovy, still recovering from its collapse at the beginning of the century, had acquired some prospect of a stable future.

Immediately after the birth the baby was measured, washed, and swaddled; then delivered into the arms of a wet-nurse who had been carefully examined both for the quality and abundance of her milk and her freedom from any taint of witchcraft.[1] It was shown to its delighted father and blessed, with particular fervour, by the aged Filaret, Patriarch of Moscow – for Filaret was also the baby's grandfather. A magnate and politician who had turned cleric late in life, he was reputedly the most powerful man in Russia, more powerful even than his son the Tsar, and it was Filaret who arranged the christening and who chose the baby's name. The name he lighted upon conjured up all the qualities he hoped the infant prince would be endowed with: it was Alexis.

There were two saints of that name: St Alexis the Man of God, whose day was celebrated a week after the birth; and another with two feast days in the Russian calendar, a saint revered for qualities beyond mere godliness – a scholar and a Russian patriot who in the fourteenth century had schemed and striven to bring stability to the

5

realm and increase its territories.[2] It was in this saint's monastery – the Miracle Monastery – that the infant was to be christened.

The palace was abustle long before the christening. Cooks and cellarmen prepared a series of elaborate celebratory banquets; seamstresses in the palace work-rooms laboured over decorative wraps and bedding suitable for an infant prince; clerks in the palace treasury took careful note of all the gifts that streamed in – gem-encrusted crucifixes and caskets fashioned out of precious metals; reliquaries (including one containing the supposed remains of the martyred princes Boris and Gleb) and a pair of tiny pistols; jugs of silver gilt and crystal; golden drinking dishes; the figure of a bird inlaid with gold; bundles of sables, rolls of precious cloths, and from Filaret a purse containing 150 gold pieces.

On the day of the christening the church bells, the greatest in Christendom, rang all day. The baby, ten days old, was brought to the Miracle Monastery in a closed carriage escorted by boyars and noblemen. His godmother, Filaret's sister, carried him into the nave, where, before a multitude of dignitaries, the Tsar's chaplain immersed him in the font three times, placed a little salt in his mouth, anointed his forehead, chest and hands with oil, and placed a golden cross with the image of St Alexis around his neck. The ceremony concluded, the prince was borne back to his swansdown cot with its fur-lined coverlet bedecked with velvet ribbons.

Everything possible was done to promote the baby's contentment and his healthy growth. Under the supervision of *boiarina* Arina Nikitichna Godunova (a widow noted for her piety and common-sense) a bevy of nursemaids tended the infant, bathed him, played with him, sang him lullabies and rubbed him with sweet-scented lotions prepared in the palace pharmacy. But although the baby lived separately from his parents, he was by no means isolated from them. Indeed before he was four months old little Alexis accompanied the rest of the family on its annual pilgrimage to the Trinity–St Sergius monastic centre some fifty miles from Moscow.

By the time he returned special quarters had been fitted out for him in the palace, and there, during the months that followed, screened from the rude gaze of the public, he steadily extended his acquaintance with the world. His environment was a bright one, full of colour: drapes with intricate patterns of plants and animals; the glitter of jewels; and, through windows, the sight of the busy river that flowed beside the Kremlin walls and, farther off, the rolling, wooded countryside. Gradually his ear became attuned to a variety of human voices, to the sound of musical instruments, and to snatches of sung liturgy that drifted in from the palace chapels. His fingers explored an increasing variety of objects – the carved wood of furniture, the decorative tiles that encased the huge stove in the corner of the room, and a succession of toys designed to improve his manipulative skills and provoke his curiosity.

Alexis's babyhood was brief. He was quickly weaned and soon out of swaddling clothes – whereupon he was immediately dressed as a miniature adult. By the time he was a year old his wardrobe included a red silk-satin cap lined with sable, a fur coat two feet in length and sixteen inches across the shoulders, a silk coat for the spring and a stock of vests, breeches and stockings. Precocity was almost forced upon him: he was equipped with a special frame with four stout iron wheels to help him learn to walk; with his own salt cellar and drinking scoops to encourage him to feed himself; with games (including one that involved hurling silver darts at a target on the ground) to improve his coordination and with a fine rocking-horse of German manufacture complete with velvet saddle and all accoutrements. The processes of learning and amusement went hand in hand. One day his father took him to see the wonderful gilded organ he had had installed with its mechanical cuckoos and nightingales that popped out and sang upon command; there were play-times with his older sister Irina, running about the palace gardens; watching the caged goldfinches and linnets; poring over intriguing prints and pictures imported from Germany, with which they were regularly provided; listening with rapt attention to stories told them by retainers skilled in telling tales.

The Tsar's jesters in their red and yellow liveries were also deputed to amuse them; there were romps with the palace dwarfs, and performances by conjurors. In the autumn of 1631, when Alexis was two and a half years old, one of the palace guards showed him some tricks, the precise nature of which goes unmentioned in the sources, and at about the same time he watched, together with his father, while the jester Ivan Lodygin performed an act with falcons designed to make them laugh. This was the little prince's induction to the royal sport of falconry, which was to be one of his chief passions later in life. Indeed from that point on every experience he was exposed to seems to have been planned with his future role in mind.

Martial qualities were especially encouraged. In September 1631 he was given a miniature sabre and a fine bow with a quiverful of arrows. And by the time he was three he was the proud possessor of a truly royal outfit: a coat of gold atlas, decorated with pearls; a long-sleeved riding coat with fastenings made of pearls and crystal; a magnificent pearl-studded collar; and a pair of pearl-encrusted velvet boots. He was also allotted his own chaplain, a priest called Alexander, who conducted evening and morning prayers for him and for Irina in a special chapel, explained Christian observance to them, and the significance of each different saint whose icon was brought out each day. Henceforth Alexis attended early mass on festivals with his parents and observed the dietary restrictions during the four great fasts of the Orthodox year.

Religious practice inured the child to routine and discipline; it gave him a sense of the way in which God had shaped the year; it lent a rhythm to his life through regular prayer and the observance of fasts and festivals, and it provided ritual outlets for emotion. It also helped equip him to be Tsar, for, as with the Byzantine Emperors of old, a Russian Tsar was legitimized by his Orthodoxy: he was God's agent on earth, the secular shepherd of the Muscovite flock, and only his piety allowed him to carry out the sinful business of government without endangering his soul.

By the time old Filaret died in October 1633 he must have been well satisfied with his grandson's progress, for Alexis at four and a half was a promising and eager child. Indeed the time was already deemed appropriate to launch him into the society of other boys and to prepare him for his formal education. Thus it was that the regime of Governess Godunova gradually gave way to a new one, supervised by a man of prominent family who had many years' experience as a functionary at the court. His name was Boris Ivanovich Morozov. Boris's shrewdness (not least in money matters[3]), his acquaintance with the machinery of state and his progressive views, exemplified by his predilection for western European expertise and fashions at a time when the vast majority of Muscovites viewed all things Western with suspicion, fitted him for the responsibility of bringing up the prince. Curiously enough, although Boris had a genuine respect for learning, he was a man of little or no education himself. But then his task went much wider than mere book-learning: he had to induct Alexis into the adult world and equip him generally to be a Tsar.

Boris had already come into contact with the child. In February 1633, for example, he had accompanied the family on its annual pilgrimage to the Trinity–St Sergius monastic centre at Zagorsk.

But their meetings now became more frequent. Later the same year Boris brought the child two toy swords, perhaps to have him taught the elements of fencing. He also arranged for the child to see a performance of bear-baiting. (We know this because the huntsman who baited the bear had his caftan torn and indented for a new one.) And meanwhile Boris, in association with Vasily Ivanovich Streshnev, a kinsman of Alexis's mother, selected eighteen small boys as playmates for the prince, and had them fitted out in uniform liveries and equipped with drums and tambourines. Alexis, who was also the proud possessor of drums and sticks, could now march about at the head of his own band. And companions were now available, at his bidding, to play ball, to admire his German pictures or his model ship, and, in winter, to go tobogganing with him (two toboggans were made for him that autumn and five sleds the next).

Despite the forty years that separated them, a firm friendship was to develop between the Prince and his Governor. Alexis was always to regard Boris with affection, gratitude and respect. As for Boris, his appointment was to prove the gateway to power and to incredible wealth. Their relationship established, Boris was elevated to the rank of boyar, took his place on the Tsar's Council (the Duma), and launched Alexis in earnest on the path of learning. One day in May 1634, shortly after the boy's fifth birthday, he entered his charge's room bearing a book bound in yellow silk. It was a primer; and with the primer came the tutor, Vasily Prokofiev, who was to teach Alexis the alphabet and how to read.

The primer was almost certainly a version of that compiled under Filaret's supervision two years before[4] (the actual book which Alexis used has disappeared long since), and it emphasized an ordered, step-by-step approach, beginning with an admonitory verse:

Take this book, thou clever boy
And start to climb from the lowest to the topmost steps.
Be not lazy or careless in thy studies
And always pay attention to thy teacher . . .
Begin with the letter A that thou seest here.
Afterwards, under teacher's guidance, thou wilt proceed to others.

Every letter was accompanied by sayings associated with the life of Jesus, and the readings were graded for difficulty. The primer was also equipped with an elementary grammar, and since numbers were still represented by letters rather than Arabic numerals, the basic elements of mathematics were taught at the same time.

In the same month that his schooling started Alexis was given a swing, presumably as a sweetener. He was also furnished with his own court in miniature and taught how to be the master of it. Twenty boys of good family (several of them very probably seconded from his corps of drummers) were appointed to serve him as gentlemen-in-waiting and gentlemen of the bedchamber. They were at once his servitors and friends; and they may have shared in his lessons. Some of them, like his kinsman Afanasy Matiushkin, were to become life-long friends.[5] Yet he was already hedged about by protocol. He now had an ante-room where his guests sat in order of precedence on benches placed around the walls – although he was still to sleep in a cot until he reached the age of eight.

By September 1635 Alexis had mastered the elements of reading (for which achievement his teacher was rewarded with a pair of sables), and he proceeded to the next stage: learning the Book of Hours – by rote and in a sing-song fashion. Five months later he started on the Psalter, and three months after that he was launched into the Acts of the Apostles. By the time he was seven he could read quite fluently, and was deemed ready to embark on the next stage of his education: learning how to write.

For this he had a different teacher – Gregory L'vov, an Under-Secretary in the Foreign Office (a department of state noted for its calligraphy); he was provided with a pen, paper, ink and sand, and with a different primer, which set out each letter in its different forms, provided lively colour illustrations of key words, and short passages to copy out. Inevitably, these were chosen to instil proper attitudes and moral precepts: 'A wise man not given to books is like a bird without wings'; 'He who wishes to learn much must sleep little and please his master'; 'Charity does not consist merely in the giving of alms, but in offending no-one and offering no-one evil for evil'; 'He is of strong mind who is not given to strong drink'; 'Turn thy face from strange women and do not converse much with them'.

Such extracts from the Church's wisdom and literature were interlaced with Bible stories, about King David the Psalmist and King Solomon the Wise – stories which demonstrated that successful rulers were those who pleased God; meanwhile his reading was extended to embrace the Books of Proverbs and Ecclesiastes (which he was often to quote in later life), the wisdom of Solomon and of Joshua. He also became well acquainted with the lives of Russia's favourite saints – St Stephen of Perm, who had mastered all learning within a year; St Abraham of Smolensk, who had fasted ceaselessly and was devoted to books; St Sabbas, who exemplified the harmony of prayer, work and charity; the holy patriot St Sergius, of course, and others. But riddles were also used with didactic purpose:

Question: What is the height of the heavens, the breadth of the earth and the depth of the sea?
Answer: The Father, the Son, and the Holy Ghost.

No doubt Alexis would proudly communicate such discoveries to his sisters (besides Irina there was also Anna, a year younger than himself), though his infant brother Ivan, more than four years his junior, was too young and too sickly to appreciate such cleverness.

Meanwhile, Alexis was introduced to other activities designed to further his physical proficiencies and heighten his mental agility: riding (on a succession of ponies carefully graded to suit his size); archery and swordsmanship; backgammon and chess. Deportment too: when he was eight a certain Ivan Semenov was deputed to teach him and some of his companions 'how to walk about rooms, and dance, and play various games'. But although Alexis owned a Polish lexicon there is no evidence that any foreign language featured in the curriculum. At the age of eight, however, a new subject was introduced: cantillation. It was taught by three singing deacons (presumably to illustrate the harmonies), and Alexis took eagerly to this subject too, for he liked music. Two stringed instruments had been numbered among his toys for three years now; his sense of rhythm had long been fostered by the songs his nurses had sung to him, and, more recently, by playing with his band of drummers. He also owned a set of seventeen copper bells and, later on, he was to acquire a rebeck, though there is no evidence that he ever learned to play it. But church singing did fall within his capability and music was to remain an abiding interest throughout his life.

According to Professor Platonov, Alexis's education 'in effect ended' with his study of cantillation.[6] But this was not the case at all. Musical studies had a purpose beyond mere entertainment or the reinforcement of piety. As in the Byzantine Empire (from whose educational principles Alexis's own schooling obviously derived), savants regarded music as a science akin to mathematics, and the gateway to astronomy and other advanced subjects.[7] So far from his studies ending at the age of nine, they were extended, given a more secular orientation, and apparently quickened in their pace – for at this point Boris Morozov allotted a boy of exceptional intelligence and four years Alexis's senior to share his lessons and so bring him on the faster. This was Artamon Matveev, the son of a non-noble official in the Foreign Office,[8] and despite Matveev's plebeian origins he was to enjoy Alexis's friendship and his deepest trust until death parted them.

Together they now embarked on a course of studies which can be reconstructed in outline from occasional references in palace and ministry records. We know that books and experts were assigned to the Tsarevich on a temporary basis from various government departments – chiefly those concerned with military and foreign affairs, for these were the main repositories in Muscovy of know-ledge about the wider world and disposed of the expertise to trans-late foreign works of learning. The principles which guided Boris Morozov in structuring these studies were doubtless utilitarian – a sufficient knowledge of military organization and weaponry, of international affairs, and of governmental precedents to equip Alexis, some day, to take charge as Tsar. But since so many of these things required explanations in some detail, the two boys were soon immersed in quite extensive studies, including the elements of several sciences as well as history and geography.

As early as 1637, for example, no fewer than twenty-nine scien-tific works, dealing with mathematics, mechanics, hydraulics and astronomy, had been borrowed from the Artillery Office library for this purpose.[9] And references to such subjects in Alexis's writings in later life lend support to the view that he received some grounding in them at an early age. We know, too, that among the books he owned in childhood was a cosmography describing the world as it was then known; and use was also made of the extensive survey of Muscovy drawn up for the government two years before Alexis was born. This listed every town in the realm, with its distance (in travelling time) from Moscow, and was a mine of information on the human and economic, as well as the physical, geography of the Tsardom, besides including data on its neighbours, the Khanates of Central Asia, Persia, and the Ottoman Empire.[10]

Alexis's geographical studies were given life by objects made in foreign lands, by personal accounts of travellers abroad, and by the sight of foreigners. Some impressions of the worlds of the West, and of the Orient, were conveyed by German engravings, by various artefacts in his possession (like the figurine of a lion holding a snake in its paws presented by an English merchant in 1629, and his

Persian inkwell), by items of furniture about the palace and the famous Kremlin clock built by Christopher Galloway. Such things also gave Alexis some appreciation of the best of both western and oriental workmanship. And, thanks to Boris, he sometimes wore clothes and shoes which were made in the German fashion. Furthermore, Matveev's own father had visited foreign lands, and presumably Alexis also met other officials who had been abroad. When he was ten, Boris arranged for him to have sight, from a secret hiding place, of formal receptions of foreign embassies. Thus, at a relatively tender age, the future Tsar was able to observe the dress, manners and physiognomies of representatives of such diverse states as Poland and Persia, Turkey and Sweden, besides learning about the niceties of diplomatic protocol.

History formed an important segment of his education, though it was of the patriotic rather than the critical sort. Since childhood Alexis had heard stories of the half-mythical past of the Russian land and of the heroes who had defended it. This knowledge was extended by readings from selected Russian chronicles, and supplemented by smatterings of ancient history (it is clear that he knew about Alexander and Julius Caesar, for example). Then recent history came to figure more prominently, and merged with current affairs. He was surely acquainted with the monk Avraamy Palitsyn's account of Russia's period of chaos earlier in the century – a work redolent of the deep-felt xenophobia those times had produced. He certainly learned about that traumatic juncture when law and order had broken down so completely that Catholic Poles had come to rule in Moscow, from Boris himself and others of his generation who had lived through it. And what Alexis learned from them gave him a firm purpose for the future: to protect the Russian land from foreign predators and to regain all those territories which it had lost.

Such considerations undoubtedly preoccupied the adult world about him. Only a few years before, Muscovy had fought an expensive and unsuccessful war in an attempt to wrest the city of Smolensk back from the Poles; and since 1638 the Tatars had been mounting destructive raids into southern Russia. Three years later the Cossacks, who had captured the citadel of Azov from the Tatars' overlords, the Turks, offered it to the Tsar; but in January 1642 it was decided that Muscovy could not afford to go to war in order to hold it, and young Alexis shared the general disappointment. (Boris had furnished him with wooden clogs which had been made in Azov.)

There was no lack of examples of heroic and victorious monarchs which the boy might take to be his models. Many were depicted in the murals which at that time decorated the state reception rooms in the Kremlin. There he saw Gideon battling with the Amalekites, King David and the other Kings of Israel, depictions of the Emperor Augustus and of Constantine the Great. But if Alexis felt a special affinity to one image above all others it was to one on the right-hand wall immediately by the entrance to the Hall of Gold. It was a picture of a young Tsar, in full regalia, looking towards the figure of Christ the Saviour, who was stretching out both hands to bless him and his sceptre. The young Tsar was Ivan the Terrible – Ivan who had conquered the Tatar Khanates of Kazan and Astrakhan; Ivan who had led his victorious armies to the shores of the Baltic Sea (territories which had since been lost). Here was an example for Alexis to emulate, and a recent one at that, for Ivan had been Muscovy's last effective and successful ruler. Reminders of Ivan were to be found almost everywhere. Even when he went on pilgrimage to the tomb of St Sergius at Zagorsk, for the Cathedral of the Assumption hard by it had been built to commemorate Ivan's victories.

The murals in the state rooms (not least the one which glorified Ivan) also helped the young Tsarevich to grasp some essential elements of political philosophy: that a Tsar's authority derived directly from God; that he was responsible to God for the welfare of his flock; that a Tsar's authority was (or should be) absolute, but that he must dispense charity and mercy as well as justice, and protect the Christian faith if he was to earn success and gain a place in heaven. It was a concept which consciously derived from Byzantium. And Alexis learned to understand it through books as well as iconography. A copy of the Emperor Basil I's supposed advice to his son and successor Leo VI, which emphasized the moral behaviour expected of a monarch, came into his possession. Indeed, some passages from it had been included in his father's coronation speech. Advice of a more practically political kind derived from *The Secret of Secrets* – advice supposedly given by Aristotle to Alexander the Great.

Although the book is thought to have been black-listed in Muscovy, several copies existed. Alexis's father certainly owned one of them and no doubt Alexis had, or came to own, one too. From Alexis's actions, and the phrases which tripped off his pen in later years, it is certain that he was well acquainted with its contents

– though one cannot tell precisely when he first read it. Among a
host of other recommendations concerning matters pertaining to
health and the occult, *The Secret of Secrets* in its Muscovite versions
suggested that a monarch should command obedience by inspiring
awe and obtain loyalty through dispensing kindness; that he heed
the advice of his counsellors; that he uphold the law and be even-
handed in administering justice; that he concern himself with the
welfare of his soldiers, promote men, including commoners, to
high rank on the bases of merit and loyalty alone, and keep the
nobles under control. It also urged a ruler to employ foreigners as
spies, to make use of maps and inventories and, somewhat less
practically, told him how to forecast the outcome of a battle by
means of numerology.[11]

So, Alexis's education continued well into his teens. Indeed, since
he had become a voracious reader and retained his curiosity, it
continued, albeit on an informal and unstructured basis, well into
his manhood. But how effective was his education? Insofar as it
produced an alert, inquiring mind in a healthy, active body it was
splendidly effective. It was effective also in providing Alexis with a
sound moral sense and a religious discipline which was to promote
psychological stability and a holistic outlook on the world. It has
been characterized as unsystematic,[12] yet from what is known about
the order of Alexis's studies it had a system, albeit traditional, that
was well suited to its purpose. It did, however, create certain intellectual impediments. These were inherent in the state of the Russian
language at the time. An amalgam of Old Church Slavonic and
demotic speech, this language was by no means the precise instrument for the communication of ideas that it was later to become.
Moreover, educated Russians had inherited the rhetorical style of
the middle Byzantine period, using words for the sheer pleasure of
them, so that sheer verbosity often tended to obscure a line of
argument. Learned clerics tended to lavish adjectives on nouns and
to load texts down with learned quotations. Instructions drafted by
bureaucrats were tediously repetitive. Furthermore, Alexis had to
straddle two distinct value systems: one that was theologically and
morally oriented; the other which was secular, practical, and down-
to-earth. The authority of a Tsar rested equally on both; and it
would be Alexis's essential function to maintain them both in
harmony.

On 1st September 1642, the date of the Muscovite New Year, the
thirteen-year-old Alexis made his first public appearance. Until

then, as at his christening, he had always been sheltered from the public gaze, but now, resplendent in a red tunic, yellow silk caftan, pearl collar and gem-encrusted cloak, and holding a bejewelled staff made in India, he sat upon an ivory throne beside his father to receive the season's greetings from some of the greatest men in the land.[13] Alexis's entry on to the public stage was a formality; but it was useful politically and had a constitutional purpose too.

The regime was under pressure. Tsar Michael, no longer protected by Filaret's authority, was not perceived to be a charismatic figure; and so the appearance of this well-made, gracious youth beside him lent some glamour to his rule. The other reason was the problem of succession. Alexis's younger brother Ivan had died four years before; his mother had borne another male child but it had not survived, and she was now past the age of bearing children. Alexis had three sisters – Irina, now in her sixteenth year, Anna, aged twelve, and little Tatiana, aged seven – but in male-dominated Muscovy it was inconceivable that any of them could succeed. Hence all hopes of continued Romanov rule rested with Alexis alone. But even here there was a problem.

Ever since the original, Riurikid, dynasty had died out at the end of the previous century, Tsars had been elected by an Assembly of the Land. This had been the case with Boris Godunov, with Vasilii Shuiskii, and with Michael himself. But to make the succession subject to an election might invite party strife and perhaps another civil war. On the other hand, for Michael simply to bequeath the throne to Alexis in his testament, which had been the procedure under the old dynasty, might not prove enough to guarantee a smooth and unchallenged transition of power to Alexis when Michael died. It seemed advisable, therefore, to associate him publicly with his father (rather as Byzantine Emperors of old had associated their chosen successors with them in government) in the hope that in the course of time Alexis would come to be generally regarded as the natural, obvious and hence legitimate successor to the Tsardom.

Alexis's role was purely ceremonial, but the number of his ceremonial appearances was soon increased. On 6th January 1643 he went with his father in open procession to the Cathedral and down to the bank of the River Moscow for the traditional Blessing of the Waters ceremony held every Epiphany.[14] During the following spring he was frequently to be seen with the Tsar, riding out to hunt on the royal estates around Moscow; and on 6th January 1644 he actually took his father's place in the Epiphany ceremony.

There is reason to suppose that this increasing weight of duty thrust upon a lad barely into his teens was also due to the Tsar's poor health. It also helped to mask a general sense of insecurity which pervaded the inner sanctums of the court – an insecurity which found expression in the fear of plots. The year before a full-scale enquiry had been launched into an alleged attempt to harm the Tsaritsa;[15] and in June 1643, when Tsar Michael was bled for St Anthony's Fire, the blood was carefully buried in the garden outside his room by two of his most trusted boyars,[16] presumably to prevent any possibility of its being used for witchcraft by anyone who wished him ill.

Nonetheless Alexis seems to have carried out these official duties without any sign of tension – indeed with panache and charm as well as dignity. And his charm was particularly evident in carrying out one duty of some diplomatic importance – the entertainment of Valdemar, Count Guldenlere, the morganatic son of King Christian IV of Denmark. Valdemar arrived in Moscow on 21st January 1644, and Alexis undertook a prominent role in his reception. He extended formal greetings to him at a great banquet, held in the Kremlin's grandest state reception room, known as the Hall of Facets, and attended by the Danish and Habsburg Ambassadors;[17] he had a number of informal and friendly conversations with him through an interpreter; and he took him hunting.[18] Alexis's role was purely social, but important political issues hung upon the visit.

The idea of a marriage between Valdemar and Alexis's sister, Irina, had first been broached two years before and Tsar Michael was delighted with it. Such a union would cement a friendship between Muscovy and a state which not only occupied a strategic position on the flank of rival Poland but commanded the straits between the Baltic and the North Sea, and thus the trade routes to the West – invaluable for Russian commerce should a foothold on the Baltic be regained. It would also provide Irina with a husband and, it was hoped, with male children who might continue the line should Alexis die prematurely. Michael's assurance that Valdemar would be accorded the same honour as was due to Alexis himself, and his words of welcome to him: 'You will take the place of my son who died', lend some credibility to this view.[19] But one major obstacle stood in the way: Valdemar was a Protestant and, while happily accepting the considerable sums provided by his hosts to maintain him and his entourage in Moscow (they numbered three hundred), he adamantly refused to be baptized into the Orthodox Church.

The Patriarch was equally insistent that he should be. So was Boris Morozov; so was public opinion insofar as it was cognizant of the affair. But Tsar Michael had his heart set on the alliance, and he would not let go. Repeated efforts were made to persuade Valdemar – a programme of cajolery and blandishment in which Alexis himself took some minor part. Disputes were held between Valdemar's chaplain and Orthodox priests, and, as the pressures upon him increased, Valdemar asked permission to return home. It was refused. The Danes tried to suborn Russian courtiers. One suborner was discovered, and banished to the Arctic north. Valdemar tried to escape, and was restrained. The atmosphere grew extremely tense. Valdemar, though officially a guest, was in fact a prisoner in the Kremlin. Everyone involved (not least poor, hopeful Irina) felt anxious and sour.[20]

It was in these circumstances that on 28th March 1645 Alexis tried to raise his father's spirits by staging a little entertainment for him. It took the form of a comedy act of the slapstick variety – a mock fight between one of his mother's footmen and a jester called Isai. Alexis was pleased enough by the performance to award the footman cloth to the not inconsiderable value of two rubles;[21] but the Tsar, though doubtless appreciative of this sign of his son's affection for him, remained out of sorts and depressed. Alexis had been representing his father on several public occasions recently,[22] and the need was to continue.

On 23rd April the Tsar was examined by his doctors. They diagnosed a scurvy, a chill and congestion; attributed his condition to restricted blood-flow caused by mucus accumulating in the stomach, spleen and liver; prescribed a concoction of herbs and roots mixed with hock, and put him on a diet. The treatment failed to work, however, and after a month they examined him again. He was complaining of pain in the upper abdomen. They decided that this was due to malfunctions of the liver and spleen, which had been weakened by the Tsar's 'lack of activity, cold drinks, and melancholy'. More medicines and an embrocation were prescribed and, a few days later, fumes were applied to his ear to relieve his headache.[23] The Tsar's condition did not improve, but when the end came it was unexpected.

On the evening of 12th July 1645 Alexis was sent for. His father

had collapsed. He rushed to join his distraught mother at the bedside. It being obvious that the end was close, the Patriarch and the
senior boyars were summoned urgently. It was reported that on his
death-bed Michael declared Alexis to be his successor and entrusted
him to the care of Boris Morozov,[24] but it is impossible to tell for
certain what, if anything, he said. What is certain is that Michael
died that night.[25]

A solitary bell began to toll; the Tsaritsa and the womenfolk
broke out in seemingly endless sobbing; and a bemused Alexis
noticed (as he reported some years later) that his father's belly had
'stirred and rumbled' just before he died.[26] He was as close an
observer of death as he was of life.

Meanwhile urgent business had been attended to. Alexis's second
cousin, Nikita Romanov, had at once been sent into the ante-
chamber to take the oath of loyalty to him and to his mother, and to
press the assembling notables to follow his example. Throughout
the rest of that night and in the days that followed, oaths of allegiance were administered to every member of the Council, every
court servitor, soldier and civil servant that could be found in the
city.[27] Clerks laboured ceaselessly copying out messages to be sent,
in Alexis's name, to every local governor in the realm, informing
them that Michael had 'left the earthly kingdom for the Kingdom of
Heaven' and that Alexis had 'been made Tsar' in accordance with
his father's command, with the approval of the Council, and with
the blessing of the Patriarch. Central government's representatives
in the provinces were further enjoined, having sworn loyalty themselves, to assemble 'all ranks of service people' in church and see to it
that they also swore to serve Alexis and his mother as they had
served his father.[28] There was no question of Alexis being elected
Muscovy's Tsar by a parliamentary Assembly of the Land (*Zemskii
sobor*), as wishful-thinking historians trying to trace Russia's
chances of a democratic evolution have sometimes imagined.[29] It
remained to be seen, however, if his assumption of the crown would
be recognized as legitimate.

There were certainly some Muscovites who did not think it was.
Ten years before, an abbot of a monastery, Archimandrite Feodorit,
had suggested that Alexis might be a changeling, and there had been
investigations into other seditious mutterings as well. People had
been overheard saying that the Tsaritsa Evdokia had been too old to
bear a male child when she married, and that Alexis was 'a spurious
Tsarevich'. Peasants in one district were said to have been seen

carrying a man on a litter, who wore a 'crown' and whom they addressed as 'Tsar';[30] and now, in 1645, a hermit near the city of Suzdal' was to be denounced for claiming that Alexis was 'no Tsar but the horn of Antichrist', and one Michael Pushkin for saying that Alexis had 'made himself Tsar . . . without their electing him'.[31]

As yet Alexis knew nothing of this; and in any case he was absorbed in the ritual of mourning: receiving the condolences of the black-clad notables as they filed past the open coffin to pay their last respects; trying to console his mother and sisters; following the Patriarch and bishops, and the coffin, in the funeral procession; dipping a spoon into the honeyed porridge which constituted the traditional funerary meal; and attending daily prayers beside his father's tomb. Attempts were made to shield him in his grief. Official orders and requests were made that he should not be troubled during the forty-day period of mourning. Nonetheless he was. The question of what to do with Valdemar was still outstanding and had to be resolved and so, five days after his bereavement, Alexis was advised to give the Dane an audience and once more broach the subject of his conversion. But Valdemar was still adamant and, later the same day, submitted another formal request for permission to return home. The matter was referred to the Council and the Patriarch. Not surprisingly, they decided to let him go.[32] Irina, having lost her father, had now lost her hope of marriage too.

A less forgivable intrusion on Alexis's privacy was attempted by the Polish Ambassador, who demanded that Alexis give a dinner in his honour. When reminded that he had just been orphaned, the Pole retorted that his King had invited Muscovite ambassadors to dine after his Queen had died. It was pointed out that grief at the loss of a wife only lasted till re-marriage and that a man might marry several times, whereas Alexis had only one father. Nevertheless, on 9th August, he was required to grant the Poles a farewell audience with the full formalities in the Hall of Gold[33] – a task which must have been all the more difficult to carry out, burdened as he was with concern about his mother.

The Tsaritsa Evdokia had fallen into a decline since her bereavement; and on 18th August she, too, passed away. The sixteen-year-old Alexis had been doubly orphaned within five weeks. On 1st September he made his first public appearance as Tsar when, dressed in black from head to toe, he played his part in the New Year celebrations, for which he could have had but little heart. A few days later he left Moscow for Zagorsk, on pilgramage (going the last few miles to St Sergius's tomb on foot). There he prepared himself, through prayer and fasting, to assume the burden of the crown.[34]

The coronation, already once postponed, was fixed for 28th September – the very first day after the conclusion of his mourning. Such haste was necessary. Until he received God's sanction by being anointed and crowned (and until all those who mattered had pledged their loyalty all over again) his authority as Tsar was only provisional, and the government remained in limbo. The old administration, dominated by the powerful Sheremetev family, and especially by Fedor Sheremetev who ran two key departments of state – the most important finance ministry and the *Streletskii Prikaz* which controlled the guards regiments – still lingered on. But Alexis trusted Boris above all the rest and, although a Council member, Boris as yet held no such important post. Alexis dared not dismiss ministers and appoint new ones until he was crowned; until he was crowned those in office were shy of exerting their authority to cope with the problems that confronted the state. And these were urgent.

The Tatars had resumed their raids that year. They were repulsed, but there was mounting discontent among the gentry servicemen who bore the main burden of the country's defence. They were complaining that they could not afford to equip themselves or turn out for active service as long as so many of their peasant serfs, who were supposed to maintain them, were flitting. If they were to fulfil their duty to the state, therefore, these peasants must be bound to them by law for ever. The peasant serfs, on the other hand, looked to the Tsar to liberate them from bondage. And, waiting in the wings, hoping to exploit another social upheaval, was a Polish pretender to the throne of Muscovy, funded by the Polish King.[35] Chroniclers noted 'many portents' on earth and in the sky that year which boded ill for Russia.[36] And the sixteen-year-old Alexis seemed but a frail protector.

But on the day of his coronation, he emerged from the palace clothed brilliantly in red, white and gold, and walked in procession between lines of *strel'tsy* guardsmen to the Cathedral of the Dormition in the Kremlin. As he entered, the choir struck up, intoning the prayer for longevity, and, as he climbed onto the dais, the Patriarch sprinkled him with holy water and pronounced a blessing. The ceremony had begun and ushers ensured that the congregation, which included representatives of a wide section of society, were silent and attentive. In due course Alexis read out his coronation speech. He referred to his illustrious predecessors – to Riurik, legendary founder of the Russian state, to St Vladimir, who had brought it Christianity, to Vladimir Monomakh, grandson of the Byzantine Emperor Constantine IX, and to others. There were two significant omissions, however: Boris Godunov and Vasilii Shuiskii. Alexis was creating the impression that he was somehow inheriting the crown from Ivan the Terrible through his son, 'our ancestor', the childless Tsar Fedor. There followed an implicit warning in the form of a reminder about 'the state of ruin' into which the country had fallen after Fedor's death; and then a tribute to his late father, the pious Michael, who had kept 'all Orthodox Christians in peace and tranquillity'. Finally, he justified his succession by saying that his father had 'blessed' him 'with the Tsardom' and that the Patriarch was crowning him in obedience to his father's command.

The speech took over fifteen minutes to deliver. Then the Patriarch spoke, and at even greater length. Alexis, he told the congregation, was 'beloved and chosen by God' to be Tsar and Autocrat. He wished him spiritual and bodily prosperity; expressed the hope that he would 'shine forth like the sun among the stars'; that he would preserve the Christian faith, keeping the Tsardom in the same state of piety and purity as he now received it from God; and that he would love truth, and rule justly and mercifully. He also said something else which was to stick in Alexis's mind; 'Thou art set up as Tsar. Strive also to be a Tsar inwardly, over thyself.'[37]

The climax of the ceremony arrived. Alexis was blessed with a crucifix made from the True Cross. All the bells began to ring. At last Tsar Alexis emerged from the Cathedral to confront the cheering crowd. He paused while his cousin Nikita Romanov poured three dishes of golden coins over him. He then proceeded to the Cathedral of St Michael the Archangel, burial place of Tsars including his father; then to the Church of the Virgin, and finally up the Golden Staircase to the Hall of Facets for the feast, pausing briefly at the entrance to be smothered once again with showers of gold. Blessings and gifts were heaped upon him. Representatives of the merchant class, the service ranks, even the humble townsmen paid him their tribute.

Alexis was no doubt bemused, but he had sustained a day of ritual splendour, and was now truly and legitimately Tsar. But it was one thing to reign; another to rule. He was blessed with many qualities – intelligence, vigour, charm and presence. He had been taught many things necessary to the art of governing. And he had a sense of duty. But as he himself had perhaps begun to realize, he lacked the worldly wisdom and experience to succeed (perhaps even survive) in so harsh a world. Wisdom was, eventually, to come. But for the moment the vulnerable Alexis could only put his trust in God – and in Boris Morozov.

Chapter II

In the Shadow of Morozov

Immediately after the coronation Alexis relieved the aged Fedor Sheremetev and two others of his family of their ministerial responsibilities, gave Boris Morozov control of several key departments and put friends and relatives of his in charge of others. All the main levers of power were now responsive to Boris's touch. So far as practical policy was concerned the Tsar himself was, in effect, his puppet. The forms and trappings of autocracy were carefully maintained: ministers humbly submitted petitions to the Tsar inviting him to order action;[1] Alexis's florid signature was needed on documents; his presence was required at certain ceremonies. Nonetheless Boris arranged that public affairs should not obtrude too much into the young man's life, and Alexis himself was grateful for the older man's protection.

Adjustment was difficult. He had reverted to the black of mourning immediately after his coronation, and the Patriarch's homily about his mission as Tsar weighed upon his mind. He knew he could not become as wise as Solomon overnight and he felt daunted by the awful weight of his responsibilities. So it was that, with Boris's encouragement, he decided to seek solace and inspiration in a series of pilgrimages. He went to pray at Mozhaisk, where his mother had been born, at Zvenigorod, whose great monastery dedicated to St Sabbas contained the icon of his namesake, Alexis the Man of God, and, in all probability, to Borovsk as well.[2] Gradually he began to recover his spirits, but he remained restless. As a contemporary noted later that year, he was rarely to be seen in Moscow 'since he began to reign, but is always going on outings'. And with the approach of spring 1646 he put his mourning clothes aside,[3] and launched himself with enthusiasm into the season's sport.

At the beginning of April he wrote from his lodge at Pokrovskoe to his childhood companion and servitor Afanasy Matiushkin in Moscow. There was plenty of duck about, he reported, though he had not had much luck since his hawks had 'not yet got into their catching stride'. But he persevered. Six days later he wrote again, this time calling for an embrocation to relieve an ache in his arm – caused by carrying heavy falcons on his wrist all day – and he was still away hunting at the end of the month, when he asked Matiushkin to call on his sisters and report on how they were (since his bereavement he had come to regard his sister Irina as his surrogate mother).[4]

His sporting tastes were catholic. He enjoyed hunting with hounds, chasing wolves and foxes, trapping bears, tracking elk, and racing pigeons (betting on them too),[5] but falconry had become his passion. The appearance and behaviour of these predatory birds fascinated him – the fierce black eyes of a gerfalcon blazing out from the whiteness of its plumage when its hood was removed; its powerful, soaring flight with its long, pointed wings outstretched. He would watch intently as it floated high up in the distant sky; catch his breath as it suddenly dived (almost vertically and at amazing speed) towards some unsuspecting bird below; then spur his horse into a gallop towards the falcon's expected point of landing to see if its powerful claws still clutched their prey. But Alexis was no less absorbed by the challenge of training young falcons. It was a task demanding considerable powers of observation, patience and persuasion – qualities which were to serve him well in later life.

Yet, for all his devotion to sport and pilgrimage, he also found time to extend his knowledge of the complex machinery of state and of the sort of men who ran it. Every morning when he was in Moscow councillors would attend on him to brief him (and each other) on the progress of affairs, to discuss alternative policies, and to commend lines of action to him. They would bow down low when he entered and when he left, though for all their great show of deference it was they, not he, who were effectively the masters. These men were members of the Boyar Council, or Duma, which comprised those who held, or had held, the most important ministerial portfolios, provincial governorships and military commands. By no means all its members attended these sessions, however – not those who had been retired, like the Sheremetevs, nor those carrying out duties at a distance from the capital. Nor did all of them hold the exalted rank of boyar. Three other ranks also qualified for membership: sub-boyar (*okol'nichii*), gentleman-councillor (*dumnyi dvorianin*) and secretary-councillor (*dumnyi d'iak*), these last being titles reserved for those few members of the provincial gentry and the bureaucratic class who managed to forge their way through to the top.

Many members of the Duma came from families which were as old as the Romanovs themselves and no less prominent than they had been before Michael's election to the throne. Several were Alexis's relatives (his uncle Simeon Streshnev was a member and both Vasily Streshnev and Nikita Romanov were soon to be promoted boyars). Several more were protégés of Boris (his brother-in-law P. T. Trakhoniotov was now a sub-boyar and his brother Gleb was soon to attain the rank of boyar). Nonetheless many of them owed their preferment rather more to their service records than to nepotism or ancestry,[6] so that the Duma contained a considerable store of ability, wisdom and experience. And one member was Alexis's tutor Gregory L'vov, who had been newly promoted Secretary-Councillor.

It was through Gregory especially that Alexis learned about the bureaucratic machine which implemented the Council's policies and carried out the routine administration of the realm. It was, as he discovered, a complex, labyrinthine machine. The departments (*prikazy*) into which it was divided were housed inside or just outside the Kremlin walls and staffed by a professional bureaucracy about a thousand strong, supplemented by others who disposed of particular expertise, such as merchants who understood the niceties of commerce and finance and foreigners who could serve as interpreters and translators. Among the more important departments were the Foreign Office (*Posol'skii prikaz*); the Office of Muster (*Razriadnyi prikaz*), which kept records of all men liable to state service and rostered them; and the Great Treasury (*Bol'shaia kazna*), which, under Boris's personal direction, controlled foreign trade, weights and measures and the minting of money, and collected dues from certain sectors of the population and a variety of indirect taxes too (including one for the privilege of washing clothes in the Moscow river). Beyond these were clutches of departments concerned with revenue-collection in particular regions (*cheti*), with the administration of professional army units – the Musketeer, or Guards, Office (also run by Boris) and the Artillery Office (run by his brother-in-law) – and with the administration of the palace (*Bol'shoi dvorets, Kazennyi prikaz*, etc.). And there were separate departments to administer the state monopoly on liquor and to supervise non-Orthodox foreigners in the service of the Tsar (both also supervised by Boris); to keep down brigandage; to run the city of Moscow; to liaise with proconsular governors of distant Kazan and Siberia; to judge civil actions involving service gentry; to control service estates; to maintain postal communications; to implement the laws concerning bond-slaves; and many more.

It was a bewildering jig-saw of a system, and to modern eyes irrational. No single department exercised overall financial control (there was no budget); many had their own individual sources of revenue; some had their own agents in the provinces while others operated through local governors; several combined administrative with financial and judicial with police functions; and there was considerable overlap and fragmentation of authority between individual ministries.[7] And yet, for all its apparent irrationality and confusion, for all that the bureaucrats wrote on their knees rather than on tables and had no acquaintance with decimals, the system worked.[8] It may have been less sophisticated than that of the Vatican or of Venice, but Alexis disposed of a more advanced civil service than his contemporary Charles I.

If the Muscovite bureaucrats were professionals,[9] however, they were also corrupt. They accepted bribes like Samuel Pepys accepted presents from the captains he appointed to the command of ships – as a matter of course. And ordinary Russians also took the practice for granted.

> When you go to see the Secretary [so one man practised in the art of bending officialdom to his will instructed his agent] make sure that he is in a good mood before you enter his quarters and when you do so make sure that you greet him with the utmost respect . . . If he accepts the letter be sure to give him three rubles and promise more, but give the chickens, beer and ham to his cook rather than to the Secretary personally.

Nonetheless there was resentment at the scale of extortion and misappropriation. Some officials, it was soon claimed, were 'buying hereditary estates and building stone houses for themselves . . . with the proceeds of their unjust peculation'.[10] Some of their political masters, however, did even better, and Boris himself was accumulating tremendous wealth. By 1647 he owned more than 6,000 peasant households, and although much of his fortune derived from devices tantamount to misappropriation and from using officials to serve his private interests (often regardless of the law) the bulk of it came in the form of gifts from his grateful master.[11] Young Alexis was a soft touch; and Boris was a greedy man.

On the other hand, he was by no means a bad mentor for a Tsar needing practical instruction in the art of government. Despite the lack of a budget he realized that the state's expenditure had long been outrunning its income, and that the imbalance must be urgently corrected. Hence measures were taken to increase taxation income and to pare down costs. In March 1646 the tax on salt was quadrupled and tobacco, banned as satanic in 1634, was put on sale again, like liquor, as a state monopoly. Tax enforcement was tightened up, smuggling combatted and savings made through cutting posts in the state service and the salaries and allowances of those who were retained.[12]

Understanding the purpose, Alexis played his part as a good husbandman. The number of palace servants was reduced, the wages of the remainder cut. He even saved on clothes by having much of his father's wardrobe altered to fit his own strapping frame (at six feet he was a good three inches taller than his father and much broader in the shoulders).[13] He also took an interest in foreign trade and especially in the great trading expeditions to the Orient that were mounted by the crown. So Alexis came to appreciate the difference between loss and profit – although he never was able to distinguish at all clearly between his private property and that of the state. For a titled autocrat with the entire realm as his patrimony such distinctions were not easily grasped. It was more natural to conceive of his role as that of a farmer and of Russia as his farm.

There was one sector of expenditure, however, on which Boris, with Alexis's strong approval, did not stint funds: the modernization of the armed forces. In 1646 a new department was established to organize the formation of dragoon regiments; a mission was sent to Holland to recruit mercenary officers to discipline and train Russian conscripts; and considerable expenditure was sanctioned for the importation of firearms. Then, in 1647, another department was set up to organize the manufacture of gun-barrels and arrangements were put in train to publish an illustrated translation of one of the most famous military textbooks of the age, Johann von Walhausen's *The Art of Infantry Warfare*. Muscovy was to have a new model army.[14]

Boris's policy of financial retrenchment was bold and prescient, but various groups among the population were soon squealing with discontent as they felt the bite of it. State employees complained that they had not received the pay that was due to them;[15] townsmen grumbled about the rising cost of food (a consequence of the bad harvest of 1646 as well as of the salt tax), and merchants were up in arms about concessions enjoyed by foreigners which allegedly allowed them to compete on unfair terms.[16] The provincial gentry were restless too. They were also the worst hit by peasant flights and, despite the completion in 1646 of a new fortification system in the south, they were repeatedly called out for duty against the Tatars. This service obligation threatened many of them with impoverishment. Furthermore, they resented the Department of Service Estates allotting some of the best tracts of provincial land to careerists in Moscow, especially when some of these same careerists were working these estates with peasant runaways from their own much more modest holdings.[17]

Such resentments were feeding underground streams of subversion which the government treated seriously every time they surfaced. Complaints coupled with 'indecent words' about the Tsar (that he did 'not stand up for' the lower serving classes or that he paid no regard to their petitions) were rigorously investigated. A man was arrested and interrogated under torture for asserting that Alexis was not legitimate and that the Tsarevich Ivan (his late brother) represented the true line of succession. And there was no shortage of people ready to denounce others for sedition – for whispering that Morozov had placed Alexis upon the throne; for declaring that Valdemar would have made a better Tsar; or for 'intending' to break their oaths of loyalty, defect abroad and raise rebellion, as Alexander Nashchokin, a scion of the Moscow gentry, was in 1646.[18]

How much Alexis knew about such cases is uncertain. He may well have been apprised of some of them through Boris himself, through others close to him like Gregory L'vov (who had sat on a commission, headed by Boris, which investigated the case concerning Ivan), or through his kinsman Vasily Streshnev, who ran the Office of Muster. On the other hand, although he was occasionally presented with lists comprising abstracts of petitions (mainly from members of the palace staff), great care was taken to keep his movements secret so that he should never come face to face with any common petitioner, and, having no contact with the people, he was in no position to appreciate their points of view. But he could not but be aware of disturbances among his own retainers.

These men were drawn from the ranks of the nobility and the Moscow gentry and they stood at his beck and call night and day. There were those who helped him dress and undress; those who escorted dishes from the palace kitchens, who held them until he called for them, and who tasted them before he ate; those who carried his chair, his carpet and his faldstool when he went to church, and his gear when he went hunting; and some were always standing by to carry messages and run his errands. Gentlemen-in-waiting and of the bedchamber, stewards, chamberlains, ushers, couriers and supervisors of the palace menials, most of them served in the palace on a rota system for a few months in the year;[19] and each of them held a rank that accorded with his duties not only at court but as a soldier when he was called for army service and as a governmental functionary when he was posted to a job in Moscow, the provinces, or on some mission abroad.

Such men were as jealous of their honour (and many of the younger ones as rowdy) as any Montague or Capulet. They would protest boisterously, sometimes violently, if they were allocated a duty which did not accord with the honour they thought due to their lineage. Rarely did a week pass without someone protesting that he could not serve under, or on a par with, someone else who was allegedly inferior in terms of ancestry and precedent – at which the other party would usually protest that the objection dishonoured him and his family. The Office of Muster would carry out an inquiry, but obstinate complainants would refuse to accept an adverse decision and would have to be forced to comply on pain of imprisonment, beating, official disgrace and confiscation of property. Even when the Tsar formally announced that the rules of precedence would not apply on a particular occasion or campaign there would be storms of outrage resulting from hurt pride – refusals to serve, which could disrupt military operations, and unseemly scenes and even brawls at the court,[20] which were harmful to the Tsar's own honour.

Alexis himself was acquiring a goodly store of invective (the patristic literature, to which he was devoted, provided models), though he was sparing in his use of foul language until he was provoked. But his patience and his bookishness did not accord with the earthy sentiments of the rowdier elements at court; and his piety seemed exaggerated to those of a more secular cast of mind than he. Such people would sneer at him behind his back and call him 'the young monk'.[21] And the epithet was earned, because under the influence of his new chaplain, Stefan Vnifant'ev, Archpriest of the Kremlin's Cathedral of the Annunciation, the Tsar seemed to be growing almost fanatically religious.

Every morning at the crack of dawn (in winter well before dawn) Stefan would be waiting in the chapel to bless the Tsar and conduct morning prayers for him. Later in the day Stefan (according to his friend Ivan Neronov, Archpriest of the Kazan Cathedral on Red Square) was 'always entering the Tsar's apartments to read him extracts from edifying books, to admonish the young Tsar . . . to [perform] good deeds of every sort' and guard his soul 'from every kind of evil inclination', and Stefan also encouraged Alexis to call on him at night to talk and to borrow books. Stefan nourished Alexis's youthful idealism, convinced him that the level of Christian observance among the people must be improved, and inspired him with the vision of a united Orthodox world in which Greeks and Russians would be perfectly aligned in worship. Stefan, in fact, was a zealot and the leading light in a circle of reformist clergy which was to become known as the 'Zealots of Piety'. And it was through Stefan that Alexis met other members of the group who, in their different styles, also brought influence to bear upon him. One was Neronov, whose sermons attracted huge audiences which sometimes included the Tsar himself.[22] Another was a man who was subsequently to play an immense role in Alexis's life. His name was Nikon.

Nikon was the abbot of a monastery in the far north who came to Moscow in 1646 to collect alms. His reputation had preceded him. A towering figure of a man, six feet and five inches tall, he was rock-like, stern, passionate and charismatic. He had also known suffering. Orphaned as a child, he had been prompted to take monastic vows by the deaths of his three children eleven years before, since when he had been guided by the rule of St Sabbas in his extreme asceticism and by St John Chrysostom in his charity. The impression he made upon Alexis, twenty-four years his junior, was considerable. So great a spiritual treasure could not be suffered to return to the bleak sub-arctic wastes. He must be kept close by in Moscow. As it happened, the abbacy of the New Saviour Monastery (a Romanov endowment which contained the tombs of Filaret's parents and his wife) was vacant and lay within Alexis's gift, and Nikon was given the preferment. Henceforth Nikon was to attend the Tsar in his chapel every Friday morning, discuss affairs of the spirit with him and intercede with him for orphans, widows, prisoners and the oppressed. Word of this got about and before long Nikon was besieged everywhere he went by petitioners trying to gain his ear, and through him the Tsar's.[23]

Stefan and Nikon inspired the impressionable Alexis to act. On the eve of Lent 1647 the Tsar was instrumental in having an encyclical issued enjoining the clergy to pray reverently, live purely and (since drunkenness was the besetting sin of Russians, monks as well as laymen) to keep sober. A sabbatarian decree was also issued ordering the closure of inns and shops on Sundays; and the Tsar was persuaded to abandon certain amusements he had formerly enjoyed. Although his dwarfs Ivashka and Ortiushka were retained, the court musicians disappeared, their places being taken by a group of beggars and foundlings, several of them crippled or infirm, who sang and chanted spiritual verses about the palace. He was also encouraged to share the enthusiasm of a like-minded young courtier, Fedor Rtishchev, who was planning to bring a number of learned monks from Kiev to Moscow – men who understood Greek as well as Slavonic and who could therefore help align Russian with Greek religious texts.[24] The native religious fundamentalism combined with ideas, or stances, picked up at first or second hand from Greek Byzantine authors, coalesced in Alexis's mind to build up a more or less coherent notion of an ideal order. Had not the Emperor Justinian the Great proclaimed that nothing so pleased God as the unanimity of all Christians in the true faith? Had not subsequent Byzantine Emperors (his spiritual predecessors) insisted on standard religious observance? In a well-ordered realm, surely, all the people would devote themselves to God through prayer, good deeds and obedience. And obedience to God implied obedience to the Tsar, his representative.

It was a vision, however, which few Russians of the time could easily be prevailed upon to share. Indeed Joseph, Filaret's successor as Patriarch, was not enamoured of all Stefan's ideas. Alexis was persuaded to temper his enthusiasm for the moment, and meanwhile Boris Morozov, in his wisdom, smiled indulgently on his youthful commitment and considered the next, and obvious, step on Alexis's road to maturity. Now in his eighteenth year, he was a well-built, lusty young man, proud of the handsome red beard which he had grown. He was clearly ripe for marriage, and early in 1647 the procedure for selecting a suitable bride was set in train. The procedure was Byzantine in origin and like a fairy tale in character. Two hundred maidens, all of them of gentle, though not aristocratic, birth were listed as eligible and brought to court to have their beauty, health and dispositions assessed. Gradually, by a process of elimination, their number was reduced to six. How far Alexis himself was free to choose is not certain (the process of selection was carried out under shrouds of secrecy), but it is probable that he was given the opportunity to view the candidates, perhaps from some secret point of observation in his sisters' apartments, and to state his preferences. Eventually a choice was made – the daughter of a provincial nobleman called Euphemia Vsevolozhskaia. But this fairy tale was to have no happy ending.

On hearing the news of her good fortune the girl fainted. This was interpreted as being due to a 'falling sickness' which at once rendered her ineligible. It is not impossible, however, that her chances were sabotaged by supporters of a rival. People were soon whispering that she fainted because her head–dress had been bound too tightly, that she had been poisoned, and that Boris himself had connived at the girl's undoing (though this is doubtful). But there is firm evidence that one of Nikita Romanov's peasants was investigated for witchcraft in connection with the affair.[25]

Alexis was evidently much upset. He is said to have sunk into a mood of adolescent depression and to have eaten nothing for several days. Another prospective bride was to be found for him within the year, and meanwhile he turned to God and to his spiritual advisers for sustenance and immersed himself in charitable work. In the autumn of that year he was taking meticulous note in an elegant hand of how much he disbursed in small sums day by day to the needy, on candles bought to commemorate the dead, on payments made to redeem a prisoner in gaol for debt, on food for the hungry, and of where he took the money from and whether he handed it out personally or through an intermediary. Thus on 1st November, out of money remaining after the purchase of books and a further ten rubles taken from the treasury of the Great Palace Department, he gave ten kopeks apiece to two hundred beggars and three kopeks each to a hundred more, besides having food distributed to a thousand. Next day, he wrote, 'myself gave six rubles, ten kopeks each, to sixty people', but since anonymous charity was doubly meritorious he usually left the disbursement (the coins wrapped up in twists of paper) to others, and the record of it remained a matter between him and his Maker.[26]

His surviving papers from this time show that economic and military affairs also drew his attention. Following the precept of that mirror of princes, *The Secret of Secrets*, which recommended the use of inventories, he had extracts copied out from the new census books. These listed the number of peasant households within the state domain in seven districts, and on them Alexis carefully noted the number of young men taken from them to serve in the guards or as soldiers in the new-formation regiments which were being set up.[27] For all the breadth of the vision he was forming about a victorious Muscovy in which all his subjects would show a uniform and proper fear of God, Alexis also appreciated the importance of mastering detail. He was never to lose it.

Yet with this concern for mundane detail went a constant expectation of the miraculous, and he had been excited that summer by unlikely news from a distant province. A plough-boy on a court estate had found an icon in a field. It had a silver cover and a Greek inscription, and had worked a miracle. When the boy's companion, who was a Cheremis and not a Russian, had burst out laughing at the sight of it he had been temporarily struck blind. On recovering he had begun to pray fervently (he confirmed this under questioning). Furthermore, when placed in the local church the icon had effected a number of miraculous cures, all of which were duly recorded. At once an order was issued in the Tsar's name calling for the icon to be brought to Moscow under escort, together with the plough-boy, the Cheremis, a priest and a deacon,[28] and a solemn reception for them was arranged in the capital. If the discovery was an omen, it was a good one, for not long afterwards the efforts to find a suitable bride for Alexis were crowned with success.

The matchmaker was Avdotia, the wife of Boyar Prince Nikita Odoevskii, commander-in-chief of the army of the south, and Alexis first met the girl in his sisters' apartments.[29] Her name was Maria and she had qualities other than comeliness to commend her. She was modest in bearing, religious in temperament, and at twenty-three years of age more mature than her prospective husband. Moreover, she was the daughter of one of the 'new men' whose careers had been flourishing under Boris's patronage – Il'ia Miloslavskii. Il'ia belonged to the Moscow gentry but his forebears had never held exalted office. His uncle, Ivan Gramotin, was Secretary in the Foreign Office, however, and his own sphere of expertise was foreign affairs and the purchase of Western technological and military expertise. He had served on an embassy to Ottoman Turkey and in 1646 had been sent to Holland to recruit metallurgists who could produce iron suitable for making gun-barrels, wire, iron sheeting and water-powered mills; captains well-versed in military formation; and twenty of the very best-trained soldiers.[30] Henceforth Alexis would have someone close to him who had some acquaintance with the new technology and who knew Western Europe at first hand.

The wedding was fixed for 16th January, a few weeks before Alexis's nineteenth birthday. The arrangements were supervised by Boris himself and, since he had no wife, by his sister-in-law. Disputes about precedence were banned on pain of death. The best man was Boyar Prince Iakov Cherkasskii, who, after Nikita Romanov and Boris himself, was the richest of all Alexis's subjects, and a prominent role in the ceremony was allotted to Nikita Odoevskii. Fedor Rtishchev had charge of the wardrobe, and since Alexis knew that he and his father were men of modest means he gave them 160 sables so that they should have something to present to the bride on the occasion of 'our Tsarish joy'. The wedding procession was spectacular. It was mid-winter and Moscow glinted under snow. Alexis rode on horseback to the ceremony, alongside the bride, who was tucked up in a sledge and flanked by sixteen footmen bearing lanterns. The wedding was followed by four days of lavish banqueting at which all the great came to offer their congratulations and their gifts to the bridal pair, who sat on the same cushion on the capacious throne in the Hall of Facets. The food was elaborate. Swan cooked with saffron and wood-hen with lemon and goose giblets for him; roast goose, sucking-pig and hens cooked in three different ways for her; and there were dishes of larks, cheese and egg pies, pancakes, crucian carp with mutton, and cheesecakes, besides many kinds of bread, confections and unseasonable fruits and berries.[31]

There was one break with tradition, however. Former weddings at court had been marked by noisy singing, dancing, merriment and excessive drinking. But his chaplain, the puritanical Stefan, had persuaded Alexis to prevent the occasion being marred by braying trumpets, lewd songs and excessive laughter. So the Tsar married 'quietly in the fear of God'. He and his bride quaffed kvass from a huge silver goblet rather than wine or vodka. The only music heard was 'spiritual chants and hymns' sung by choirs. The occasion, in short, was unwontedly dignified – and not only for religious reasons, for Alexis intended that 'everyone should be amazed by and wonder at his . . . sense of proportion and good order'.[32]

By all accounts the routine of their married life together followed the strict canonical rules concerning sex. After sleeping together they would invariably wash and submit to the blessing of a priest before entering church or kissing an icon; nor would they come together on holy days, nor during Lent, nor (following rules similar to the ancient Jewish laws of *Niddah*) during her menstrual periods,[33] their observance of these laws of sexual purity being facilitated by their having separate quarters and separate bath-houses. At all events their union was immediately successful. By the time they left for the annual pilgrimage to the Trinity Monastery on 24th January (as subsequent events were to demonstrate) Maria was pregnant.

Two days after that Boris married the bride's sister, Anna. No doubt his primary motive was political for it created a family tie between the Tsar and himself. It also strengthened his ties with Il'ia Miloslavskii who could not but become influential at court in his own right now. (Il'ia had been promoted sub-boyar the day after the wedding and on Alexis's return from his honeymoon-cum-pilgrimage he was made a full boyar.[34]) Boris's marriage brought him little joy, however. According to Samuel Collins, Alexis's personal physician some years afterwards, Anna was 'a succulent black young Lass' who did not care for him 'so that instead of children jealousies were got'.[35] Nonetheless, from Boris's point of view the union, as events would soon show, was a wiser move than even he expected.

For Alexis, marriage added a new and delightful world of intimacy to all those other worlds which made up his universe. There was the world of the *terem* (that part of the palace reserved for women and small children), which was still dominated by his sisters, where life was mainly given over to gossip and good works; the world of high policy, dominated by Boris; the world of the Church, headed by the Patriarch and adorned by the likes of Stefan and Nikon; the world of the court itself; and all those other, more distant, worlds that together made up Russia. Some of these worlds already overlapped through family connections, but it was Alexis's role as Tsar to bind them all together. One symbolic means of doing so to which Alexis attached great importance was ceremony. Ceremonies great and small punctuated the Muscovite year as they had in Byzantium, and if Alexis had not read the Emperor Constantine VII's book upon the subject he certainly shared his view that, through ceremony, 'We shadow the harmonious movement of God the Creator around the Universe, while the Imperial Power is preserved in proportion and order.'[36]

The formal dinners he exchanged with the Patriarch symbolized the diarchy of terrestrial and heavenly power; the distribution of special pies to selected servitors and churchmen on his name-day and the name-days of his immediate family strengthened personal links between his family and the establishment; the levées he gave for great merchants, prominent bureaucrats and even the representatives of the Moscow hundreds forged links with other classes. And his stately appearances, as at the Blessing of the Waters rites in January or on Palm Sunday (when, recalling Christ's entry into Jerusalem, he would lead an ass bearing the Patriarch in solemn procession round the Kremlin), not only linked the worlds of the Church, the court and government, but huge numbers of the lower orders too, if only as spectators.

Yet for all the demands of duty and for all the time he now devoted to his wife, he found time, too, for other activities that provided outlets for his energy, provoked his curiosity, and fed his mind. Towards the end of February 1648 he made time to watch one of his huntsmen, Sila Zertsalov, confront a wild lion, and then a wild bear,[37] and as soon as the weather allowed he plunged into another season's falconry. Methodically, he started a record – a 'List of falconers who accompanied the birds and caught them'. In this he wrote down the names of every man he had sent with gifts of falcons to boyars and others whom he thought deserved some favour, and how much he gave them as rewards for running the errands: 'Gave them two rubles each'; 'Gave Peter a gold piece and a half-ruble to Mikhaiko'.[38] Rewards fortified loyalty, of course, but he was always measured in his largesse, and a careful accountant.

He always made time for reading, too – most recently a 'Book on the Faith', a worthy compilation commended by Stefan which contained telling polemics against the Catholic religion, and which was published at his command that May.[39] And the inquiring spirit which soon gained him the reputation of having read every book published in Slavonic also led him to take a keen interest in diplomacy and hence in developments in the wider world outside Muscovy. He had recently presided over the conclusion of a defensive alliance with Poland against the Tatars – an unlikely achievement in view of the grievances each state harboured against the other. (Poland resented Muscovy harbouring peasant runaways from their lands; Moscow resented Poland's continuing occupation of Smolensk and her failure to counter the smuggling of liquor and tobacco across the frontier.) But it was clearly more important to cut the cost of defending Russian lands against the Tatars (whose Khan was no more effective in restraining his hungry people than Moscow was effective in restraining the Cossacks on its southern frontiers) than to avenge pride lost in former wars with Poland. As Alexis now understood matters, his realm needed time to conserve and increase its strength before it embarked on any military adventures.

Similar considerations dictated the maintenance of good relations with Queen Christina of Sweden, who controlled access to the Baltic, Muscovy's most convenient gateway to the West; and Alexis also took an interest in developments in distant England, whence came disturbing news of King Charles I's surrender to Parliament. The Kremlin had been besieged by competing envoys from both sides, and in February 1648 one arrived from Charles's heir in Holland. Alexis could not be other than sympathetic to his request for Russian aid to sustain a loyalist campaign in Ireland designed to save the King.[40] There were men close to Alexis who well remembered Muscovy's own civil wars, and the spectre of sedition still hovered, albeit distantly, over the Russian crown.

Indeed it was this fear, along with some few signs of increasing restlessness among the population (there had been recent riots in the town of Tot'ma), that had prompted Boris to temper the government's harsh domestic policies. In December 1647 the hated salt tax was repealed and steps were also taken to placate the provincial service classes. A law protecting lands in the frontier steppe zone of the south from being taken over by high-ranking men in Moscow was revived; large tracts of land in those areas which had passed into the hands of such people were confiscated; and the time limit for the return of runaway serfs was abolished (although the problem faced by serf-owners with small resources in tracking them down remained). Plans were also prepared to protect tax-paying townsmen from competition from town residents who were tax-exempt by virtue of their being ascribed to great landowners and monasteries.[41] And so when Alexis went out on pilgrimage again in the late spring of 1648 it is likely that he thought a great deal more about Ukraine whose Orthodox population had raised a rebellion against Polish rule and were asking his protection, and about his wife Maria who was now quite big with child, than about any danger from his own subjects.

Yet, on Thursday 1st June 1648, when he was returning to Moscow, he was unexpectedly confronted by a crowd.[42] From their dress they appeared to be common citizens of Moscow. Some of them held on to the bridle of his horse, but others held out bread and salt to him (a peaceful sign of hospitality) and someone began to read out a petition. It complained of bloodsuckers and tormentors who were oppressing them, and in particular it called on him to replace Sub-Boyar Leontii Pleshcheev, who was in charge of the Land Department, which supervised the running of Moscow, with a just official or with their own elected representatives. Alexis seemed nonplussed. He had evidently received reports of complaints (probably abbreviated and tendentious versions prepared by officials) but they had not allowed him to gauge the intensity of feeling involved. Alexis promised to look into the matter and provide them with satisfaction. This appeared to content them and Alexis rode on into the Kremlin.

But then some members of his entourage – perhaps friends of Pleshcheev – began to ride their horses into the dispersing crowd, shouting abuse and laying into them with whips. They also snatched written petitions out of their hands, tore them up and threw the fragments in their faces. This provoked resistance. Some of the petitioners picked up stones and hurled them at their assailants, forcing them to flee into the Kremlin. Half an hour later the Tsaritsa's procession approached and the crowd attempted to petition her, but Boris Morozov was with her. He ordered the escort of *strel'tsy* guards to clear them out of the way. The crowd fought back with sticks and stones, but Maria's carriage was rushed through to safety. Sixteen members of the crowd were arrested.

When Maria enquired what the commotion was about Boris had told her that it was caused by trouble-makers who should be executed. But there were many in Moscow who thought otherwise. Rumours spread like wildfire through the narrow streets; crowds gathered at churches; crude handbills were nailed on doors; tub-thumpers gathered sympathetic crowds around them. Anger about food prices (still rising despite the withdrawal of the salt tax), unemployment, taxation and haughty and corrupt officialdom welled up into a single stream of protest. The inexperienced Alexis was about to confront his first major challenge as Tsar.

No doubt he took pains to reassure his wife that night and no doubt Boris talked confidently of a firm hand bringing the situation quickly under control. Some officials in the Land Department may have been high-handed, but the complaints against Pleshcheev, a valued if junior member of the Council, were unjustified. However, on the following morning a sizeable crowd met the Tsar as he came down the Red Staircase on his way to church. Voices urged him to grant their petition. Alexis replied that petitions should be submitted in the proper way, in writing; but when they told him that they had tried to do so yesterday with no result he agreed to look into the matter. They also called for the release of those who had been arrested the day before, at which (according to one report) Alexis turned angrily on Boris and asked him why he had imprisoned anyone without his orders. By the time the service ended a considerable crowd had gathered outside the church and it pressed in so closely behind the Tsar's procession that the guardsmen had great difficulty in forcing a passage through it. Sensing danger, Boris ordered the Kremlin gates to be closed as soon as the procession had entered, but a mob of several thousands surged through before they could be shut and they followed Alexis all the way to the palace shouting their demands.

In his private dining room Alexis held a hurried conference with those boyars whom he had invited to dine with him that day. It was decided to call out six thousand *strel'tsy* available in the city to clear the Kremlin and otherwise to play for time. Boyar M. M. Temkin-Rostovskii was sent out onto the staircase to try and pacify the crowd, but they seized him, saying they wanted to talk to the Tsar in person. Another boyar appeared (probably Nikita Romanov), but the crowd insisted that they would deal only with the Tsar. At last Alexis did appear. He asked what they wanted (well knowing what answer they would give), and when they called for the release of the sixteen prisoners he granted their wish. At this Temkin-Rostovskii was released (and immediately took to his bed for several days recovering from the shock of his rough handling). But the crowd now pressed their demand for Pleshcheev to be handed over. This offended Alexis's sense of order. If Pleshcheev was to be punished, the punishment must be judicial. He told them he needed more time to investigate the charges, but that if Pleshcheev were found guilty he himself would arrange his punishment. At this some of the mob threatened to seize Pleshcheev themselves.

Meanwhile, some of the *strel'tsy* had arrived. They brought no deliverance, however. Many of them were sympathetic to the crowd and they told Alexis so. They would willingly protect him in accordance with their oaths of loyalty, but they did not want to shed blood on account of the tyrannical and traitorous Pleshcheev and his arrogant officials at the Land Department. Some of them fraternized with the crowd and told them that they had nothing to fear. As a result the calls for Pleshcheev became increasingly insistent. To Alexis and those around him it became obvious that some further concession must be made.

Once more the Tsar came out onto the porch at the head of the staircase. This time he reminded them that it was Friday, a fast day, a day on which no blood should be shed. But he promised to have Pleshcheev punished publicly on the morrow. This seemed to mollify the crowd somewhat, but meanwhile a scuffle had broken out between some of Boris's retainers and a group of *strel'tsy* whom they had accused of disobeying orders. One *strelets* was knifed to death and his companions rushed to Alexis seeking redress. They found him tense and irritable from the strain of the last, harrowing, hours. 'Why should you need protection from Morozov's servants?' he is alleged to have snapped. 'You are as strong or stronger than they are. If they have wronged you take your own revenge on them.'

If this answer is construed as encouraging a dangerous brawl within the palace (and we cannot be certain of his actual words), then it was injudicious. But in view of what happened next it seems as if Alexis was trying to deflect their attention away from the palace. This group of *strel'tsy* at least, for all their protestations of loyalty, could not be relied on; and he could not allow himself to be used as a wedge between them and Boris who was both his chief minister and their commander. If it was indeed his purpose to get them out of the palace then he succeeded – for they rushed off towards Boris's residence followed by remnants of the crowd.

They stormed into the house and when Boris's steward, Mosei, interposed himself, they beat him to death. Thanks to her close connection with the Tsar, however, they did no harm to his wife Anna. But they ransacked the house and from their behaviour it is evident that they were more intent on punishing the man who had cut their pay, was responsible for the death of one of their companions, and whom they were coming to imagine as a satanic figure, than on merely plundering his goods. They broke open chests and coffers and hurled their contents out of the windows; they tore the clothes they found to shreds and scattered household goods and even coins about the street outside. By the time they had finished 'not even a nail was left in the wall'. But success only whetted the mob's appetite. They moved on to the residences of other enemies, real or imagined. They looted Pleshcheev's house and Trakhoniotov's, and the residence of Nazar Chistoi. The unfortunate Nazar (who was now Counsellor-Secretary at the Foreign Office, though he had once been Secretary at the Great Treasury Department) was caught as he came home, at which (according to a foreign visitor to Moscow) they 'knock him on the head with an axe [saying] this is for the Salt [tax]. Then, the Man being halfe dead, they haled him down the stayres by the heeles, dragg him like a dogg over the whole Court, and having stripped him, they flung him starck nacked upon the dunghill . . . [where] they put him qu[ite] to death.'

In all, the crowds sacked about seventy houses that day, including those of Boyars Nikita Odoevskii and A. M. L'vov (who directed the Palace Chancery) and of the great merchants Vasilii Shorin and Vasilii Gusel'nikov. There would have been more damage still had not loyal units of *strel'tsy* been sent to guard some of the more obvious targets; and with the main focus of disturbance deflected elsewhere the government managed to regain control within the Kremlin. By dawn on 3rd June, with the assistance of some of the new-formation troops, whom the crowds let pass unhindered and even with good humour (perhaps believing they were allies), the Kremlin had been cleared and the gates were safely closed.

Nonetheless, so far from the troubles being over, the crisis point had not yet been reached. Early that morning crowds gathered again outside the Kremlin walls. An attempt was made to disperse them by firing blanks. It failed. Some protesters got into church belfries and began to ring the bells. Their sound brought countless thousands into Red Square. They were made up of all sorts – tax-paying townsmen, a few renegade *strel'tsy*, household servants, visitors from out of town and even contumacious monks. All the pent-up grievances and resentments of recent years welled up through them into a gigantic tidal wave of anger. The crowd wanted blood and were determined to have it – Pleshcheev's, Trakhoniotov's, Morozov's too. Trakhoniotov had been spirited away to the safety of a monastery outside the city; the other two were safe inside the Kremlin. But the regime was under pressure now from forces other than the crowd outside. The *strel'tsy* wanted their eight-ruble cut in pay rescinded, and did not want to take orders from Boris; the merchants themselves wanted reform, if only to avert further disturbances which threatened their fortunes and their lives; petitions were coming in from gentry and the lower serving classes demanding concessions; and now even members of the Council began to argue that the Tsar had no alternative but to replace Boris and his coterie, and even to throw some of them to the raging wolves outside.

Alexis evidently resisted. Nikita Romanov was sent out to test the temper of the crowd, to promise them satisfaction in general terms, and to ask them to go home. He came back to report that they said they bore no grudge against the Tsar, only against his evil ministers, and that he had promised them that these would be punished. Meanwhile fires had broken out at several points in the city and since most of the *strel'tsy*, who also constituted Moscow's fire brigade, were otherwise engaged they began to spread. There is no reason to suppose that Boris was responsible, but rumours to this effect spread among the crowds and it raised their anger to a fever pitch. The rioting flared up again and Alexis, who had remained stubbornly loyal to his chief minister, now had to concede that Boris had become a magnet attracting opposition from all sides. There was no alternative but to relieve his friend of office. Boyar Prince Iakov Cherkasskii took over, which mollified the *strel'tsy*; a number of other ministerial changes were made; and that evening the reviled Pleshcheev was taken out onto Red Square for execution.

The crowd grabbed him from his escort and beat him to death. Nor was this enough for them. As the fires and the looting continued to spread, they bayed loudly for Morozov's blood. Alexis's chief purpose was now to save Boris's life. He prevailed on the Patriarch and on his chaplain Stefan to intercede with the mob. They duly appeared at the Saviour Gate, the Patriarch holding up the revered icon of the Virgin supposedly painted by St Luke to reinforce his plea for pity. They would not heed him. Twice more he tried – then went back to report his failure to the Tsar. Alexis now made his last throw. He went out to confront the crowd in person.

Bare-headed and in a state of high emotion, he kissed the golden cross which the Patriarch held out towards him and, turning to face the sea of people, he begged them in the name of God to calm down and to spare Boris's life. He spoke with tears in his eyes of the debt he owed the man who had brought him up and been a second father to him; and the sight of the Tsar, so young, so vulnerable and Christ-like in his projection of humility, did have some effect. Their hatred of Boris was clearly still intense but many of them appeared to be prepared to listen. There were calls for Peter Trakhoniotov (who was also thought responsible for the salt tax), and Alexis replied that he was not in the Kremlin, that the man must first be found, and his offences properly investigated. Meanwhile they must be patient. Finally, in response to another uproar about Boris Morozov, he suggested that justice might be done if he sent Boris into exile. The fires still raged; a large element of the crowd was still excited and suspicious; and there is some evidence to suggest that Alexis may have been forced to promise to hand Boris over to them, but if he made the undertaking he did not keep it.

Peter Trakhoniotov was eventually found and brought to Red Square for execution. But, as Cherkasskii and his helpers firmed up the loyalty of the *strel'tsy* (their pay cuts were restored) and units of the gentry levies approached the city, Alexis wondered if he might not yet manage to keep Boris near him. The mob's fury had been terrible. They had exacted vengeance even on the corpses of their victims (they had trampled on Pleshcheev's head, steeped it in vodka and thrown it onto a fire; they had burned Trakhoniotov's body, and disinterred the remains of Nazar Chistoi to abuse them too). But for a moment it seemed that their fury, like the conflagrations in the city, might soon burn itself out. It even became possible to make a few arrests. But the citizens of Moscow had not forgotten the Tsar's promise, and Cherkasskii and his associates were also anxious to be rid of Boris. Alexis, however, was nothing if not obstinate. He could not bring himself to do the deed.

The pressures on him mounted. Calls for reform were mounting on all sides, and on 10th June a petition from merchants, gentry and other groups was received. It reminded Alexis of his duty to govern justly and to protect the poor; and quoted from the Psalm of Solomon:

> . . . Judge Thy people with righteousness,
> And Thy poor with justice . . .
> Save the children of the needy,
> And crush the oppressor . . .

The storm, they submitted, was a manifestation of God's anger at injustice. They humbly suggested that Alexis call an Assembly of the Land which would provide representatives of various classes with an opportunity to air their grievances and suggested that he carry out a re-codification of the laws. They also called for Boris to be exiled. Alexis hesitated for at least twenty-four hours. Then he finally gave way.

On 12th June Boris was taken under a strong guard of *strel'tsy* on the first stage of his exile to the St Cyril Monastery at Beloozero, over three hundred miles to the north. A few days later, the worst of the disturbances having subsided, Alexis took the opportunity of a holiday to visit a church outside the Kremlin and to make a political speech on the way.

> I was distressed to hear of the abuses [of power] committed by Pleshcheev and Trakhoniotov. It was done in my name but against my will. Honourable men have been appointed in their place – men who will be pleasing to the people and who will administer justice equally to all. . . . I shall see to it personally that this is strictly done.

He also undertook to lower salt prices and abolish monopolies. The crowd bowed to indicate their gratitude, and he took advantage of the moment.

> I promised [he said] to hand Morozov over to you. But, while I must confess that I cannot altogether justify him, I cannot bring myself to condemn him. The man is dear to me; he is the husband of the Tsaritsa's sister. It would be very hard to hand him over to death.

And as the tears streamed down his face people shouted 'Long live his Majesty. God's will and the Tsar's be done.'[43] A combination of procrastination, good timing and the charisma of office had served, it seemed, to save his friend.

But he did not let Boris go without doing all he could to protect him, and in the weeks that followed, with a series of disturbances being reported from the provinces, he continued to watch over him. On 6th August he dictated a letter to the abbot, provost and bursar of the monastery where his friend was being held ordering them to take all measures necessary 'to ensure that our Boyar Boris Ivanovich Morozov is protected from harm' and, more especially, to consult him as to whether he should remain inside the monastery during a forthcoming fair, which would probably attract all sorts of undesirables who might well make trouble; or whether it would be safer for him to leave the place while it was on. He added a postscript in his own hand:

> You should believe this letter. See to it that you protect him from harm. . . . Do not let anyone know if he should decide to [leave] . . . If anyone should be so informed and I should find out you will be punished. But if you keep him safe you will be doing good to me as well as him and I shall reward you accordingly. . . . Show this letter to my friend.[43]

They did keep him safe, and they were rewarded. Indeed, although the Moscow uprising had spread to the provinces, the issue of the order summoning an Assembly of the Land in July helped to calm the population, and on 29th August Alexis felt able to dictate another letter to those in charge at the St Cyril Monastery: 'Now, by the grace of Almighty God and to our Tsarish pleasure, the time of confusion is receding . . .' It was now safe for Boris to leave for his estate in the province of Tver. They should provide him with an escort, who should be instructed to respect and obey him, and with horses or boats, depending on whether he decided to travel overland or by the river route. Again Alexis added a personal postscript:

> Tell my friend and father-substitute . . . that the time has come for him who brought me up to go to his village at Tver . . . I have added this in my own hand . . . and my seal is on it, so you should believe this letter and release him with great honour and with caution so that his health is well preserved.[44]

Boris got to Tver safely and shortly afterwards moved to another of his estates nearer Moscow. By nightfall on 26th October 1648 he was back in Moscow itself, Alexis having offered each member of the *strel'tsy* a further ten rubles, perhaps more, as a bribe to ensure their complaisance.[45]

Shortly after Boris's return, his successor Prince Cherkasskii was dismissed from office. Since a complete restoration of the old order was out of the question Alexis placed his father-in-law Il'ia in charge of the *strel'tsy*. But he restored Boris to control of less exposed departments, and though Boris was never again to wield such power as he had done formerly, he was to remain something of an *éminence grise*. Alexis had salvaged something from the storm. It remained for him, with God's help, to find ways of establishing a new order that would prove less fragile than the last.

Chapter III

The Pursuit of Good Order

Throughout the summer of 1648 the population had been restless and the atmosphere in the Kremlin remained tense. Demands for reform continued to stream in; rebellions flared up spasmodically in the provinces; shrewd men considered that the slightest spark might set a new conflagration raging in the capital itself. The situation called for the utmost caution — but it demanded action too. Somehow the government had to reassert its authority; somehow it had to find a way of building lasting social peace. It was a daunting challenge, and Alexis confronted it with a confidence that betrayed his youthful innocence.

While most of his advisers thought in terms of shady political trading and manipulation, he conceived of a solution in terms of two clear-cut principles: justice and autocracy. He meant to honour his promise of reform by carrying out a thorough revision and updating of the laws. But he was equally determined that his autocratic rights should in no way be diluted. Muscovy must never go the way of heretical England where Parliament now ruled the King. Yet on 12th July, at the height of the crisis, Alexis had been prevailed upon to call an Assembly of the Land. It was due to meet on 1st September and the representatives were already beginning to trickle into Moscow.

They comprised all sorts (except peasants, who, as in other countries of the time, counted for nothing in the scales of politics). There were bishops and magnates who knew Moscow well and who understood how things were managed there; but there were also provincial servicemen and townspeople who, though officially designated 'good and sensible men . . . experienced in the affairs of state and of the land', wandered about Moscow eyes agape at the wonder of the place. It was huge — more than ten times as populous as any other city in the country — a maze of bustling streets, each specializing in particular commodities: caviare and boats and books;

wines imported from the West and damasks from the Orient; weapons, cooking pots and huge church bells. Almost anything that a man might crave or his imagination might conceive of was to be had here. But the visitors could not help but notice, too, the ugly gaps left by the recent fires, even though these were already being fast filled in (for prefabricated timber housing was another of Moscow's specialities). And there, in the centre of it all, capped by golden roofs and domes, they glimpsed the fabled Kremlin, their destination.

Over 300 representatives eventually assembled there. They included 14 prelates, 40 members of Moscow's lay elite, 3 great merchants and 4 lesser ones. But these were heavily outnumbered by the humbler sort – 15 *strel'tsy* and 12 spokesmen from the Moscow hundreds; about 80 from other towns (5 from Novgorod and 1 or 2 each from others according to their size), and some 150 representatives of the provincial gentry and the lower serving classes.[1] No doubt many of them were awed by the occasion and its setting, but they knew what they wanted and, as events were soon to demonstrate, they were not afraid to speak their minds. Nonetheless, although they were divided into an 'upper' house (in fact the boyar Duma) and a 'lower' one, this was to be no parliament of the English sort, still less a revolutionary one. The 'lower house' was allowed only to discuss business placed before it and to present petitions relevant to the Assembly's central purpose: to establish what the laws of the land were and what they should be. The government took good care to retain the initiative throughout. Rather than a parliament, then, the Assembly assumed a character not altogether dissimilar from a latter-day party congress. It was used as a sounding-board for the regime, to approve rather than initiate policies, and to provide popular legitimation for the decisions that the Tsar and his government would actually take.

Alexis himself was excited by the enterprise. The prospect of gaining the reputation of a legislator, like Justinian the Great or Ivan the Terrible, appealed to him, and he participated in the work with great enthusiasm. He not only presided over the 'upper house' but closeted himself 'with his collaborators every day in order to construct good [legal] arrangements whereby the people should, so far as possible, be satisfied'.[2] His chief collaborator was Boyar Prince Nikita Odoevskii, a senior Council member in his late forties who had acquired considerable experience as a provincial governor and earned something of a reputation as a military man as well. But it was Nikita's position at the head of a special secretariat set up to prepare the complete codification of the laws that made him Alexis's closest companion during these days.

The secretariat had the task of carrying out the necessary research to define what the law actually was (no easy business in view of the hundreds of orders and judicial decisions, some of them conflicting, that had piled up in the decades since the last, and only partial, codification), and to ensure that the best precedents were followed. To this end they had been ordered to consult the rules of the Apostles and the Fathers of the Church, and 'the civil laws of the Greek [i.e. Byzantine] Emperors', selecting those which were appropriate to both the state and the land, as well as collating all of Alexis's own enactments, those of his predecessors and the judgements delivered by 'the boyars' (the nearest Muscovite equivalent to case law). They had to reconcile all of this, act as a clearing house for the petitions, draft such new legislation as was deemed necessary, and submit the whole to the Assembly for its consent.

The first twelve chapters of the draft Code were ready for Alexis's consideration when he returned from his regular autumn pilgrimage on 3rd October. They dealt with blasphemy and order in the Church; with the Tsar's own honour and security; with order at the court; with regulations concerning servicemen on campaign, communications, and other matters. But for all his natural inclination to immerse himself in detail Alexis was above all concerned about one overriding legal principle, which he was to refer to with some frequency in his personal correspondence. The principle was defined succinctly in the preamble to the Code: '[that] the administration of justice in all cases be equal for all . . . ranks of people from the greatest to the least'.

The idea was Byzantine in origin. It had figured more than once in the legislation of Leo the Wise, and was commended by that popular manual for the guidance of princes, *The Secret of Secrets*. Yet it was a strange notion in the context of seventeenth-century Muscovy where there were no trained lawyers, no distinctions between the executive and the judicature; where it was natural for decisions to favour the powerful and go against the weak, and where the people had no comprehension of due process. Nonetheless, as is clear from his personal correspondence,[3] Alexis was captivated by the idea, and equality of justice was enshrined in the Code as a major tenet of Russian law. This is not to imply that Alexis ever regarded himself as bound by laws, even those he was about to sanction. As an autocrat he stood above such things. Nor did he ever imagine that the phrase should imply that the laws themselves should favour all sections of the population equally. Like another Byzantine Emperor he considered it necessary at times to favour the rich at the expense of an arguably over-favoured poor.[4] But he was intent that the laws themselves be applied accurately and even-handedly.

A clearer idea of his understanding of the phrase 'justice equal for all' emerges from the long tenth chapter of the Code. It laid down that his boyars and other, lower-ranking, agents were to 'treat all the people in the state of Muscovy from the greatest to the humblest in rank according to the law (*vpravdu*) . . . and not to add nor take away anything from [it] in the process of judging, whether by their own fancy (*vymysl*) [or] on account of friendship or enmity [to a party involved in the case]; not to favour a friend nor take vengeance on an enemy, nor to act in the interest of any person in any case for any reason whatsoever. [Furthermore, they were to] carry out the Sovereign's business without being shy of powerful personages, and deliver the wronged from the hand of injustice.' Procedures were laid down for appeals and punishments for judges who infringed the principle: deprivation of honours for those of Councillor rank; dismissal without re-employment coupled with public disgrace for others.[5]

Alexis's obsession with justice, fed by his idealism and his respect for Roman precedent, was politically opportune since injustice and maladministration had been among the major grievances of the protestors. Even so it was not enough to satisfy them. It was also necessary that certain of the laws of Muscovy be changed in order to conform with current social needs. This was another principle that had informed the legislation of the Emperor Justinian and of other codifiers since, but it involved political dilemmas. It was clear from the petitions that the economic grievances of certain sectors of society – notably the townsmen, who had been the backbone of the Moscow uprising, and the provincial servicemen, who had been involved in the riots in the provinces which followed, must be redressed. The question was, at whose expense should they be satisfied?

It was during the earlier stages of deliberation over these issues that on 22nd October Alexis was interrupted during an all-night service at the Kazan Cathedral by the sudden arrival of his father-in-law, Il'ia. The choir was just starting the anthem for matins as he rushed in with the news: the Tsaritsa had been safely delivered of a child – and it was a boy! A euphoric Alexis briefly acknowledged the congratulations of those present and abruptly left the service to visit his wife and heir.

He decided that his sister Irina should be the godmother;[6] that his son should be christened Dmitrii, after the last, unfortunate, Tsar of the Riurikid dynasty; and that next spring he would make a pilgrimage to Uglich, where the boy-Tsar Dmitrii had met his death. A few days later Boris returned to Moscow and shared his joy. Boris's arrival coincided with a moment of critical decision over the forms that the concessions to the townsmen and the gentry should take, and although there was little love lost between Boris and Cherkasskii it was Cherkasskii's stance over policy rather than any personal factor that led Alexis to dismiss him as his chief minister.

In order to satisfy the provincial gentry, a law abolishing the time-limit on the return of runaway serfs had been mooted for inclusion in the Code. This would have harmed the interests of great landlords like Cherkasskii who, in conditions of a general labour shortage, were making good use of runaways who had sought refuge on their estates. Others, including Boris, would also suffer from it; so would the Church. Indeed the Church was threatened with an additional blow by being forbidden to accumulate any more land, whether by purchase, gift or legacy,[7] in order to prevent any further drain on land available for allotment to those who served the state. Hard though these measures were, however, most members of the 'upper house' were persuaded to accept them as a modest price to pay for peace in the countryside. That the law on runaways also barred the last legal escape route for serfs and placed them firmly under the jurisdiction of their lords seems to have worried no one; but the legislators should not be blamed for failing to foresee the dire effects that serfdom would have, nor for offending the moral standards of a future age. In terms of the moment they were following a trend already set by other states in Eastern Europe,[8] the ethics of the age, and the dictates of necessity.

But what seems to have angered Cherkasskii even more than the compulsory return of runaway serfs was the means proposed to placate the townsmen. One of their chief grievances concerned urban traders and artisans who were exempt from tax by virtue of being ascribed to the Church or to members of the secular elite. This presented them with competition on unfair terms. It also increased the tax burden they had to bear since taxation was levied on the group as a whole and increasing numbers of their enterprising fellows were escaping their shares of the collective obligation by seeking the protection of some magnate or monastery. Thanks to Alexis and Odoevskii the tax-paying townsmen got their way. Traders and artisans with premises in Moscow, its environs and in other urban centres were henceforth to pay their obligations to the state and forbidden to ascribe themselves to anyone on pain of dispossession, flogging and exile to Siberia. Peasants who had set up shop were forced to sell and return to their former homes, although, to prevent any further increase in the price of food, peasants from the countryside were still to be allowed to bring their produce in for sale. As for the untaxed urban properties of the Church and the magnates, they were simply confiscated for the crown.[9] Alexis as well as the townsmen reaped the benefit; the Church, cousin Nikita Romanov and Cherkasskii paid the price, and it was considerable.

Nor did the work of codification end there. The laws were also clarified in respect of service estates[10] and oaths of loyalty;[11] slavery[12] and taverns[13] were regulated; penalties were defined for crimes against the person,[14] and measures were enacted for the preservation of order in the realm. Retired servicemen were to act as provincial magistrates (provided they were literate) and provisions were made for the construction and maintenance of prisons.[15] By 29th January 1649, after less than four months' deliberation, the task was completed, endorsed by all except Cherkasskii, Nikita Romanov and a handful of others, and sent to the printing house for publication. The representatives dispersed for home.

Alexis was well pleased with the outcome, as well he might have been. He may not have become a new Justinian, but his new Code represented a considerable achievement in knitting principles and practical decisions together. Furthermore, the Assembly of the Land had served as a means of strengthening the crown's authority, not of weakening it.[16] Alexis might not yet be in a position fully to exercise his theoretical rights as autocrat, but the rights had been preserved. He would be able to hand them on to little Dmitrii not one whit diminished.

No doubt the achievements were largely the product of Nikita Odoevskii's secretariat and of the collective wisdom of his other advisers, most of whom displayed an acute political sensitivity and some deft manoeuvring to match. Nevertheless Alexis also deserves a measure of credit, inexperienced though he was. It was his philosophy as much as anyone else's which informed the Code, and he had made a political contribution too. By no means all his Councillors had been agreed on all the issues; some of the most important measures had been violently opposed by powerful interests. It was largely due to Alexis's firmness that Cherkasskii and his allies did not get their way, that the Church took its reverses like a lamb, and that the discord was no greater than it was. And for all the refusal of some powerful men to sign it, Alexis's Code was to remain Russia's basic law book until well into the nineteenth century.

The mere enactment of laws, however, does not in itself guarantee their observance or enforcement. The Code was not to produce equal justice for all even within Alexis's understanding of the term. Those in authority continued to accept bribes, albeit less openly than before. According to one Moscow bureaucrat of the time, they did so 'on the back stairs, through their wives or daughters or through a son, a brother or a bondman, pretending that they know nothing about it and are not taking bribes at all'.[17] A governor accused of maladministration or of accepting bribes might be forced to repay them and even be dismissed his post,[18] but the Tsar and the more honest of his agents were not easily accessible to complainants – and a commoner who petitioned the Tsar direct could expect a flogging even if his case was looked into, so great were the continuing fears for Alexis's safety.

The new laws, though they satisfied substantial and hitherto dangerous sectors of society, were by no means universally popular either. As late as January 1649 there were fears of serious disturbances on the part of tax-exempt townsmen who did not want to join the category of taxpayers, and even though a number of the less reliable *strel'tsy* had been safely packed off to Siberia a conspiracy was uncovered among those who remained.[19] Some new elite palace guard was clearly necessary, but the idea of forming such a force, 5,000 men strong, to be trained by a Dutchman, Colonel Boeckhoven, foundered on the rock of xenophobia and had to be abandoned. Eventually about 3,000 recruits were mustered to replace the men who had been exiled from Moscow and a *strelets* elite of six regiments, each about 1,000 strong, was organized. Every man was hand-picked; every officer a man of impeccable loyalty. Artamon Matveev, Alexis's childhood friend and school companion, was commissioned into one of them. Henceforth this life guard mounted watch over the palace and the approaches to the Kremlin on a rotation basis, day by day.[20]

Yet all these measures failed to satisfy the Tsar. The selective concessions to strident groups among the population, the unmasking of sedition, the suppression of disturbances and the tightening of his personal security were all reactive or precautionary measures to counter the epidemic of disorders that was afflicting Muscovy along with the rest of Europe. They dealt only with the symptoms of the disease; Alexis wished to cure it. He wanted to seek out the very sources of dissent; to destroy the cancerous tree of rebellion root and branch. Indeed, he was beginning to find his way towards a solution. It amounted to nothing less than a campaign for moral regeneration.

On 5th December 1648 he had issued an instruction which was to be read out on Sundays and festivals in every church throughout the land. It contained a solemn warning to the people to desist from spiritually rebellious and devilish acts. They were not to listen to the mockery of itinerant minstrels or buskers; they must shun sorcerers; they must not play immoral and devilish games, nor bait bears or dance with dogs, nor sing diabolical songs. Nor must anyone wear a mask, indulge in moon-gazing or take part in an orgy of mass bathing. Lewd processions and rites which smacked of witchcraft were forbidden. Popular musical instruments were to be confiscated and burned. Offenders were to be thrashed with switches and suffer exile for a third offence; and the wandering minstrels themselves (the notorious *skomorokhy*, popular throughout the realm for their satires and barbs against authority) were to be flogged for a first offence, heavily fined and flogged for a second.[21]

The onslaught on popular customs and entertainments did not stem simply from an excess of religious puritanism; it had a serious political purpose akin to that which informed the Counter-Reformation in the Habsburg Empire and elsewhere.[22] Then as now, satire was regarded as potentially subversive. The pagan practices (sometimes so much more enjoyable than Christian ones) were widespread and deeply rooted, and they faced the Church with competition which made its task of supporting the secular power more difficult. Paganism might also afford a counter-ideology, of however primitive a kind, that was conducive to disobedience and hence a challenge to the central authority. A shaman or witch who enjoyed some local respect stood in the way of a Tsar who wished to monopolize his subjects' deference. On the other hand, to force people to go to church, and to ensure that parish priests were appointed by the bishops and not chosen by their parishioners (a traditional practice, still widely honoured, which preserved local autonomy at the expense of Moscow's control), were measures conducive to political obedience.

Alexis was not unaware of the disreputable behaviour that went on in the countryside. He learned about it from the clerics who had served as parish priests, among them a new acquaintance introduced to him by his chaplain Stefan. His name was Avvakum. Avvakum (as he himself was to record in his memoirs) once confronted a troupe of godless travelling entertainers who wore masks, played damnable lutes and drums and had two performing bears in tow. He had torn into them full of righteous zeal. 'I drove them out and broke the buffoons' masks and drums on a common outside the village, one against many, and took away the two great bears.'[23] Such zealous behaviour did not endear the likes of Avvakum to their parishioners; it did commend them to the Tsar. They were good recruits for his crusade to promote good order.

Following the trauma he had experienced in 1648, Alexis's concern for 'good order' (*blagoustroistvo, uriadstvo*) was becoming obsessive. This was evident in his anxiety to extirpate rebellion, whether political or spiritual; but it began to find expression in other ways and was even to affect the conduct of his recreations. His taste for ceremonial became increasingly theatrical; and a suggestion of the martinet emerged in him as well as he groped for ways to make every activity orderly, deliberate, concerted, measured; to free them from any taint of anarchy or individual self-will. He could not yet find words adequate to express his all-embracing vision (though he was to make such attempts), but his vision was also reflected in another campaign on which he now embarked – to bring order to the liturgy. It was a campaign that he was inspired to mount by his love of music, his sense of theatre, and his religious proclivities as well as his new-found passion for good order, but it was to bring him into conflict with the Patriarch of Moscow.

Alexis wanted to eliminate the common practice of shortening church services by gabbling various parts of it off simultaneously, one priest racing through a Psalm while another rushed off a prayer and a deacon chanted a canticle in the background. The practice smacked of spiritual anarchy; it offended his sense of harmony and of decorum. Instead he wanted to enforce a rule by which the liturgy was sung in proper order with every word of it clearly enunciated so that its beauty should be apparent to all – and if his subjects had to spend longer in church as a result, so much the better for them. His chaplain Stefan, Nikon and others of his clerical friends were enthusiastic in their support; but there were also those around him, not least the Patriarch Joseph, who were distinctly cool.[24] The simultaneous gabbling of prayers might offend the Tsar's aesthetic sensibilities but it was a practice honoured by time. True, it had been banned almost a century before, but the ban had been widely ignored and to reintroduce it now would make for trouble among the clergy, and probably make church attendance even less popular than it already was. Such was the Patriarch's opinion and he was head of the Church.

Nonetheless the Tsar had the right to convoke a church council to decide the issue and Alexis did so. It met in the palace on 11th February 1649. The Patriarch presided but Stefan and Nikon were among the twenty-eight others who attended and Alexis was confident that they would win the day.[25] He was wrong. The Patriarch could not bring himself to do more than recommend that monasteries be instructed to adopt the proposal. Parish churches should be exempt in his view – and the majority concurred. At this Stefan burst out in a tirade against the assembly in general and the Patriarch in particular. He called them 'wolves'; he accused them of being 'destroyers rather than shepherds'; he said they would destroy God's true Church. Together with Nikon and Ivan Neronov he refused to sign the resolution, and stalked out of the hall to report the matter to the Tsar. The aged Joseph, understandably angry and distressed, promptly submitted a petition calling for Stefan to be punished. Alexis ordered both men to attend him.

It was an acrimonious meeting at which Stefan and the Patriarch gave vent to violent emotion. Stefan railed on about the decision, claiming that it showed the Church in Muscovy was not a Church of God; the Patriarch called for Stefan to be punished, preferably by death. 'It is written in your Majesty's Law Code', he said, referring to the very document he himself had set his hand to with such heaviness of heart to please the Tsar, 'that anyone uttering such insults to the ecumenical and apostolic Church should suffer death, and Stefan has insulted both the Church and me.'[26] Fortunately, the old man's excitement had got the better of his memory. The Code did prescribe the death penalty for blasphemy, for interrupting mass, and for committing murder in a church; but it did not do so for Stefan's offence. Alexis tried to make the peace. Stefan was reprimanded; no order concerning the conduct of church services was issued.

Given the assembly's decision, there was little that Alexis could do. Yet he would not let the matter drop. Instead he found a means of outflanking his own Patriarch by applying to another. He consulted the Patriarch of Constantinople, the senior prelate of the Orthodox Church. The answer to his letter was not to arrive for many months, but when it did so it was pleasing. Constantinople approved. With that ruling to brandish at Joseph it was no longer difficult to persuade him to change his mind, and through him, those of the other doubtful clerics. Another church assembly was summoned. It duly endorsed the reform.[27] But it took Alexis two years to get his way – two years over one measure.

His frustration reflected both his youthful impatience and the limits of his power. There were so many things he wanted to do yet could not, nominal autocrat though he was. If only he had more men about him who shared his objectives and showed vigour in pursuing them; men who would not place obstacles in his way, men who would not drag their feet. He needed fewer Josephs and more of Nikon's calibre. In Nikon, it seemed, he had found someone of real stature – a man at once pious, fearless, learned and politic; a man who shared the vision flowering in his mind, and who would help to make it real. So it was that in March 1648 he had had Nikon installed as Metropolitan of Novgorod, the second most important see in all the land. At the same time he had urged Nikon (like some latter-day political commissar) to report directly to him on any sign of corruption or disloyalty in the civil administration of the province.[28] Nikon did so. He understood very well that to gain the Tsar's trust was to gain the keys to power.

Much has been made of Alexis's susceptibility to Nikon's influence, but it should not be overstressed. What earned Nikon particular favour, other than his impressive personal qualities, was the fact that Alexis found him to be of one mind with himself about so many things. And if Alexis found many of Nikon's ideas congenial, the influence was by no means one-sided. Nikon himself changed his mind over several matters in order to bring his views into alignment with the Tsar's. He was subsequently to claim that he had subscribed to the Law Code against his better judgement; he was also to trim over another cause which Alexis had espoused – the idea of making the Muscovite Church truly ecumenical by bringing its texts and liturgy into line with their Greek originals.

Alexis's purpose in this was as much political as religious. For Muscovites to pray in the same way as other Orthodox Christians would reinforce the Tsar's claims to be the protector of all those Christians from Ukraine to Alexandria. Alexis had evidently taken to the idea in the course of conversations with Stefan and with his friend Fedor Rtishchev; and he was spurred on by the fear that if he did not assume this role some Orthodox Balkan princeling might claim it by default. (As recently as 1642 Basil Lupu, Prince of Moldavia and a vassal of the Ottoman Sultan, had presided over an Orthodox Church Council attended by the Archbishop of Kiev and was reported to have visions of being crowned an Emperor.) And the arrival in Moscow towards the end of January 1649 of Patriarch Paisos of Jerusalem added more fuel to the fires of Alexis's ambition.

Like other visiting Greek clerics before him, Paisios's main purpose was to raise funds for the Church, and the Holy Places, in Palestine (although it was also pleasing to be treated deferentially by a Tsar and to live in luxury at his expense for several months). But if the clever Greek had come to Moscow cap in hand, he knew how to pander to his host's susceptibilities, and he was honey-tongued about it. His address to the Tsar at their very first meeting struck just the right inspiring note:

> May the Most Holy Trinity . . . bless your sovereign empire, exalt you above all monarchs, and make you victorious over . . . all enemies, both visible and invisible, like . . . King David, King Hezekiah and the Emperor Constantine the Great. May he grant you strength and increase your years into deep old age. May he deem you worthy to mount the throne of the great Emperor Constantine, your predecessor, and to liberate pious Orthodox Christians from the clutch of the infidels, from the ferocious wild beasts that consume us. . . . May you be a new Moses who will liberate us from captivity as he liberated the Children of Israel from the hands of Pharaoh. . . .[29]

Alexis was not unmoved by the prospect of becoming an all-conquering, ecumenical Emperor who would one day drive the Turks out of all the Christian lands they occupied and re-create Constantine's Empire, ruling it, perhaps, from Constantinople which had been the centre of Christendom for a thousand years. It was a distant dream, of course, but a dream which was to linger at the back of Alexis's mind for years to come. And so he listened with particular attention to certain criticisms which Paisios offered concerning Russian Orthodoxy. Not only did there seem to be divergences from the original Greek in the liturgy, there were differences in ritual as well. Among other things Muscovites made the sign of the cross with two fingers and not three. Such divergences drove a wedge between Orthodox Christians, separating Russians from the rest. Already predisposed to do so, Alexis now resolved to rectify the matter. Nikon was not so predisposed. Like so many other zealots of piety, he tended to be a religious nationalist, defensively suspicious of Greeks like Paisios. Nonetheless Nikon was persuaded to concur.

Developments in Ukraine heightened interest in the project at this time. The Orthodox Ukrainians had rebelled against their Polish overlords and had applied to Muscovy for protection and support. In February 1649 another emissary from the Ukrainian leader, Bogdan Khmelnytsky, was in Moscow pressing Alexis to intervene. Ukraine was not only a great territorial prize; its possession would give Muscovy a spring-board from which to launch a war to liberate the Orthodox populations of the Balkans. For the moment, unfortunately, Muscovy was in no position to risk a major conflict with Poland, though everything short of that was done: a mission was sent to Bogdan at his headquarters in the town of Chigirin to explain that although Muscovy could only accept Ukraine as a protectorate if the King of Poland acquiesced, economic aid and covert shipments of arms would be provided, and any Orthodox Ukrainian who might want to cross the border would be given refuge in Muscovy.[30] Meanwhile Alexis set out to prepare Muscovites ideologically for a great crusade of liberation; and the alignment of Muscovite religious texts and practices with those of other Orthodox communities formed a part of those preparations.

The task appealed not only to Alexis's ambition to become a conqueror, but to the scholar in him, to his centralizing instincts and to his ecumenical ideals. If Moscow was indeed the Third Rome, the rightful successor to Byzantium which had been the Second Rome, as some Muscovites had liked to believe for generations past,[31] then it must break out of its provincialism or fail to seize its destiny. The problem was how the task might be accomplished; how the necessary expertise to align the Greek and Russian practices might be acquired. Fedor Rtishchev already had his scheme to bring learned monks from the Ukrainian city of Kiev to Moscow, but this was evidently considered insufficient, for Alexis himself now sent to the Bratskii Monastery in Kiev requesting the services of scholars who would be equal to the task. And meanwhile the Patriarch Paisios recommended a member of his own entourage, called Arsenios, to the Tsar. Arsenios knew no Russian, but he could learn it, and in all other respects he was well qualified to help the project forward. Alexis accepted the offer. The move stirred up a hornets' nest.

Arsenios the Greek provided a splendid focus of opposition for those Muscovite nationalists and obscurantists who disliked foreigners in general, 'clever' Greeks in particular, and feared 'foreign' learning as a threat to all that they held dear. In the opinion of such people (and there were many of them both at court and among the clergy) foreigners would turn Moscow into a Tower of Babel, and the likes of Arsenios meddling with their religion would introduce confusion and heresy into what had always been a safe and comfortable spiritual fortress. It was said that Arsenios had studied medicine at Padua, that he had sojourned in that den of iniquity which was Rome, and been trained up for his subversive mission by the Jesuits.

Unfortunately the rumours seemed to be well based. Early in July 1649 Arsenios was denounced as a secret convert to Catholicism – and, for good measure, a forced convert to Islam too – by none other than Paisios himself (in what circumstances we know not) as he made his way home to Jerusalem.[32] Arsenios had become an embarrassment. Yet Alexis had a use for him. The Greek was sent off to Solovka in the far north of the country to learn Russian and Church Slavonic; and in due course, once the dust had settled, he was to be brought back to Moscow and set to work on the task for which he had been engaged. Meanwhile the Bratskii Monastery in Kiev had responded to Alexis's request. Two monks, Epifany Slavinetskii and Arsenyi Satanovskii, arrived in Moscow during 1649; a third, Damaskin Ptitskii, followed a year later. These men were conversant with both Slavonic and Greek. Moreover, as Ukrainians, they were more acceptable to the xenophobes than Greeks. The work of reconciliation went ahead.

Indeed, the activity of these scholars was to have an importance extending beyond the religious sphere. Slavinetskii in particular was to produce a number of translations from Latin as well as Greek concerning such subjects as cosmography, medicine, mineralogy, philosophy and politics[33] – works which were to broaden the intellectual horizons of such Muscovites as had access to them, and so help breach the dyke of mediaeval conceptions which were holding new, western, influences at bay. For the moment, however, the dyke held firm. Innovation of any sort aroused screams of protest. Anyone who knew Latin was widely assumed to have turned aside from the path of righteousness, and heresy was considered to be an inherent ingredient of Greek. Even many who accepted the necessity of correcting the church books preferred them to be compared with early Slavonic texts rather than with the Greek originals. As Alexis was discovering, there was no point in trying to impose reforms and innovations in the teeth of such widespread and violent opposition; to do so would guarantee failure and perhaps invite political disaster. To succeed he had to cultivate patience, play the fox.

It was a relief, therefore, to turn occasionally to pursuits in which he could not be baulked – to falconry, of course, and to the management of his personal estates. His first step towards imposing his own order on these was to find out precisely what assets he disposed of. This much is shown by the instructions he set down in his own hand for Peter Khomiakov, one of his trusties in the Falconry Office. They required Peter to draw up a complete inventory of two villages which had recently reverted to the crown. Alexis's approach was thorough, although the manuscript of the original draft with all its scratchings out and reformulations suggests that he had no pre-existing model on which to base this domestic census. Peter was to list every household in the villages; note whether they belonged to a peasant, a cottar, or a tradesman; question each of them 'carefully as to how long he had been resident . . . and [to] write down their Christian names, their surnames and their ages'. From human capital he was to proceed to other assets. Alexis instructed Peter to log the number of animals each possessed, their stocks of grain and flour, and 'question them as to how much arable they ploughed' on their old master's demesne and how much seed they sowed upon it. Alexis also wanted to know what they had been used to paying in quit-rent and what the total income from quit-rents was; how much hay was produced; whether there were any ponds and lakes on the estates, and the acreage of forest-land upon them.[34]

The approach was that of a good husbandman, a sound enough foundation upon which to build ambitious farming plans. And that Alexis had such plans, and agricultural innovations generally, in mind is suggested by the arrival from Stockholm in December 1650 of a Frenchman, Pascal Poitevin, who entered his service as an expert in horticulture, irrigation and the cultivation of vines.[35] The interest was prompted by more than recreational or academic interests; the purpose, as it transpired, was to increase production and profits. Alexis evidently understood that money provided a basis for success in statecraft; that it was the sinews of war. And to the same end parallel efforts were continued to find deposits of silver which could be used for minting money (of which Muscovy was chronically short), and of other precious metals, and to secure a favourable balance of trade.[36]

Nonetheless, Alexis was beginning to spend much more freely than he had done before. Over the winter of 1649–50 he had new quarters built on his estate at Kolomenskoe, a favourite haunt of Ivan the Terrible, sited on a bluff overlooking the River Moscow only a few miles from the Kremlin.[37] He was also dressing more sumptuously, partly as a means of impressing those who saw him with the grandeur of his office. His hunting establishment was growing too, and so was expenditure on his family and on entertaining. In February 1650 Maria gave birth to a second child, a girl he decided to call Evdokia to commemorate his mother,[38] and this occasioned another series of dinners and receptions, given by the Tsaritsa as well as by himself.

It was at a dinner given for him by Maria, to which a few members of the Council had been invited, that Sub-Boyar Prince Ivan Romodanovskii created a stir by objecting to being seated below his colleague on the Council, V. V. Buturlin. This Ivan had behaved objectionably, for the same reason, at a dinner given by the Patriarch on Palm Sunday. He had slipped under his seat and had had to be hauled up by the arms and held forcibly in his place, protesting loudly all the while.[39] The man was punished and forced to submit, of course, but it was hard for Alexis to witness such a blast of personal pride. It affronted his dignity and spoiled the joy of the occasion. It also added to his difficulty, already considerable, in holding his inner ring of servitors together.

Inevitably there were jealousies and rivalries between the members of his Council. But outsiders also attempted to set them at each other's throats and to arouse Alexis's own mistrust of them. The conspirators who had been unmasked in January 1649 had tried to implicate Prince Cherkasskii.[40] Six months later a gentleman with a grudge against Bogdan Khitrovo, another member of the Council, had accused him of conspiring with Boyar Prince Alexis Trubetskoi and Fedor Rtishchev to murder Boris Morozov.[41] Fortunately the allegations proved false, but they had had to be taken seriously, and although the liars were punished (two had their tongues torn out; another was flogged) suspicions tended to linger. Alexis had ordered every member of the Council to attend the trial of those accused in the first case; he had personally delivered judgement in the second. But he was anxious to do more to dispel the doubts; to build up trust and accord between his helpers, to demonstrate that he himself harboured no suspicions of his boyars, even those who had lost office.

He continued to invite members of the Cherkasskii and Sheremetev clans, as well as the Morozovs, to dine with him from time to time. He also used his precious leisure time to show them and others favour. On one occasion he asked Boris Morozov, Iakov Cherkasskii, Nikita Romanov (who had been so incensed about the Law Code) and Prince A. M. L'vov (with whose direction of the Palace Office he was becoming increasingly dissatisfied) along with several others to a bear hunt. The invitation took the form of a mock petition that began 'Your Tsar prostrates himself and requests'. Would they ride with him to Ozeretskoe in pursuit of an old bear that had been reported in that vicinity? Would they have dinner with him afterwards, prior to their return to Moscow? He ended by wishing them 'spiritual salvation and bodily health' – and asked them to acknowledge his 'petition' by signing their names upon the back.[42] This jocular reversal of roles reflected more than high spirits; more, even, than a warm and friendly disposition; it was another means of inviting loyalty to his person and of promoting harmony among the prominent.

Alexis also took the senior boyars with him, as well as his entire family, when on 22nd May 1650 he left on the pilgrimage to Uglich which he had vowed to make when Dmitrii had been born. Kashin and the Koliazin Monastery had since been added to the itinerary, which also included Zagorsk, so that the pilgrimage was of unusual length; and it was vast in scale. The palace stables office was busy with the arrangements for weeks beforehand, ensuring that the necessary equipages would be in good order, that the hundreds of horses needed would be ready, and that oats and hay would be available in sufficient quantities along the route. Functionaries saw to it that everything the party might want was carried in the expedition's baggage, and others were sent ahead to ensure that the roads were adequately prepared and that appropriate lodgings would be ready at each staging point.

The pilgrimage itself, which was to last over a month, served as a holiday for the royal party too and predictably falconry played a prominent part in their activities. Alexis supervised the arrangements personally, sending regular instructions and requests to Afanasy Matiushkin in Moscow, and giving him news of what happened along the way. The pace was leisurely. The hunting began on 23rd May at Alexis's lodge at Rostokino. Two days later they reached Taraskova, still only fifteen miles from Moscow. From Taraskova Alexis wrote to Afanasy, exhorting him to train the birds in his charge 'as hard as God allows' and calling for exact reports of their condition – especially one called 'Little Corporal' (*Karpun'ka*) which was ailing. The only news of interest which he conveyed was that a new falconer, Mishka Semenov, had nodded off beside a fire and fallen into it, though he had been pulled out quickly enough for him to escape a serious burning.[43]

It was an idyllic time, providing balm for the spirit. Only occasional showers of rain interrupted the party's sport. Maria and the ladies, wearing silk scarves and white hats to give them shade against the hot spring sun,[44] enjoyed the rural scene, though they were also encouraged to take part in the hunting. They were provided with merlins for this purpose – small birds that would not overtax their strength as would the large ones handled by the men. The party had more good sport in the neighbourhood of the Trinity–St Sergius shrines, and beyond. But after they moved northwards to the Koliazin Monastery on 4th June they met a fifty-mile stretch of densely-wooded country where there was no prey to be had – not even little forest birds, as Alexis informed Matiushkin. His luck changed at Koliazin on the upper Volga, about two hundred miles from Moscow, where there was some good open country and plenty of wild duck, though, in order to give variety, Alexis had arranged for birds of other species to be brought up and released as prey. The hunting there was first class and Alexis was pleased with the performance of his falcons. Even 'the foolish "Cossack" made a catch'.

The Koliazin Monastery was the base from which they visited their other points of pilgrimage – Uglich, which was forty miles farther up-river, and Kashin, twenty-five miles to the north-west. Both had been chosen as much for their political symbolism as for their spiritual associations. Uglich was where the boy-Tsar Dmitrii, last of the Riurikid line, had met his death, and thus served to connect the old dynasty with the new in the public mind. It also contained the Alexis Monastery, completed in the year of Alexis's own birth, with its marvellous Church of the Assumption: three steep-pitched, red-brick towers soaring heavenwards to symbolize the hoped-for spiritual and political union of all the Russias – Muscovy, Belorussia and Ukraine. Kashin, however, was no less important than was Uglich at that moment. The remains of Princess Anna of Tver, whose prayers were believed to have saved the city from the Poles during the Time of Troubles, had recently been found at Kashin. Alexis took a prominent part in the ceremonial reintombment of her remains, which amounted to canonization. It was another proclamation of Muscovy's hardening attitude towards Poland. Only recently Alexis had sent a formal protest to Warsaw about Polish treatment of Orthodox Ukrainians, and their continuing occupation of Smolensk and other territories formerly belonging to the Muscovite crown. A sizeable indemnity had been demanded – and the withdrawal from sale of certain books which attributed sovereignty of those territories to the Polish crown. But the pilgrimage might have seemed an even clearer indication of Alexis's attitude. It was meant to encourage Russian patriotism and hostility to the oppressive Poles. It was also, perhaps, a harbinger of war.

Nonetheless falconry was never far from the forefront of Alexis's mind throughout the expedition. On 11th June, a week after his arrival in Koliazin, he dictated another letter to Afanasy giving detailed instructions for the care and training of the birds and patiently repeating others, though he had to leave some things to the man's discretion since 'I shall not return from the expedition for some time yet'. He warned that falconers could expect a flogging if any of the sick birds should die through their neglect or carelessness, asked a series of detailed questions about the condition of particular birds, and communicated the names he had chosen for five new falcons. He also instructed Afanasy to set up a new falconry base at Kolomenskoe and to make arrangements for another hunt which he intended to make from Pokrovskoe on 30th June, after his return. But the letter also reflected his concern for order and discipline among those who served him. Afanasy was to ensure that 'accord and friendship' was maintained among the falconers, 'that there should be no discord of any kind between them', and that the junior staff be held 'on a tight rein so that they behave respectfully to you and . . . Peter Khomiakov'.[45]

For all the work upon the Law Code, for all the concessions to the malcontents, and for all his attempts to impose religious obedience upon his subjects, many of them were still forgetting their duty towards God and the Tsar. The great pilgrimage had taken place against a background of further serious disorders, this time in the north-west of the country, in Novgorod and Pskov. Triggered by grain exports to Sweden which seemed to threaten increased food prices, the crowds had railed against oppressive officials as well as against foreign merchants, and had shouted the name of Boris Morozov. Worse, it was rumoured that the rebels were seeking the protection of Poland.[46] Troops under the command of Prince Ivan Khovanskii had been sent and Pskov was placed under siege, but there were fears that the rebellion might spread, and in order to find a means of defusing the explosive situation another Assembly of the Land was called. Presided over by Alexis, it met on 4th July and again on the 26th, and eventually a solution was found through negotiation. The townsmen and servicemen involved in the rising were persuaded to submit and take oaths renewing their allegiance. Few punishments were meted out.[47] It was a relief that so threatening a problem had been solved with the shedding of so little blood. But what gave Alexis particular satisfaction was the behaviour of his friend Nikon during the riots at Novgorod.

When the mob had come roaring round his house, baying for the Governor, Prince Fedor Khilkov, who had taken refuge there, Nikon had gone out to confront them. A stone hurled by a rioter had knocked him senseless to the ground. But he had saved Khilkov, and as soon as he recovered he had gone to the Cathedral, where he had solemnly called down the wrath of God upon the rebellion and then admonished the crowd for three hours, promising to intercede with the Tsar on their behalf, reminding them repeatedly of their duty towards him, and finally persuading them to disperse. He had performed admirably after Khovanskii's arrival, too, advising him to adopt a soft line in subduing the population, and protecting him when he was criticized for so doing. He wrote to Alexis taking the responsibility upon himself and commending the Prince for 'working in a quiet, unprecipitate way to promote your interests so that unnecessary violence might be avoided'.[48]

The public order crisis had been weathered by a judicious mixture of force, persuasion and concession. Yet the art of maintaining social peace and of governing by consensus did not altogether accord with Alexis's temperament. It restricted his range of movement, like a king's on the chess-board. But the frustration caused him by the self-will of so many of his servitors and the seemingly incorrigible indiscipline of the population at large was still worse. Even when he succeeded in making a good law it was evaded or ignored. His famous Code, though intended to be 'fixed' and 'immutable', could not always be enforced and his principle of 'justice equal for all' remained a phantasm. Nor were his policies on religion or the army any more successful. Despite his injunction of 1651, services continued to be gabbled off confusedly in many churches;[49] a plan to train up gentry levies in the new techniques of warfare failed when, in November 1649, two thousand of them had refused point-blank to take orders from foreign officers, and attempts to encourage an interest in modern weaponry and tactics met with supine indifference: of the 1,200 copies of *The Art of Infantry Warfare* published, complete with fascinating illustrations, in 1649, only 134 were to be sold by 1659.[50]

For all their fawning professions of respect and obedience many of those who were supposed to serve him obstructed him at almost every turn. This made him angry – but it also helped him visualize his ideal order – an order which would mirror the order in Heaven, where everything moved with grace, beauty and decorum; where there was neither collective anarchy nor individual self-will. But to attain it he would need to promote more like-minded helpers to positions of authority. Nikon was one such, and there might soon be an opportunity to instal him as Patriarch in the place of Joseph who was old and ailing. Nikon would be a bulwark in support of order. He would be his instrument in bringing the people to a proper respect for God; he might even serve as a useful counter-weight to some of those smooth-tongued boyars, like Prince L'vov, who were so deferential to his face, and failed him once his back was turned.

In the autumn of 1650 little Dmitrii died. It was a grievous blow, if not an entirely unexpected one. But the Tsar was young and there was every hope that Maria would bear him other sons. They did not mourn too long. Nor did his loss dampen Alexis's ambitions – to tame his own unruly subjects, and to make his name ring through the world as the saviour of all Orthodox Christians.

Chapter IV

Spiritual Rearmament

From the early 1650s the 'eternal peace' between Muscovy and Poland, concluded in 1634, seemed increasingly likely to belie its name. Moscow was angry with the Polish government for failing to suppress books that contained passages insulting to the Tsar's honour; the Poles were infuriated by Muscovy's insistence on the Tsar's titles, some of which represented claims to territories they regarded as rightfully their own. Mutual fears reinforced their anger. Poland was afraid that Muscovy would intervene in Ukraine (the insurrectionaries were still clamouring for Alexis's protection); Moscow was afraid that Poland would strike up an alliance with the Crimean Tatars and try once again to destroy the Russian state.

In February 1651 Alexis had presided over another Assembly of the Land. Its general purpose was to prepare the country for the possibility of war, and more specifically to obtain the Church's sanction to break a solemn peace treaty should a pre-emptive strike against the Poles prove necessary. Sanction was obtained. If Poland failed to give way over the question of the Tsar's honour, Alexis might break the peace and accept the Ukraine under his protection; and even if it did he might nevertheless resolve the Ukrainian question as he judged necessary.[1] Negotiations with Poland continued, but in June Polish forces defeated the Ukrainians, whereupon the King became less tractable and the Ukrainian leader, Bogdan Khmelnytsky, grew more importunate than ever in his demands for help. If protection was not granted, he was ultimately to threaten, he would have no alternative but to conclude an alliance with the Tatars and become a vassal of the Sultan. For the moment, however, he did not go so far and, aware that a commitment to use force against Poland involved incalculable risks (not least of Swedish intervention), Moscow decided to drag out negotiations.

But as the months passed expectation of war gradually hardened into virtual certainty.[2]

Alexis used the respite as best he could, mindful of the warning his childhood idol, Ivan the Terrible, had once given: 'How can war be waged with bravery if there is no good order in the realm beforehand?'[3] He pressed on, therefore, with his plans to impose his own order and, not least, to prepare his subjects spiritually for war. He wanted to see all his people at one in prayer. Such unanimity would promote morale and induce God's favour when battle was eventually joined. Hence the whip was cracked against religious dissenters: an iconoclastic monk was dealt with;[4] members of an apocalyptic sect, the Kapitons, who denied the necessity of secular institutions, were sent scurrying for shelter into the deepest forests.[5] More positively, priests were urged to deliver proper sermons from their pulpits rather than merely reading out selected homilies from the Church Fathers and, having persuaded the prelates to introduce single-voice cantillation in February 1651,[6] Alexis played an active part in enforcing the rule. When music books arrived from Kiev he took pains to master them,[7] and thereafter made a point of instructing officiants in the proper mode at services he attended. A visiting cleric from Syria saw him in action more than once interrupting divine service to correct mistakes and to issue orders: 'Chant this; sing that canon, or that hymn, to such-and-such a tune.'[8]

But the spiritual preparations did not stop at that. He began to plan a series of great religious demonstrations designed to promote popular enthusiasm and patriotism. The main demonstrations were to centre round the ingathering and re-burial in Moscow of the remains of certain Russian clerics who had acquired an odour of sanctity and around whom cults of a distinctly anti-Polish nature had grown up. The plan was formulated in talks with Nikon and the Patriarch Joseph who accompanied him and the Tsaritsa on visits to the St Sabbas Monastery at Zvenigorod in the autumn of 1651 and in January 1652.[9]

St Sabbas himself had been a Russian patriot, a disciple of that super-patriot St Sergius, and Alexis had formed a passionate attachment to him. Indeed, he believed that Sabbas had intervened personally to save his life. Once out hunting he had outpaced his entourage when a bear attacked him. His situation was desperate – but an old monk suddenly appeared and the bear lumbered back into the forest. The intervention seemed miraculous and Alexis fancied he saw the likeness of St Sabbas in the old man's face. The impression was so strong, indeed, that he ordered his tomb to be opened to establish whether Sabbas was still there or had risen from the grave.[10] The bones were still there, but this did not diminish Alexis's devotion to him nor his belief in the saint's miraculous powers. Indeed, as he told a visitor some months later, he soon gained further proof of them. While helping to re-inter the remains he noticed that one of the Saint's teeth had fallen out onto the floor. He picked it up, put it in his pocket, and thereafter rubbed his own teeth with it whenever he had toothache. And always, so he reported, 'the pain ceased instantly'.[11] Such was his own faith, and now, advised by Nikon, he set about directing and intensifying the faith of others.

The subjects of the great religious processions and magnificent reintombment ceremonies in the Kremlin's Cathedral of the Assumption were the first two Patriarchs of Moscow – Job, who had been deposed and imprisoned by the impostor-Tsar Dmitrii during the Polish occupation, and Hermogen who had died of starvation having been imprisoned by the Poles in 1612. The implications would be clear. Both had been martyred by the prospective enemy. Furthermore, their presence would enhance the sanctity of the Kremlin, citadel of both religious and secular authority. Like Tsar Ivan before him, Alexis considered centralism to be essential to good order. Ivan's drive, over a century before, to search out the remains of provincial saints had added more than forty to the Muscovite pantheon, thus symbolizing the triumph of the state over provincialism and reinforcing Moscow's claim to be the Third Rome.[12] Once again, Alexis was following in Ivan's footsteps.

He must have been embarrassed, therefore, when his friend Nikon urged him to give similar honours to the late Metropolitan Philip, Job's predecessor as head of the Muscovite Church. Not only would Philip's name fail to conjure up any patriotic sentiments, but he had been deposed by Ivan himself for challenging his authority and for remonstrating with him publicly from the pulpit. Worse still, it was widely believed that Ivan had had Philip murdered. The honouring of Philip's remains, then, would run quite counter to Alexis's political intentions. On the other hand, the cult of Philip had probably become too widespread to be ignored. Miracles had long since been reported from his tomb and a service to his memory had been included in the book of martyrs since 1636.[13] The transfer of Philip's relics from the Solovka monastic centre on the White Sea would inevitably draw general attention to

Tsar Ivan's cruelty, but it would deprive the far north of a focus for localist sentiment (which, as events were to demonstrate, existed in some strength there) and perhaps a way could be found of preventing the occasion from carrying any imputation against the principle of autocracy of which Ivan had been champion. As the preparations went ahead Alexis pondered how this might be done.

Certainly, far from contemplating any restriction of his personal authority he was presently trying to increase it. It was to this end that in February 1652 he dismissed Boyar Prince A. M. L'vov who headed the Great Palace Office and as such was his right hand in day-to-day administration, in charge of his personal secretariat and of liaison with the Church. For some time Alexis had become increasingly dissatisfied with the man's performance. L'vov was slow to obey instructions; on occasion he seemed to ignore them. At first Alexis had begun to by-pass him, especially in the administration of the crown estates, choosing to act through Vasily Bot'vinev, his personal secretary for falconry affairs, rather than through normal channels,[14] but L'vov's incorrigible slackness and his tendency to make his own decisions had at last proved too much for him. Relieved at the old man's departure, he was delighted by the performance of the man he soon appointed to succeed him – V. V. Buturlin (one of those trusties, or confidential private agents, Alexis was to make increasing use of), whom he soon raised to boyar rank. As he reported to Nikon, with Buturlin in place his word was now feared in the palace, his orders obeyed 'and everything is done without delay'.[15]

There were some who reviled the name of Tsar Ivan because of his cruelty, but Alexis aspired to such a reputation. Indeed, he was intent on building up a popular image of himself as a harsh man – and not without effect. As a foreign agent reported to his government not long afterwards: 'the Tsar is barbarously cruel . . . [and] capable of anything. [He should] find satisfaction in tales from the history of Ivan . . . and his tyranny.'[16] In fact Alexis was by disposition kindly, but he had set it as his mark to be obeyed without delay, evasion, protest or slovenliness, in matters great and small. Thus when Peter Golovin protested at not being made a full boyar on grounds of precedence Alexis cancelled his promotion to sub-boyar and had the man imprisoned and disgraced; when a falconer failed in his duty he had him thrashed and demoted to be stirrup-groom in the suite of a prince from Persian-occupied Georgia who had sought asylum in Moscow.[17]

He was also capable of expressing terrible anger on occasion, anger, however, which was deliberate, controlled. It was aroused in the spring of 1652 by the steward (*kaznachei*) of the Sabbas Monastery, the object of Alexis's particular care and devotion. He lavished money on the place and gifts on its inhabitants. He had built an infirmary there and regularly visited its sick inmates; he lit and snuffed out candles during services there; he made a point of serving the monks at formal dinners; he not only donated bells for it, but personally composed the inscriptions to be cut into them; he even supervised its accounts.[18] The monastery was his pride and joy, and so when he heard that its steward Nikita, no doubt in a fit of drunkenness, had ordered out a section of *strel'tsy* he had stationed there, assaulted the corporal in charge and beaten some court peasants, he ordered the man to be dismissed from his office and put in irons under guard. Nikita dared to complain. At this Alexis decided to emulate Isaiah's Prince of Peace and slay the wicked with the breath of his lips. He sat down to compose a letter which he ordered to be read out publicly in the presence of the errant Nikita and the entire fraternity:

> To Bursar Nikita, enemy of God, God-hater, Christ-seller, bringer of disorder to the house of the Miracle-worker [St Sabbas's Monastery], single-minded little Satan, damned scoffing enemy, wicked, sly evil-doer. You are like the evil-loving Judas [Iscariot], for just as he sold Christ for thirty pieces of silver so you, damned enemy, have betrayed the Miracle-worker's house and [disregarded] my instructions by your . . . evil drunkenness and artful, underhand, scheming intents. Satan himself rejoices in you. . . . Who asked you to exercise authority over the Miracle-worker's house and over me, sinner that I am? Who gave you this power to by-pass the Abbot and without his knowledge to beat my *strel'tsy* and peasants . . .? Remember what the Gospel says: the arrogant loses grace in the eyes of God. O damned enemy. . . . obliger of Satan, you write to your friends . . . [complaining] that *strel'tsy* stand guard outside your cell – but it is a good thing that they should guard your carcass! *Strel'tsy* guard better and more honourable men than you. Even Metropolitans have been [confined] on our orders [an allusion, this, to Tsar Ivan's imprisonment of the Metropolitan Philip]. . . Do you imagine that I consider your threats of any account? You should know . . . that I consider the threats even of my brother sovereign [Poland] as but a cobweb – because I fear the Lord, my enlightener and Saviour, and thanks to the help of the most holy

Virgin and the prayers of the Miracle-worker Sabbas no threats are terrible to me. . . . I shall disgrace you for your arrogant muttering . . . and I warn you that if you should repent to the Miracle-worker and submit to me insincerely . . . you will be expelled, rejected and excommunicated by our God Jesus Christ, by his most pure Mother, by Sabbas the Miracle-worker, and by me, sinner that I am.[19]

The letter reflected more than angry disappointment in a monastic official who should have known better; it reflected Alexis's faith and the autocratic philosophy which it justified. Nikita's punishment came directly and publicly from the Tsar – not through the medium of his monastic superior. The Patriarch was given no locus in the matter; nor did Alexis mention it in his letters to Nikon, which provided an otherwise full account of what was going on in the Church. His friend, who was by then on his way to distant Solovka accompanied by a large retinue of lay dignitaries (and by one of Alexis's own pensioners, the holy fool called 'Basil Barefoot') to fetch the relics of St Philip back to Moscow, found out about it anyway, at which Alexis apologized:

Do not be upset about my not writing to you about the Sabbas business. . . . I forgot, truly. I had to deal with so much correspondence that day I became tired. Forgive me for this, holy master. The omission was not due to any ill-intent.

Alexis believed in his right to punish the errant monk; but he also felt a great need for Nikon's support and wanted to retain his trust.

'Pray for my wife [he asked him] so that . . . God may deliver her of a child. Her time approaches and I should be beside myself with grief if there should be any misfortune.'[20] He also asked Nikon's prayers for his little daughter Evdokia, who 'is extremely fond of you'.[21] The same month he wrote another letter to his friend addressing him in terms of particular respect and affection as 'preceptor of our soul and body . . . lover and confidant of Christ and shepherd of the sheep who speak . . . valiant warrior and labourer for the heavenly Tsar . . . cherished favourite and friend'. Again, in time-honoured fashion, he was openly repentant of his own sinfulness (which was assumed to be the inevitable consequence of wielding secular power): 'By the grace of God . . . I am called the true Christian Tsar, though because of my own evil, worldly actions I am not worthy [to be called] a dog . . . yet though sinful I regard myself as the slave of that luminary by which I was created.' The

point of the letter, however, was to inform Nikon of the death of the
Patriarch Joseph:

> Because of the sins of all Orthodox Christians and because of
> my own impious sins, it has pleased our Creator . . . to take our
> father and shepherd . . . Joseph, Patriarch of Moscow and all
> Russia, from this world of temptation and hypocrisy, and place
> him in the bosom of Abraham, Isaac and Jacob. . . . Our
> mother, the ecumenical and apostolic Church, is widowed, and
> grieves very tearfully and deeply at the loss of her groom . . .
> like a dove in the desert having no companion.

The loss was serious for the state as well as for the Church, he
added, for it deprived it of spiritual direction, and he urged Nikon to
return to Moscow as quickly as possible in order to take part in the
election of a new Patriarch. The letter was signed in his own hand as
'God's slave Alexis of all Russia'. But it was written several weeks
after Joseph's death.[22] The delay was probably occasioned by
Alexis's wish to carry out informal consultations as to who the new
Patriarch should be, and whether his own choice would be acceptable – for such elections were customarily pre-determined and
effectively dependent on the wishes of the Tsar. In fact Alexis
provided Nikon with a hint as to his choice, telling him that the
election could not be held without him and intimating that the new
Patriarch would be *Theognost*, 'known to God'. Nikon would guess
what he meant by that.[23]

There was another hint to the same effect in the long account,
appended to the letter, of the ceremonial reintombment of St Job on
5th April and of the subsequent illness and demise of the Patriarch
Joseph – one of the most closely observed descriptions of a death in
mediaeval (that is, pre-Petrine) Russian literature and an account
which reveals much about the 23-year-old Alexis's own attitudes
and perceptions. It begins with a description of Job's reception. A
delegation of prominent men of affairs as well as prelates greeted the
procession at Tushino, seven miles from Moscow, and from there
strel'tsy carried the coffin on their heads into the city, where Alexis
and the Patriarch met it. The crowds which he had hoped for duly
materialized:

> It was so crowded [he reported] that there was no room for an
> apple to fall. The roofs and alleyways and the area which had
> been gutted by fire were packed so full of people that it was
> [almost] impossible to get through on foot or horseback. . . .

Even old people more than threescore years and ten in age
could not remember such a throng.

The aged Patriarch was clearly moved. With tears in his eyes he
remarked: 'Behold, Tsar, what a fine thing it is to stand for righteousness; there is glory in death.' Many others also wept. But Alexis
was also struck by a request the Patriarch made just after the
entombment. A space was vacant next to the new shrine. It was
intended for the remains of St Hermogen, which were to be the
subject of a similar ceremony a few weeks later. The Patriarch
requested that he be buried there instead, and in retrospect Alexis
took this to be prophetic;

> His . . . words . . . struck me . . . with great wonderment,
> since he . . . prophesied his own death. For later he fell sick
> with a fever . . . and though it abated by Palm Sunday he was
> still affected by a pain in the loins and a rupture, and he only got
> through the ceremony of riding the ass that day [symbolizing
> Christ's entry into Jerusalem] by dint of great effort.

He was unable to officiate at the service which followed, and
though he made light of his indisposition to an emissary whom
Alexis had sent to enquire after his health, when he eventually
emerged from the Patriarchal Palace to conduct a funeral service he
looked extremely grey. It was reported that he was very ill, but
Alexis did not yet realize quite how ill he was.

> I sent Vasily Buturlin to ask after him . . . but they said he was
> well. That same Wednesday evening I thought of visiting him,
> but then thought, why not tomorrow? But, by God's grace,
> the first thought took such a strong hold of me that . . . I went
> that same evening, arriving an hour before nightfall.

Eventually they brought the sick Patriarch to him. He was trembling with fever and half delirious:

> He went past me to bless Vasily Buturlin. Vasily told him: 'The
> Tsar is standing over there' but he looked right through me and
> asked: 'But where is the Tsar?' I said 'I am standing in front of
> you, bishop' at which he recognised me and said 'Come to be
> blessed, Tsar' and held out his hand for me to kiss.

The two of them began to talk. Alexis asked how he felt and
whether he needed anything, but the Patriarch replied absent-
mindedly, in brief snatches, between long silences, and eventually
intimated that he expected to recover. 'I suppose it will pass,' he

said. 'It was like the last year.' Alexis thought it proper to suggest that he make a will. 'Such is our life,' he began clumsily, 'healthy one day and dead the next.' But then he stopped, and now he blamed himself for not persevering.

> Forgive me, great prelate, sinner that I am . . . for not remind-
> ing him about the will – to put his spiritual affairs in order and
> to arrange for the disposal of his treasure. . . . I deceived
> myself. It was not that I did not expect his fever to be fatal . . .
> but this in itself made me hold back since I felt that I might
> upset him if I mentioned his will . . . So I simply thought: 'I'll
> see him tomorrow' which I fully expected to do.

With great effort the old man had said some prayers and tried to accompany Alexis to the door, but he could barely drag himself along, so Alexis dropped to his knees to kiss Joseph's feet and the cherubim embroidered on his slippers while the Patriarch pronounced the triple blessing over him and gave him absolution. Then Alexis made the old man turn back.

Half an hour before dawn the next morning, the Thursday of Passion Week, Alexis was interrupted at matins and told that the Patriarch was dying. He immediately rushed to his bedside. The old man lay silent with staring eyes. Alexis joined the Archbishop of Riazan in trying to bring him to his senses so that he could confess and receive the last rites in a proper state of consciousness.

> The Archbishop and I shouted at him and shook him by the
> arms to make him speak, but he said not a word. He only
> stared. His entire body was racked with fever and his teeth
> were chattering. . . . One could see that he wanted to speak,
> but could not.

Soon the Archbishop of Kazan, the Bishop of Vologda and other hierarchs rushed in, but all their shouting brought no response either. They turned him onto his back and raised his head. It was decided to give him communion and administer the sacraments, holding his mouth open to receive them, for he was unconscious. Alexis helped to lift him up while they gave him extreme unction. At this the dying man glanced to the left, towards the clerics who were consecrating the oil, then raised his eyes upwards. Alexis concluded that he was having a vision – perhaps watching all his good and evil deeds pass before him (he had read somewhere of such things happening). He told the others so but they were sceptical. Nonetheless, Alexis wrote,

He looked upwards for a quarter of an hour, keenly observing everything on the ceiling, obviously aware of what he saw. Then he covered his face with his hands and shrank back into the corner hard against the wall, tearing himself free from the arms of the archpriest . . . and began to cry out loudly but unintelligibly, and so he tried to hide himself, pressing into the corner. It was very much like someone trying to protect himself from a physical assault coming from above. His whole body shook the while as he wept and cried out, looking upwards. He was like this for a quarter of an hour, after which he began to sink. . . . They said the prayers for the dying . . . and his eyes became very dull. . . . I said my farewell, kissed his hand and bowed to the ground, and went home towards six o'clock, having sealed up the [Patriarchal] treasure.

Little more than an hour later report reached him that the Patriarch had died, and the great Tsar Bell rang out three times.

And just as sheep without a shepherd do not know where to turn, so now we sinners do not know where to set our heads, for our former father and shepherd has died and we do not yet have a new one.

He asked Nikon to pray for a successor but intimated that he, the Metropolitan of Kazan and his chaplain, Stefan, already knew who it would be. 'They say he is a holy man.' His letter to Nikon then continued the story.

When Alexis had gone to pay his respects to the late Patriarch, he had found him well laid out, his beard perfectly combed, almost as if he were still alive. But that same evening when Maria and his sisters were due to attend his lying in state in the Annunciation Cathedral and he had gone on ahead to send away the watchers, he had found the doors open and no one there except for a terrified priest weeping over a psalter. He at once arranged for those who had deserted the dead Patriarch to be punished, and then tackled the priest, who told him that the corpse's abdomen had suddenly begun to swell up and the face to move – at which he had supposed 'he was coming to life again. So I opened the doors and wanted to flee.'

Alexis sympathized, 'for what he said made me so afraid that my legs almost gave way under me'. Nonetheless he approached the bier to see for himself. The belly was indeed projecting a foot above the bier and the hands were not placed together 'as is done with other dead people'. The corpse was in a fast state of dissolution. He actually saw the stomach move as if it were alive. If this was the fate of a Patriarch what horrific end awaited a sinning Tsar? He struggled to keep command of himself.

> The devil planted an idea in my mind: run away from here at once. . . . But I crossed myself and took his reverend hand and kissed it, remembering the words 'From dust ye came and to dust ye will return' . . . then I looked at his face . . . His beard was shrunken and his face was swelling up. At that moment pus dropped onto his moustache and the mouth began to open as I looked. And pus ran from the mouth and fresh blood from the nostrils. I was very afraid and stood back a little so as to lessen the fear. That gave me new life so that I took his hand with a prayer, and my spirits rose. And my wife and sisters were not at all frightened and . . . went up close.

Alexis helped make the arrangements for the funeral, which was held next afternoon. The corpse and the surrounding area were drenched with incense to reduce the stench during the final lying-in and the face, which in the Orthodox rite is customarily exposed to view, was covered – which some 'small-minded people', as Alexis termed them, promptly attributed to the late Patriarch's evil life. However, a hand was left out to receive the customary certificate of absolution, praying for compassion and for a place in Heaven for him when the Day of Judgement came, and a certificate of his career and behaviour also went with him to the grave. But no one had remembered to arrange for the bells to toll during the burial, and Alexis himself had to send an urgent order that they be rung.

He wept during the ceremony, of course, 'remembering my own sins', but he observed the behaviour of others too, and took care to tell Nikon that the Councillors closest to him, Vasily Buturlin, Michael Odoevskii and Michael Rtishchev, had also wept, and the old military specialist Prince Trubetskoi more than anyone. It was a way of commending them to his friend. One further matter disturbed him. It emerged, as secrets so often do tend to emerge in the course of talks at funerals, that the late Patriarch felt that he and Stefan Vnifant'ev wanted to be rid of him, and that, rather than be dishonoured, the old man had thought of petitioning to be retired. His secretary had told Vasily Buturlin so. In retrospect one can well understand why he might have felt so, though Alexis protested that neither he nor Stefan had ever thought 'so terrible a thing'.

Having failed to remind the dying Patriarch about his will, Alexis took on the chore of acting as his executor. It was a complicated task on which he spent the best part of ten days. As he told Nikon, this was partly due to the old man's propensity to engage in financial deals without keeping proper records. Besides quantities of coin, there were many fine pieces of plate, rolls of cloth and other valuables about the place – even some arms and armour. But it was often virtually impossible to tell whether an item formed part of the Patriarchal treasure, or his private fortune, or whether it had been pawned as security for a loan. Eventually, however, he completed the task and disposed of the property. He took the trouble to provide his friend Nikon with an account of the disbursements. Much went for charity – 2,000 rubles to Michael Rtishchev for redeeming impecunious debtors; other sums for the relief of prisoners, alms for the poor and for the maintenance of monasteries and churches. Yet more went to buy back pawned church plate and altars and for masses of commemoration for Joseph's soul. Every patriarchal servant also received something: at a special ceremony Alexis handed over ten rubles apiece to the staff in Moscow, exhorting them to pray for their late master and (reminding them of the biblical adage 'the first shall be last and the last shall be first') telling them not to resent the fact that they were all getting the same. They seemed grateful, he reported – as they should have been, for it was a far bigger sum than had been given on the death of any former Patriarch. Alexis confessed to satisfaction at discharging the duty – not least because he had himself coveted some items of the plate – and he congratulated himself on resisting the temptation.

Finally, there was a delicate disciplinary matter to deal with. Boyar Prince Khovanskii and other secular members of the expedition to fetch St Philip back to Moscow had been complaining that Nikon had been trying to impose religious discipline upon them. Although it was Lent and their mission was primarily religious, strict fasting and taking orders from a churchman, however senior, accorded ill with their inclinations and their sense of honour. One of them, Vasily Otiaiev, had even written to his friends that 'it would be better for us to fall [fighting] in the new territory beyond Siberia with Ivan Ivanovich Lobanov [who had recently been sent on an expedition to the river Amur] than to be with the Metropolitan of Novgorod, because he makes [us] fast by force. No one can make one believe in God by force.'

This placed Alexis in a quandary. He could not afford to antagonize the service gentry. In all likelihood they would soon be needed to fight a war. Yet he did not want the authority of Nikon, his chosen instrument for bringing the realm to spiritual order, undermined. He therefore suggested to Nikon privately that there was a difference between exhorting and forcing people to obey the rules, but provided him with a formal letter addressed to the expedition as a whole which in effect supported him.

> We have been informed [it read] that various gentry and serving men sent . . . to fetch back the remains of the great prelate, the Metropolitan Philip, are failing to observe Lent and are eating without decorum. Now you, our intercessor [Nikon], should force everybody to fast upon St. Peter's Day . . . since God has given you the power to deal with matters of good order; and you, our Boyar [Khovanskii], are to discipline any offenders and order them to travel in good order, without levity, for they should travel with fear and trembling both on account of us, the earthly Tsar, and because it is fitting to do so on a mission to such a great luminary [as Philip].

Nikon was advised to promise rewards for the obedient. For the rest matters would be settled face to face with him when the expedition returned to Moscow.[24]

Its return was not expected before July and meanwhile Alexis must have wondered how the ceremonial transfer of Philip's remains to the Kremlin would be received. Philip, after all, had been the enemy and victim of his hero Tsar Ivan, the champion of autocracy. In effect he had been an enemy of state power, in contrast to the patriotic, state-supporting saints Job and Hermogen whose memory was also being honoured. He had been persuaded to sanction the translation of Philip by Nikon and partly also through the intercession of his wife Maria. The problem was how to do it without besmirching Ivan's memory, without discrediting the authority which he himself now wielded. He had expended a good deal of thought, therefore, in composing a letter to Philip, which he had given to Nikon to read over the grave before the remains were disinterred.[25]

It began with a customary panegyric:

> To Christ's imitator who abides in heaven, to the celestial, sturdy angel and our most exquisite, most wise spiritual teacher, shepherd and intercessor, great lord, father of fathers, most reverend Philip, Metropolitan of Moscow and all Russia, thy son Alexis, by the grace of Almighty . . . God . . . greets thee.

Alexis then explained his reason for removing Philip to Moscow:

Nothing causes me such spiritual sorrow as your absence from
. . . the Cathedral of the Assumption in . . . Moscow which is
filled with the prelates who preceded and succeeded thee.

His presence there, together with the others, would enable their
collective prayers to keep the Church and the Tsar firm in the
Christian faith and 'protect the flock of thy saintly pasture from the
all-devouring wolf'. It would also serve to strengthen Muscovy in
war, for

We cannot be made secure by our own might and by heavily-
armed forces [alone]; it is with God's help and the prayers of
you saints that fate is turned to our advantage.

But not least he implied that Philip's transfer to Moscow would
wipe out all traces of the sin that Tsar Ivan and the secular power had
committed against him, and thus bolster the harmony between
State and Church and help unite the nation:

I beg thee to come [to Moscow] so that the sin of my forefather,
the Tsar and Grand Duke Ivan, which he committed against
thee in a fit of mindless spite and uncontrolled anger, may be
forgiven and thy indignation against him and against us . . .
may be assuaged . . . I bow my Tsarish dignity before thee on
behalf of him who sinned against thee in order that thou
shouldst relieve him of his sin which has come down to us.
Forgive it; remove the disgrace he incurred by exiling thee; let
everyone know that thou art truly reconciled to him. . . .
Come, forgive even him who offended thee to no purpose, for
he repented the action at the time. . . . Restore things to rights,
for as the Gospel, for which thou didst suffer, says, 'A house
divided against itself cannot stand.' There is no-one to contra-
dict thee now . . . there is no discord among thy flock nowadays, and if there had been [the house] would not have stood
till now. . . . O saintly chief, holy master Philip, our shepherd!
Do not despise our sinful prayer. Come to us in peace . . .[26]

Alexis took care to make as little as possible of Ivan's offence. He
represented the ceremony as an act of reconciliation that would
serve to rehabilitate Ivan. Nikon, however, took a somewhat different view. When the expedition finally reached Solovka on 3rd June
1652 and he addressed the monks there, he not only accused Ivan of
having 'felt hatred for and imposed unjust punishment on' Philip,
but of having had him murdered. If this gave rise to any doubts
about Nikon's attitude if and when he became Patriarch, there is no

evidence of its being remarked on at the time; and Alexis learned
with some satisfaction that three days afterwards when Nikon read
out his letter (which had meanwhile lain on Philip's tomb) to the
assembled congregation it had had a considerable effect. 'There was
weeping and great sobbing from all present,' reported Nikon.
Indeed, 'I could hardly read from our weeping.' Philip's remains
had then been disinterred and taken on their way to the ringing of
bells and the flickering of candles.[27]

On its return the expedition met with a disaster. One of the boats
on which they were travelling sank in a storm and several lives were
lost including that of Secretary Leont'ev who had played an active
role on the secretariat which had prepared Alexis's law code.[28] But
the long journey was completed without further mishap, and on 9th
July all was ready for their entry into Moscow. Having arranged for
the Polish embassy, which was in Moscow for further negotiations,
to have a clear view of the proceedings, Alexis prepared to welcome
the returning saint.

He wore a cloth-of-gold caftan for the occasion and a cap
encrusted with gems and pearls. Yet when Varlaam, the hoary
Metropolitan of Rostov, overcome by the great heat and the intense
emotion of the occasion, collapsed and died, Alexis did not allow his
sense of majesty to overcome his spontaneous sense of what was
most necessary, and he immediately rushed forward to help support
the relics on his own shoulders. He gave an account of the ceremony
some weeks later to his friend Nikita Odoevskii who had taken up
an appointment as Governor of the huge province of Kazan. Within
an hour of reaching the approaches to Moscow, he asserted, St
Philip had wrought a miracle:

> He cured a woman who was dumb and possessed, and she
> suddenly began to speak and be well. . . . He wrought another
> cure upon a girl in the presence of the Polish ambassadors. . . .
> And when we carried him into the square opposite the Hall of
> Facets he effected yet another cure, of a blind man. . . . There
> were so many people all along the route . . . that there was no
> room to drop an apple. There were innumerable sick people
> lying about and crying out to him, and an immeasurable groan
> went up from all the lamentation and the wailing. And he lay in
> state in the Cathedral for ten days in order to receive the
> supplications of petitioners, and the bells rang continously
> throughout those ten days from morning until night. At least
> two or three and as many as five, six or even seven were cured
> every day. . . . He cured Stefan Vel'iaminov's wife. She had

asked for the prayer for the dying to be said for her and her mind was wandering, but the miracle-worker appeared to her and said: 'Have yourself carried to my tomb.' And she is blind and has not heard a thing these eight years, and has had a migraine all those years. Yet the moment they brought her in she recovered her sight and hearing, and she stood up and went away a well person. Indeed he made whole people who had been sick not only for eight years but for twenty or thirty. And he cured women suffering from excessive [menstrual] bleeding, and the possessed, and people with all sorts of infirmities.

But pleased as he was by the apparent moral effects of St Philip's return to the Kremlin, he was delighted by another of its consequences – for in his view it also served to rehabilitate Ivan, removing the shadow that had been cast over his memory.

Where is the persecuted and the false counsel now? [he asked Nikita triumphantly] Where are the slanderers and the tempters? . . . Has not all the evil perished? Has it not disappeared for ever? Has not all desire for vengeance been taken from my forefather . . . Ivan?[29]

Immediately after Philip's reintombment, the election of the new Patriarch took place. Alexis had set his mind on Nikon, who was now the senior prelate in the Church, but he was not the candidate preferred by everyone. In June the Metropolitan of Kazan, the Archpriest Avvakum and others presented a petition addressed jointly to Alexis and Maria asking that Stefan Vnifant'ev be chosen.[30] It was not heeded. Alexis wanted not only a close and trusted friend and a committed reformer, but a good administrator and a strong disciplinarian. Nor were those, like Khovanskii, who had experienced Nikon's authoritarianism enthusiastic. Indeed Nikon himself had doubts. The Tsar had friends whom he regarded as anti-clerical. Nikita Odoevskii, for example, had persuaded him to transfer much of the Church's jurisdiction to the civil power. On the other hand, the Tsar had shown good-will by restoring much of that jurisdiction to him in the Novgorod diocese the year before,[31] and by sending Odoevskii away to Kazan.[32] The fact that some of the reforms which Alexis wanted him to introduce as Patriarch would prove unpopular with many of the clergy might also have been expected to make Nikon somewhat diffident about accepting the patriarchate. Nevertheless he took good care not to alienate any of the electors. According to Avvakum, Nikon 'Played the fox with us, and it was all bowings and scrapings and "Good morrow to you!" For he knew he was to be patriarch and wished to remove all obstacles thereto.'[33] So Avvakum and other potential opponents were all prevailed upon to sign their names calling Nikon to the patriarchal throne.

Yet on 22nd July when a formal delegation called on Nikon and asked him to go to the Cathedral of the Assumption, where Alexis and the rest of the conclave awaited him, he declined to come, and he refused repeatedly. It was only when Alexis sent some leading boyars with orders to fetch him there that he at last went and even then he would not accept appointment until the Tsar himself knelt down next to St Philip's tomb and begged him to accept.[34] A show of modesty, of course, was becoming; but this excessive show of reluctance had another purpose – to extract a promise of obedience from all those present, not least the boyars. Would they promise to respect him as their archpastor and spiritual father? Would they allow him to put the Church in order? Would they obey him in all matters ecclesiastical and spiritual? They duly swore that they would do so.

The scene was obviously rehearsed and no doubt Alexis and Nikon had planned it together. Bolstering Nikon's authority as Patriarch was, after all, another means by which Alexis could advance another step towards the distant vision of good order.[35] So, on 25th July, Nikon was duly installed as Patriarch by the Metropolitan of Kazan and by Alexis himself, who gave him his pastoral staff and made a public address. Nikon's reply reflected his understanding of the Tsar's ambitions. He prayed that God would increase his empire 'from sea to sea and from the [sources of the] rivers to the ends of the earth. May He restore your scattered and pious Tsardom and keep it united, and may you be raised to be Christian Tsar and Autocrat over the world, shining forth like the sun amidst the stars.'[36]

Alexis was confident that the administration of the Church, so lax and fumbling under Joseph, would henceforth be firm and efficient. He was sure that the liturgical reforms he wanted would now be speedily introduced and properly enforced; and that Nikon would see to it that every parish priest became an agent of the Kremlin. Furthermore, he now felt able to leave virtually all ecclesiastical matters – even the appointment of bishops – to the new Patriarch. It would free his time for other business, not least military business. However, the two continued to work very closely together. Indeed Alexis promptly gave Nikon a site on which to build a new

Patriarchal Palace which would connect with his own apartments.[37] Harmony between State and Church seemed to be assured.

Nikon lived up fully to Alexis's expectations. His firm grip was soon felt by the Church; the scholars at the Printing Office, led by Epifany Slavinetskii, were set to work at full pelt re-translating and editing liturgical texts for publication; and the reforms designed to bring Russian practice into line with that of the rest of the Orthodox world were swiftly introduced. Some signs of arrogance were soon remarked in Nikon. He became difficult of access to many of his erstwhile friends. He also had a translation of the Donation of Constantine included in the edition of canon law (the Nomocanon) to be issued in 1653. This might have excited the suspicion that Nikon was preparing to arrogate more power to his office than he should. But, as yet at least, it did not.[38]

The summer and autumn of 1652 formed a blissful interlude for Alexis before the coming storms. In August Maria gave birth to another daughter called Martha;[39] and there were many opportunities to escape the stuffy Kremlin, to enjoy long days under the hot sun in the countryside and to visit his estates. He had projects in mind for some of them – to grow oranges, and to make wine which would be as good as any that was imported.[40] There was also time between his ceremonial functions and other duties for sport, and to enjoy the company of friends. On 1st November he called in on Nikita Odoevskii's sons, Michael and Fedor, at their father's estate at Veshniakov. It was a happy, high-spirited occasion which got off to an excellent start when the brothers led out a fine grey stallion to present him with as he rode in.

'Do you think I've called on you to rob you?' Alexis responded, but Michael, visibly moved by the honour of the visit, answered: 'I never expected to see you here, Sovereign. Accept it for Christ's sake and gladden father and us for we have never had such an [illustrious] guest here.' Seeing (as he later recalled) that their plea was not meant to flatter and that their joy at seeing him was genuine, he accepted the gift. 'It was not that I valued the horse so much, but their straight, unfeigned service and obedience and their heartfelt joy at seeing me.' They showed him round the estate, the house, even the outbuildings. 'I went everywhere and saw everything,' he told their father, 'even the stables.' Later he was their guest at dinner, after which he 'sent word to Pokrovskoe that he would go hunting in the woods over Karachel'ska way'. They went on together to Alexis's hunting lodge where he plied them with vodka, presented them with gifts including goblets to mark the occasion and sat down with them to a supper which they washed down with sweet wine. Before they had quite finished, however, Michael rose to his feet and begged leave to go. He had a severe headache, felt unwell, and wanted to reach home in Moscow by morning. Permission was granted. Less than three weeks later Michael was dead.

Two days afterwards Alexis dictated a letter of condolence to his bereaved father, Boyar Nikita Odoevskii, which is one of the foundations of his reputation as the most attractive of Russian monarchs.

> By the judgement of our almighty and beneficent God [he wrote] and by his terrible command your first-born son, Michael, was taken to join the inhabitants of heaven on Friday, 19th November, five hours after day-break.

He proceded to describe the circumstances of Michael's last illness (having gathered the details by his brother Fedor) and gave a moving account of the death:

> He was passing from this life of temptation to life eternal . . . and was unconscious when they brought him the sacraments. But when they shouted at him [to rouse him] so that he could partake, he opened his eyes, saw the priest with the eucharist, and said 'I am quite unworthy . . .' But he [eventually] accepted the holy gifts for the journey to Christ the Lord in sound mind, and then grew calm. They gave him extreme unction three hours after daybreak, and after that he said nothing; that is, he fell asleep. There was no sobbing whatsoever, and no pain.

But the greater part of the letter was taken up by Alexis's attempts to console Nikita.

> Do not grieve too much. Of course you must grieve and shed tears to some extent, but not immoderately lest Almighty God be angered. You must imitate the righteous Job. He was tempted by our common enemy Satan; he suffered so many calamities. Yet did he not bear them [patiently] and did not God give him sons and daughters again? And why? – because he did not sin in his mouth; the deaths of his children did not make him resentful. . . . You know that everything God does is for our good. Besides he was in a state of grace when he was taken. . . . How would you feel if your son had died by falling from his horse without an opportunity to repent?

He bolstered this attempt to raise old Nikita's spirits by reminding him of a parable about St John Chrysostom (which in fact he himself mis-remembered) and of another about St Varlaam – one of those moral riddles so beloved of the mediaeval mind. Varlaam, when granted the privilege of reprieving one of two men who had been condemned to death, had pardoned the guilty one since he was in any case doomed to damnation, but had allowed the other, who had been unjustly sentenced, to die since as an innocent he would go straight to paradise. Furthermore, Alexis promised that the Odoevskiis would continue to enjoy his favour. He would care for the orphaned Yuri, Michael's son, and would arrange masses to be said for Michael's soul. He had already consoled his brother Fedor and represented Nikita himself at the funeral. 'You must trust in God . . . and rely on us, for God willing, we shall not abandon you, nor your children and grandchildren. . . . God has commanded us to help the helpless . . .' Finally he added a postscript: 'Prince Nikita Ivanovich! Do not feel aggrieved. Just trust in God and depend on us.'[41]

The letter reflected his gift for friendship, his deep sense of religious duty, an instinctive appreciation, perhaps, of how important it was to command loyalty through love. The morale of those who served him was certainly very much in his mind as war with Poland became virtually certain and the pace of military preparations was stepped up. Strenuous efforts were being made to provide all servicemen with firearms (preferably flintlocks) and to modernize the organization and training of a large part of the army.[42] Alexis was concerned with this; but he was as much concerned with the problem of how he might prepare his subjects morally and psychologically for war. He has left us an account of his decision to make war on Poland which sheds some light upon the matter.

One day, probably later the same year, he sat down with quill and ink and a booklet of blank paper and set about trying to formulate or reconstruct his thoughts about the impending military business. For some moments he simply sat and doodled. (The cover bears a few disjointed letters and squiggles, and in the centre a flowery motif, possibly a monograph of his name, which concludes in a repetitive scrawl laid on with a very heavy hand. Together they suggest a man gearing up to define some elusive idea in plain words.) At last he turned over the page and started to write, beginning with a customary acknowledgement to God:

By the grace of this most benign, mighty, generous and merciful God of ours and through the intercession of our most holy,
chaste and merciful intercessor and protectress, the Virgin, and
through the prayers of all the saints, this happy idea came to us,
the Great Sovereign, our Tsar and Grand Duke Alexis
Mikhailovich of all Russia.

Concerning the military business of how to protect the true,
Orthodox, Christian and pure faith and the holy, ecumenical
and apostolic Church and all Orthodox Christians, and of how
the enemy might be put in dread; and concerning my own,
with . . . God's help . . ., successful appearance before the
armed forces in giving a brave and valiant impression; likewise
to make the announcement to my men in the armed forces [in
such a way as to inspire them] with bravery and valour.

He recorded having begun to consider 'this blessed affair' (as he
termed his decision to go to war) on the first Monday in Lent,
having consulted his advisers about it, and decided the matter a
fortnight later. The venture had Nikon's approval. He had given it
his blessing at a formal meeting of the Council, whereupon the
relevant department issued orders for a general muster of the
Moscow service gentry, *strel'tsy* and conscripted men. Alexis
reviewed some of them on the meadows near the Devich'e nunnery
towards the end of June. A podium was erected there for him to
stand on. It was equipped with columns and balustrades, painted
in gold and covered with purple velvet. He wanted to make as
impressive a show as possible.[43]

In fact the review took place on 28th June 1653 after fifteen days
of exercises and manoeuvres, and it culminated in a speech that was
read out to the serried ranks in Alexis's presence and in his name. In
it he urged them to be courageous, praised their turn-out, and told
them to be no less orderly when, at God's behest, they marched into
battle against the foe. He reminded them, too, that 'greater love
hath no man than to lay down his life for his friend' and assured
them that death in battle would be sure to bring them eternal bliss.[44]
Following that, all present were called upon to swear new oaths of
loyalty to him (the boyars promising to obey 'without any evasive-
ness or obstinacy').[45] Only six days earlier Alexis had written to
Khmelnytsky informing the Ukrainians that he had finally decided
to accept them under his 'high hand', and that preparations for war
were already under way.[46]

These preparations took many forms. All foreigners who would
not be converted to Orthodoxy (apart from certain experts in

Alexis's employ) were forced to live in a special ghetto, which was known as the Foreign Suburb, beyond the river Iauza outside Moscow, and their places of worship in the capital were torn down.[47] Measures had also been taken to limit the sale of liquor. This brought a double benefit. It promoted public order by reducing drunkenness; it also released more grain, which would otherwise have been used by the distilleries, for the export market to help pay for the importation of military supplies.[48] The precaution was also taken of obtaining the approval of representative members of society in May, June and again in October 1653, when it was used to make a formal declaration of war against Poland (which, as anticipated, had just rejected Moscow's demands) and for union with Ukraine (at which a mission, headed by Buturlin, was sent to administer an oath of loyalty to Khmelnytsky and his lieutenants).[49] All these measures served to prepare the country materially and psychologically for war. But another measure taken to promote spiritual good order was less well received.

In February 1652 a new, revised, Psalter had been published and Nikon had issued a general instruction for obeisances in church to be made from the waist rather than from the knees and for the sign of the cross to be made with three, rather than with two, fingers folded. These and other measures were the fruits of the work designed to bring Muscovite worship into line with that of the rest of the Orthodox world; but there were many who reacted to the news like Avvakum: 'Our hearts froze, our limbs shook.' He and his like were vociferous in their protests, and unrestrained in their abuse of the reformers (Avvakum accused Nikon of 'belching out venom'). Stefan Vnifant'ev tried to calm them in vain, and Nikon's firmness made them revile him the more. One objector, a priest called Login of Murom, was denounced and condemned by a church assembly. At this the popular Archpriest Neronov spoke out, and when he was confined for disobedience, two other Archpriests, Avvakum himself and Daniel of Kostroma, rose up in his defence and petitioned Alexis and Maria on his behalf. Alexis had them arrested and handed over to Nikon. With war impending matters could not be allowed to get out of hand. Attempts were first made to persuade the dissenters to conform, but they were adamant. Nikon's answer was to force them to become monks so that they could be incarcerated in monasteries and subjected to the strictest discipline. Alexis made a point of being present at their ceremonial defrocking with Maria (he saw Login spit in Nikon's eye). Only in the case of Avvakum himself and perhaps at Maria's intercession did he intervene. They had a liking for the man, even though Alexis disapproved of his having abandoned his provincial parish (he had been beaten up and driven out by a great crowd who objected to his zealotry). Instead of being forced into a monk's habit, Avvakum was exiled to Siberia, eventually to serve as chaplain to an expedition sent to the cold and dangerous regions of farthest Dauria.

The purge was well timed and, for the moment at least, seemed to have succeeded in its purpose. Of the prelates only the Bishop of Kolomna seemed sympathetic to the rebels. The remainder did as they were told and kept their mouths shut.[50] Unity and good order, which for a moment seemed to have been seriously threatened, now appeared to have been firmly re-established. It was the more important since Alexis had taken the decision to accompany his troops on campaign in person, just as Ivan himself had done. It was for this reason that he now conferred a title on Nikon that no Patriarch of Moscow other than his own grandfather, Filaret, had ever borne. It was a title of his own – 'Great Sovereign' (*velikii gosudar*').[51]

This has since been interpreted as a sign that Alexis was wholly under Nikon's influence, but there is no substance to the allegation. His prime purpose in conferring the honour (which was to last only so long as he was absent at the front) was to ensure that a prospective regent would be in place should some disaster befall him. It was a Byzantine tradition that the Patriarch of Constantinople should rule the city in an interregnum or when the Emperor was absent on campaign; moreover, Tsar Ivan himself had appointed the Metropolitan Makaryi as regent when he had led his army against Kazan and Astrakhan. Alexis was also to leave a commission of boyars in Moscow to deal with routine administration while he was away, but it was as well to have Nikon keep an eye on their activities. The title also enhanced Nikon's authority in carrying out a task that was vital to the success of Muscovite arms: to mobilize the considerable resources of the Church in order to provide the army with a flow of recruits, means of transportation and supplies.[52] Yet for all his trust in Nikon, Alexis had other confidants. His old school-friend Artamon Matveev may not have been the only one among them to whom he was to entrust a cipher book for use in communicating 'secret matters' to him directly while he was away.[53]

With good order now imposed on Church and State and with his authority as autocrat strengthened (never again, after 1653, was he to summon an Assembly of the Land), Alexis now felt able, in the words of Tsar Ivan, 'to fight a war with bravery'. His mission was a holy one. He was launching a crusade to protect all Orthodox Christians; he was about to take possession of a vast and rich new province (the Ukrainians swore allegiance to him in January 1654). As winter approached he plunged himself into preparations for the campaign which was to start the following spring. The first main objective had already been chosen: the old Russian city of Smolensk which the Poles had held for over forty years; a subsidiary force would be sent to Kiev.

Two days after the formal declaration of war on 25th October Alexis rode out to Kolomenskoe where many of the troops were ordered to muster, and immersed himself in arrangements and inspections. He had ordered all commands to be held without any consideration of family honour. Merit and ability alone were to determine rank; and he issued a warning that anyone who petitioned against his posting on grounds of ancestry or precedence would suffer immediate punishment: permanent disgrace and exile.[54] That winter he also went through lists of provincial gentry and junior servicemen, minors and converts who were to be enlisted in the new-formation regiments of infantry, cavalry and dragoons.[55]

Then in February 1654, joy of joys, Maria gave birth to a son. He was named Alexis after his father. It was a grateful, excited, confident Tsar Alexis who prepared to go to war – a war which was to change his outlook on the world and the fate of Russia.

Chapter V

Alexis Goes to War

During the winter months of 1654 every wheel and lever in the Muscovite war machine clanked into action, ready to move against Poland as soon as the spring thaw had passed its spate. The new-formation regiments stepped up their training; artillery in the Kremlin armoury was checked and tested; all necessary resources for the campaign were mobilized. Every town, village and monastery in the country was soon involved. Part-time servicemen were ordered to report for duty; crowds of auxiliaries were raised among tribesmen subject to the Tsar; and recruits – one from every twenty households – were brought into assembly points, issued with arquebuses, spears and halberds, and hastily taught the elements of battle drill.[1]

Extraordinary measures were taken to ensure that this vast and motley army, perhaps 140,000 strong, would be able to move at the appointed times and be fed along the lines of march. Horses as well as men were levied, not least from the church domain;[2] butchers, bakers and brewers were drafted into regiments, together with their wares, to ensure that the men would be fed, and victuals were stockpiled in state granaries at forward points for sale to the troops in case supplies from other sources should run out.[3] A rudimentary army medical service was also organized and of course priests were allocated to all units to act as chaplains under the supervision of the Metropolitan of Kazan.

Alexis, meanwhile, was planning the strategy of his campaign. A primary aim was to ensure that the enemy remained diplomatically isolated, and so embassies were rushed out to Poland's neighbours to announce the Tsar's sovereignty over Ukraine and elicit assurances that they would not intervene on Poland's side;[4] steps were taken to coordinate the operations of the Cossacks under Bogdan Khmelnytsky with those of the Muscovite armies, and meanwhile

92

the finishing touches were put to the plan of operations. The main thrust, led by the advance guard under Nikita Odoevskii and followed by the 'Great Regiment' commanded by Iakov Cherkasskii, was to strike at Smolensk and the territory beyond it. The right wing, led by Vasily Sheremetev, would concentrate at Velikie Luki and move in the direction of Vilna, guarding against the possibility of an intervention from the north by Sweden. The left flank was to be protected by another army under the command of Nikita Trubetskoi which would march south-west to Briansk and link with Khmelnytsky's Ukrainians. The rear-guard under M. M. Temkin-Rostovskii was given the task of supporting the Ukrainians and fending off any strike on the part of the Crimean Tatars. The object, apart from regaining Smolensk and helping the Ukrainians to expel the Poles, was to capture the region between the Dnieper and the upper reaches of the Western Dvina, that part of the Grand Duchy of Lithuania known as Belorussia (White Russia).[5] The strategic aim was therefore ambiguous. If the plan succeeded, Ukraine would be secured and the Belorussians, many of them Orthodox, would be united with all the other Eastern Slavs. But success would also prepare the way for a Muscovite advance up the Dvina to the Baltic Sea.

Alexis himself was to participate in the march on Smolensk at the head of the 'Sovereign's Regiment', an elite corps which included the cream of the *strel'tsy* and several regiments of new-formation troops. Boris Morozov and cousin Nikita Romanov were to accompany him, together with most of the remaining Councillors (only a small commission of boyars was to stay in Moscow), so that his campaign headquarters were to house the essential nub of government as well as the high command. Meanwhile, in the weeks preceding his departure, Alexis maintained a high level of activity – inspecting units, scrutinizing endless lists and reports, presiding over innumerable meetings. In March growing opposition to Nikon's liturgical reforms forced him to divert his attention briefly to ecclesiastical affairs, and in an attempt to put an end to the dissension he called yet another church council, over which he himself presided. Nikon made an impassioned appeal for aligning Russian rituals with the Ukrainian and Greek, but the Bishop of Kolomna was no less impassioned in his opposition. No agreement could be reached over the matter of genuflection and though Nikon was authorized to proceed with the correction of church books he was urged to pay as much attention to the old Russian as to the

Greek models. Neither Tsar nor Patriarch was content to leave matters there, but in view of Alexis's imminent departure further action was entrusted to Nikon.[6] Having made over a generous endowment to his friend's new foundation, the Iveria Monastery,[7] Alexis returned to the compelling military business.

Yet the war itself had an important religious dimension. This was clear from the ceremonies held to see the troops off to the front. On 23rd April the entire court was assembled in the Assumption Cathedral to hear Nikon admonish Nikita Trubetskoi and his staff to fight joyfully for Church and Tsar, after which Alexis entertained them to dinner and to a speech in which he urged them to keep God's commandments, to show compassion to the sick and needy, but not to spare 'God's enemies'.

> I hand you these muster-rolls of your warriors. Keep them like the apple of your eye. Love them, and defend the fatherland with them. Be good to them . . . if they behave well, but do not spare the evil among them. . . .

Then, turning to the assembled warriors he warned them to be alert and obedient, not to offer 'lame excuses', and to keep themselves 'pure and chaste, for you know not when your hour will come'. Later, after dinner had been cleared away, he personally administered a form of communion to them. Coming down from his dais he took bread and wine, and they lined up in order of rank to drink from the cup he held out to them and kiss his hand while the choir of the court chapel intoned a hymn to the Virgin. He commanded all his troops to make confession and to take communion:

> Do not neglect this . . . order when on campaign. . . . If you keep this commandment of Christ and renew yourselves with blessed repentance . . . the Angel of the Lord will take up arms about your regiment. . . . But if, through your negligence, even one man should fail to renew himself through confession, then you will answer for it at Christ's terrible court.

The old warrior Trubetskoi replied in appropriate terms:

> Most illustrious, gracious and wise Sovereign, our father and teacher, we are delighted by your words of useful spiritual admonition. They have provided us with that very spring [of inspiration] which we sought. Just as the Israelites were fed with manna through the divine foresight of Moses, so we have been nourished by the sustenance emanating from your lips, O Sovereign, and our hearts and souls rejoice. . . . We may be

small in spirit and of little faith but we shall strive to attain perfect obedience and God will be our helper.

At this, Alexis took Trubetskoi's grey head in his hands and pressed it to his breast, commending him aloud as reverend, full of grace, 'fortunate in war and terrible to enemies', and the old man, in an emotional frenzy, prostrated himself no fewer than thirty times before his Tsar.

When Alexis left the hall to address the junior commanders of Trubetskoi's force, who were drawn from the gentry of Moscow and Iaroslav, about the reasons for war and to regale them with white mead, they also received him with enthusiasm. And when he declared himself ready to shed his own blood for the sake of Orthodox Christians they shouted back that they would give their heads for the cause, for their soveriegn, and for their fellow Christians. Alexis was touched by this show of devotion. 'The Lord God [he told them] will grant you life for your good intentions, and we shall be ready to reward you . . . for your services.'

Three days later Alexis watched Trubetskoi lead his command out of Moscow. Maria stood beside him and Nikon sprinkled them with holy water as they marched, banners flying, below the stand.[8] Soon afterwards he went to prepare himself spiritually for the coming campaign by praying at the tombs of Sts Sergius and Sabbas at Zagorsk and Zvenigorod. For him this was a holy war, and his main armament religious. This much is borne out by instructions he issued to a general:

> Keep to single-voice cantillation. . . . When battle commences you and your men must go forward on God's business singing.
> . . . Keep the Jesus prayer in mind. . . . Go into battle joyfully, without any doubt and your singing will be such that despite yourselves . . . you will not be defeated . . . and you will seem terrible to every enemy.[9]

He seems to have devoted almost as much attention to the choice of icons to accompany the troops[10] as to inspecting various segments of the army and praising them for their discipline and drill. On 15th May he authorized one of Muscovy's greatest treasures, the icon of Our Lady of Iveria, to accompany the advance guard of the main army commanded by Nikita Odoevskii. Three days later he himself followed it, leading his elite troops out of Moscow towards the front.

Rarely had Muscovites been treated to so noble and colourful a sight. Twenty-five battle standards were carried at the head of the parade; then Alexis's personal ensign, a golden eagle over a ground of black and white stripes bearing the motto 'Fear God and Obey the Tsar'. It was followed by six horses so richly caparisoned that even their hoofs were set with pearls. Alexis himself rode in a gold-decorated carriage, upholstered in crimson velvet. He wore a gown smothered in pearls and was carrying his orb and sceptre. A personal escort of twenty-four hussars, led by two officers with sabres drawn, flanked his carriage. A Tatar prince of Siberia with his attendants preceded it; behind it rode Boris Morozov and his father-in-law Il'ia; and behind them came rank upon rank of soldiers in a seemingly endless, multi-coloured stream. Here and there an icon bobbed up and down above the river of marching men, and banners of multifarious and intricate design calculated to inspire courage fluttered before them. There were representations of Jesus, St George and St Michael the Archangel; there were cherubim with flaming swords, more modest pennants bearing coloured crosses, but there were also some of transparently secular design. One of them showed the figure of a mermaid, representing the arms of Warsaw and bearing the motto 'Come fetch my booty'.[11]

The 25-year-old Alexis set off to war as a crusader, as a St George whose mission it was to save Orthodox Christians from the Polish dragon, as an avenger who would win back stolen lands. But the campaigns were to change him. His going to war freed him from the close embraces of his wife and sisters; it was to give him sight of other lands, open his eyes to other cultures, and broaden his horizons. The war, in short, was to be his university.

At first, however, his progress was slow and unexciting. He had to stop for three days at his estate at Vorob'evo near Moscow to transact urgent business. It was there that he took the necessary but fateful step of approving sample castings for a new devalued coinage, including copper money, there being no other acceptable recourse at the state's disposal to finance the vast expenditure of the war.[12] Then he had to kick his heels at Mozhaisk for two days waiting for the horses to be properly fed. The delay made him impatient, for scouts had reported that Smolensk had been left virtually undefended and he was anxious to make all speed to reach it before it was reinforced.[13] By the end of May he had reached Ostrozhka, over half-way to Smolensk, and, as he wrote to his family, he was determined to move on at once; but for all the efforts of the local peasants drafted out to clear the way the road was almost impassable because of the spring mud. He prayed intensely that conditions might improve.[14]

Slow progress was not his only problem. Some of his lieutenants were evidently not agreed about the strategy, nor hopeful of the outcome. For all their protestations of zealous service Alexis sensed that some of them were unenthusiastic, evasive. As he confided to Nikita Trubetskoi:

> Those riding with us exude two spirits rather than one – like the atmosphere [*lit.* a cloud] which sometimes exudes cheerfulness, reliability and hope, but sometimes seems sultry, stormy and foul with every kind of evil, sly Muscovite trait. . . . As God is my witness, how can one trust such two-faced men? . . . There is no relying on them at all. . . . But for the bright spirit He has given me, their cowardice would crush my heart.[15]

He mentioned no names, but it is not improbable that Il'ia Miloslavskii was among those he had in mind. His father-in-law was an ambitious sycophant, who overrated his own abilities and underrated his luck. But Alexis dared not offend, still less harm or punish, Il'ia for fear of distressing his own Maria. Instead he began to take into his own hands certain matters which were the nominal responsibilities of both Il'ia and others whom he did not trust to act with sufficient accuracy and despatch, issuing direct orders and calling for direct reports. Alexis was no stranger to personal administration, of course. He had long since used falconers and personal secretaries to help him supervise his hunt and his favourite estates rather than let court and governmental functionaries run them for him. This practice was now extended, however, to diplomacy and military affairs, particularly logistics: the provision and movement of men, horses, equipment and food for his armies. But effective personal control of such matters demanded an adequate secretariat and so, in addition to his campaign chancery run by Counsellor-Secretary Larion Lopukhin, he set up what was in effect a private office headed by another trusted bureaucrat called Tomilo Perfil'ev (who bore the title of 'Secretary in the Sovereign's Name') and including two under-secretaries, one of whom, V. Botvin'ev, had been his Falconry Secretary for the last five years.[16]

This practice of by-passing normal channels, of taking matters into his own hands, was to grow, and as it grew, his Private Office (Office of Secret Affairs as it was also known) was to expand as well. But what was to become the instrument of Alexis's distinctive style of government emerged during the early stages of this, his first campaign, and it was inspired by his long-felt urge for autocratic efficiency, his reluctance to allow the Council to discuss every matter of importance, and his dissatisfaction with the performance of certain ministers. But if he had hinted at his worries to Nikita Trubetskoi, he breathed no word of them to his wife and sisters. On 3rd June he perhaps came near to doing so when he admitted having had a headache all day (whether physical or not we cannot tell), and on that account dictated a letter to them rather than writing it himself. But that same day good news reached him which raised his spirits and made his headache disappear. The main Polish army was moving towards Ukraine, and though there were 10,000 enemy troops some seventy miles to the west of Smolensk prisoners had reported that the city itself was garrisoned by few more than 2,000 men and did not anticipate a Muscovite attack. With God's help the enemy could still be caught by surprise.[17]

Next day there was more good news: Dorogobuzh, a town only fifty miles from Smolensk, had fallen to his troops. On 10th June he left Viazma and for the first time in his life crossed the frontier of the state of Muscovy. By the evening of the 29th he was encamped upon a hill less than two miles from Smolensk itself.

The reports arriving at general headquarters continued to be excellent. The right wing under Sheremetev had reached the Dvina and taken the city of Polotsk; the left wing under Trubetskoi soon announced the capture of Roslavl'; a force detatched from Temkin's command was moving to support Khmelnytsky;[18] everything was going according to plan. It was decided that the Great Regiment under Cherkasskii should advance to deal with Janusz Radziwill, Hetman of Lithuania, who commanded the largest enemy force operating in the region, while Alexis would stay with the Sovereign's Regiment, the siege engineers and the artillery to supervise the taking of Smolensk. On Wednesday, 5th July, he moved his camp to another hill even closer to the walls. He stood there, like a predatory falcon, eyeing his prey.

Although there was only a motley force of some 3,500 men to defend the city, although they were short of artillery and supplies, and although many of its bastions were in a poor state of repair (preparations to withstand a siege had only started in May), its capture was not to be an easy task. There were three miles of high, stout walls for the besiegers to contend with, and resistance was determined.[19] For his part Alexis had 30,000 men, most of them

crack troops and many of them led by foreign officers (including
Colonels Butler, Gibson and James English). But his right hand in
this enterprise was the elderly general Alexander Leslie, seasoned
campaigner and expert in siege warfare. Leslie had already begun
preparations before Alexis's arrival. Baggage wagons had been
ranged outside the walls to offer the sappers some initial protection;
trenches were being dug opposite the weakest points in the walls;
saps were being extended to within twenty-five yards of them; and
a bombardment had already begun – thanks to a notable achievement on the part of F. B. Dalmatov-Karpov in getting the guns
through (which earned him a personal letter of commendation[20]).

Nor were the powers of religion neglected. Alexis had ordered
the Metropolitan and other prelates to walk, Gideon-like, around
the walls of Smolensk, carrying icons aloft.[21] Nonetheless he
attended assiduously to the technicalities, filling sheet upon sheet of
paper with calculations of his own forces and those of the enemy,
with orders of battle and plans for storming operations.[22] Afraid of
squandering his expensive elite troops, he decided not to risk a
general storm until a Ukrainian force, under Colonel Zolotarenko,
arrived. Meanwhile every effort was made to soften up the
defences. On the 26th and 28th the walls were subjected to a heavy
bombardment. On the 29th and 30th the bombardment was more
intense and several bastions were damaged. Day after day the
pounding continued. Alexis was spellbound – and not merely by
the flashes and the boom of guns (he had seen these before at
artillery trials); nor by the sight, through his telescope, of bricks and
splinters flying off the walls (though he formed a love of artillery
beyond all other arms, and a keen interest in ballistics). He was
excited by the brisk translation of plans into actions. How satisfactory it was to see such immediate and tangible consequences of the
exercise of power!

Yet all the power let loose upon the city was not to yield the
desired results at once. The besiegers erected mobile fortifications,
and two of Smolensk's towers were demolished in the days that
followed, but resistance continued. An attempt to run trenches
along the riverside was beaten off, and when, on 16th August, a
storming operation was finally mounted, it proved to be a costly
failure. It was a week before he could bring himself to write home
about it:

By God's grace our troops stormed Smolensk very bravely.

They broke into one of the towers and onto the walls and there
was a great battle. . . . But the Poles had mined the tower with
gunpowder, so many of our men were forced to come down
from the walls and others were set on fire by the explosion.
More than two hundred Lithuanians were killed. We lost three
hundred killed and a thousand wounded.

He added a postscript: 'Do not grieve about the storm. Our men
fought stoutly and famously, and gave them a beating.'[23]

Plans for another storm were immediately drawn up and four
huge 40-pounder culverins, made in Holland, were brought up to
increase the besiegers' fire-power.[24] But it was attrition rather than
assault that doomed the garrison. They had sustained many casualties; their stocks of food and ammunition were running low, and
then their last hope of being relieved died with the defeat of
Radziwill's army. When the Muscovites planted the captured Polish
banners outside the walls, morale inside the city crumbled. Against
the wishes of the Governor the inhabitants sued for peace. Surrender terms were eventually agreed and on 23rd September Alexis
entered Smolensk.

It was the crowning moment of a campaign blessed with glitter-
ing success. In all, some thirty cities had been captured; a huge slice
of the Grand Duchy of Lithuania had been occupied, including the
larger part of Belorussia. The forces of Catholic Poland had been
comprehensively defeated. But the moment of triumph was marred
by the receipt of grievous news from home. The plague had struck
Moscow earlier that summer and had since become epidemic. As
Prince Michael P. Pronskii, head of the boyar commission left in the
Kremlin reported, more than half of the population had fled the
capital, including most of the clergy, and terror had taken hold of
almost all who had remained.

> Orthodox Christians [he wrote] are . . . being buried without
> priests, and corpses are lying about in the city and outside it to
> be mauled by dogs. . . . All government offices are closed;
> many secretaries and under-secretaries have died, and our
> homes, Sovereign, have been emptied, almost all the people
> having died.[25]

A visitor from Syria has left an account of the plague which, if not
clinically accurate, conveys something of the terror it induced:

> Persons might be standing erect in full health, and in an instant
> would drop down dead. A man riding on a horse, or sitting in a

carriage, would roll back and expire, and swelling like a bladder, would turn black, and assume the most hideous expression of countenance.[26]

Loyal Pronskii stayed at his post where he himself was struck down by the disease on 11th September. The next day his colleague Khilkov died. The Kremlin was sealed up. Moscow was desolate.

Fortunately, however, Alexis's family was safe. In July, at the first signs of danger, Nikon had spirited them off to Zagorsk, and when the plague intensified and began to spread he took them farther away to the Koliazin Monastery.[27] But Nikon's own departure from Moscow had provoked popular anger.

> The Patriarch [people said] should have had the decency to stay in Moscow and pray to God on behalf of Orthodox Christians. But he has abandoned Moscow, and, seeing this, many parish priests have also fled leaving Orthodox Christians to die without confession and without the sacraments.[28]

Worse, many had begun to regard the plague as a scourge sent by God to punish Muscovy for abandoning the true religion by allowing Nikon to carry through his reforms. Some even claimed to have had visions forbidding the printing of the new prayer books.[29]

Nonetheless Nikon's departure had been essential, and the decision was endorsed by Alexis. The realm had to be governed from a place of relative safety and this Nikon had been doing, issuing orders in the names of the Tsaritsa and the infant Tsarevich. The enforcement of quarantine regulations received priority. The doors and windows of the Tsar's quarters in the Kremlin had been bricked up to prevent any emanation of the plague wafting in to infect his possessions; a *cordon sanitaire* had at once been placed across the road between Moscow and Smolensk; and eventually Moscow was sealed off altogether. Fires were lit across the main roads and essential correspondence coming out was dictated across the flames and the originals burned. Where a bearer of the plague had passed along a road an area of seventy feet on either side was burned, the ashes mixed with earth and carted away, and fresh earth laid down on the once affected spot. And anyone breaking quarantine was to be executed.[30]

At last, in October, the plague began to abate, and Alexis left Smolensk for Viazma, where he arranged for his family to join him. He was looking forward to their arrival, he told them, much 'as a blind man rejoices at [the prospect of] light',[31] and, indeed they were reunited shortly afterwards, whereupon in January Maria was to give birth to another daughter. Meanwhile a member of the Council had been sent to Moscow to report on the condition of the City. His account, written in December, made grim reading. Only fifteen servants remained in the palace; the survival rate among the city's monks was barely 15 per cent; only half the translators in the Foreign Office had survived, and the toll among other government servants had been heavy. The leading boyars had suffered grievous losses among their domestic staffs. Of Boris Morozov's 362 household servants, only 19 remained – the rest had died or fled. Nikita Trubetskoi had only 8 left out of almost 300, Nikita Odoevskii 15 out of 310; Iakov Cherkasskii had lost 423 people dead; cousin Nikita Romanov 352. Among the city's tradesmen only one in five seemed to have survived.[32]

Alexis called for reports of losses in other cities, and the answers were almost as sombre. In Kaluga the death rate was over 70 per cent; half the population of the city of Tver had perished; almost half in Uglich and Suzdal'. Kostroma and Nizhnii-Novgorod had each suffered over three thousand deaths; many monks in his precious Sabbas Monastery had perished too. . . .[33] As a contemporary was to recall: 'God poured forth the vials of the wrath of his fury on to the Russian land. The plague was great exceedingly; none can even now forget; we all remember.'[34]

Yet, however despondent he felt inwardly, Alexis felt it to be his duty to raise his people's spirits. He was soon urging Boris and indeed all his servitors to abandon '*sadness and be merry*', stressing the message by underlining the words.[35] And partly for the same reason he decided to make his return to Moscow particularly spectacular – a thanksgiving after the storm, and one that would assault all the senses of those who watched. His entry, early in February 1657, was heralded by great blasts of gunfire. Sixty battle-standards, each with an escort of *strel'tsy*, led the procession. Then came two icons borne aloft on long poles illuminated by great golden lanterns and followed by priests carrying candles, swinging censers of burning incense, or bearing holy books. Behind them walked the staff of the Foreign Office, and Nikon with the visiting Patriarch of Antioch, both with silver croziers in hand and jewel-studded golden mitres upon their heads. They halted outside the Kremlin and took up their stations ready to greet and bless the Tsar.

Alexis himself was preceded by seven companies of dragoons, a bevy of colonels, the Master of the Horse, forty splendid horses with long saddle-cloths, a band of trumpets, pipes and drums, and two of Alexis's favourite horses each with a sabre hanging from its saddle-bow. Then came a choir of white-clad boys, and finally Alexis himself – on foot, bare-headed despite the freezing tempera-ture, and wearing a long coat of white sable. There, watched by an embassy from Sweden, Alexis received the blessings of the Patriarchs, the welcoming gifts of the surviving citizens and the prostrations of the multitude.[36]

The demonstration pleased the crowds, and his arrival seemed to restore confidence, but it could not make good the disastrous ravages of the plague. The yield of a special levy imposed by the government the previous autumn was accordingly disappointing, forcing Alexis to step up the minting of copper coins, and to send his agents to extract forced loans from any monastery which he learned had stores of gold or silver money.[37] At all costs the means had to be found to prosecute the war. The need to conquer more territory, and, even more important, to control a larger productive population, was greater now than before. Captive Belorussians, Lithuanians and Poles could make up the depredations of the plague.[38] Orders had already been issued in October for his forces to reassemble in March, before the thaw set in this time. Despite continuing Polish resistance in desultory winter operations and raids made by their allies, the Crimean Tatars, he sensed that the enemy could not prevent Muscovy consolidating her gains, and indeed making new ones, provided the strength of effort was main-tained. However, enthusiasm was by no means universal. Many members of the elite were anxious for more time to rearrange their affairs after the plague, and not a few were reluctant to have their old bones shaken again by the discomforts of another campaign.

Alexis was not sympathetic to such pleas. When Vasily Sheremetev petitioned for leave from duty at Vitebsk on account of his age and ill-health, permission was refused. A general edict was issued condemning such 'grumbling' petitions. Only those in finan-cial straits might ask for leave; there must be 'no deserting service'. Everyone was to 'serve with joy until his release.'[39] Nonetheless, not a few were to fail to appear at the appointed place and time, offering all kinds of excuses, some of them good. But even these were warned that although on this occasion the Tsar would hold his hand, if it happened again he would certainly ruin them: confiscate their estates and pack them off in disgrace to Siberia.[40]

His own few weeks in Moscow had been filled with activity. The arrival of the Patriarch of Antioch occasioned a vast celebratory dinner, which, despite the fact that no meat could be eaten, the palace kitchens contrived to make quite sumptuous, dressing up minced fish to look like stuffed lamb and geese and providing an amazing variety of pastries, puddings, and other dishes which were washed down with vodka, Cretan wine and mead.[41] There were gifts to distribute, and gifts to receive, including a curious variety brought by the Patriarch Macarius: pistachios and 'manna' (which Alexis had never seen before), dates, angora wool and cinnabar; candles made in Jerusalem and musk-scented soap from Constantinople – besides an impressive collection of relics. There was a fragment of the true cross 'tested by fire and water', a rock from Golgotha spattered with the blood of Jesus and a bone of John the Baptist. For Maria there was part of the veil of St Anastasia to guard her against enchantment; for the infant Tsarevich Alexis a finger of Alexis, the Man of God, and a 'small quantity of his hair'; for his sisters, various limbs of holy women.[42]

Inevitably, Alexis was drawn into church affairs again. Nikon was working resolutely to bring order to the Church, to drive through the reforms in the teeth of growing opposition, and to raise the respect in which the Patriarchal office was held (to which end he kept even boyars waiting in his ante-room). Resentment of him was increasingly apparent among the elite and common folk alike, but a grateful Alexis remained steadfast in his support for him, and Nikon took advantage of his presence in Moscow to explain and justify his reforms in a public sermon. He spoke of the three-fingered cross. He also condemned icons that reflected western styles of painting, and had some examples carried in. Announcing the names of the noble owners from whom they had been confiscated, he hurled them one by one onto the floor, and ordered them to be burned. This proved too much for Alexis. He jumped to his feet and intervened. 'No, father,' he remonstrated. 'Do not burn them.' Whatever their faults these icons should be treated with some respect, and given a decent burial.[43]

Furthermore, his cousin Nikita Romanov had recently died and a grip had to be taken of his considerable properties which Alexis now inherited;[44] and the affairs of the court pharmacy had also to be taken in hand. Since Pronskii's death it had lacked a director, but, rather than appointing Il'ia, who made a veiled request for the post, he appointed another in-law, Ivan Miloslavskii, and even so he retained a large measure of personal control. The pharmacy, after all, was the only medical, indeed scientific, centre in the realm and although its primary purpose was to serve the health of the Tsar and his court, both war casualties and the recent epidemic of the plague prompted Alexis to take an active interest in it. (He had just founded a medical school there to train physicians for the army.[45]) But above all it was the prosecution of the war which claimed most of his attention and kept him working at his desk through much of the night.

The plan was simple: a great advance from Velikie Luki and Smolensk to Borisov on the river Berezina and beyond – to take the cities of Minsk, Vilna, Kovno and Grodno; another force to operate from the south through Slutsk; both forces to converge on Brest in a pincer movement and thus sweep the enemy out of the entire Grand Duchy of Lithuania. A smaller force was to move on Dünabork to offer a shield against any Swedish interference[46]; Khmelnytsky's Cossacks would also advance in conjunction with other Muscovite forces sent to Ukraine. But the operations could not be conducted in a diplomatic vacuum. Sweden was worried, not so much at the prospect of the extinction of Poland (which seemed increasingly possible) as at allowing Muscovy to carry off all the spoils. Alexis was well aware of the situation. In January he had written to his friend Artamon Matveev, who had served under him as a colonel of *strel'tsy* at Smolensk and whom he had since sent to Ukraine, about an encounter with a Swedish envoy, Udda Edda. It contained no reference to God, nor to his personal worthlessness and dependence on the prayers of others, nor even of his own exalted Tsarish dignity. In private, ciphered, correspondence with a close friend there was no need to maintain the usual masks and they were all discarded – to reveal a direct Alexis, Alexis the strategist, the machiavellian statesman:

> I have not set eyes on such a stupid envoy in ten years. This fool was sent to find out what we . . . will do for love of the King [now Carl Gustav]. . . They are really afraid of us, the Swedes. . . . It is not Smolensk that vexes them so much as [the capture of] Vitebsk and Polotsk because it gives us the route up the Dvina to Riga. The King writes suggesting that an eternal agreement should be confirmed by [our] ambassadors, and that he is sending his ambassador to us . . . and that, as if out of love for me, he has sent a Councillor as an envoy to inform [me]. But I think that fear was twice as much involved as love. . . . In another letter he writes that we should not carry the war into Courland for the sake of his royal friendship, since [the Duke

of] Courland is a friend of his, the King's. But we . . . declined
on the ground that he was subject to the King of Poland. . . .[47]

Alexis set out from Moscow again on 11th March. It was
evening, and his way was lit by hundreds of blazing torches. Two
days later and only a few miles out he reported to his sisters that the
going was rough. 'I have never seen a worse road in my life.' There
were immense snow-drifts and the track was so uneven that, for all
the efforts of the sweepers and stirrup grooms, he felt shaken and
bruised from the jolting as his sledge shuddered over the bumps.
Nonetheless he reached Viazma on the 16th and was at Smolensk by
the end of the month.[48]

He kept up a stream of brief messages to his family, urging them
not to pine for him too much and to be at peace with one another.
His sisters had a clinging tendency, but he did not love them the less
for it, and it was hard for the family not to be together at Easter, the
main holiday in the Orthodox calendar. They sent each other Easter
eggs, however, and he took care to celebrate their name-day feasts.
He told Irina that he had 'feasted joyfully' on her birthday, and
thanking them for the Easter egg they sent him he wrote that he had
'kissed it with tears of joy for want of kissing you yourselves'.[49]
Presumably he wrote even more often and intimately to Maria,
though these letters have not survived. He also gave them snippets
of news about the course of the campaign, but these gave no
impression of the range and intensity of his work. There were all
manner of problems to cope with and couriers in their dozens were
leaving his headquarters daily bearing his solutions.

One problem concerned desertion. Men were fleeing into the
forests, many of them aiming to reach Ukraine and obtain registra-
tion there as free Cossacks. At once Alexis wrote to Vasily Buturlin
ordering him to make sure that Hetman Khmelnytsky did not
accept them and that one deserter in ten captured be hanged.[50] He
was in constant correspondence with his commanders in the field,
and with Moscow – ordering the raising of more recruits, the
sending of more money, the direction of supplies, the treatment to
be accorded to captured cities. He even found time to instruct
Falconer Tobolin to discipline a man who had failed in his duty,
telling him to address the culprit as 'son of a heretic, son of a bitch' –
but then, thinking these to be too strong for the offence, crossed
them out and substituted a mild 'damned villain'.[51]

At first the campaign promised well. The enemy had not
expected the offensive, least of all so early in the year. But by the end

of April the Dnieper at Smolensk broke its banks, flooding the baggage camps and setting the only bridge awash. It was bad luck. Nothing like it had been seen at Smolensk for thirty years.

This reverse, coupled with the appalling mud, made movement so difficult, especially for the artillery, that the entire offensive was put behind schedule. Nonetheless, by 10th June Alexis had moved his headquarters forward to Shklov where the great assault across the river Berezina was set in motion. On the 15th he took communion in preparation for the enterprise; then the armies moved forward. While Bogdan Khitrovo advanced to Borisov to secure a passage across the Berezina, the bulk of the forces set out to secure the city of Minsk. Nikita Odoevskii's advance guard marched on 20th June, followed by the 'Great Regiment' on the 24th and the rear-guard, now under the command of Boris Alexandrovich Repnin, a day later. Zolotarenko's Cossacks also moved to join them. Alexis had intended to proceed to Borisov, but as he reported to his family he had remained at Shklov to solve a logistical problem: 'We did not go because supplies of bread were short.' Since the Dnieper was still in flood he had sent 600 wagons overland to Smolensk to fetch supplies. They were expected back on St Peter's Day, the 29th, whereupon he intended to cross the Dnieper and move on to Borisov 'without an hour's delay'.[52]

The opposition seemed to be small-scale, locally-based; there was no news of the main Polish army and the King. This worried Alexis. But no royal army emerged and so in July he swung his forces north-westwards towards the River Nieman, Vilna and the forces of Radziwill and Honiewski which defended it. He himself followed close behind. Still things went well. Towards the end of July the Lithuanian forces were confronted and beaten. Vilna fell, and although its castle held out, on the 30th Alexis made his solemn entrance into the city riding in a velvet-upholstered carriage built in France driven by a coachman dressed in brown and yellow livery and escorted by halberdiers in brown velvet caftans with ruby-coloured collars. Guns boomed out a salute.[53] He had little appetite for the dinner that had been prepared for him there, however.

The streets along which his procession had passed had been carpeted with red cloth, but he could not help but notice that the side-alleys were littered with corpses and smell their stench which mingled with smoke from burning buildings. The carnage had been terrible – not only in the fighting of the day before but in its aftermath, when swarms of undisciplined fighting men (and notably

Zolotarenko's Cossacks) had indulged in an orgy of looting, rape and murder, more especially of Catholics and Jews. Such was the norm of warfare. Had the city surrendered it might have been spared. But it had not surrendered. Besides, this was a crusade. Nonetheless, Alexis was horrified. He ordered the bodies to be buried (though many of them were merely piled away farther out of sight) moved the Cossacks up to the most dangerous posts around the hill-top castle (which fell a few days later), and threatened death to any soldier found misbehaving.[54]

Yet during his stay there Alexis could not but be impressed by the city. For all that the more prudent of its inhabitants had packed up their treasure and departed before the invaders came; for all the destruction and the burning, Vilna was visibly a centre of civilization. It contained the marvellous Radziwill Palace with its marble columns and gilded cupolas and domes. Many of the other buildings were of Gothic, Renaissance or Baroque style; its riches and its art were above the ordinary even for Lithuania, reflecting its strength as a commercial centre and as a great store-house of crafts and manufactures (in which Muscovy was so sadly lacking). In all, Vilna gave the impression of a Western city to Muscovite eyes, and Alexis was clearly enthralled by it.

The silver tomb of St Casimir was carted off to Moscow, of course; the gold was stripped from the roof of the Radziwill Palace, and the contents of these as well as other buildings in the city were plundered. Carts which had been used to transport supplies for the campaign returned laden with clocks and furniture, tapestries and marble columns – and twenty of the local wild buffalo, a gift to Nikon from the grateful Tsar. But more significant were the skills which the capture of Vilna and of other Lithuanian and Belorussian towns put at Muscovy's disposal. When Alexis needed 2,000 small copper bells for his falcons he was to send to Vilna for them,[55] and in the months and years that followed hundreds of skilled men – woodcarvers, physicians, gold- and silversmiths, leather-embossers, printers, painters, gunsmiths and tailors – were to find their way to Moscow; and many more were to be carried off as labourers to help make up the losses from the plague.[56]

So it was that the captured territories made a contribution to the Russian economy and to Russian culture. What he saw there also stimulated Alexis's aesthetic senses and enlarged his aspirations. His English doctor, Samuel Collins, was later to observe that since the Tsar had 'been in *Poland* and seen the manner of the Princes' houses there and ghess'd at the mode of their Kings his thoughts . . . [have] advanced and he begins to mode his Court and Edifices more stately, to furnish his Rooms with tapestry, and contrive houses of pleasure abroad.'[57] Yet it was not his campaigning that first opened Alexis's eyes to the material culture of Western Europe.

He had been surrounded by Western objects since he was a child; he knew something of the mode of foreign kings from the reports of Muscovite ambassadors and from Western officers in his service. Moreover, a glance at the orders given to his English buying agent, John Hebdon, testifies to the fact that he was already avid to acquire the best samples of Western artifice and invention.[58] Nonetheless, there was a world of difference between objects which had been divorced from their context and the sight of an environment complete and entire. What he saw of those Renaissance and Baroque interiors especially – their symmetry, their grandeur and their humanity – moved him. So did the thought of his own success in war, and it was with satisfaction that by early September 1655 he was adding 'White Russia' to his tsarish and autocratic titles.[59]

Not only Minsk and Vilna fell to him that year, but Kovno, Grodno, Homel and Mogilev too. Alexis had thought of continuing the campaign into the winter in order to round off his plans and then return to Moscow for good. However, he began his slow journey home in early September. Many assumed that this was due to an epidemic among the horses which severely reduced the troops' mobility,[60] but there were other reasons. Since June the international situation had changed rapidly, and Alexis needed to re-think his strategy. The catalyst of change was Sweden.

Swedish troops had invaded Poland in June. By the end of August they had occupied Warsaw itself and Cracow. The Polish court had fled to the monastery of Częstochowa in Silesia. The once powerful state of Poland-Lithuania had collapsed and crumbled. Alexis had delivered the blow that had first cracked that brittle but imposing edifice; and yet, ironically, he was to be instrumental in restoring it. It was a decision he did not take hurriedly, however. That autumn and winter he received a succession of foreign ambassadors and held countless discussions with his aides.

Envoys came bearing the congratulations of their monarchs from Denmark, from the Habsburg Emperor, even from the Republic of Venice. At last, it seemed, Muscovy had won recognition by her peers as a European power. But these emissaries, as he well knew, were anxious to urge policies upon him that would serve the

interests not of Muscovy but of their masters. The Venetians, while
they wanted to develop trade with Russia (as indeed Alexis wanted
to with Venice), invited him to turn his attentions to the south and
join them in an alliance against the infidel Turks.[61] The imperial
ambassadors were anxious to act as mediators between him and
Poland. The Danes also urged an anti-Swedish stance upon him,
while Khmelnytsky preferred Sweden to the Poles, and the Swedes
themselves tried to counter their enemies by offering him a tempt-
ing commercial alliance. Opinions among his counsellors were
divided and unstable. And to add to the complications, Polish–
Lithuanian magnates were trying to secure their own positions by
offering their allegiance to one or other of the occupying powers.
Radziwill ingratiated himself with the Swedes; others inclined
towards Muscovy, and before long even mooted the idea that
Alexis might be elected the next King of a restored Poland.[62]

By the end of the year the die was cast. Alexis, while holding onto
his conquests, acceded to a *rapprochement* with the Poles and prepared to turn his forces against Sweden. Several considerations
weighed in this decision, but one more than any other. A too-
powerful Sweden would be in a position to cut Muscovy off from
access to the sea routes to Western Europe and Alexis had come to
wish desperately for a sea-port of his own on the Baltic coast. This
had led him in June 1655, almost as soon as he knew of the impending Swedish intervention, to offer protection to the city of Gdansk,
Poland's great foreign trade emporium. Unfortunately for him,
however, Swedish forces had overrun the city's hinterland and his
secret agent (a merchant of Pskov) charged with smuggling the
message through failed to reach his destination.[63]

The decision to engage Sweden had much to commend it in the
altered circumstances. It also had a wealth of precedent behind it.
Protestant Sweden was as heretical to Russian eyes as Catholic
Poland: Sweden, too, had an Orthodox minority which it
oppressed; and Ivan the Terrible's long Livonian war had been in
part directed against her. Furthermore the state of Muscovy was in
severe financial straits and the revival of its economic fortunes was
considered to depend in large measure on the acquisition of a Baltic
port, through which it might grow rich (as so many of the Polish
nobility had grown rich) by the export of bulky goods like grain
and potash to the West, and where it might create a shipbuilding
industry and a fleet of its own. Alexis's subsequent activities suggest
that the dust had been blown off a plan presented to him in 1651 by a

Frenchman, Jean de Gron, which had drawn attention to the profits to be made, among other things, by the construction and the sale abroad of ships.[64] Muscovy had the timber, tar, hemp and flax for such an enterprise; it lacked the port, the shipyards and the expertise in building large seagoing ships. These Alexis now set out to acquire – for the chief objective of the forthcoming campaign was to be the great old Hanseatic port of Riga (to which Alexis had already alluded in his secret letter to Matveev a year earlier).

Meanwhile, despite rumblings of discontent among the mercantile classes, the production of devalued silver and copper coins was stepped up, their acceptance as legal tender insisted upon,[65] and military expenditure continued unabated, not least on the *strel'tsy* guards regiments, which Alexis now took under his personal direction, enlarging the Private Office to provide himself with the necessary assistance.[66] But if military and strategic matters commanded the centre of his attentions, as the all-seeing Tsar he could not afford to neglect matters that held less interest for him, and his return to Moscow for five months embroiled him once again in church affairs (whereupon he tried to avoid the rough language he had become accustomed to while on campaign and fall into his former style, suffused with religious imagery).

Nikon and he had many dealings, not least over property. Alexis continued his generous sponsorship of Nikon's building projects and, for his part, the Patriarch sanctioned the transfer of two attractive villages, Dmitrevskoe and Stepanovskoe (once the property of the Patriarch Joseph), to the Tsar, who had long coveted them.[67] Nikon was also anxious for the Tsar to invest him with a white cowl of the Greek style in place of the customary black. It was Alexis's understanding, confirmed by the Patriarch Macarius of Antioch, that the white cowl symbolized purity of faith. It was worn by the other Orthodox Patriarchs, and was associated with the idea of Moscow as the Third Rome, to which Alexis had long subscribed. To Nikon, however, it may also have carried with it some idea of the primacy of Church over State. Certainly his face beamed with pleasure as he put it on.[68] Alexis supported his old friend, too, in his final enforcement of the revised liturgy and ritual.[69] Nonetheless, it soon became apparent that all was not well in their relationship.

There was no rupture between them as yet, but the incident a year before, when Tsar had remonstrated with Patriarch about the burning of icons, was to prove more than a straw in the wind. Nikon, of course, was not entirely popular and he suspected that the Tsar had been drawn closer to his enemies in the course of his campaigns. Indeed, some of Alexis's companions, including his kinsman Rodion Streshnev, despised Nikon, and the Tsar had been isolated from the influence of others like his sister, the hero-worshipping Tatiana, for whom Nikon could do no wrong. But this counted for little. The real divergence between them stemmed not from the influence of third parties but rather from differences in personality and political style. Nikon (partly at the Tsar's own urging) had set out deliberately not only to enhance the dignity of his office but to strengthen his authority to the point (as many regarded it) of tyranny. Alexis, on the other hand, for all his autocratic principles, had developed sufficient political sensitivity not to invite opposition gratuitously. He preferred persuasion to force, and knew how to invite obedience; Nikon, by contrast, lacked discretion; he only seemed to understand the stick.

Alexis's great success was to persuade the dissenter Ivan Neronov to make his peace with the authorities. He sought to set the seal on their reconciliation one day at service when he asked Nikon to give Ivan a special blessing. Nikon objected that this was not an appropriate moment. Alexis told him sharply to be quiet, at which Nikon retorted that he had no need of the Tsar's advice in liturgical matters, least of all in the middle of a service.[70] The penitent Neronov was nevertheless rehabilitated, but this was not the only case of a public altercation between Patriarch and Tsar. On the eve of Good Friday Alexis upbraided Nikon in church for saying the prayer for the Feast of the Immersion once only, instead of twice, as the Patriarch of Antioch had assured him it should be. An argument ensued during which the Tsar was heard to call the Patriarch 'a quarrelsome peasant'. 'I am your spiritual father,' replied Nikon, standing on his dignity. 'Why, then, do you revile me?' 'It is the holy Patriarch of Antioch, not you, who is my spiritual father,' retorted Alexis, and immediately sent after the Patriarch of Antioch who had just begun his homeward journey, and asked him to return. The quarrel was patched up, and late in April Alexis was present when Nikon formally anathematized the use of the two-fingered cross and confirmed the various other changes in practice.[71] Good order demanded that there must be only one standard way of prayer; and Alexis, preparing to leave on his third campaign, still needed Nikon.

The troops and wagons were already on the move when, on 15th May, two days prior to the formal declaration of war on Sweden, Alexis left Moscow for his third campaign. This time he was helped by an enlarged personal secretariat with an additional Secretary, Dementii Bashmakov, who was to keep the campaign journal, provide him with daily abstracts of reports and map out the lines of march.[72] Evidently his use of his Private Office for confidential correspondence made for some confusion among his family, for in writing to them from Viazma on 23rd May he felt constrained to tell them that although they might correspond with whomsoever they pleased, their letters were only to be penned by those trusties he had left with them (presumably his private secretaries remaining in the Kremlin), and that it was 'not fitting' to address letters to a mere secretary or under-secretary,[73] implying that they had been addressing letters for him to his private staff rather than to him personally.

Once again movement was slow, partly because of the mud, but also because of the weight of supplies which accompanied the army, not least luxuries without which, apparently, so many great men could not survive. Boris Morozov started out that year with gallons of Rhenish and other wines, not to mention mead and vodka, a dozen dried sturgeon, twenty salmon, nearly a hundred dried chickens, preserved goose, more than five hundredweight of butter and fat, fifty hams, barrels of caviare and lemons – in addition to simpler foods to feed the humbler of his retainers. Further supplies were bought locally or sent for on the way.[74] That the luxuries enjoyed at home must be available on campaign was taken for granted, but Alexis had become intolerant of anyone who seemed to place his personal comforts before his duty towards him.

He had found a form of punishment for such malingerers which also afforded him amusement. It had evidently started one day when Alexis had forded the River Moscow at a deep and difficult point and then forced his entourage to follow, laughing at their discomfiture. When they upbraided him, he had told them it was meant to lessen their huge paunches, the product of too much rest and idleness. Nor would he allow them to change their clothes until they had attended mass and downed three successive draughts of vodka.[75] What had started as a boisterous prank evidently became a habit. Paul of Aleppo reports Alexis registering the names of all those who had failed to attend him at morning prayers, having them fetched from their homes with their hands tied behind their backs and hurled into the water in all their finery, saying: 'This is your reward; which you have invited, by preferring to sleep with your wives to the splendid lustre of this blessed day, and not coming forth to assist at morning prayers with your Emperor.'[76] The anecdote has support in the records, for the names of those who failed to appear on time for such occasions as his name-day service in October 1655 were indeed registered;[77] and in a letter to his kinsman Afansy Matiushkin Alexis himself admitted: 'I have made it my custom to duck [errant] courtiers every morning in a pond. The baptism is well done. I duck four or five, sometimes a dozen of them – whomever fails to report on time for my inspection.' Then, perhaps ashamed of his coarseness and wanting to portray himself in a more sympathetic light, he explained that he entertained them afterwards and claimed that many of them came late on purpose in order to secure an invitation to dinner.[78]

All the punishments he meted out were exemplary, however, whether ducking courtiers for lateness, hanging peasant soldiers by the dozen for desertion, confiscating the estates of a nobleman who dared to protest about his posting on grounds of precedence and having him knouted and sent to Siberia, or ordering a courier who had lost a falcon to be knouted and chained to an iron ring.[79] But the Tsar's grace, his rewards for good service, were the obverse of that coin, and many of those who marched were anxious to do their duty well. By the beginning of July 1656 advanced units of his army had begun to inch forward down the Dvina towards Riga.

Alexis arrived in Polotsk on 5th July, there to be greeted by the abbot of a local Orthodox monastery and told that his presence there was 'a cause of sweet rejoicing and of unspeakable happiness to all'. It was not the truth. Catholics who had survived the city's capture the year before still trembled; no professing Jews survived. Nonetheless Alexis had dealings with Catholics there, receiving the Habsburg Ambassador Allegretti with every sign of good grace to discuss preliminary terms for a forthcoming peace with Poland, and on the 15th, taking a local icon with him as reinforcement, he moved northwards towards the fighting zone.[80]

This time it was Boyar Simeon L. Streshnev who led the vanguard and Alexis ordered him to keep to the right bank of the river so far as possible in order to give no offence to the inhabitants of Courland, subjects of the Polish crown, on the other bank. The Courlanders were not to be plundered; provisions needed from them must be purchased at a fair price and their crops must not be trodden down. Streshnev claimed to be obeying orders and by 19th July was laying siege to Dünabork (now Daugavpils). Alexis, however, had reports of Streshnev's men leaving a trail of plunder and killing through the Duke of Courland's territory. He ordered him to hang the worst offenders, knout the rest and write to the Duke in his name promising compensation for lives lost and damage done. But Streshnev's task was difficult. The enemy had entrenched himself on the Courland bank, blocking the river to his boats, and he was forced to send troops over to dislodge them. Eventually, he managed to proceed with his advance, though at the cost of many casualties, and he was soon deluged with petitions for compensation from the wounded.

Alexis gave precise instructions on how to deal with them. Compensation (in addition to monies already provided to pay for their treatment) was to be made on a scale of between two and four rubles according to the gravity of the wound sustained and whether the wounded man belonged to the service class, was a cavalryman, convert or foreigner, or merely a common soldier, dragoon, Cossack, monastery serviceman or conscript from the tax-paying classes. Valid claims were to be registered and paid out after the campaign had ended. Progress continued, despite the loss of some boats in the river rapids. By the end of July Streshnev had captured Dünabork, and Alexis soon set up his quarters there.[81]

On 3rd August he wrote to his family describing the town's capture after a dawn assault and how the place had been ravaged by fires caused by Russian grenades. He mentioned the casualties his men had sustained, but not the massacre of the inhabitants which they had perpetrated. And he promptly Russified the place by ordering a church to be built in the ruins and re-naming the town after the martyred infant princes Boris and Gleb. By mid-August he was at the siege and storm of Kukenaus. The place, he wrote good-humouredly, was 'immensely strong with a deep moat, the younger brother of our moat at the Kremlin, and a fortress which is the son of the Smolensk citadel'. He had celebrated the martyrdom of the Tsarevich Dmitrii and the entire besieging force had attended mass before the storm, which had cost 500 men dead and wounded.[82] Afterwards he ordered an Orthodox church to be built there by way of thanksgiving and ordered the name to be changed to 'Tsarevich Dmitrii' in honour of the murdered prince. Before long he was outside Riga with a vast force, artillery to back it up, and General Leslie to supervise the trench works.

But for all the efforts expended, for all his hopes and spiritual preparations, this time, at long last, his luck was to run out. Indeed circumstances had been against him from the start. The desertion rate had been increasing and more men had had to be spared to form search parties to track them down. Although Cossack experts in the art of boat-building had been ordered up,[83] the flotilla was too small to supply, still less blockade, the city from the sea, and in mid-September a large part of it, containing vital supplies, was lost through enemy action. Not least, the spring mud and the determined resistance of the Swedes upstream of Riga had delayed progress by a month or more and, as it proved, too little time was left now to press the siege to a successful conclusion before the onset of winter.

Seven batteries of cannon sent hundreds of rounds screaming into the city; the heads of officers killed in sorties were paraded within view of the defenders in an attempt to lessen their morale; there were two attempts to storm. All to no avail. With losses mounting, discontent on the increase, and no sign of any weakening of the garrison's will and ability to resist, his generals advised Alexis to raise the siege. He refused. A Swedish raid on his encampment which caused many casualties and carried away over a dozen battle standards at last persuaded him to change his mind. The October winds were biting sharply as a disconsolate Alexis began his homeward journey. The soldiers left in a much happier frame of mind. Years later a song about the siege was still being sung in Russia:

> Do not leave us poor men to besiege Riga.
> Riga has already wearied us,
> Riga has tired us; Riga has plagued us.
> We have suffered much cold and hunger here.

They plead with the Tsar not to leave them there, and the Tsar grants their wish. Riga, he tells them, has wearied him as well.[84]

Although the great prize had eluded him, there were consolations. Large parts of Latvia, Estonia and Finland were in his hands, and after months of hard negotiation at Vilna his representatives, headed by Nikita Odoevskii, had at last reached a measure of agreement on peace terms with the Poles. Alexis was to become Poland's King when the present King died. This huge concession was hedged about with conditions. Alexis must not interfere in Polish affairs until he became King; after his own death the Polish nobility would revert to their normal practice of electing a successor; the constitution of the state must not be infringed; the rights of the Catholic Church must be preserved. The agreement had yet to be ratified; many points of disagreement had yet to be resolved.[85] Even so, Alexis now had the prospect of becoming one of the very

greatest monarchs in the world; new and alluring vistas of aggrand-
isement had opened up before him.

Principle withered in the face of ambition. The Orthodox Tsar
began to contemplate defending the faith of Catholics. Yet this was
merely another flowering of those contradictions latent in him since
childhood – the clash between isolationism and the lure of the West;
between Byzantine exclusiveness and a yearning to be accepted on
equal terms by his European peers; between Muscovite obscur-
antism and the more rational world of technology and science;
between the immutable world of the spirit and the turmoil of
change and innovation in the real world. If Alexis had ever had
doubts about surrendering himself to the charms of Western civilization he now abandoned them; yet he did not abandon his heritage,
and he made no obvious mental effort to reconcile the two. Perhaps
he sensed the essential futility of such an exercise.

In any case, less philosophical and more pressing problems filled
his mind: how to break through to the Baltic; how to counter
Sweden's ally, the Crimean Khan; how to bring the Ukrainians to
heel (the ailing Khmelnytsky had been showing too much indepen-
dence of late); how to manage the pro- and anti-Nikon factions; and
how to solve the perennial problems raised by the indiscipline of
Russians.

Chapter VI

The Autocrat Asserts Himself

Alexis was almost twenty-nine and in the full flower of manhood. Red-bearded, bright-eyed, tall and muscular, he looked the image of an ideal prince, and if he was beginning to show signs of corpulence this only added to the dignity of his appearance. His demeanour reinforced the image. He could give those who met him an impression of terrifying sternness or of melting graciousness. He could exert charm or inspire awe almost at will, and although he occasionally showed signs of youthful impetuosity he had become altogether more deliberate, more manipulative, and more effective as a ruler. The change owed much to his experiences on campaign.

The failure at Riga had been a disappointment, but he realized that with patience and perseverance he might yet achieve his strategic aims. His forces were still well established near the Baltic; negotiations were soon under way to bring Courland under Muscovite protection; he still had prospects of becoming King of Poland, and his victories over the last three years seemed enough to earn him recognition as the equal of Europe's greatest monarchs. Indeed, territorial aggrandizement was not his only claim to be treated on a par with the Kings of France and Spain. They were absolutists and so was he. The war had helped him find his feet as autocrat. Not only had he earned a reputation for dealing fiercely with anyone who contested his opinions, he was issuing more and more edicts without consulting the Council, still less an Assembly of the Land.[1] Yet Alexis had not sought absolute power solely out of vanity or ambition; power was also the means of creating his ideal order.

He had recently found time to give expression to this vision in a curious document intended to set a new standard 'for the honour and improvement of the Sovereign's beautiful and celebrated bird-hunt'. Repetitive in the Russian way and ponderously didactic, this

118

rule-book on falconry nevertheless reflects Alexis's philosophy as autocrat. Its readers were exhorted at the outset to respect the book, to learn and understand the rules it contained, and to 'praise us who made them'. The rules themselves, he explained, were based on four principles: 'Measure, proportion, composure and strength'. If these were applied with good order, proper organization and thorough preparation, they would produce the desired result: stateliness and harmony. Indeed, the rules were intended to bring his falcon hunt to such a state of perfection that anyone who saw it, or even heard about it, would 'be astonished' that not only great occasions of state but secondary activities such as hunting were conducted 'with honour and order, to standard, and in proportion'. Even the Tsar's sport was to proclaim his values and his objectives, for 'without honour the mind is diminished . . . without order nothing can be made secure'.

Falconry was a 'glorious sport'. It was a pleasure to hunt with a young gerfalcon; the sight of a tercel catching another bird in flight gave satisfaction and amusement, and the high flight of the merlin was also 'gladsome and beautiful to watch'. The pastime provided consolation too, driving cares and sorrows from one's mind. And it was quite proper to spare time for it. There was, after all, 'a time for work and a time for play'. Nevertheless Alexis did not confuse recreation with relaxation. Even sport must have its discipline, and its distinctive tsarish ceremonial.

The procedures to be followed were all set out in detail – even to the positions of carpets, cushions and chairs. Each chair was to be attended by a falconer (wearing a special livery consisting of a long-sleeved, collarless coat, a curved tricorn hat, a monogrammed shoulder-belt and gauntlet) and when the Tsar arrived the under-falconer in charge of the section on duty (there were five, each with its complement of men and birds) was to doff his cap, report everything ready, and await permission to proceed.

From then on everything followed the style of a military drill. The rules specified the forms of command to be used; who was to hold the lure-bag and who the towel; who was to affix a falcon's golden foot-strap and bell, and who was to remove its silken hood. They even laid down how the huge gold-embroidered elkskin gauntlet was to be pulled on, how a bird's feathers should be adjusted, and the manner in which a falcon was to be held, high up, for everyone to see. The birds were often adorned with jewels and each one had its name – 'Sultan' and 'Warrior', 'Diamond', 'Star' and 'Snake', 'Achilles', 'Boyar', 'Kopek' and 'Little Friend'. No aspect of a falconer's training, duties and entitlements was left undefined either.

Upon induction into the elite corps of falconers a man had to swear a special oath which Alexis had composed. It summed up what he expected of a servitor – to serve him and the imperial hunt 'faithfully, honestly and joyfully' so long as he should live. But the initiate would receive an appropriate admonition too:

> If, in accordance with our imperial command, you carry out all your duties with joy, you will be rewarded. . . . But if you are . . . careless or neglectful . . . lazy, drunken, bad, ill-behaved . . . disobedient, foul-mouthed, evil-tongued, slanderous . . . or behave evilly in any way, then you will be clapped in irons . . . or even sent to Siberia.[2]

In the spring of 1657 Alexis was out hunting two or three times a week, and to judge from his letters[3] it was one of his chief talking points with family and friends.

But if falconry was one obsession, another was the West. Like a child snatching at his elder brother's toys, he was determined to acquire every Western contrivance, artefact and skill that might improve his army and provide him with luxuries as fine as the Emperor's or the King of Spain's. The commissions he gave to his foreign buying agents that year prove as much. He called for 'engineering equipment with which one man could sap a distance of fourteen feet a day in the most difficult terrain and seventy a day in open country'; he wanted the most accurate artillery, every sort of optical aid, including trench telescopes; books on warships, on the use of fire-power in taking or defending a citadel, on the handling of a baggage train 'with speed, skill and safety'.[4] His domestic requirements ranged wider still.

He ordered John Hebdon to buy him fine tapestries and furniture in Western Europe, trees for the palace gardens, sets of pistols engraved with griffins' heads, hunting scenes and flowers (and with the double-headed eagle chased in gold near the lock). He called for velvet holsters, musical boxes, 'parrots of the very finest plumage which can speak; clever parakeets, the very best singing canaries, other foreign song-birds and wild birds with ornamental feathers'. He wanted 'lace such as is worn by the Kings of France and Spain and by the Emperor', gloves and gauntlets sewn with pearls and precious stones, a glass summer-house, silver tableware, canteens of cutlery with lace and velvet handles, fingerbowls and candlesticks (some presumably to give away) and a vastly expensive cuirass 'for a man of moderately stout girth' (presumably to wear himself).

Nor was this all. Hebdon was instructed to obtain samples of the seals used by the King of Spain (so that he could make ones just as fine); 'three fine royal carriages'; 'halberds such as are carried . . . [by the bodyguards of] the Kings of France and Spain and of the Emperor' – plus the uniforms to go with them. In due course most of the stuff arrived (though Hebdon sent only two 'royal' carriages and had difficulty in finding furniture of sufficient quality).[5] And in due course building works were put in hand to create an appropriate setting for them. A Swedish engineer colonel with a reputation as an interior designer was instructed to fit out a new, grander, dining hall in the Kremlin 'in the new foreign style'; the best painters that could be found were set to work redecorating Alexis's private quarters, and a rose garden was planted just outside them.[6] Alexis's aspirations were also made evident by the new throne he had made with a Latin inscription declaring him to be 'The Most Powerful and Invincible Emperor Alexis of Muscovy', and the fine portrait of himself which he had painted by a Western artist (probably the Dutchman Daniel Vuchters) and which bears a Latin motto proclaiming the purity of his autocratic power. Indeed in 1657 he went so far as to set up a special department charged with the task of establishing the genealogy and the titles proper to the Tsar of Muscovy and the achievements, and the likenesses, of all his predecessors.[7] If it would help to establish his status in the West, Alexis was fully prepared to claim descent from the Emperor Augustus, from Constantine the Great or even from Philip of Macedon (two of the sets of tapestries he ordered from the West were to picture Constantine and Philip). It was therefore with some satisfaction that, in the autumn of 1657, Alexis received a letter from the Doge of Venice, couched in the very warmest terms and bearing a golden seal.

The letter was brought back to Moscow by the embassy he had sent to Venice some eighteen months before, and he read its reports with particular interest and attention not so much because of the business it had transacted but on account of the story of the journey and the ambassadors' accounts of what they had seen. The mission had failed to promote direct trade relations with Venice on preferential terms, which was hardly surprising in view of the length and excitements of the voyage. The two Dutch ships which Hebdon had arranged to carry them from Archangel to Leghorn were buffeted and holed by storms (which ruined the cargo of rhubarb they were to sell in Italy on Alexis's behalf) and had a narrow escape in an encounter with Moorish pirates. Nor was Venice prepared to accede to Alexis's request for a hard currency loan. (For that matter, Alexis had no intention at that moment of accepting Venice's invitation to join her in an alliance against the Turks.) But the considerable honours which had been accorded to the ambassadors satisfied some of his yearning for prestige, and he was fascinated by their descriptions of the curiosities they had seen.

Through them Alexis learned about the exotic 'Marriage with the Sea' ceremony which the Doge performed each year, about the notorious Venetian Carnival when everyone went about in masks, and how much it had cost to build the Rialto. But their account of Florence, where they had made an unplanned visit, interested him at least as much. He was given accounts of Florence's *palazzi*, of the giant magnet that hung in the Duke's armoury, of the stuffed crocodile that graced the Ducal apartments, and of the fountains and statues in the Ducal gardens.[8] All these things, and many more, stuck in Alexis's mind and in due course were to prompt further embassies to Italy and the mounting of a diplomatic offensive to gain due recognition from France, Spain and other states. For the moment, however, diplomatic resources had to be concentrated nearer home. The negotiations with Poland were reaching a critical stage; Brandenburg and Denmark had to be persuaded to join the struggle against Sweden; the Ukrainian Hetmanate must be prevented from succumbing to the blandishments of the Tatars, Swedes and Poles. And both grand strategy and the projection of his imperial image abroad had to take second place to the maintenance of political harmony and autocracy at home.

The chief problem was Nikon. The Patriarch had justified all Alexis's original confidence. He had been energetic and fearless in imposing order on the Church; he had supervised the civil administration of the realm during Alexis's absences on campaign; he had helped him put the boyars in their place. Yet in doing so Nikon had become something of a political liability. He had become unpopular among all sectors of society. Traditionalists hated him for enforcing the liturgical reforms; he was reviled for having left Moscow during the plague; churchmen feared him for his harshness; ministers resented his high-handedness. In fact Nikon had few friends left. He had even managed to fall out with Alexis's almoner, the equable Fedor Rtishchev, who had supervised care for the wounded on campaign;[9] and with the environment of hostility towards him extending to members of the Tsar's own family, his friendship with the Tsar himself became difficult to sustain.

Alexis's sister, Tatiana, might still be devoted to the Patriarch; the Tsaritsa (like the Tsar himself) might be grateful to him for saving her and the children from the plague, but Alexis's cousin, Simeon Streshnev, clearly despised him, and his unreliable father-in-law Il'ia was reputedly at the centre of a clique of boyars intent on bringing Nikon down. As the climate of opinion hardened against the Patriarch, others, of lowlier rank, dared to urge the Tsar against him publicly. At an all-night service in the Cathedral in January 1658 the old zealot Grigory Neronov came up to Alexis as Nikon was approaching the altar, and asked him straightly:

> How long will you tolerate such an enemy of God, Sovereign? He has brought discord to the whole house of Russia. He has trampled your Tsarish honour underfoot. He doesn't heed your authority any more. He makes everyone afraid.[10]

Alexis, clearly irritated, said nothing and moved away.

In fact Nikon had twice offered to retire, and twice Alexis had refused the offer. He could see no obvious candidate with the firmness, administrative skills and spiritual authority to succeed him, and he did not want to add the burden of administering the Church to all his other responsibilities. On the other hand the Patriarch had tasted (and obviously relished) the exercise of authority, and Alexis was beginning to suspect that he might try to encroach on his own, secular, sphere and challenge the principle of autocracy which he was determined above all things to maintain. In the revised edition of the canon law published in 1653, Nikon had inserted a passage from the Donation of Constantine which asserted that the authority of the Church was superior to that of the State.[11] It had had its uses in bolstering the Patriarch's authority in the Tsar's absence at the front and so far Nikon had not invoked it to challenge Alexis. But if ever he did so, if ever he should try to play the Metropolitan Philip to Alexis's Ivan, he would have to be restrained.

Nikon, in fact, had no intention of challenging the Tsar, and though he had formed the view that the Church should form a sacrosanct enclave within the body politic, he made no attempt to withhold from the state taxes and levies raised on Church property. For his part Alexis was content to allow Nikon a free hand in the

Church domain, even though this ran counter to his own Law Code, provided that Nikon acted as his agent. Both men accepted the traditional view that Tsar and Patriarch constituted a duality that must work in symphony together. Hence, everything depended on their close personal cooperation, and the readiness of each to be persuaded by the other. But the relationship was not easy to maintain. Alexis was no longer the hero-worshipping youth that he had been when first they had met, and Nikon (who was old enough to be his father and was, by temperament, authoritarian) found it difficult always to defer to his once devoted pupil. Nonetheless both men tried hard to maintain the relationship and both made compromises.

Throughout 1657 and the early months of 1658 they were frequently in each other's company – at services and the round of receptions, dinners and ceremonies that themselves symbolized the ideal accord that was supposed to exist between the two. Alexis also invited Nikon to his estate at Pokrovskoe. No record exists of their conversations and most of the rumours about them cannot be trusted, but they no doubt touched on matters affecting Church–State relations and involved a struggle of wills between the two, a struggle which Alexis seems to have won, for if Nikon pressed for complete judicial autonomy for the Church he did not get it. On the other hand, Alexis continued to allow him, rather than the Monastery Office, to manage Church taxation (a signal sign of trust) and in February 1657 he exempted the Patriarch's own properties from tax. Moreover, he was generous in his endowments of Nikon's new religious foundations, the Monasteries of the Cross, of the Iverian Virgin, and of the Resurrection.[12] Vast sums were lavished on them, sums which Nikon was to use in order to make them monuments to his talents as a patron of the arts and learning. These monasteries, then, were themselves to be expressions of the harmony and friendship that still existed between Nikon and Alexis, and it was appropriate that they should be the scenes of attempts to maintain that harmony.

In October 1657, a few months after Nikon had christened his fourth daughter Sophia, Alexis attended the consecration of the Resurrection Monastery some thirty miles from Moscow and stayed there for five days as Nikon's guest. The church he planned to build there was to be modelled on the Church of the Holy Sepulchre in Jerusalem, and its situation, on a bluff overlooking the river Istra, was an absolute delight. As Alexis stood with Nikon taking in the view he remarked: 'This is truly a blessed place. The Lord God must always have intended it to be the site of a monastery. It is as beautiful as Jerusalem.' The name stuck. Henceforth the Monastery of the Resurrection was always to be known as 'The New Jerusalem'. Nikon had been most solicitous for Alexis (who showed some signs of being unwell) and pressed him to come again. He must have been delighted, then, to receive a letter from the Tsar soon afterwards expressed in warm and affectionate terms:

> You pity us and grieve about us, but, God willing, we shall survive thanks to your most holy prayers . . . We shall not refuse to come again. . . . Tsar Alexis, with much joyous love, kisses thy honourable hand, and greets thee.[13]

Alexis also intimated that he would accept an invitation to visit another of the new foundations, the Iveria Monastery, shortly after Christmas, and, desperately anxious that the Tsar should be impressed and pleased with his reception, Nikon immediately sent frantic orders to the Archimandrite in charge there. Everything must be done, he told him, to create an impression of harmony, decorum and wonder. A finely carved chair, upholstered in velvet and gold, must be provided for the Tsar. The church itself must be decorated in such a way as to amaze all who set eyes on it, and since the bell-tower was unfinished it was to be demolished and a timber structure at least thirty feet high erected in its place. He would be extremely angry, he added, if it were not completed before the Tsar arrived. Furthermore, the entire compound, including the walls, should be finished or at least made to look as if they were; a guard of honour of a hundred musketeers must be provided (if not available, peasants must be drafted in, dressed up and taught how to perform for the occasion). Supplies of food, drink, candles, and hay must be laid up, and the pond should be cleaned out and filled with fish. Moreover, monks, chosen for their voices and appearance, must be formed into a choir, dressed beautifully, and rehearsed in special polyphonic chants which were to be sung to the Tsar in greeting and farewell. Not least, the Archimandrite must establish good relations with the Monastery's neighbours and ensure that the Tsar was not troubled by petitioners while he was there.[14]

But by the beginning of 1658 their relationship was again under strain; by May they had ceased to dine in each other's company; and in June Alexis stopped attending services at which the Patriarch officiated. There is no lack of speculation as to the reason: Nikon's general unpopularity, the boyars' determination to be rid of him, Alexis's reluctance to confront the man. But there was another, more probable, occasion for the break: Nikon had been disobedient.

The Metropolitan of Kiev had died in 1657 and Nikon had been asked to ordain a successor. At that juncture it was vital that a man loyal to Alexis be installed and that the Ukrainian Church be integrated into the Muscovite Church without delay. Since the death of Bogdan Khmelnytsky in the summer of 1657 the situation in Ukraine had been deteriorating rapidly. His successor, Ivan Vyhovsky, while professing loyalty to Alexis, was strongly suspected of flirting with the Tatars and with Poland. Unless firm action were taken he might defect and Ukraine might be plunged into chaos, perhaps lost. Yet, knowing that the Ukrainian Church, given proper direction, could serve as a bulwark for stability, Nikon adamantly refused to sanction the appointment of a new Metropolitan. Nor did he help matters by asserting that he knew how to handle Vyhovsky if others did not. His ground for refusal seems reasonable enough. Kiev fell within the province of the Patriarch of Constantinople, not of Moscow. But Alexis had no reason to suppose that the Patriarch of Constantinople would object if he knew it was the wish of the Tsar, the Protector of all Orthodox Christians. Nikon had thwarted an essential political move. Furthermore, in defending the position he had taken up he had (by his own admission) been 'irritating' Alexis by reminding him of the oath he had taken in 1652 to obey the Patriarch in all matters spiritual.[15] Yet, as Alexis had learned, it was not possible to separate the spiritual from the political. The symphony (that almost mystic term conveying the ideal concord that should exist) between Tsar and Patriarch had been shattered.

From Alexis's point of view, if Nikon would not recognize him as the senior partner in areas where temporal and spiritual authority overlapped, then it were best for him to resign. In July Nikon would have completed his sixth year as Patriarch. For friendship's sake Alexis was prepared for Nikon to depart voluntarily and with honour on that anniversary, but by progressively breaking off relations with him Alexis was dropping more and more obvious hints that he should proffer his resignation. They were hints, however, which Nikon refused to take. At last, early in July 1658, matters came to a head.

A state banquet in honour of King Teimuraz of Kakhetia, in Georgia, was given on 4th July. No invitation had been extended to

Nikon, and he sent one of his officials to ask the reason. The man had reached the Red Staircase to the Palace when Sub-Boyar Bogdan Khitrovo who was clearing a way for the guests struck him on the head with a staff. The man protested, explaining that he had been sent by the Patriarch. Khitrovo retorted that he should not make so much of himself; that the Patriarch was not to be regarded so highly – and struck him again, harder. The account is Nikon's, but there is no reason to suspect its truth. Khitrovo had no reason to love Nikon. He had been on a mission to Ukraine earlier that year, a mission which had turned out to be particularly difficult. He knew how much harm Nikon's intransigence had done to the Tsar's interests there. And anyway Nikon's man was making a nuisance of himself. Nikon reacted by sending a message to Alexis demanding an enquiry into the incident. Alexis claimed to be too busy to deal with the matter immediately. He is said to have promised to give Nikon an audience shortly, but if so he failed to keep the promise. He did not attend the Cathedral for the Feast of Our Lady of Kazan on 8th July and he ignored Nikon's invitation to attend another service two days later. Then, in order to step up the pressure, he sent word that Nikon must cease using the title 'Great Sovereign'.[16]

However, no indication of submission, and no letter of resignation, arrived. Only a message that the Patriarch was minded to leave Moscow because of the Tsar's anger against him. The game of cat and mouse continued. Alexis sent no reply to Nikon's threat. Next day, despite pleas from his secretary and from Ziuzin, his one remaining friend among the boyars, Nikon made his way to the Cathedral of the Assumption to celebrate liturgy and to preach a sermon. The rift was about to become public – and at the Patriarch's initiative, not the Tsar's.

His text for the sermon concerned the prime requisite of the true shepherd, love of one's flock. In emotional terms he declared that he no longer felt able to discharge his patriarchal duties. Yet his humble plea of inadequacy provided but a thin gloss on what amounted to a bitter attack upon Alexis. He recalled that he had accepted his post reluctantly and only because the Tsar, the boyars and the bishops had all promised to obey him in matters of divine law. For six years the Tsar had kept his promise 'in so far as he could' and, for his own part, he had shown 'patience'. But it had become impossible for him to go on. The Tsar was weak, he declared, the helm was rotten; the ship could not be steered. He referred resentfully to the odium that had attached to him on account of his liturgical reforms and his abandoning Moscow to the plague (both done for the Tsar's sake). He found unpopularity difficult to bear; but the Tsar's displeasure was even worse than that. Nevertheless, he then proceeded to displease the Tsar still more. He accused him of permitting all sorts of offences against the ecclesiastical order; of refusing him justice; of disregarding his promises; of preventing the Church being administered according to the canons; of depriving him of ecclesiastical jurisdiction; of abrogating to himself the right to judge the clergy. Even in his anger against him the Tsar was unjust, he claimed. 'And so, remembering the divine command "Turn away from wrath", I shall now leave this place . . . and go into the wilderness, for the Tsar's wrath has engrossed everything, and we are accounted as nothing.'

It is not entirely clear what effect Nikon thought his tirade would have on Alexis. Presumably he felt forced to act in order to escape from an impossible situation and needed to justify his action. Yet his review of events was tendentious. He accused Alexis of breaking with Byzantine imperial traditions, but those traditions (had he but known) favoured Alexis's position, not his own. The outburst might have been calculated to provoke rather than persuade the Tsar; and it must have been obvious, even to him, that the performance was unlikely to trigger off a surge of public sympathy for him. More probably it was simply an expressive act – the roar of a wounded lion and of a forsaken friend. And there was a streak of malice in it too. Nikon was intent on vengeance. He wanted to embarrass Alexis – not merely by making a public statement about him in immoderate and disrespectful terms, but by abandoning his office without actually resigning it.

A letter he sent Alexis confirming his intention to leave Moscow makes this clear. 'So I . . . shall now shake off the dust that clings to my feet, and leave it to you. You will have to give account to the Lord God for everything.' Nikon was transferring a moral burden to Alexis; attempting, perhaps, to blackmail him into submission. If so, Alexis proved a match for him. He sent the letter back with Nikita Trubetskoi with a message saying it was not acceptable and would he please explain. Nikita told Nikon that the Tsar had no personal animus against him, but that he must not interfere in matters of state and he must cease using the title 'Great Sovereign'. But it was no use. Nikon replied that he had no personal grudge against the Tsar, that he had not interfered in matters of state, and intimated that he had no intention of dropping the title either.

Shortly afterwards he moved to the house which the 'New Jerusalem' Monastery kept in Moscow. There he waited, hoping even now, perhaps, that Alexis might capitulate, or at least see him, but the Tsar only sent to ask why he was leaving Moscow without his permission – to which he retorted that he was going no great distance and that if the Tsar would only 'lay aside his wrath' he would return.[17] On 12th July, Nikon left Moscow.

He did not go, however, without leaving a letter behind addressed to Alexis and his family. In it he took a humbler and apologetic tone, asking forgiveness for leaving without permission, and referring to himself as 'the former Patriarch'. Alexis was grateful for that small mercy, and he showed it by sending his cousin, Afanasy Matiushkin, after him to convey his personal forgiveness and to offer Nikon a personal bodyguard of *strel'tsy*. The break with his old friend came as a severe blow to Alexis. 'It seemed,' he was to say in retrospect, 'as if I was asleep with my eyes open and saw it all in a dream.'[18]

But if he was unprepared for the shock emotionally, politically he was ready for it. No wave of sympathy for Nikon was expected from the public. None came. His biographer refers to weeping crowds following him on the first stage of his journey into self-imposed exile, but there was no mass reaction, except, perhaps, of slight bewilderment. Traditionalists rejoiced at his departure (hoping, in vain as it turned out, that his liturgical reforms would now be annulled); most churchmen sighed with relief; so did ministers. Petitions accusing him of oppression, maladministration and unfair exactions had been flowing into government offices for some time,[19] and there were many who had simply been unable to bear the sheer pomposity of the man. Simeon Streshnev trained a huge mastiff to stand up on its hind legs and wave its paws about as if in patriarchal blessing. When Nikon heard of this, he pronounced a solemn curse on Streshnev.

As soon as Nikon left Moscow, the day-to-day running of the Church was entrusted to the Metropolitan Pitirim, some imprisoned clerics were released, patriarchal estates (though not those monasteries and properties ascribed to Nikon personally) were taken over by the state, and papers in the patriarchal palace were commandeered. This had to be done if the affairs of the self-confessed 'ex-Patriarch' were to be taken in hand, and Nikon had had ample time to carry away with him any private correspondence of a sensitive nature. Yet he protested at Alexis seizing

my poor and humble property, which was left in my apartments, and my papers, in which there were many private
matters which no secular person has any right to see . . . I had
. . . many of thy Majesty's secrets of state, as likewise secrets of
other persons, who needing perfect absolution for their sins,
wrote letters to me. . . . I am astonished at how soon thou hast
come to such audacity.

But moral outrage was mixed with petulance. He complained at
having been excluded from the name-day feast of Alexis's sister
Anna and at having been denied a piece of her name-day pie which
was customarily sent to him if he could not attend. 'I alone was
excluded from thy rich table, like a dog. . . . If I were not regarded as
an enemy, I should not have been left without some little morsel
from it.' Had Alexis forgotten the injunction to 'feed the hungry'?
He prayed that Alexis be no longer angry with him, claimed that he
had been maligned without cause, and then immediately provoked
Alexis again by objecting to his judging the clergy. He rebutted any
charge that he had absconded with any treasure, and finally begged
to be forgiven – but only in order that Alexis himself might earn
forgiveness. [20]

This letter did not please Alexis. Nor did the reports that the old
man had taken to wearing heavy chains – punishing himself, it
seems, for Alexis's failure to punish him. Yet, though he lived
humbly and ate simply, Nikon continued to lavish money on
learning and the arts (among other projects, on what was to become
one of the most celebrated of Russia's historical chronicles) and,
above all, on the prison in which he had chosen to incarcerate
himself, the beautiful, but as yet far from complete, 'New Jerusalem' Monastery. Alexis was content to leave him in possession of
it. Indeed, he sent him presents from time to time, sometimes
substantial ones of as much as two thousand rubles in cash –
evidence not only of his residual affection for Nikon, but of his
ability to turn the other cheek. Besides, he had no intention of
making a martyr of Nikon as Ivan had of Philip.

The affair was messy and unfortunate, but Alexis felt no moral
responsibility. As he once explained, had Nikon submitted to him
he would gladly have allowed him to retain a free hand with the
Church. Instead, Nikon had demanded Alexis's submission and
that was impossible, [21] not only for practical political reasons but
because it ran counter to his duty to defend his own honour and to
uphold the autocracy. Even so, Alexis took good care to play his

part as the 'angelic prince' – visiting prisons and almshouses ten times or more a year, giving charity to the inmates; visiting monasteries where he would kiss the heads, hands and mouths of sick men in the infirmaries; staging, and attending, special feasts for beggars; and making spontaneous acts of charity to the needy. (Once, out hunting, he caught sight of a ragged carter, whereupon he snatched the cap off the head of an attendant falconer and handed it to the man along with two rubles.) Alexis was generous by temperament, but he was not unaware of the value of such gestures. They made for popularity; they gave him a saintly aura, and they helped cut the ground from under Nikon's feet, tending to give some the impression that he was at once both Tsar and Patriarch. It was not an unacceptable image to many Muscovites and some churchmen were soon addressing him as 'our Christian head'.[22] But Nikon's departure was not the only difficulty he confronted that July.

It was in July 1658 that the diplomatic and military situations, which had seemed so promising at the beginning of the year, suddenly began to slip and then slide towards catastrophe. That month his hopes of becoming King of Poland were dashed. The Papal Nuncio had denounced the idea; the Polish bishops protested when the proposal was formally laid before the Sejm; and the negotiations at Vilna broke down (at which Alexis gave vent to some harsh words about his old friend Nikita Odoevskii who was in charge of them). Then, in September, Hetman Vyhovsky abrogated his oath and threw his hand in with the Poles.[23] Muscovy could still count on considerable support among Ukrainians (which it promptly exploited), but the development threatened to open up her southern frontier to Tatar attack, and, given the increasing hostility of a resurgent Poland, endanger her gains in Belorussia and Lithuania as well as Ukraine. Alexis could not hope to hold all these fronts and fight the Swedes. Reluctantly, he had to abandon any immediate hope of securing a seaport on the Baltic and come to terms with Sweden. That December a three-year truce was duly signed.

Even so, military preparations had to be stepped up very sharply. Available forces were redeployed and fresh troops raised. Indeed, by November 1658 a special department had been set up to organize recruitment and arrangements had been put in hand for the first time ever to conscript men on a countrywide scale. Six men were raised from every hundred households that year; in some areas such as Novgorod even more, though in regions of low population density the draft was commuted to a special tax of a ruble per household. It produced 18,000 men.[24] This was not to prove sufficient and in succeeding years the levy was to be repeated and increased. But since Alexis was convinced of the superiority of troops organized and trained in the Western fashion, he wanted all of them made into new-formation soldiers (two-thirds of them infantry; one-third cavalry), and there were not sufficient officers available who were schooled in the new methods to absorb a larger intake. This circumstance explains Alexis's care to prevent the cream of his army, on which so much extra expense was being lavished, sustaining excessive casualties (on at least one occasion he gave personal orders to a general not to use the crack *strel'tsy* units at his disposal for storming operations[25]). It also explains the attention he now lavished on his existing cadre of trained professional officers and his efforts to recruit more from abroad.

It had become his practice to hold levées for officers of new-formation troops (the vast majority of them foreigners) on their departure for a war zone or to the provinces, where they were to train intakes of raw recruits. Soon he was making a point of receiving, and talking to, mercenaries newly arrived in Muscovy seeking junior commissions and even non-commissioned rank in his service. And meanwhile efforts were redoubled to attract even more of such men from the West. In 1658, for example, Colonel Franz Trafert was sent to Holland to recruit engineers, and John Hebdon was instructed to engage an unspecified number of competent officers plus 'a good general who is capable of commanding large forces operating independently'.[26]

This did not reflect much confidence in the military skills of native Muscovites and indeed Alexis watched over his commanders and the remodelling of his army like a hawk. Although as titular head of the Musketeer and Foreign Servicemen Departments his father-in-law Il'ia had nominal charge of the modernization programme, in fact Alexis kept him on a tight rein. Sometimes he countermanded orders Il'ia had issued; he supervised the pay and provisioning of certain units personally; and he sent direct exhortations to his commanders urging them to use the new expertise, hectoring them about good formation, discipline, the importance of musketry drill, the need to hold fire until the enemy was well within range, and not to fire too high.[27]

Technology and method fascinated Alexis and by no means only in the military sphere. He determined to bring all sorts of expertise to Russia. Why import German mechanisms or Venetian glass, after all, if the means to make such wonders in Muscovy could be acquired? Why struggle with perennial problems such as disease, or lack of money, or the costs of war if Western magicians could be found to solve them? Something of this emerges from the curious rag-bag of his wants which he drew up for John Hebdon early in 1659:

1. The very best sort of doctor who can find cures using herbs available in Muscovy
2. Concerning Dr. Johann Balau;
3. An alchemist of the very best kind and an amiable fellow, who understands these herbs and can concoct with them;
4. A reliable herbal book that deals with Russian and Polish as well as foreign herbs;
5. Mineralogists expert in all kinds of silver, copper, lead and iron ores;
6. A goldsmith who can gild;
7. A German to make all sorts of clever heads for springs;
8. The book for the Gunnery Court;
9. An illustrated book in four volumes on trajectories and someone who can make them all work;
10. A pamphlet about the Tsar's campaign;
11. And about all three of the Tsar's campaigns;
12. Monthly news-sheets from all states;
13. Good birds – singing parrots, finches and canaries;
14. A master glass-maker who knows how to make clear glass and all kinds of embossed and cut-glass vessels, and who knows the sort of earth [silica] from which such glass is made;
15. $2\frac{1}{2}$cwt. of camphor.[28]

Apart from the birds, the camphor and items 10–12 (which reflect his concern to ensure that his achievements were properly appreciated in the West and to gain up-to-date intelligence of developments there), they all concern the acquisition of scientific and technological expertise. Yet by no means all of them mark new departures for a Tsar of Muscovy. Almost a hundred years before, Ivan the Terrible had applied to Queen Elizabeth of England and sent to Italy for architects, engineers, doctors, apothecaries and 'experts at finding gold and silver'. Nor was the engagement of foreign scholars and craftsmen something new for Alexis. Not only Hebdon but others of his agents (like Jan van Sweden and Jagan van

Horn who was based at Lübeck) responded to regular requests from him to send him experts of various kinds. But Alexis also made it his habit to stock-pile craftsmen's tools of all kinds (every sort and size of hammer, saw, plane and pincer was imported besides complete sets of implements used by gold and silversmiths);[29] and there is reason to suppose that, perhaps because of the impression the great plague of 1654 had made upon him, Alexis had acquired a particular interest in medicine and cognate sciences.

Like Tsars before him, Alexis kept Western physicians (usually Germans) in the Kremlin and he valued them for their supposed abilities in areas that stretched far beyond the confines of what would be regarded as medicine today. One of them, Dr Andreas Engelhardt, who came to Moscow in 1656, was admired as much for his talents as an astrologer (he was able, for example, to forecast from the movement of comets the likelihood of Muscovy suffering another outbreak of bubonic plague) as he was for his purely clinical learning (he had written a highly-regarded work on epilepsy). Dr Samuel Collins, on the other hand, an alumnus of Leyden and Padua as well as Cambridge, whom Hebdon engaged to be one of Alexis's personal physicians in 1658, specialized in anatomy (in the broadest sense) and indeed was to publish an impressive work upon the subject in two folio volumes on his return to England after ten years in Alexis's service. It was probably through conversations with such men, and with his foreign apothecaries (such as Robert Binyon, who was engaged in 1657, and Robert Tuohy, who arrived somewhat later[30]), that Alexis's interest in experimental and speculative science (as opposed to the mechanical sort) was stimulated and extended. Nor is it surprising that he should have concerned himself with aspects of astrology, alchemy and the occult. His hero Ivan had dabbled in them and such learning was still respected among educated Westerners even though it was soon to fall out of fashion with them. Furthermore, the Byzantine character of his education, combined with his religious convictions, might have been expected to have given him some notion of the 'wholeness' of nature, a unity in all creation and hence of the existence of a key which might unlock all the secrets of the universe. Yet Alexis was a severely practical, as well as a spiritual, man. The combination led him to take an approach to science that was both utilitarian and catholic. Though he respected the astrological expertise of a man like Engelhardt (just as he respected the engineering skills of General Leslie), he did not despise the powers of well-disposed saints, and he was not contemptuous of popular magic.

One April, for example, he wrote down instructions for peasants in some villages belonging to the Stables Office to collect specified quantities of mint, clovers, lingwort, gout-weed roots and St John's wort on the following 24th June. The precise purpose for which he wanted them is not known. They may have been used for heating and scenting his steam bath; he may have had some prophylactic or aphrodisiacal purpose in mind. But the fact that he insisted that they had to be gathered on Midsummer's Day shows that he subscribed to the popular magical belief that herbs gathered that day were endowed with mysteriously heightened powers.

Yet more curious is the experiment he had conducted aimed at increasing the crop yields on some of his personal estates. He made out a prescription, consisting chiefly of consecrated oil and holy water from the wells of the Sergius and Sabbas Monasteries (which was sent for in the greatest secrecy and hauled out to the accompaniment of a special prayer). The resulting concoction was then applied to the ploughland at the time of the autumn sowing in a ceremony which Alexis devised specially for the occasion. A special tent was erected on each estate; those participating, including a priest, were fully briefed as to the precise part each should play and the special prayers to be recited, and the precious fluid was sprinkled over the earth in the form of a cross.[31] How effective this method turned out to be in increasing the harvests is not known, but Alexis was clearly prepared to go to great lengths in order to counter the sharp fall in agricultural yields which had taken place following the plague. Alexis, then, was quite open-minded in his approach to solving problems and curing ills. He would exploit an ingenious machine, a prayer, a prescription from his doctors, witchcraft – anything which seemed to him might produce a desirable result.

If he found a cure that seemed to be effective he would apply it widely, enthusiastically and without discrimination. Thus, having been bled for the first time and feeling better for it, he ordered all his closest courtiers to be bled too, assuming that they also would derive a similar benefit from the treatment. Furthermore, when one of them, his old uncle, Rodion Streshnev, demurred, Alexis became extremely angry. 'Perhaps you consider your blood more precious than mine? Why should you think yourself better than anyone else?' Then he struck the old man.[32]

The assault on Rodion Streshnev was but one sign of the growing violence of Alexis's temper. This violence, which belies the popular legend of his being the gentlest of Tsars, was usually provoked, however, and often by his own servitors. Foreign observers of the Muscovite scene at the time comment unfavourably on the characteristics of most Muscovite officials. The Venetian Ambassador found them to be unlettered, crude, and lacking both discretion and conscience; a Swedish envoy reported that most of the Tsar's counsellors were lazy and had poor understanding. 'General interests of state inspire but few,' he remarked. 'The Tsar remains alone.'[33] If not completely true, it was substantially so, and Alexis knew it. That is why he had begun to create a new executive elite, promoting loyal, able and conscientious men of comparatively humble status whom he had noticed to positions of importance usually deemed to be way above their station. One such was a poor but educated gentleman from the Pskov region of north-western Muscovy called Afanasy Ordyn-Nashchokin.

Afanasy had first emerged from obscurity in 1650 when he had played a useful part in coping with the Pskov rebellion, but it was on his mastery of the complicated affairs of the Swedish frontier and Swedish relations that his career was founded. Alexis had appointed him Governor of the Baltic territories (in what is now Soviet Latvia) captured from the Swedes in the campaign of 1656, and he had since been involved in negotiations with both Sweden and Poland. His piety and charity no less than his industry, shrewdness and originality of mind commended him, and in April 1658 Alexis promoted him to the exalted rank of Gentleman-Councillor.[34] It was soon justified. That December he concluded a truce with Sweden by which Muscovy was to hold onto Livonia for three years. In the circumstances it was a triumph.

Unfortunately, there were all too few men of Afanasy's calibre, and their preferment attracted strong resentment from high-ranking men of superior social status. Alexis had to take good care not to estrange them. He had enough problems without inviting more. Hence, in 1658 he wrote to the aristocratic V. B. Sheremetev, assuring him that boyar rank was, or at least had been, hereditary. On the other hand, he also explained to him that the son of a boyar might never reach the rank and that in any case one who had it was wrong to boast about it. Certainly he was making fewer promotions to the Council than he had in the first years of his reign, and a declining proportion of those he did promote belonged to the old nobility.[35] At the same time he was by-passing normal governmental channels of communication with increasing frequency, instructing trusted officials in sensitive posts to report directly to him rather than to the relevant department, and he was taking more and more matters out of the hands of ministers in order to deal with them himself.

As a result the staff of his Private Office, now headed by Secretary Dementii Bashmakov, was steadily increased (in 1659 there were nine under-secretaries working there). But Alexis's tendency to by-pass his own administration created a certain degree of confusion on occasion, both among those officials whom he trusted (both Afanasy and Nikita Odoevskii were at times uncertain as to whether they should report directly to the Private Office or through normal channels) and those judged to be less competent, like Prince Ivan Khovanskii, a descendant of the Grand Princes of Lithuania. Alexis once told him straightly that although he had sought him out for promotion despite the fact that 'everyone called you a fool' (Ivan earned his nickname of 'the braggart') he should never presume upon his favour.[36]

His dissatisfaction with traditional structures was given impetus by news of a disaster which reached him towards the end of June 1659. A Muscovite force under Boyar Prince Trubetskoi had been defeated near the fort of Konotop by a combined force of Ukrainians and Tatars under Hetman Vyhovsky. Upwards of 5,000 men, mostly gentry levies, had been lost, and the road to Moscow was opened to Tatar attack. The quite unexpected news caused consternation, even panic. Alexis appeared in public wearing mourning; people of all ranks were drafted to strengthen Moscow's defences, and the Tsar himself was often to be seen inspecting their work. People fled into the city from the countryside and rumours spread that the court was to withdraw to the safety of Yaroslav, beyond the Volga.[37]

In fact the attack never materialized and the panic subsided. Nevertheless, although Trubetskoi had managed to keep the remainder of his force intact and to retire in good order to the citadel of Putivl, and though Muscovy's position in Ukraine was soon stabilized, the losses had been serious enough to persuade Alexis to speed up the army modernization programme. He was by no means alone in this resolve. Afanasy wrote to him that year urging him to station armies of trained professionals, commanded by competent generals, permanently on the country's frontiers. The resources were not available, however, to effect such a root and branch transformation, at least not yet. Nor was it politically possible to replace Russian commanders with such senior foreign officers as were available. Nevertheless Alexis was encouraging such experts to put their opinions to him direct rather than through their commanding officers. That September, for example, three senior officers of Prince Khovanskii's north-western command, Lieutenant-General Thomas Dalyell and Colonels Heinrich Hulets and Robert du Glassis, produced a critique of military dispositions in their sector and made nine proposals for their improvement. Alexis accepted all but one of these, rewarded them, and instructed their commander, Khovanskii, not to conceal any information regarding the military situation from Dalyell in future.[38]

Such steps, necessary though they might be, did not endear the likes of Khovanskii to the foreigners, nor to such jumped-up advisers as Afanasy Ordyn-Nashchokin. Yet Alexis remained unwavering in the support he gave to those whose counsel he valued. No stronger challenge to his loyalty could have been provided than the defection abroad, at the beginning of 1660, of Afanasy's son, Voin, with a sizeable cache of government funds. Even though Afanasy was about to embark on critical peace talks with Sweden, through which he hoped to regain the Baltic port of Narva, the pressure on Alexis to dismiss him must have been immense. Indeed, as soon as he learned the dreadful news, Afanasy himself submitted a petition to be retired from service. Alexis, however, would have none of it. So far from accepting the resignation, he sent Afanasy a personal letter designed to restore the man's self-confidence, assure him of undiminished favour, and assuage his personal grief. In it he praised Nashchokin's loyal and efficient service and his high moral attainment:

> We have learned that your son, by God's wish and his own madness, has absconded to Gdansk, causing you . . . terrible grief. . . . We the sovereign Tsar have been affronted by this bitter affliction, by this evil dagger which has pierced your soul and body, just as you, our faithful slave, have been. The sorrow and anguish are great indeed. We grieve also on account of your wife . . . whose only-begotten child was wrested from her womb in vain. . . . As to your petition to be replaced, upon what precedent do you propose such a course? I think it can only have been made out of unconfined grief. You talk of being dishonoured – but consider the glory that awaits you in heaven on account of your suffering. . . . It is not hard to fall so much as, having fallen, not to rise up again; so you should . . . rise up again quickly, become strong, have trust. . . . As to your son's

treachery, we . . . know that he acted against your will. . . . He is a young man who wants to make his mark upon the world and so, like a bird, he flits here and there; but, like a bird, he will get tired of flying and return to his nest . . .

The letter was taken to Afanasy by Yuri Nikiforov, one of the Private Office under-secretaries, with Alexis's personal instructions to console him in every way he could, to reassure him that he retained his trust, and to urge him to ignore the rumours circulating in the world that he was somehow implicated in his son's defection.[39] The balm worked. Nashchokin was deeply moved by Alexis's message and agreed to soldier on. As for his son Voin, Alexis (who had met him and judged the sort of man he was) proved right again: he was eventually to return to Muscovy and, for his father's sake, received no greater punishment than to be sent in disgrace to one of his father's estates. But all Alexis's shrewdness, all his adroitness in managing men, could not avert the series of reverses that he and his cause were about to suffer.

At times during the spring and summer of 1660 it seemed as if the very fates themselves were conspiring against him. First, Afanasy's peace talks with the Swedes began to falter, and then, in May, Sweden concluded a peace with Poland, leaving the Poles free to turn all the power that they could muster against Muscovy. Alexis had been willing to sacrifice much in order to hold on to his bridgehead to the Baltic in Livonia, if only for some years and not in perpetuity. But that hope now began to recede, and especially after June when Khovanskii sustained a serious defeat in Belorussia at the hands of Hetman Sapieha. Alexis was not only disappointed; he was furious – because Khovanskii had invited disaster by his 'pointless boldness'. He had attacked a far superior force with only three new-formation musketeer regiments and two thousand horse. Furthermore, the cavalry had failed to keep formation. They had broken and fled, leaving the precious infantry to be slaughtered. As Alexis confided to his cousin Matiushkin, this news had completely ruined his summer sport with the falcons.[40]

Meanwhile the problem created by Nikon's abandonment of the Patriarchate remained. Insofar as it had helped to dissipate widespread resentment against the regime, Nikon's departure had been politically advantageous and Alexis had been in no hurry to replace him. But to leave the post vacant for too long would smack of scandal, and so Alexis began to sound out possible candidates (often using his friend Fedor Rtishchev for the purpose). He wanted someone who would maintain the reforms Nikon had introduced, be firm in control of the Church, and unwavering in his obedience to his own person. Few seemed to be so qualified. Even the Bishop of Viatka, though satisfying most criteria, opposed some of the reforms.[41] On the other hand, the Archimandrite Paul of the Miracle Monastery and Bishop Hilarion of Riazan seemed to understand what was needed, and above all the Archimandrite Joachim who, when canvassed for his opinions, is said to have replied in terms which Alexis found ideal: 'I know neither the old faith nor the new, but I am ready to do whatever those in authority order to be done, and to obey them in everything.'[42]

Unfortunately, Alexis was by no means certain that he could proceed to an election. Nikon's departure had no precedent. It was unclear if in abandoning his see he had abdicated or not; nor, if he were still Patriarch, whether he could be deposed; nor yet, if he were willing to abdicate, whether anyone else but he could install his successor. In February 1660 a church council assembled in the Hall of Gold to thrash these questions out. It tried first to determine, on the basis of depositions from over seventy witnesses to his departure, whether Nikon was still Patriarch or not. No conclusive answer emerged, however. The depositions and the witnesses were re-examined. It was decided that Nikon had voluntarily relinquished his post, and that a successor should be appointed. But a tangle of unresolved questions remained. A committee of four was set up to establish what the answers were. It was packed with Alexis's supporters (both Riazan and the Archimandrite Paul sat on it), yet its conclusions were neither clear-cut nor satisfactory to him. Three times he sent the report back for reconsideration, and meanwhile the deliberations dragged on from February into August.[43]

Nikon himself was being as awkward as he could be. He condemned the Metropolitan Pitirim, who was administering the Patriarchate, as 'a spiritual adulterer'; claimed to have no intention himself of returning to his patriarchal duties 'like a dog to its vomit', yet insisted that he must officiate at the installation of his successor. But to accept this would be to give Nikon an implicit power of veto over the choice of his successor. Besides, it was politically undesirable that he should become a legitimate focus of attention or that he should be associated in such a way with his successor.[44] Alexis had one success when the synod was recalled in August 1660, for it endorsed his wish to extend the autocratic principle by making his pre-eminence in Church affairs explicit. Its conclusions (which he had taken care to amend in his own hand) contained references to the Tsar having 'lordship over his Church' and responsibility for its 'good order'.[45] Nonetheless, since Nikon obstinately refused to make a formal act of abdication, the question of how to depose him, and to depose him in an irreproachably canonical way, remained.

Alexis had turned for advice on this to Slavinetskii, as an expert in canon law. But Slavinetskii had wavered. At first he had been sure that the synod lacked the authority to depose Nikon and that, if he persisted in his refusal to resign, the Patriarch of Constantinople must be asked to degrade him. By mid-May he had been persuaded to change his tune, and had duly signed a synodal act deposing Nikon. But then he had retracted, claiming to have misunderstood a canon.[46] In June the problem was almost resolved when an attempt was made on Nikon's life. His tailor and an archdeacon to whom he had given shelter tried to poison him. But the attempt failed. Nikon was taken ill, but he recovered. The government set up an enquiry. Alexis's hands might have been clean, but he thought it important that they should be seen to be clean. Suspicion fell for a time on the Metropolitan Pitirim and the Archdeacon Paul, but it transpired that the perpetrators (who were examined under torture) had acted on their own initiative.[47] Nikon remained to be disposed of and Alexis began to cast about for another, more amenable and more ingenious adviser on canon law than Slavinetskii, an adviser who could find a way of deposing the Patriarch. But that autumn his attention was diverted by another series of military disasters.

First Yuri Dolgorukii sustained heavy casualties on the western front and had to retreat to Mogilev; then news arrived that forces in the south had failed to dislodge a Tatar army which had been extending a grip over the estuary of the river Don under cover of a Turkish fleet.[48] Worst of all was the news about the army under Boyar V. B. Sheremetev in Ukraine. He had been besieged in Chudnovo by a far superior force of Poles and Tatars since early September. His predicament had not seemed desperate since a substantial force of loyal Ukrainians under their new Hetman, Bogdan's son Iurii Khmelnytsky, was nearby. But when confronted by the enemy, Iurii came to terms with them, leaving the Muscovites without help or hope. Early in October Sheremetev capitulated. An entire army was led off into captivity; control over the greater part of Ukraine had been lost.

Fortunately the enemy was unable to exploit the success which came so late in the fighting season; and in retrospect the debâcle was in one sense, perhaps, to prove a blessing in disguise, for the core of the lost army consisted predominantly of the old-style gentry cavalry.[49] Its loss was to discredit military traditionalism in Russia for good. But in the short term the surrender at Chudnovo seemed all the more ominous since it coincided with mounting social restlessness in Moscow over the rising price of food. Alexis's fortunes had reached their lowest point since 1648 and seemed to be falling even further.

Abandoning any idea of bringing the business of the Patriarchate to any swift resolution, Alexis moved fast and sure-footedly to save what he could. His first step was to fend off any chance of another Moscow rising. To this end the views of all classes in Moscow were canvassed. Predictably, fingers were pointed at any number of culprits – profiteers and hoarders, high taxation, the amount of grain going to make vodka, harvest failure, the fact that so many of the Tsar's servicemen, formerly paid in grain, were now paid in cash. Steps were immediately taken to keep prices down by reducing the output of the state distilleries, requisitioning more grain from church estates to distribute among the *strel'tsy* and so reduce market demand, and by other measures.[50] It amounted to no more than a stop-gap solution, more useful in demonstrating concern than for its economic effect, but it was enough to avert the immediate threat of riots, and bought Alexis some precious time to devote to shoring up the military position.

Kiev, at least, was secure with a garrison of some 18,000 men (though they were short of food) and a hold was regained over eastern Ukraine with the help of Iurii's uncle, Somko, and other pro-Muscovite elements. But Alexis had lost confidence in the stability of Ukrainian loyalties. As he told Afanasy Ordyn-Nashchokin that autumn, 'It is impossible to depend on them, nor trust them in anything. They move like reeds with the wind.' The position in Belorussia was also vulnerable. A truce would have to be arranged on that front; and since it was now obvious that his forces were over-extended and that he must retrench, Alexis instructed Afanasy to convert the truce with Sweden into a permanent peace at almost any cost – though he was to try to hold onto a part of Livonia if he possibly could, albeit just one town.[51]

Fearing an adverse reaction in the West to Muscovy's reverses, and in an attempt to control his image there, Alexis told John Hebdon (whom he had entertained to dinner the previous February) to obtain copies of all reports of the recent defeats appearing in the West and to arrange for the publication of rebuttals. Alexis supplied him with a text.[52] At the same time he intensified his campaign to recruit more western officers, indeed to raise troops wholesale in the West, stepped up arms importations and mobilized as much as he dared of Muscovy's own remaining resources. Making a point as he did of checking every casualty list (he had recently berated a commander because of a discrepancy in one of them[53]); caring as he did about the wounded and the families of those killed in action (seeing to it that the widows and mothers of fallen musketeers were cared for in nunneries[54]), he knew precisely how much manpower had to be replaced, and was more than ever determined now to westernize the army whatever the cost.

At the end of November 1660, instructions were sent to van Horn in Lübeck to engage what amounted to an entire corps complete with support services – Colonel Maximilian von Burn plus four cavalry and four infantry colonels together with their entire formations; engineers, gunners, makers of firearms, and all kinds of inventive craftsmen; Colonel Werner de Huyck and his three cavalry and two infantry regiments; Colonel Henryk van Egerat and his regiment. . . . Hebdon was asked to help in this mission and then go on to London where he was to convey to the recently restored Charles II the Tsar's wish 'to hire 3,000 cavalry and infantry together with their officers'. Soon afterwards Afanasy Ordyn-Nashchokin was empowered to negotiate the hire of Swedish officers to train Russian troops.[55] Imports of armaments and ammunition were increased too. Another agent was sent to Holland, Hamburg and Lübeck to buy weapons. At Lübeck alone he bought 160 tons of copper, let contracts for the provision of 300 cannon, investigated a new weapon called the 'musket grenade' which had a range of 200 yards, and acquired a book on artillery (besides another on gold and silver ore). Muskets, carbines and pistols poured in by the thousand from Holland, along with slings and bandoliers and locks for gun-barrels made in Muscovy.[56] And with peace with Sweden in the offing, the government also looked forward to finding a plentiful supply of arms more cheaply nearer to hand.

Human resources were also found within the realm, of course, albeit with increasing difficulty. The levy of 1659 had yielded over 15,000 men; that for 1660, 17,000 (Alexis raising a higher proportion from the crown estates than from the rest of the country); and a similar levy was ordered for 1661.[57] In January that year he also ordered recruits to be raised from among the peasants on lands belonging to the three monasteries still in Nikon's charge. Nikon immediately complained that, given the previous levies, an intolerable burden was being placed upon his monks and peasants. Indeed he soon claimed to have had 'a vision' in which the martyred Metropolitan Philip ordered him to ask the Tsar why he enslaved the Church, depriving it of corn and cash as well as men. Alexis ignored him.[58] Most of these raw peasant recruits, each furnished with two pounds of powder, and two of lead and fitted out in rustic uniforms, were sent to be fashioned into modern soldiers by Alexis's foreign officers. Sons of the service gentry and gentry already on active service were also drafted or transferred into the new-formation regiments, and henceforth only noblemen who had been declared unfit for active service were allowed to serve in civilian posts.[59]

Alexis now dealt personally with petitions from his foreign servicemen wanting to return home,[60] granting very few of them – but he made a point of receiving, and smiling graciously at, virtually every foreign soldier entering his service. On 4th October 1661, for example, he held a reception in the Hall of Gold for a contingent of thirty-seven officers, NCOs and trumpeters under Colonel Gottlieb von Schälk, who had recently arrived from Habsburg territory; another nineteen from Lübeck; a contingent of nearly 150 officers and men (including a priest, a doctor and three trumpeters) commanded by Colonel Henryk van Egerat from Denmark; and three Scottish officers. Other wild geese from Scotland also arrived and kissed the Tsar's hand upon appointment. One whom he had received at Kolomenskoe a few weeks before was the 25-year-old Patrick Gordon whom a Muscovite agent had persuaded to transfer his allegiance from the Poles (he had also fought for Sweden). It was not the pay which attracted Gordon so much as Muscovy's reputation for paying it regularly and the chances of promotion (Gordon was promised a lieutenant-colonelcy after serving one year of a three-year term). Even so he received a gratuity of twenty-five rubles in cash, twenty-six rubles'-worth of sables, plus some lengths of cloth, as well as his major's pay.[61] And Gordon was only one of thousands.

The cost to the exchequer was enormous – more, probably, than the state's income. It was not only a matter of having to maintain so many mercenaries, but of equipping the new model regiments and finding the cash or kind to pay the service gentry's active service allowance and the peasant recruits' few kopeks a day.[62] In addition, huge bills for imported arms had to be met. It could not be afforded, and Alexis knew it. Hence his refusal to pay the huge ransom the Tatars demanded for the release of Sheremetev (though payments for the repatriation of prisoners-of-war from Poland had recently been negotiated); hence the desperate immediacy with which reports of a silver find were followed up, and the frantic efforts made to raise loans abroad on the security of future shipments of Muscovite potash, tar and hemp.[63]

But there were hidden costs of war which were no less serious. Desertion was on the increase, and although Alexis, in his humanity, recognized that 'God has not given courage to all men alike', he took forcible measures to counter it.[64] Peasants were also fleeing in ever-increasing numbers – both to escape the greater exactions due to the loss of population in the plague and to avoid conscription. As a result Dr Collins was soon to remark that

> the best of the land is harass'd, the rest untilled for want of men. For in five hundred *versts* [300 miles] travel up the River you may see ten women and children for one man. All things are there become very scarce; everything six times the rate it was formerly; and copper-money is not valued.[65]

Patrick Gordon, too, was struck immediately on his arrival in Muscovy by the high cost of living and 'the extraordinary moroseness of the people'.[66] And demoralization was to spread to Moscow itself where (as an anonymous letter which reached Alexis maintained) hundreds of deserters posing as street-sweepers lived by crime, trafficking in tobacco and liquor, plundering drunkards, gambling and committing sodomy with small boys.[67]

The impetus behind the accelerating moral decline derived from the costs and dislocations caused by war. Since there was no other way of covering the yawning deficit resulting from his military expenditures, Alexis had begun to allow the money supply (in the form of cheap copper coins) to get completely out of hand. By the end of 1661 the mint was employing well over 400 men and had become the country's largest industrial enterprise. The result of their work was to increase the rate of inflation. By November 1661, judging by the price of rye (the staple food), money bought less than a third of what it had done in 1658 and over the next months it was to fall in value by a further 70 per cent.[68] Instead of recognizing that the coin of the realm was being debased by a deliberate act of government policy, it became popular to blame counterfeiters. Some were certainly found and harshly dealt with (the list Alexis kept of those condemned in 1659–60 alone covered six pages[69]). But it was the state, not the counterfeiters or profiteers (among whom, by popular reputation, Il'ia Miloslavskii was the chief), that was the culprit, and the state now began to feel the consequences.

By 1661 the population of those parts of Ukraine and Belorussia still occupied by Muscovy were refusing to accept copper coins. Finding it increasingly difficult to obtain food, the Muscovite garrisons turned to plunder, which, in turn, provoked violent reactions. In February 1661 the townsfolk of Mogilev actually rose up and threw the garrison out; and in Ukraine too the Muscovite troops had become increasingly unpopular. It was with relief, then, that Alexis heard that peace had been concluded with Sweden. The Treaty of Kardis, signed in June 1661, secured an exchange of prisoners of war and access across Swedish territory for Western merchants, craftsmen and mercenaries; but the fleet of seagoing craft built by Cossack shipwrights and intended for the Baltic trade had to be destroyed, and all Livonia was lost.

Even now Alexis tried to persuade the Duke of Courland to let him build a ship in his yards which might take part in a joint trading voyage with Courland ships to India, but the prospects of Muscovy becoming a major maritime power all but disappeared. Having bought peace on the northern front, available forces could now be concentrated against his remaining enemies, but even though the western front was now manned by new formation units,[70] the campaigns of 1661 were not to go Alexis's way.

His troops held their own in Ukraine, but in Belorussia and Lithuania the front collapsed. The news of Khovanskii's defeat near Polotsk and of an impending advance by a strong army under the Polish King caused Alexis to call an immediate conference. The mood was sombre. Perhaps in an attempt to lighten the atmosphere, or else to ingratiate himself with his son–in–law, whose displeasure with him had become increasingly obvious of late, Il'ia Miloslavskii chose the occasion to suggest that he himself be sent to retrieve the situation at the front. If command were to be entrusted to him, he said, he would soon bring back the King of Poland as a prisoner. Alexis was not amused. He had come to despise Il'ia's character and his capabilities. Even Khovanskii seemed preferable to this fool.

MICHAEL FEDEROWITS,
Czar ou *Grand Duc de Moscovie.*

Alexis's father, Tsar Michael I

The *terem*, built 1637: Alexis's childhood home within the Kremlin

Château Kremelin, dans la Ville de Moscou, avec la célébration de la Fête de Pâques Fleuries.

The Palm Sunday procession before the towers of the Kremlin; a scene possibly from the reign of Michael rather than his son Alexis

Portrait of Alexis, after an oil painting probably done from the life

Vue du Château de Moscou par derrière.

Le supplice du fouët chez les Moscovites.

View of the Kremlin from the south, showing the place for executions

The Tsaritsa Maria,
Alexis's first wife, in
1662

Procession including
the Tsaritsa Maria. In
front of her the
Tsarevich is shown as
a babe in arms; he in
turn is preceded by
Alexis's sisters: detail

Alexis's second wedding, to the Tsaritsa Natalia, from a French engraving

The Tsarevich Fedor,
Alexis's son and immediate
successor: detail

Peter I as a child, from a
work of 1678

What? [he is said to have roared in response] Do you have the effrontery, you boor, to boast of your military skills? When have you ever borne arms? Pray tell us of the fine actions you have fought. We might then believe you could fulfil these promises. You old fool . . .

Fuming with rage, Alexis advanced upon him and grabbed him by the beard. 'Or is it that you presume to mock me with your impertinence? . . .' Then he dragged his father-in-law across the room, hurled him out and slammed the doors behind him.[71]

Urgent measures were taken to shore up the front, but the cities of Grodno, Mogilev and Vilna were all lost.[72] There seemed to be no alternative now but to try to make peace with Poland, and on much worse terms than might have been obtained that spring. All Alexis's golden dreams had dissolved. All that remained was desolation, ashes.

That autumn Boris Morozov died. Alexis had visited him on his death bed; he attended the funeral and had more than a dozen masses given for the repose of his soul. No doubt the singing gave him some consolation. But as he sat in church he might have pondered the fact that Boris, who had once been so reviled that he himself had been hard put to it to save his life, seemed to be so much lamented by the people.[73] It might seem ironic, but it was not the only irony. Alexis, the 'angelic prince', was soon to be in danger of his own life, and at the hands of his own people.

Chapter VII

Tempests and Turning Points

To an innocent onlooker in the Muscovite crowd the Tsar might have seemed oblivious of the tide of troubles mounting up around him. He did not cease to make regular appearances in public at religious ceremonies and military reviews; he continued to preside cheerfully over investitures and banquets; and in the winter and spring of 1662 he was often to be seen riding out to hunt.[1] Appearances were misleading, however. By the light of day and to an outsider's eye the Tsar might seem to be jovial and free from cares – but once hidden from the public eye Alexis removed the mask. At night, when the palace fell silent and the motionless sentries looked like statues in the flickering lights, he would prowl about his Private Office turning over the papers on his secretaries' desks and fret about the dangers that now beset him and his realm. It was usually at night too that he presided over committee meetings of the Council. (The full Council met but rarely now – only at moments of extreme crisis and when he wanted to devolve the odium of some particularly unpopular decision upon it.) And night, and the maze of passageways that led to his apartments, provided cover for secret meetings with his trusties (not least Artamon Matveev who took his turn every few days as commander of the palace guard), to send out his spies and to receive their reports.[2] By day he played the sportsman and the figurehead, appearing to hover serenely above the turmoil of life; by night he was the spider at the centre of the governmental web.

His agents now were everywhere – with his armies, with missions, at weddings and funerals – and, thanks to them, the intelligence he received was excellent. They were all men who depended on his favour – gentlemen of modest means, guardsmen and falconers. But the more important and sensitive assignments were generally entrusted to one or another of the Private Office under-secretaries. One of them, Yuri Nikiforov, was attached to the great embassy which left Moscow early in 1662 bound for Prussia, Denmark, Holland and England, and which was subsequently instructed to proceed to Venice. Among its chief purposes were to gain recognition for Alexis as one of Europe's leading monarchs and to raise large hard-currency loans. It was successful in neither. When the ambassadors rode through London in all their magnificence with retainers bearing splendid falcons on their wrists to present to Charles II they were hooted and jeered at by the crowds (such, wrote Samuel Pepys, 'is the absurd nature of Englishmen'); and Venetian senators fell about laughing when the Muscovites made extravagant demands for diplomatic honours. Apart from securing repayment of a loan Alexis had made to Charles in exile the embassy was to return home almost empty-handed.[3]

But Nikiforov had other assignments apart from keeping the ambassadors themselves under surveillance – not least the gathering of economic intelligence. He was told to collect samples of spices, herbs and vegetables, and to engage expert craftsmen, and was given a special book in which to note down everything he saw which he thought might interest his master.[4] In this way Alexis extended his knowledge of the world. His study was already hung about with maps; he was soon to acquire one of 'the Indies and other states', and yet another representing 'the entire world'. Yet so far from being frivolous or academic his curiosity was excited by his desperate financial straits, for if loans of sufficient size could not be raised abroad greater efforts had to be made to earn more from trade. Hence his attempt to persuade the Duke of Courland to allow Muscovy to build ships in his harbours and let them sail from there to Western Europe and the Indies; hence also the proclamation issued in February 1662 announcing that the export of tar, hemp, potash, sables, beef fat and leather were henceforth to be crown monopolies, as grain, raw silk, caviare and rhubarb already were.[5]

This device promised to amass substantial sums, but carried with it the risk of alienating those of his subjects who were heavily involved in those trades. They were few – a handful of huge landowners and substantial merchants who had other interests to fall back on and whom Alexis reckoned unlikely to present a political danger. Nevertheless there were also some less substantial merchants who claimed that the decision to buy up their most profitable goods at fixed prices paid out in copper coins threatened them with total ruin, and their groans were echoed by the trading classes as a whole since it was they who were bearing the brunt of the economic crisis and of inflation in particular.

Food prices had risen by about 70 per cent in the three months since November 1661, yet, while paying out in copper money, the state was collecting taxes in kind. The impact on society was uneven. Most peasants, though they were restive, could live off their own. Over large parts of the realm people were simply resorting to barter. But inflation was having devastating effects on the urban tradesman and artisan, especially in Moscow. Aware of their mood, in April 1662 Alexis sent Il'ia Miloslavskii to confer with representatives of the Moscow townsmen, to take note of their grievances and of their proposed solutions. They blamed the state's exactions and the unrestrained supply of copper money; and they demanded the summoning of an Assembly of the Land. This Alexis would not countenance. Nor would he lighten their burdens. He hinted distantly that he sympathized with them in their plight; he stepped up the campaign against counterfeiting and corruption;[6] but that was all. While taxes and conscription remained at unprecedentedly high levels the mints continued to churn out copper coins (many so poor in quality that they soon turned rusty), and prices continued their giddy upward spiral.

Astute foreign observers in Moscow at the time were apprehensive. The Emperor Leopold's Ambassador, Baron Augustin de Mayerberg, subsequently reported that 'we were in a state of continual expectation that the people, who are always very inclined to revolt, would be moved by despair to raise a rebellion which might not easily be suppressed'.[7] Yet there was no rebellion that winter, nor that spring. On 16th July Alexis and his family moved out to Kolomenskoe as they usually did to escape the height of a Moscow summer. A few days later the storm broke.

The trigger seems to have been the announcement of another levy on the movables and stocks of registered townsmen. On the morning of Friday, 25th July, crowds gathered in the streets near the Lubianka where notices protesting against the government had been posted up. Officials with an armed escort were sent to tear them down. Though jostled by the crowd they managed to snatch some of them away and returned with them to the Kremlin. The entry in the court diary for that day makes brief mention of some disturbances quelled by the guards but, having noted that the day was a fine one followed by a warm night, the account peters out, leaving a blank sheet which was never to be filled in.[8] Other sources, however, allow the events of this critical day for Alexis to be reconstructed.[9]

The arrival of a courier from Moscow bearing a copy of the offending notice may have been his first intimation of impending trouble, but the movement developed so quickly that some of the protestors may have reached him first. It was his sister Anna's name-day and he was attending mass with his family and members of the court in the church at Kolomenskoe. Distant shouts were heard, and they grew closer as a crowd of Muscovites climbed the hill towards them. From the names they called out Alexis must soon have realized that they were after blood – the blood of his father-in-law and brother-in-law, of his uncle Simeon Streshnev, and of his friend Fedor Rtishchev among others. He must have realized, too, that the guard at Kolomenskoe would not be strong enough to hold a mob at bay. Briskly he told the trembling Miloslavskiis and the other prospective victims who were with him to hide in the Tsar-itsa's apartments. Then he went outside to confront the oncoming crowd. The spectre of 1648 loomed large again. This time, how-ever, the outcome would be somewhat different.

The demeanour of the crowd was rough. They called out raucously for reductions in taxation; they told him to hand over the corrupt and 'traitorous' boyars so that they could punish them; they trampled all over the carefully-nurtured plants in the gardens. Alexis mustered all his patience, all his guile. The tone he took with them was quiet, conciliatory. He promised them redress, but insisted that he, and not they, must dispense justice. He said he would return to Moscow, meet with his Council, and deal with all their grievances – but first he must complete his duty to God and hear out the end of mass. Apparently satisfied, the crowd turned back.

Alexis had bought some precious time, and he exploited it. He summoned two regiments of guards from Moscow and sent the popular boyar Prince Ivan Khovanskii there to restore order. He also sent to the Foreign Suburb to call out all available new-formation troops. He could not know, however, if these measures would suffice or if relief would come in time. The garrison was under strength (several guards regiments had recently been posted to the front), and the reliability of some units was in doubt (he had noticed the occasional uniform among the crowd). Indeed, the forces of disorder still held the initiative, and crowds returned to Kolomenskoe sooner than he feared they might.

By now Moscow was in uproar. Shops and houses were being looted and elements among the mob were in a lynching mood. The great merchant Vasily Shorin, one of Alexis's chief financial advisers and tax farmers, was prominent among the 'enemies' they were looking for. They failed to find him, but they found his son, and a number of them set off for Kolomenskoe taking him with them as a hostage. They met the crowd which had confronted Alexis earlier streaming down the hill and urged them to turn back – so that the mob that confronted him a second time was larger, and more belligerent, than before. They found Alexis on horseback, apparently about to return to Moscow. No help was at hand; he could not know if rescue would come, nor even if his messengers had managed to get through. The motley array of bakers and butchers, artisans and piemen, servants, vagabonds and soldiers was seemingly unarmed, but with only a handful of retainers at his back it was pointless to resist them.

This time they backed up their demands with a curious show of patriotism. They claimed that Shorin was in league with the 'traitor boyars'; that he had fled to Poland; that he was plotting with the enemy. They pushed his terrified son forward and told him to confirm the tale. The lad duly stammered out a garbled story supporting their allegations. Alexis knew it was not true, but he played out a charade with them, hoping against hope that a regiment or two would ride up to his rescue before it was too late. He asked young Shorin a few questions; suggested that he be taken into custody. Still no help came. They demanded that the 'traitor boyars' be executed immediately and he did his best to stall them. But the heat, their excitement, their anger (and, no doubt, the vodka which many must have taken to give them courage) made them impatient. They became more threatening by the moment. If the Tsar would not hand over the culprits, voices screamed, they would seek them out themselves – and as Alexis knew, and they probably suspected, the 'culprits' were hiding only a few yards away. Alexis promised satisfaction. It was not enough. What guarantee could the Tsar give of his good faith, asked one who seemed to be a leader? Alexis swore by his wife and children. A plebeian hand stretched out to touch his own – and then the brittle peace was shattered. 'Indecent words' (unspecified in the sources) were uttered about the Tsaritsa Maria; Alexis was jostled; rude fingers tugged at the buttons of his coat. Two or three members of his suite moved forward in the vain hope of protecting him. . . . At that moment, the troops arrived. They had come round by the rear to avoid driving the crowd onto the Tsar. At once Alexis turned his horse around and shouted: 'Save me from these dogs!' The troops moved forward.

It was all over within minutes. The crowd, several thousands strong, was trapped between the advancing soldiers and the river below. Some were struck down; some were arrested. Many more were trampled to death, and about a hundred drowned in the river trying to escape. In Moscow, too, order was quickly restored. Later that day Alexis received a list of those arrested, and he at once ordered 'ten or twenty of those villains' to be hanged. Next day he confirmed the order – and eighteen men, apparently selected at random, were duly hoisted onto gibbets beside the main roads leading into Moscow.

A full investigation into the riots followed, and Alexis took a personal part in it, going down to the torture chamber to listen to the interrogations. On the 4th and 5th of August he prescribed the punishments. Some who had participated had limbs cut off or their tongues ripped out; others were knouted; and some soldiers and members of the service gentry who had engaged in looting or had been heard comparing their pay and conditions unfavourably with those of the pampered elite regiments were demoted and exiled to distant Astrakhan. Everyone arrested had the first letter of the word 'rebel' branded on his left cheek. These punishments were a good deal harsher than those of 1648, and the indiscriminate executions and mutilations reflect something more than the need for exemplary punishments. There was an element of personal vengeance in them. The 'gentle' Tsar was angered enough by his encounter with the rabble; but the unmentionable things they had said about Maria had evidently infuriated him. The affair had undoubtedly distressed her deeply. Indeed it was to take her more than a year to recover from the shock of it.

If in this instance Alexis's cruelty mirrored his fury with the disobedient masses, it was also in part the obverse of his love, for he was an affectionate, and apparently a faithful, husband. The Venetian Ambassador, having no doubt enquired about the matter, had reported that 'the Tsar has no other love; nor is he given to sensual pleasures'. It is true that some months prior to the riots it had been rumoured that he might send Maria to a nunnery and remarry, though for reasons of state: because of her apparent inability to bear another son – but in May 1661 she had presented him with a new male child, Fedor, and the rumour ceased to circulate. Puritanical as well as uxorious, Alexis would not tolerate promiscuity in those around him, either. He had once warned his father-in-law to cease his scandalous behaviour or quit the court. He is said to have told Bogdan Khitrovo much the same when he learned of his taste for Polish girls and that he kept a harem of them.[10] For Alexis marriage, like the autocracy itself, was a sacred institution and a bulwark of good order – that ideal condition so hard to establish, so difficult to maintain.

The effort of defending it was beginning to take a toll upon his health. The failures of recent years; the increasing frequency of crises (which so often involved personal relationships); the impossible choices he had to make; the cheerful image he had to sustain despite the blows that God (or a malicious fate) had rained upon him; the sheer volume of work that autocracy entailed, coupled with his unwillingness to delegate through the established machinery of government; and now, perhaps, the delayed shock of those desperate moments at Kolomenskoe – the combination of all these things threatened to undermine his constitution. He began to experience digestive troubles, hypertension, racing pulses and sudden nosebleeds (one of these was to force him to make a sudden exit from a banquet given the following February for the English Ambassador, when he toasted 'that glorious martyr Charles I'). He consulted his physicians, Doctors Engelhardt and Collins. They recommended leeches. Indeed Collins was subsequently to produce a paper for him indicating the days which were astrologically the most propitious for letting blood, as well as more general rules on maintaining health and a report on the curative properties of valerian and burdock. More immediately, however, it was Engelhardt's prescriptions that seemed more appropriate. He tried to counter Alexis's symptoms not only with laxatives and emetics laced with modest quantities of opium, but with extract of hellebore, which slows the heart-beat and lowers blood pressure.[11]

Rest would also have helped, no doubt, but he was to have no rest. The riots were only a symptom of a deeper malaise which was beginning to shake the whole realm. As Samuel Collins was to remark, without much exaggeration, 'This Empire is impoverish'd, depopulated and spoil'd so much in ten years, as it will not recover its pristine prosperity in forty.'[12] The war was at the root of Russia's problems and Alexis himself was now yearning for peace (another 10,000 men were lost that August and mutiny in the army of Ukraine was only staved off by rushing a considerable sum of unaffordable cash there). But he was not for peace at any price. After all, the war was also an economic investment. It might yet secure profits in terms of valuable land, population and access to commercial routes.[13] The religious and social strife rending the country called for the continued exploitation of Russian patriotism, or xenophobia, which had found expression even among the rioters at Kolomenskoe (in their assumption that their perceived enemies were in league with the Poles). Peace on humiliating terms could endanger the dynasty. Yet his refusal to capitulate forced Alexis into a series of desperate twists and turns in economic policy.

A few weeks after the uprising the recent measures increasing the number of state export monopolies were rescinded, but duties on sales to foreign merchants, payable in silver, were increased, and the 'musketeer tax', payable in grain, was doubled. A month later another extraordinary levy of 20 per cent was imposed on the stocks and movables of his urban subjects. On the other hand, the minting of copper coins was stopped and in June 1663 they were withdrawn from circulation altogether.[14] This broke the vicious spiral of inflation, but created temporary difficulties, especially for the poorer strata of the urban population who had no stake in the land. In the short term it compounded the threat to public order, while the combination of urban poverty and poor harvests also served to reduce taxation income. Yet money had to be found. The funds lavished on the elite units of the army had saved his regime during the riots; those insurance premiums still had to be paid, and paid lavishly. In 1663 Alexis was to make a special gesture of gratitude to the musketeer guards for serving him 'in the time of trouble' and for not joining 'the rebels, traitors and criminals' who had risen; and that was only one gesture among many.[15] As a Swedish observer noted that year, the popular mood in Moscow was still dangerous. 'They are discontented with the new taxes. . . . Murmurings are heard everywhere. . . . The Tsar's hands will always be tied by internal disorders and rebellions.'[16]

Under Alexis's personal direction the Private Office had begun to collect reports of seditious talk about the Tsar, from the provinces as well as Moscow,[17] and to take an active interest in what were to become known as 'The Sovereign's word and deed' cases, by which subjects, however lowly, were encouraged to denounce their superiors if they had reason to suppose they intended harm to his 'honour' or his 'health'. Sometimes Alexis removed such cases from the hands of the regular authorities and gave them to special investigators who enjoyed his personal trust; sometimes a new enquiry was set up. Furthermore, as a recent study of the Private Office papers concludes, after 1662 Alexis's investigators were engaged in nothing short of a war with popular and subversive movements.[18] Nor did he take any chances with his personal security as he had done that day at Kolomenskoe. Guards and escorts were increased;[19] the law forbidding petitioners to approach the Tsar directly was rigidly enforced; surveillance of doubtful elements stepped up. And if Collins is to be believed, Alexis's fear for his own safety led him to commit at least one homicide.

On one occasion during an expedition into the countryside, a stranger suddenly appeared at the door of his coach. Fearing that the man intended to assassinate him, Alexis thrust at him with the staff he carried – the same pointed staff, we are told, with which Ivan the Terrible had slain his own son. But when the body was searched, no weapon was found upon it – only a claim for three years' arrears of pay.[20]

Yet Alexis's reactions to the crisis were by no means wholly negative. Indeed, the year 1662–3 saw him switch a major part of his attentions to an interesting and positive economic experiment. Realizing that agricultural productivity was a pivot on which success and failure ultimately turned, he had already taken steps to exempt peasants from military service; but now he began a radical reorganization of some of the crown estates with the aim, not only of obtaining increased supplies to help maintain the court and the military units on which his security depended, but of providing a model of efficiency for the country as a whole. The experiment was masterminded and supervised by Alexis personally, operating through the Private Office, through bureaucrats in other departments who had once worked directly to him,[21] and using agents seconded from the ranks of the falconers and guards as well as foreign experts of all kinds.

An economy within the economy (reminiscent of Ivan the Terrible's *oprichnina*, his state within the state), it drew on his earlier excursions into estate management as well as on the traditional rules of running a household which he had learned as a boy. But it also resembled some of Colbert's 'mercantilistic' ideas and, in some respects, was surprisingly modern. Originally involving only a handful of estates, it came to embrace two dozen tracts of country, some of considerable size, and tens of thousands of peasant households. It saw the development of fish-farming and stock-raising, the introduction of new crops, new systems of crop-rotation and the application of up-to-date farming technology including the use (and manufacture) of iron ploughshares, the building of dams and irrigation networks and the use of wind and water power. It came to involve not only agriculture but transportation and the development of industries, most, though not all, of them agriculturally based. The chief centre of these activities was the Izmailovo estate near Moscow.

This property saw intense development in 1663. There, next to his new summer residence on the bank of the little River Serebrianka, Alexis built storehouses (one of them three storeys high), quarters for his servants, and a tower from which he could survey the progress of the work. A vast area of wasteland was cleared that year, and his horticultural experts Heinrich Kasper, Gregory Hood and Valentine David were set to work laying out model gardens, including a physic garden, along the river-bank. Viticulturalists brought in from Astrakhan set down a large area with vines; and orchards were planted, not only with apple, pear, plum and cherry trees, but with mulberries too, for Alexis hoped to create a silk industry. Other men with special skills were brought there from Ukraine to establish apiaries and to grow melons, and nearly seven hundred peasant families from other estates were settled there to serve as common labourers. In the same year a consignment of 300 ploughs, 600 iron ploughshares, 400 axes and 600 sickles was sent there from the state ironworks for them to use. Horses were also sent to Izmailovo, and cattle, and seed-corn (taken from the storehouses of the Patriarchate); and fishponds were dug there and stocked with various kinds of fish.[22] For all that he built labyrinths, summer-houses and fountains in the grounds there can be no doubt that Alexis regarded Izmailovo primarily as a centre for agricultural development.

But Izmailovo was only the chief among several model estates which Alexis created that year and in the years that followed. Each was developed in accordance with a plan which was drawn up on the basis of a thorough survey and assessment of the potential. In June 1664, for example, Prince Ivan Dashkov presented Alexis with a report on development prospects in the Simbirsk area. In it he considered the advantages and disadvantages of its situation, its access to markets, its soil characteristics, and the availability of labour and of water power. Although it took more than four weeks to reach Moscow by river, Dashkov concluded that it was a most convenient point from which to supply Astrakhan with cheap grain. The soil was admirably suited to agriculture; parts of it could produce cheap wine; the area had plenty of running streams whose power could be harnessed by water-mills; and there were good prospects, too, for developing salt and silk production and for establishing fisheries. True, labour was scarce in parts of the area, but with hired labour brought in from outside, the project should prove profitable, despite the extra expense involved. Another survey was carried out on Alexis's properties in the Mozhaisk area, more specifically to find a spread of good arable land on which 150 peasant families could be settled – but at the same time the district's rivers, lakes, forests and communications, and the capabilities of the local peasants, were all assessed. Several more such reports reached Alexis in the months that followed.[23]

It was on the basis of these that estates, tracts of wasteland and of forest were designated for particular kinds of exploitation – grain at Bogoroditsa, boat-building at Domodedovo, salt extraction at Rostov and Pereiaslav-Zalesskii, potash production for export at Sergach (this was to increase seven-fold in as many years after 1664). And it was also on the basis of such reports that new estates or tracts of wasteland were acquired. Sometimes they were bought through intermediaries (often, evidently, below their true market price); sometimes they were appropriated with payment of compensation in the form of money or of lands elsewhere; sometimes they were rented, sometimes simply confiscated.[24] Detailed plans for their development would then be drawn up, sometimes by Alexis himself. The instructions he wrote out for the Romanovo and Skopin estates may serve as an example.

Thirty-five thousand bushels of rye seed were to be sown, the more prosperous of the local peasants being given the responsibility of sowing two and a half to four acres each, the poorer of them an acre and a quarter. If the target could not be reached in this way extra labour should be hired, but peasants unwilling to fulfil their norms were to be coerced. Landless cottars were to be set to work, but helpless widows were to be exempt from obligations. Hired labour was to be taken on to build grain silos by navigable rivers or at the nearest convenient point for shipment. Thirty stacks of hay must be laid up for the winter (presumably to feed the livestock on the demesne); a suitable site must be found on which to build a mill, and the local salt ponds were to be properly exploited.[25]

Some of the arrangements may have a mediaeval ring about them (for example, stipulations as to the number of chickens a peasant should provide for the demesne), but some reflect an economic radicalism. Specialization was introduced, dairy-farming and stock-raising developed, and in 1663 horses were supplied to six estates for use in ploughing (a distinct advance for most of rural Muscovy). New crops were also introduced – not only spring-wheat, peas, rice, vines and melons, but flax and (less successfully) hemp, cotton and mulberries. Care was taken to use the best of all known strains – Turkish wheat, Persian cucumbers, Bokharan melons, Hungarian pears. A five-field system of crop-rotation was put into operation on at least three estates, so that only a fifth of the land (instead of a third or even more) remained uncultivated at any one time. Dams, irrigation systems, windmills and water-mills were built (Izmailovo had as many as nine mills); forests were cut down, wastes brought under the plough; fenlands were drained to provide both more arable land and fishponds (thirty-seven were dug at Izmailovo alone); peasants were equipped with better implements (over the winter of 1662–3 the state ironworks turned out thousands of them, which were promptly distributed), and trained in new techniques.[26] Such improvements represented distinct advances for backward, rustic Muscovy. So did the industrial developments which went on side by side with them – not only of salt and potash, but of leather, textiles, brick-making, glass and even shipbuilding.[27]

The system was built on the rational principle of putting idle or under-used resources to work – wasteland, landless labourers and the indigent (some of them in the cotton and hemp 'work-houses' set up near Moscow[28]). But it also involved the transportation of people and the use of forced labour in the interests of efficiency. In 1664, for example, Afanasy Ordyn-Nashchokin was ordered to send 'good, surplus peasants', experienced in raising flax, from the Pskov area to central Muscovy, and more than a hundred peasants were moved from Domodedovo to another estate because they were bad ploughmen.

The labour force reacted badly. Troops had to be sent to the Romanovo estate in 1664 to cope with a rebellion; many of the peasants transferred from Domodedovo bolted on the way; and peasant families fled from Izmailovo in their hundreds: it was subsequently to be reported that of 664 families there, 481 had fled and the rest seemed to be waiting a chance to escape.[29] That many of Alexis's bailiffs were cruel and extortionate is undeniable – even though inspectors were sent out regularly to counter their dishonesty and maladministration. But given his insistence on results and the Russian peasant's sloth and resentment of change, harsh discipline was necessary. Workers sent to one of the Izmailovo farms from April to October one year show what problems the bailiffs confronted: most of the labourers failed to make an appearance at all. The sixty or seventy who did turn up arrived late, left early, and were lazy and disobedient while they were there.[30] The anarchic, conservative nature of the Russian peasants invited the oppressive treatment meted out to those of them unfortunate enough to fall under Alexis's net.

Despite the wide use of serf labour, these schemes involved considerable investment. So did Alexis's trading ventures. In 1663 the Private Office organized a huge commercial expedition to Persia (keeping careful accounts in leather-bound ledgers).[31] Alexis was by far the biggest merchant 'capitalist' in his realm, as well as the biggest farmer and the biggest industrialist. The dominating position of the Tsar in the economy has often been assumed to have stunted the development of a large and healthy merchant class in Russia. But in fact Alexis tried to encourage entrepreneurs and even to create them. He supported the van Sweden family in setting up a paper factory, for example; and he once attempted to transform some of his peasants into traders by equipping them with boats – but they only sold off, or abandoned, the boats at their first opportunity. Then in 1665 he was to approve an experiment by which the depressed city of Pskov was given self-government, granted two fairs, and its townsmen given a string of commercial privileges – but again the project foundered.[32] While some of his economic ventures may have pre-empted the role of the private entrepreneur, and some of his taxation measures may have stifled enterprise or driven it underground, most of his initiatives filled a vacuum caused by Russian torpor.

But if the pursuit of wealth for the realm as a whole and for the crown in particular became a major preoccupation for Alexis in the middle 1660s it was by no means his only one. The search for peace both with his neighbours and within the Church remained his constant care. Having tried and failed to come to terms with Poland in the aftermath of the Moscow uprising of 1662, Alexis was trying, terrier-like, to keep a grip on Ukraine – even though the war with Poland was sapping Muscovy's life-blood, and even though he now had to cope with rebellions and incursions by tribesmen in the east, which called for the diversion of scarce military resources. In 1662 guards units had to be sent to counter Bashkirs rampaging near Tobolsk and Kazan, and troubles with plundering Ostiaks and other Siberian aborigines were to take several years to quell.[33] Meanwhile Muscovy's grip on eastern Ukraine had slackened and Alexis depended heavily on his commander in the field there, Prince G. G. Romodanovskii, to restore it. As with his other generals, Alexis managed him rather as he would a horse, spurring him on and reining him in by turns. At about this time he sent him a letter full of wise military and political advice.

Romodanovskii was never to neglect his staff work, which, Alexis reckoned, had contributed to the defeats both of Sheremetev and Khovanskii. He was to be ceaselessly watchful, like the Argus with its hundred eyes, cautious at all times and humble too (the proud Sheremetev, he suggested, had been too ready to believe what flatterers said about him – that 'the fellow had not been borne who could overcome him in battle'; as a result, he had become over-confident, and ended up in captivity). In the field Romodanovskii was to make full use of deception and decoy, never allowing the enemy to guess the reasons for his movements; and politically, he was to take care of Ivan Briukhovetsky, the only Ukrainian leader on whom he should rely. Alexis had met the man and trusted him.[34] Bruikhovetsky, in fact, was his candidate to be Hetman, and in June 1663, after a year of turmoil in Ukraine, Alexis's agents managed to secure his election. 'We can all sleep soundly now,' remarked Alexis when he heard the news; but he was mistaken. The following winter King Casimir of Poland, together with his own Ukrainian allies and a force of Tatars, led an invasion of eastern Ukraine.

Shortly before this Alexis had consulted his leading ministers concerned with military and foreign affairs to decide on what terms negotiations with Poland might be resumed. They offered contradictory advice. Alexis took a careful note of the issues and sent a secret account of the meeting in his own hand to a friend (probably Artamon Matveev) in order to elicit another opinion before reaching a decision.[35] There was certainly no obvious path to peace, and Alexis was as ever cautious about coming to a conclusion, though once he made up his mind he maintained the line unwaveringly. Afanasy Ordyn-Nashchokin, whom Alexis had appointed to be his chief negotiator, argued that, rather than concluding a peace with Poland, a 'union' should be contracted with her. His arguments were ingenious:

> If a simple peace is concluded with Poland we should have to
> repatriate all our Polish and Lithuanian prisoners-of-war, very
> many of whom have taken service in all parts of Great Russia
> and Siberia [and] married here. . . . [But] if a union is effected
> they would be able to remain, and we have great need of them.
> . . .

Furthermore, he argued, 'union' was an essential precondition of
protecting those Orthodox Ukrainians who would remain under
Polish rule. Besides, a friendly Poland would help protect the
southern frontier against the Tatars, and provide Muscovy with a
bridge to the Orthodox Moldavians and Wallachians, who, if such a
bridge were to be established, would surely shake off their subjection to the Turks and allow a political union of all Orthodox
Christians to be created.

Alexis recognized the strength of some of Afanasy's arguments,
but he would not accept the implication that Orthodox Ukrainians
be abandoned to Polish rule whatever conditions might be made
about their treatment. He called it 'wavering in the wind'. He told
Afanasy that his advice on this score was praiseworthy and 'much
appreciated', but inappropriate and not to be raised again. 'A dog,'
he told him, 'is not worthy to eat a morsel of Orthodox bread,' and
there could certainly be no justification for allowing the Polish
Catholic 'dog to gnaw eternally at both morsels of this bread' – that
is eastern as well as western Ukraine. 'Go in the Tsar's peace by the
middle road,' he added. 'Do not deviate either to the right or the left.
And God go with thee.'

But there was at least one other point which Afanasy had made
that must have struck a sympathetic chord with Alexis. It concerned
what he saw as Sweden's machinations to deepen Muscovy's
troubles. According to Afanasy,

> The Swedes are plotting with the Khan for Russia's ruin. They
> write up our bad news, print it in Stockholm and send it all
> around the world, belittling the Muscovite state. . . . And that
> is why the Polish senators have become so proud and un-
> reasonable over the peace negotiations. They have begun to
> stab us in the eye with this Swedish composition, as if it were
> true that Russia was suffering terrible weakness and disorder. It
> is because of the news put about by the Swedes that all
> Muscovy's forces have been sent against the Bashkirs that the
> King [of Poland] has invaded [eastern] Ukraine. . . .[36]

It was probably this that prompted Alexis to arrange for news published abroad to be monitored on a regular rather than on an occasional basis. Certainly in February 1665 he commissioned one of his agents to have foreign news reports sent from Riga twice a week; and within a year frequent digests of foreign news reports that touched on developments not only close to home but in places as far-flung as Smyrna and Mecca were available to him.[37] It proved a useful intelligence tool and an aid to Muscovite diplomacy. But meanwhile the damage caused by Sweden's deliberate and successful attempt to mislead the world about Muscovy's true strength and military disposition had been done. The Polish invasion of eastern Ukraine in January 1664 had re-opened a desperate struggle. The peace talks started that spring broke off the following September, and, having rejected Afanasy's advice, Alexis continued his dogged quest to save his morsel of Orthodox bread from the Catholic devourer.

He took an active part in directing operations to this end. Distance left him no alternative but to grant some measure of discretion to his generals; nonetheless he expected his orders to be followed to the letter, and was excoriating when he found that any particular had been neglected. Romodanovskii himself once received a broadside reminiscent of that famous one that Alexis had sent many years before to the errant steward of the St Sabbas Monastery. Addressing it to 'The enemy of Christ's cross and new Achitophel, Prince Gregory Romodanovskii', Alexis began: 'a curse on you instead of God's blessing'. Then thinking this too strong he scratched it out and proceeded in somewhat milder fashion, falling at once into a fine rhetorical stride.

> May the Lord God reward thee for thy right satanic service to us. . . . Thou hast . . . corrected God's will and our tsarish order just as Judas sold Christ for bread. . . . Thou wast ordered to send a detachment to . . . Simeon Zmeev's command [but ultimately failed to do so]. . . . And since thou didst neglect God's and our tsarish business, the Lord God himself will neglect thee; and thy wife and children will weep such tears as orphans weep when beaten for no reason. Thou thrice-damned and shameful hater of the Christian race, our faithful traitor, most true son of Satan and friend of devils, thou shalt fall into the bottomless pit whence no-one returns for failing to send those troops. Remember, traitor, by whom thou wast singled out [for promotion], by whom thou wast rewarded, and on whom thou dost depend. Where canst thou hide? Where canst thou flee? Whom dost thou disobey? On

whom dost thou use thy wiles? Patently thou dost slander
Christ himself and neglect his business. . . .

Should thou wish for God's grace and blessing in future and
. . . to regain our tsarish favour, thou must obey our every
order, and send Simeon Zmeev a regiment each of cavalry and
dragoons at once . . . having given them their pay.[38]

Meanwhile the Church in Muscovy itself was in disorder; the
unity of faith by which Alexis set such store as the ideological
bulwark of the state was crumbling. As the new (and expensive)
service books came to be distributed throughout the country they
aroused more and more opposition, even though their use was not
yet compulsory. Furthermore, religious opposition to the Church
reforms had begun to merge with social discontents – a sinister
development which threatened to produce a political explosion of
some kind. There were even Old Believer sympathizers at court –
Prince Ivan Khovanskii, Feodosia, the widow of Boyar Gleb
Morozov, and the Princess Urusova, both of them relatives of
Fedor Rtishchev, among them. Increasing numbers of religious
dissenters and social renegades of all kinds were forming communities in the forests which resembled cancers within the body politic.
Some of them said dreadful things about the Tsar; some of them
offered violence to representatives of both Church and State, and on
occasion to themselves, burning or starving themselves to death in
protest against what they regarded as the rule of Antichrist and in
anticipation of the Second Coming. On the other hand, there were
prelates committed to the reforms who criticized Alexis for his
apparent hesitation to enforce them.[39] And the confusion was compounded by Nikon's anomalous position, neither Patriarch, nor yet
deposed from office.

The longer he remained in limbo the more dangerous he became.
He had begun to object fiercely to the way in which the Church was
run without him, to inveigh against the decisions of the 1660 synod,
and he had publicly pronounced anathema on the Metropolitan
Pitirim for carrying out patriarchal duties at the Tsar's behest and
for intervening in the affairs of the Ukrainian Church,[40] an intervention which Alexis deemed essential in order to shore up Moscow's
political authority there. The crisis in the Church had become
extremely grave, but its very gravity led Alexis to move towards a
solution with extreme caution. He wanted to maintain the
Nikonian reforms (which in essence were his own) and to maintain
religious order; yet he also wanted to reconcile the Old Believers if

he possibly could (to this end, as soon as Nikon had quit the patriarchate, Alexis had recalled the most prominent of them, Avvakum, from exile in the far distant and dangerous wastes of Dauria on the Chinese frontier). He wanted Nikon formally deposed and replaced, but he wanted to depose him in complete accordance with the canons of the Church, without any taint of oppression attaching to himself (he was still very careful to observe the feast-day of St Philip the Martyr[41]). So far he had been thwarted in this by the vacillations of his ecclesiastical advisers, but now at last he had found someone who would help him accomplish it. He was an eminent Greek, as learned in the canon law as he was in the occult – Paisios Ligarides, the Metropolitan of Gaza.

Paisios was another of those clerical mercenaries who roamed the Europe of that time in search of patronage and preferment. A man of undoubted scholarship and experience of life, his wits had been sharpened and his manner smoothed by his wanderings and by many encounters with a harsh world. Fifty years old when he arrived penniless in Moscow at the beginning of 1662, he had quickly assessed the potential of the situation, turned down an overture from Nikon, who saw him as a potential ally, and ingratiated himself with the court. Before long he was preparing answers to thirty questions presented to him by Boyar Simeon Streshnev, probably on Alexis's instructions. The questions ranged widely, but they were all concerned with clearing the way for Nikon's deposition. Should a synod be held to settle the problem? Could the Tsar convoke one? Was Nikon right to use a mirror and a comb when robing? Could he sustain his claim that he had not abandoned his diocese when he had left Moscow? Could members of a Church sit in judgement on its head? Did Nikon dishonour the name of the Holy City by calling his monastery 'The New Jerusalem'? Did the Tsar incur sin for leaving the Church so long in widowhood? Did Nikon's curses have any force? What should be done with someone who called the Tsar a tyrant?

The answers Paisios provided, though measured in tone, were calculated to please his new patron. When Nikon obtained a copy of them they certainly infuriated him. They led him to compose a thundering rebuttal, replete with biblical quotations and condemnations, and so lengthy that it must have taken him weeks to write. Alexis, however, had been well pleased with Paisios's work. On 26th November 1662 he had held a session of the Council which Paisios attended and which lasted several hours.[42] Soon afterwards he had decided to call a full synod of the Church to put a stop to schism and confusion once and for all. And, in order that its decisions should be regarded as final and beyond challenge, he had written to the Patriarchs of Constantinople, Jerusalem, Alexandria and Antioch, inviting them to attend or at least to send representatives bearing authoritative answers to the vital questions.[43] Meanwhile commissions were set up to check the controversial service books and to prepare the case against Nikon.

The plan, however, failed to work. The two senior Patriarchs were only prepared to give general advice on the relationship between Patriarchs and Tsars; they preferred not to be involved in Nikon's condemnation and they declined to come to Moscow.[44] Yet with Nikon now comparing his position as Patriarch to the sun and Alexis's only to the moon; with his asserting that the priesthood was 'in all things more honourable than the Tsardom' (since, after all, priests anointed Tsars), his continuing freedom to speak out became intolerable. In July 1663 Boyar Nikita Odoevskii, Archbishop Joseph of Astrakhan and others accompanied Paisios to 'The New Jerusalem' where he confronted Nikon. He accused him of popery, of making mistakes in the new service books, and declared that, since in his own words he had refused 'to return like a dog to its vomit', he was no longer Patriarch. Nikon responded violently. He thumped his staff upon the ground, called Paisios an unchristian knave, a dog, a peasant, another Caiaphas. At this the old man was put temporarily under close arrest in his cell while an attempt was made to find evidence against him of a variety of misdeeds including financial improprieties. Alexis received regular reports of progress through his Private Office,[45] but the results were evidently less than satisfactory and renewed attempts were made to enlist the help of the other Patriarchs.

Meanwhile Avvakum had arrived back in Moscow, and the hopes of the Old Believers soared. Avvakum lodged with Alexis's friend Fedor Rtishchev and was soon given quarters in a Kremlin monastery. 'Thus did I come to Moscow,' he was to write in his autobiography, 'and as though I was an Angel of God the Tsar and all his boyars received me gladly.' Avvakum was fêted, flattered, had money and presents thrust upon him, was offered almost any benefice he wanted. Alexis himself spoke to him several times ('he used to slip out of his carriage and come to me'). It was an imaginative move. If only Avvakum could be reconciled to the reformed Church, most of the other dissidents could probably be won over too – for Avvakum had charisma and his prestige stood so high that crowds of his adherents would follow him about the streets whenever he went out.

Avvakum was almost persuaded. Then, having heard the new liturgy being given in the Cathedral, he refused to go to mass again. Rtishchev argued with him, Prince Ivan Khilkov pleaded with him, Rodion Streshnev came to beg him at least to keep silent – and to offer him the post of corrector in the Printing Office. Avvakum was tempted. An appointment as corrector, as he himself was to admit, 'pleased me better than to be the Tsar's confessor', holding out as it did the prospect of being able to change the service books to conform to the old ways, at least in some respects. Yet in the end he could not bring himself to compromise.[46] He still believed that 'the Tsar is set over us by God' (which made him so much more acceptable than Nikon), and he wanted the dissension to end, but the revised version of the liturgy was an abomination in his eyes. He claimed that to substitute 'there is no end to His Kingdom' for 'there will be no end to His Kingdom' was to dishonour God, and that the roots of faith had been blasted by the omission of Christ's resurrection from the service books (an allegation that was strenuously denied). He even tried to persuade Alexis that he was wrong. During the spring of 1664 he bombarded him with letters.

In one of them he blamed Nikon for 'the new illegal laws' and claimed that they had 'ruined' the soul and body of the Russian people. Nikon was a heretic; he had denied Christ, and in return Christ would deny resurrection to the Tsar. He could say more, he hinted darkly, but

> I dare not say much for fear of grieving you, my light. But it is time to put the new service books aside, and all Nikon's evil plots. . . . And when we pull out this evil root, all will be well with us, and your tsardom will be serene and quiet, as was the Patriarchate before Nikon . . . and God will enable us to receive eternal bliss.[47]

Alexis sighed, and refused the audience which Avvakum requested; indeed he made no reply to him at all. At last, having received a fifth letter from the zealot, who was so likeable and in whom he had placed such hopes, he sighed more deeply still and ordered his arrest. Avvakum was exiled again, this time to Mezen in the north.

Meanwhile messages had come from the Patriarchs of Constantinople and Jerusalem urging Alexis to make his peace with Nikon and restore him to office.[48] This was displeasing. It seemed that unless Alexis took the initiative in effecting a reconciliation with Nikon, the two senior Patriarchs of the Orthodox world would not condone Nikon's trial and deposition. On the other hand it was clear that if Nikon were to be given another chance and if he were to spoil the prospect of reconciliation through his innate arrogance, the Patriarchs (as one of them said in terms) would feel bound to condemn him. Such considerations, at least, provide a credible explanation for the extraordinary, mysterious and dramatic happenings that took place in Moscow shortly before Christmas 1664.

During the small hours of 18th December ten sledges crammed with people and half-a-dozen outriders swept up to the Nikitskii Gate on the south side of Moscow. When challenged by the guardsman on watch (from the subsequent enquiry we know his name was Ivan Seliverstov) they answered that the Archimandrite of the St Sabbas Monastery at Zvenigorod (Alexis's favourite) demanded to pass. Private Seliverstov opened the gates for them. The cortège drove on to the Smolensk Gate to the west of the Kremlin, where it was challenged again, and into the Kremlin itself, past the Advanced Tower, over the stone bridge, and through the Trinity Gates. In all it was challenged four times. Each time the same answer was given; each time the gates were opened; each time the guards (who belonged to Artamon Mateev's command) failed to identify the occupants. It was dark, said the sentries at the subsequent enquiry, and the people in the sledges were too well muffled up against the cold for them to see who they were.[49]

A short while later the clerics keeping vigil in the Cathedral of the Assumption were astonished by a commotion. The north door was flung open and what seemed like 'a multitude of people habited as if for service' entered. They were followed by a man bearing a cross and a cohort of monks. Then the unmistakeable towering figure of Nikon appeared behind them.

He made his way directly to the patriarchal throne, handed the staff he was carrying to a retainer and took hold of the patriarchal crozier instead, while his choir sang the introit for the entry of a Patriarch. He made obeisance to the relics, commanded the subdeacon who was reading aloud from the Psalter to be silent and began to recite prayers. The Metropolitan of Rostov had meanwhile tried to leave and inform the Tsar of what was happening, but he found the Cathedral doors locked against him. Then Nikon summoned him and commanded him to accept his blessing. Intimidated by the presence of so many of Nikon's retainers, and with his own people in a state of total confusion (several believed that Nikon must have returned to his post at Alexis's behest), he submitted. Then, at Nikon's own behest, he went to inform the Tsar.[50]

The news created uproar in the Palace. Courtiers stood about in groups talking in excited whispers; more and more notables rushed in, some of them still only half awake; Alexis hurriedly convened a meeting of advisers. Some of them were sent to Nikon to ask the reason for his coming. He told them enigmatically that 'a vision' had commanded him to do so, and gave them a written message (or petition) for the Tsar. In due course they returned with orders instructing him to leave Moscow by dawn, before any further disturbance was created. Nikon departed reluctantly, and not before ostentatiously shaking the dust from his shoes, as if he were leaving a land of infidels, and making the members of his entourage do the same. He carried the patriarchal crozier away with him. Men were sent after him to retrieve it. He was very loath to surrender it, but finally did so – together with letters he had received which explained the real reason for his coming. They had been written by Boyar Nikita Ziuzin and they made it plain that the Tsar himself had wanted Nikon to return.

Ziuzin had once served on the patriarchal staff and had been promoted to the Council on Nikon's recommendation in 1655. Of late he had been Nikon's only friend among the boyars, but despite his exalted rank he had held no important office (his latest appointment was as second, supernumerary, Governor of Novgorod). Ziuzin claimed to have learned of Alexis's desire to be reconciled to Nikon from Artamon Matveev and Afanasy Ordyn-Nashchokin. He was interrogated under threat of torture on 22nd December. Alexis was present. As Ziuzin was held close to the fire, he and Alexis looked each other in the eye, and suddenly he knew what to do. He confessed that the initiative in calling Nikon to Moscow was entirely his own. Alexis was satisfied; the torturers retired. Ziuzin's statement had cleared Artamon and Afanasy. It had also cleared the Tsar. Ziuzin was condemned to death, but Alexis commuted the sentence. Instead, his estate was confiscated (and promptly ascribed to the Tsar), and Ziuzin himself was demoted to the ranks of the service gentry and exiled to Kazan.[51] But did the findings of the official enquiry represent what had really happened? Was Ziuzin really acting on his own initiative? Was Matveev innocent of all involvement? Was Alexis himself really amazed to hear of Nikon's sudden reappearance?

Circumstantial evidence suggests very strongly that Alexis not only knew about Nikon's return, but that he had deliberately, perhaps cynically, engineered it. Security in Moscow had been extremely strict of late, and it was well known that Nikon was never to be allowed to enter the city. Yet none of the guards at any of the four gates had bothered to hold up lanterns to the faces of those muffled figures in the sledges – and Artamon Matveev, one of Alexis's chief henchmen, was commander of the guard that night. Ziuzin's punishment was less severe than it might seem from the record, too. True he lost the exalted rank of boyar, but he had never exercised authority or power remotely commensurate with the rank, and economically his fall seems to have been cushioned. He was allowed to keep his movables and was presumably allotted a service estate in Kazan province which would have compensated him for the loss of his rather modest landholding. There was motive as well. Given the position adopted by the Patriarchs of Constantinople and Jerusalem, Alexis had good reason to engineer a reconciliation with Nikon, or at least make a show of doing so. But had he inspired Nikon to return in order to entrap him, so that he could discredit him in the eyes of the Patriarchs? Or was he genuinely seeking reconciliation and had Nikon himself somehow spoiled the plan?

The available evidence can be interpreted in a way which suggests that Alexis had deliberately spun a web to trap Nikon. Nikon had refused to be drawn by Ziuzin's first two letters urging him to return. The third letter (the crabbed original of which was eventually copied out by one of Alexis's private secretaries) insisted that it was the Tsar's wish that he come to Moscow on the appointed night, that he enter the Cathedral by the north door, that he take up the patriarchal staff and bless those who were present before sending word of his arrival to the Tsar. The letter also stressed that Alexis wished the matter to be kept secret and that he had given a specific assurance that if Nikon should follow his instructions 'I shall not fail him, nor abandon him in anything to anybody'.[52] Yet when Nikon did send word of his arrival, so far from arranging for him to enter the patriarchal palace and receiving him in order to discuss the limits to be placed on the patriarchal authority in future (as he had indicated), Alexis had ordered him out of Moscow. It might seem like a betrayal.

Yet Nikon had also been urged to come secretly and to behave in a gentle, conciliatory way so as not to arouse his enemies. He was also warned not to mention Ziuzin's name. Nikon, however, had come to Moscow with a considerable entourage and had entered the Cathedral with a mighty clamour. The uproar might well have given his enemies warning of what was afoot sooner than Alexis intended and thus made it impossible to arrive at a secret concordat with him that might then be presented as a *fait accompli*. Furthermore Nikon had compromised Ziuzin by handing over his letter. The communication of the plan at third hand certainly left room for misunderstandings. But if Alexis was only mounting a charade in order to demonstrate to the eastern Patriarchs his willingness to have Nikon back on terms, he depended on Nikon himself to demonstrate his uncompromising nature – and Nikon certainly seems to have obliged.

The petition which Nikon sent to the Tsar when his messengers came to enquire why he had come is a critical piece of evidence. It was only after this had been minutely considered by the Tsar in Council that the order was issued to send Nikon away. The petition was couched in terms of pious humility and was generally in accordance with Ziuzin's instructions. However, it also contained suggestions that Nikon still regarded the status of Patriarch to be superior to that of the Tsar, and that he had no intention of returning to office merely to be Alexis's tool:

> We have come in meekness and humility [he had written] as our Lord has taught us . . . bringing with us that peace which our Lord Jesus Christ, humbling himself and . . . coming down to earth, brought and bequeathed to his holy disciples and apostles, and after them to the bishops who from time to time minister in holy things in his Church. . . . And not only do we have this gift by the grace of God to give peace to any one, but we also have power to *remit sins*. . . . And not only thus, but we have power to bind both on earth and in heaven, and to loose. . . . If thy majesty, O Tsar, is willing to reflect on something more even than that which we have said, we will not shrink from saying, *Dost thou desire to receive Christ himself?*

As Ziuzin sighed to Artamon Matveev when he met him in the street and learned that the whole venture had misfired, 'It is his old audacity: so indiscreet!'[53]

With the failure of this last, Byzantine, attempt to come to terms with Nikon (if attempt it really was) the incident was exploited to bring about Nikon's condemnation, and the manner in which the trial was prepared involved a degree of skulduggery which reflects no credit on Alexis. He may or may not have known at this point that the wily Paisios had forged a document empowering him to represent the Patriarch of Constantinople at Nikon's forthcoming trial; but he certainly signed letters drafted by Paisios to the Patriarchs of both Constantinople and Jerusalem which deliberately misrepresented what had happened.[54] Having decided, after all, that it would be difficult to present the events of the night of 18th December as a genuine attempt to reconcile Nikon, it was submitted that Nikon's return to Moscow was an unwarranted and illegal act. Nikon, it was suggested, had come like a thief in the night to steal the patriarchal crozier, and his intemperate action in shaking the dust from his feet before he left (and making his retainers do the same) was stressed for good measure. The Patriarchs could hardly forbear from condemning him after this.

The whole business was unsavoury and some odium attaches to Alexis. Yet he himself had long since been resigned to the fact that as Tsar he had to bear a much heavier weight of sin than ordinary mortals because of the responsibilities he had to undertake in upholding the state and the peace of the realm. The desperate means to which he had resorted had been forced upon him by the urgent political necessity of countering the religious schism and the growing association of religious dissent with social unrest which threatened civil war. Yet in January 1665 the Church was still in a state of dangerous confusion and Alexis's fortunes in Ukraine were at a low point too. Enemy forces had taken Uman and Bratslav; and Hetman Briukhovetsky, though still loyally trying to cope with growing anarchy among his own people as well as fighting the invaders, was pressing desperately for more military support from Moscow. Alexis's cause seemed lost, and the comet that had recently appeared in the sky (and had excited all Europe) seemed to bode impending disasters of other kinds as well.

Alexis consulted Dr Engelhardt about it. He feared that it meant another terrible epidemic, or perhaps a famine, or that it heralded some adverse development affecting his prospects of making peace with Poland. The learned doctor consulted his astrological calendars and his muse, and compiled two learned reports. In them he related the ominous comet to the unpropitious position of Saturn in relation to Mars, and the recent damp summers. He hinted at a dry spring, and forecast another plague outbreak the following autumn. He also warned Alexis of impending 'secret sceptres of death', of rumours and agitation which would be followed by civil disturbances.[55] It all seemed extremely credible – but for once the forecast proved overly pessimistic. The plague struck London, not Moscow: and so far from facing total disaster, Alexis benefited from a seemingly miraculous change of fortune.

The first and vital development was the outbreak of a rebellion against the Polish King led by Jerzy Liubomirski in the name of 'Golden Freedom'. This unleashed a devastating civil war which put paid to Poland's advance into eastern Ukraine. Then Peter Doroshenko, Hetman of western Ukraine, abandoned his allegiance to the King and turned to the Turks for protection. This brought swarms of Tatars onto Poland's southern frontier – and an invitation to Alexis from the Pope to join a league of Christian powers against the Turks (which Alexis sensibly declined).[56] For all Briukhovetsky's vigour in suppressing opposition in eastern Ukraine, his authority there remained fragile, but Alexis now had time to engineer changes that might bring the region firmly and permanently into the Muscovite orbit.

He took the opportunity presented by the Polish collapse to invite Briukhovetsky to Moscow. There on 22nd October 1665 he raised him to the rank of boyar and arranged a marriage for him with a princess of the distinguished Dolgorukii clan. This gave the once humble Cossack social standing and a position in the Muscovite power structure. But it was only part of a radical plan to integrate eastern Ukraine. To placate its urban population, the cities of Kiev, Kaniev, and Starodub were granted the same rights of Magdeburg law that they had once enjoyed under Polish rule, and, which was more significant, the Cossack elite were granted the status and rights of Muscovite nobility. In the long term this policy of taming leading figures of an unruly frontier population by ensnaring them with the lures of a social status and a hereditary place in a larger society was probably to do more for Russian 'imperialism' than the use of force.[57] On his return home Briukhovetsky had to cope with further challenges to his authority, and the infiltration of Muscovite officials, and taxation, coupled with democratic aspirations among the Cossack rank and file, continued to foster unrest. But the 'gentrification' of the more affluent and influential among the population proved to be a vital factor in maintaining Alexis's tsarish authority. His long struggle for

Ukraine was not yet over; nor was his struggle to find a formula for religious peace at home. But he was about to impose one.

At the end of April 1666 Alexis addressed another assembly of leading clerics. The tide of reaction provoked by enemies of the Church, he said, had not only swept over the provinces, it had 'entered this very city, rushed tempestuously towards our throne, and touched the sleeve of our coat'. The 'devilish weed' of dissent must be torn up and destroyed; schism must be rooted out; mutinies against the Church must be suppressed.[58] The audience responded positively. Good care had been taken to ensure that they would. Before the proceedings had been formally inaugurated everyone present had been required to answer three questions in writing concerning the orthodoxy of the church reforms,[59] and all present had known how to answer. They thanked Alexis for his defence of Orthodoxy. The road was now open for an inquisition and, if necessary, a purge. Nikon's old enemy Bishop Alexander, whom he had transferred from the see of Kolomna to distant Viatka, was the first objector to the revised church books to be dealt with. He recanted. Subsequent sessions were devoted to other leading dissenters.

For weeks past they had been threatened and cajoled in an attempt to bring them into line. But although some, like Bishop Alexander, submitted and recanted, others, including Avvakum, would not. Despite a pleading letter from Alexis's own hand ('Wilt thou so long vex us?' he had written. 'Be reconciled to us dear old Avvakum') the man would not be moved. He was brought in chains before the synod, but remained stiff-necked. According to his own account the bishops cursed him 'and I cursed them back'. He was pronounced a heretic, deprived of holy orders, and taken away to a monastery where he was forced to become a monk.[60] Meanwhile pressure had been put on the more prominent of his secular supporters, Prince Vorotynski, Prince Ivan Khovanskii, and, not least, Boyarina Morozova. On Alexis's orders the Metropolitan Paul of Krutitsk and the Archimandrite of the Miracle Monastery paid her a visit in which, in gentle tones, they reminded her of her honour and her ancestry, and warned her that her obstinacy was putting her beloved son in danger and threatening the destruction of her entire house.[61]

The synod of May 1666 ended by condemning the Old Believers and ordering all incumbent priests to use the new service books, for hitherto the old ones had still been permissible. It remained for the eastern Patriarchs to set their seal on these arrangements, and to deal finally with Nikon. Two of them, the Patriarchs of Antioch and Alexandria, arrived at Astrakhan that June – much to Alexis's relief. The remaining Patriarchs would not come, but somehow means would be found to associate their names with the decisions of the others. When news came of their arrival Alexis saw it as heralding 'the salvation of the world, the strengthening of spiritual union, the scattering of the evil enemies of opposition; resuscitation for us all. Blessed be God who allowed this.' They were told nothing of what had transpired in recent months; nothing of Paisios Ligarides being suspected of fraud; and they were kept well clear of anyone who might inform them. When they eventually neared Moscow that autumn, Artamon Matveev, with whom Alexis had kept close counsel in all these matters, was sent to greet them with instructions to keep them closely guarded.[62]

They arrived in Moscow on 2nd November. Only then did Alexis inform them about Paisios. Two days later he gave a banquet for them; two days after that he met them again, this time in secret session, when presumably he took the opportunity to explain the position to them and to persuade them to be guided by a special brief which the industrious Paisios had prepared on his instructions.[63] The stage was now set for Nikon's trial; and the long struggle with Poland over Ukraine was on the brink of settlement as well.

The Polish government had indicated its readiness to resume negotiations and they had got under way early in 1666 at the village of Andrusovo not far from Smolensk. They had been dragging on for months. Afanasy Ordyn-Nashchokin, whom Alexis had promoted to the rank of sub-boyar the year before and sent to be Governor of Pskov, had been recalled to lead the Muscovite delegation, and again the determined Alexis had found him somewhat wanting in steeliness. While anxious for hostilities to cease, Alexis, sensing that luck was once more running with him at long last, wanted to conclude a truce rather than a permanent peace. Afanasy thought otherwise, and this earned him a rebuke. On 31st May 1666 Alexis wrote to him:

> You should conclude nothing but a truce, and that in accordance with the instructions sent to you. . . . Do not depart from those terms. . . . Leave a permanent peace to the will of God. . . . You are dishonoured by such timidity.[64]

But in July that year, despite Alexis's chanelling secret funds to him,[65] the rebel Liubomirskii was reconciled to the King. Doroshenko and the Tatars still prevailed in western Ukraine. But while it seemed as if the long-sought peace with Poland could still be reached, it remained uncertain what fruits Alexis would be able to pluck from it. By November 1666 it looked as if he would not only have to surrender his claim to western Ukraine but cede the great city of Kiev and perhaps part of Zaporozh'e as well; but within a few days he was urging Afanasy to persevere to the last in the hope of keeping Kiev.

> Be most circumspect in making the final concession. A concession over Kiev must be [treated as] a closed matter so far as what you say is concerned. It must be indicated by your face rather than directly so that [we may learn] what their intention might be, contrary to what they say. But if they should reject [our proposal] outright and insist that we move out you should ask for time to consult us. . . . Labour on! Endurance to the end will bring salvation. Greetings from both us and our new-born son [Simeon]. . . .[66]

Peace was within reach at last; and the tangled knots of Church affairs which had troubled Alexis for nine long years were about to be unravelled too. The winter of 1666–7 was to prove the most decisive of his reign so far.

Chapter VIII

Trials

By the beginning of December 1666 the stage was at last set for
Nikon's trial. On the second of that month the court assembled in
the palace banqueting hall. Alexis presided. On benches below him
to his right sat sixty-five senior Greek and Russian churchmen;
immediately to his left, on armchairs, were the Patriarchs of Alexandria and Antioch, and beyond them, in serried rows, the boyars
and other members of his Council. In the well of the court, in front
of the dais on which Alexis sat enthroned, was a table covered with a
cloth of gold. On it stood a pile of books and a silver-gilt casket
containing documents to be used in evidence. Alexis was well
acquainted with their contents – for he was about to play the part of
chief counsel for the prosecution too.

It had been arranged that everyone should remain seated when
the accused entered, but when the doors were thrown open and the
huge, cowled figure of Nikon emerged out of the shadows he was
preceded by one of his loyal deacons holding up a cross. Involun-
tarily Alexis rose to his feet; the others followed his example. The
accused came forward slowly, made the customary obeisances to
the Tsar and the assembly, intoned a prayer – and waited. Alexis
waved him towards a bench upon his right. Nikon pretended not to
notice. Alexis repeated the gesture more emphatically. Still Nikon
did not move. At last he spoke, his low voice heavy with irony:

> I did not perceive your intention, pious Tsar. I see no suitable
> place for me to sit and I have omitted to bring a chair with me.
> The proper place for me here is already occupied.

Then he demanded to know why he had been summoned. Clearly
he intended to be as difficult as possible.

Alexis came down the steps of his dais to open the case against his
former favourite. As he stood face to face with Nikon he might well

177

have felt some trepidation, for although he had mastered the case (which Paisios Ligarides had helped him to prepare) and although the two Greek Patriarchs present knew very well what was expected of them, he also understood the weaknesses of his position, the strengths of his adversary, and feared that there might be some wavering among the judges.

> Most holy, ecumenical and orthodox Patriarchs [he began]: Judge between me and this man – this man who was once a true pastor to us . . . but who subsequently, and unaccountably, deserted his flock. . . . There has been no such scandal in the Church as the ex-Patriarch created since the very foundation of the state of Muscovy. Out of his own caprice, of his own will, without the permission of our Tsarish Majesty, without the approval of a synod, and without anyone hounding him, he quitted the ecumenical and apostolic Church and rejected the Patriarchate. [Furthermore] his withdrawal has caused many disturbances and rebellions; and the Church has been widowed and without a shepherd now for nine years.[1]

There were gratifying moans and shouts of outrage from the audience. Then the Greek Patriarchs began to question Nikon: why had he deserted his post? Nikon refused to answer. Instead he challenged the composition and the competence of the court. What evidence could be produced, he enquired, that the absent Patriarchs of Constantinople and Jerusalem had consented to those present sitting in judgement over him? How could the Metropolitans Pitirim of Novgorod and Paul of Krutitsk, who, he alleged, had once tried to have him poisoned, be properly allowed to take part in the proceedings? The objections were overruled and the trial proceeded, but in an atmosphere charged with tension and acrimony.

During the remainder of that session and in the two that followed every circumstance of Nikon's departure all those years ago, and of his behaviour since, became the subject of violent exchanges, accusations and reproaches. Much was made of a secret letter Nikon had written to the Patriarch of Constantinople, which Alexis's agents had intercepted and which it was said bore false witness against the Tsar. Selected passages from his letter were read out to the court. One contained a reference to Ivan the Terrible's 'unjust persecution' of the Metropolitan Philip – at which Alexis intervened to ask Nikon why he had written 'such words dishonouring and reviling Tsar Ivan' while failing to mention his own persecution of the Bishop of Kolomna and other churchmen in his charge. Another

passage in the letter prompted Alexis to denounce him for suggesting that the comet presaged disaster for Muscovy (even though he
himself had feared as much at the time). For his part, Nikon accused
Paisios of being a heretic and an impostor (Paisios's credentials
were indeed questionable: he had been educated in Rome and first
ordained there). So the trial continued, the two chief protagonists
constantly upon their feet; Nikon ignoring, or pouring scorn on,
the charges levelled against him, and scourging his enemies on the
'jury'; Alexis trying to deny Nikon the initiative, directing the
attacks, and trying all the while to rouse all those present against
the accused. He was the general in charge of the battle; he was the
huntsman whipping in the pack.

It was appropriate that he should play the leading role, for the
issue was not simply one of Nikon's guilt or innocence, but the
defence of state supremacy, and the maintenance of Alexis's own
autocratic power. Yet the case was not altogether an easy one, and
he was to receive little support in presenting it. Apart from Nikon's
chief enemies, Paul, Hilarion and Methodius, few of the clergy
present spoke out much. Nor did the boyars. At one point Alexis
turned to them angrily and asked why they were silent, why they
left everything to him – at which Yuri Dolgorukii rose and made a
rather limp speech vilifying the accused. And when Alexis called on
the Bishop of Chernigov, whose assistance against 'the violent and
unendurable Nikon' he had invited beforehand, the learned Bishop
only mumbled excuses.

Alexis did not care for the Bishop's scruples. He knew well
enough that the case against Nikon was in some respects vulnerable
(he could hardly have forgotten that he himself had once sworn to
obey the Patriarch). But he also knew that the higher good
demanded the sacrifice of certain truths. A verdict of 'guilty' was
essential if the disturbances and rebellions in the Church, which he
had referred to in his opening address, were to be quelled; it might
prove to be a useful purgative for popular discontent as well. Yet the
trial was also a personal contest between two old friends – and
friends, in a curious way, they remained.

At one point Alexis went up to the accused and, fingering the
beads which hung around his neck, spoke to him very softly. Word
had reached him, he whispered, that Nikon had prepared himself
for death before coming to his trial. How could he believe that
Alexis would even think, still less do, any such thing as having him
condemned to death? Did Nikon not believe that he was grateful for

his former services to him? Would Alexis ever forget that he had saved his family from the plague? In reply Nikon whispered that the Tsar would have no alternative but to inflict severe 'suffering and affliction' on him. He was right. Yet the confession of error which Alexis and indeed the rest of the court so much hoped for never came. The wranglings, the imprecations, the mutual charges of heresy continued to be piled up until, at the third session, on 5th December, the trial at last moved towards its climax.

Alexis invited his adversary to accept that the two Patriarchs who were present also represented the Patriarchs of Constantinople and Jerusalem. He showed him signed documents in support. Nikon, however, would not accept the point. He was not acquainted with the handwriting of these absent Patriarchs, he said (implying that they were forgeries). The Patriarch of Antioch hastened to assure him they were genuine – at which Nikon barked back: 'You are free to say that here; but how would you answer if the Patriarch of Constantinople were present?' There was uproar again. 'He does not fear God!' they cried. 'He dishonours the foreign Patriarchs!' 'He will twist any truth into a lie.' Then Antioch rose and read out a passage from the *Nomocanon*, the book of canon law. It put Alexis's case in a nutshell:

> Whosoever troubles the Emperor and disturbs his empire has no defence.

Nikon objected that the edition was heretical. It had been printed in Catholic Venice. But his objection was as useless as all the others he had raised.

So, at last, they found him guilty – guilty of abandoning the patriarchal throne without good cause; guilty of impeding the election of a successor; guilty of dishonouring both Tsar and Church with his accusations of heresy, of latinizing, of compromising with the Church of Rome; guilty, too, of dishonouring the Greek Patriarchs; guilty of 'murderous cruelty' to Bishop Paul of Kolomna and others; guilty of 'rapine, injustice and lawlessness' in his direction of the Church. The sentence was short and, as he himself had predicted, sharp (if not quite as sharp as he had at first expected):

> In accordance with the rules of the holy apostles and the holy fathers of the church thou art deposed and cut off. Thou art no longer to be called patriarch, or bishop. Henceforth thou shalt be but an ordinary monk.[2]

It remained to draw up the formal act of deposition in Greek and Russian, and to call Nikon back to hear it read. This ceremony took place in the chapel of the Miracle Monastery on 12th December. Alexis did not attend. Having read out the sentence of the court, they told Nikon that he must henceforth live submissively, praying for forgiveness (to which he retorted 'I don't need you to tell me how to live'), and divested him of his patriarchal and episcopal insignia – the cowl with the cross of pearls and his jewel-encrusted pectoral icon of the Virgin (at which he remarked that they were doubtless needy enough to share the pearls out between themselves). He was then driven off to overnight accommodation in another monastery. On the way there he tried several times to speak. Each time one of his custodians, the Archimandrite Sergei, yelled at him to be silent, reminding him, with obvious relish, that he was no longer Patriarch of Moscow, only the humblest of monks.

Alexis had got his way at last, but it was a joyless triumph. Early the following morning he sent Rodion Streshnev to Nikon with a gift of money and a generous supply of furs to keep him warm on the journey to the Ferapontov Monastery where he was to be confined. Nikon refused to accept the presents. He also refused to give Alexis the blessing he had asked for. Later that day crowds gathered by the Saviour Gate and along Sretenka Street, for it had been announced that Nikon would leave the Kremlin by that route. They were to be disappointed. The fallen Patriarch was rushed away under a strong escort in quite a different direction. The authorities wanted no public demonstration. No doubt Nikon was disappointed too, but his spirit and his sense of moral rectitude were not to be broken. As he had remarked loudly on the day he had been sentenced, 'Blessed are the persecuted.'[3]

For Alexis, however, Nikon's fall had removed only one obstacle in the way of his plans for restoring order to the Church. A new Patriarch would have to be appointed; the norms of State–Church relations and of the liturgy would have to be defined; Old Belief would have to be declared heretical, spiritual rebellion stamped out. Hence Christmas that year provided an emotionally exhausted Alexis with scant respite. Then, in mid-January, a messenger arriving hot-foot from Andrusovo gave him new heart. He brought news from Afanasy Ordyn-Nashchokin, Muscovy's chief negotiator at the peace talks. Agreement with the other enemy, Poland, had been reached at last – and on terms much more favourable than

Alexis had feared. There was to be a truce of thirteen and a half years rather than a 'permanent peace', and although claims to much territory over which blood had been shed in torrents had to be surrendered, Muscovy's possession not only of Smolensk and part of Belorussia, but of all Ukraine east of the river Dnieper, was confirmed. Religious tolerance was to be granted to Orthodox and Catholic minorities on both sides of the new frontier, and Zaporozh'e was to become a joint protectorate, the keystone of a joint defence against Islam. Furthermore, Afanasy had persuaded the Poles to lease the city of Kiev for a period of two years (which raised the prospect of somehow holding onto it for good); to allow Polish prisoners who chose to enter the Tsar's service to remain in Muscovy; and to enter into alliance against the Tatars.[4]

Alexis showered Afanasy with rewards, honours and new responsibilities. He granted him an income of 500 rubles a year and estates with 500 peasant households. He promoted him to the exalted rank of boyar, made him overlord of the Foreign Office (with a new title, 'Keeper of the Great Seal'), and commissioned him to draft a new set of laws designed to further Muscovy's prosperity – for the way was now open for the vigorous development of trade both at home and abroad. This left Alexis free to concentrate on masterminding the changes he wanted in the Church. To this end he persuaded the two Greek Patriarchs to stay on in Moscow and kept the synod in almost permanent session. One priority was the election of a new Patriarch of Moscow; but before this could be done there was another awkward problem to settle.

Two of the bishops Alexis had counted upon most during the interregnum (and who had been among the most outspoken in their hostility to Nikon at his trial), the Metropolitan Paul of Krutitsk, administrator of the patriarchate, and Archbishop Hilarion of Riazan, had refused to sign the final act deposing Nikon. They had developed doubts after all as to whether the Church should be subject to the State. They feared for the future, they said tactfully – feared that one day a Tsar less pious than Alexis might shatter the harmony that should exist between the spiritual and political authorities, and ride roughshod over the Church. In short, these enemies of Nikon now turned out to be Nikonites themselves – and they seemed to be influencing other Russian bishops. The synod spent several days debating the issue, during which time historical precedents, quotations from the Bible and from the Fathers of the Church were piled up high, one upon the other, interpreted and reinterpreted. But despite the theological tone this was essentially a political debate and everybody knew it. The part of the Tsar's champion was played by Paisios Ligarides, and a doughty warrior (by his own account) he proved to be. He persuaded the synod not only that the Tsar was supreme politically, but that he was endowed with spiritual as well as temporal authority; that he was above the law; and that, even though the Patriarch might be spiritually pre-eminent, the Tsar (provided he was not heretical) should always be obeyed for the good of the Church itself. It was a conclusion wholly in accordance with the Byzantine tradition for which Alexis cared so deeply. Paul and Hilarion made haste to excuse themselves.[5] On the following day the synod went through the motions of electing Nikon's successor.

Alexis had already chosen his man. He was the aged Archimandrite Ioasaf from Zagorsk. Ioasaf modestly protested that he lacked sufficient learning and administrative ability for the task, but on 10th February 1667 he was duly installed. Alexis at last had a mild, cooperative Patriarch to work with, and the task of clearing up the confusions which had accumulated in the Church over recent years could now proceed apace. It was to take several months, but by the end of June 1667 the synod had produced enough decisions to fill a bulky volume.

Some amounted to a puritanical attack on popular superstition (the old ban on mixed bathing in the nude was endorsed, and priests were enjoined to educate their flocks); others to a campaign to tighten discipline within the Church itself and particularly in the monasteries. Some were designed to improve the Church's organization and effectiveness throughout the country (for example, by the creation of new sees); some to define the limits of its powers. Thus, restrictions were placed on the Church acquiring and disposing of property, and the state's authority to judge clerics was extended (the jurisdiction of church courts in civil crimes would henceforth be confined to first offences; the state was empowered to punish schismatics and heretics, and runaway serfs who had become priests or monks were to be degraded and handed back to their former masters). But perhaps the most significant of all the measures were those which concerned religious practice itself.

The rituals of the Russian Church were brought into strict alignment with those of the Greek. The conclusions of Ivan the Terrible's church council, which had cursed practices now declared to be orthodox, were explicitly abrogated; the new church books were pronounced valid (they might be Nikon's work, but he had done it 'not on his own account but by order of our most pious sovereign'); those who stirred up 'weak souls' in opposition to them, who questioned the creed, the triple Hallelujah, the three-fingered cross, or the new spelling of the Saviour's name were to be condemned as schismatics. Conformity was made compulsory.[6]

At this the hopes of Old Believers, which had soared at the news of Nikon's condemnation, sank even lower than they had been before. The main canonical support for their objections to the horrendous new prayer book and the unspeakable new rituals had been cut away. Nikon might have fallen, but 'Nikonism' had triumphed. It was clear that, having crushed the radical 'papist' opposition, Alexis was determined to destroy the conservative opposition too.

Many of the Old Believers who had been persuaded, if not to conform to the new line, then not to oppose it publicly, had since reneged, and Avvakum, of course, had persisted in his obstinacy. Now, with the work of definition completed and confirmed, in June 1667 he and three other prominent dissidents, the archpriest Lazar, the deacon Fedor and Epifany the monk, were arraigned before the synod. Avvakum subsequently recalled what happened:

> I spoke of many things in the Holy Writ with the Patriarchs. God did open my sinful mouth and Christ put them to shame. The last word they spoke to me was this: 'Why', said they, 'art thou so stubborn? The folk of Palestine, Serbia, Albania, the Wallachians [Rumanians], they of Rome and Poland, all these do cross themselves with three fingers . . .' And I answered them for Christ thus: '. . . Rome fell away long ago . . . and the Poles fell in like ruin with her . . . and among you [Greeks] Orthodoxy is of mongrel breed. It is no wonder that, thanks to the violence of the Turkish Mohammed, you have become impotent. Henceforth it is you who should come to us to learn. . . . Till the time of Nikon the apostate . . . the Orthodox faith in Russia . . . was pure and undefiled, and there was no sedition in the church. Nikon the wolf, together with the devil, ordained that men should cross themselves with three fingers, but our first shepherds made the sign of the cross . . . with two fingers, according to the tradition of our Holy Fathers. . . .' And the patriarchs fell to thinking, and our people [the Russian members of the synod] began to howl like wolf cubs and belch out words against their fathers, saying 'Our Russian holy men were ignorant. . . . How can I trust them?' . . . and I was miserable and bitter in my heart, but could do nothing.

'I abused them as hard as I could,' he added,'but at last they told him
to be silent. Then he and his companions were solemnly denounced
as heretics, cursed, degraded and transferred to the jurisdiction of
the state.

Alexis, however, did not wish to create martyrs. He therefore
sent a series of personal emissaries to try and haul Avvakum back
from the brink. First Dementii Bashmakov (who had once headed
the Private Office) went to see him, then Yuri Lutokhin, and on 5th
July, three eminent archimandrites. Two days later Bashmakov
took him another message from Alexis begging him to conform –
not only for his own sake but for the sake of the Tsaritsa and the
children too. Avvakum was moved, but he would not submit.
Further attempts were made to persuade him: in August the three
archimandrites called on him again, and on the 22nd and the 24th
Artamon Matveev went, accompanied by Simeon Polotsky, now
one of Alexis's chief advisers on religious affairs. But these missions
failed too, and so on 26th August Alexis signed an order consigning
Avvakum and his companions to imprisonment in the Arctic
monastery of Pustozersk. Many months later, still unrepentant,
Lazar, Fedor and Epifany were to have their tongues cut out for
blasphemy and their right hands chopped off for making the sign of
the cross in the 'wrong' way. Avvakum was to be reprieved at the
last moment on Alexis's instructions, but even so he was to be
placed in solitary confinement under a strict regime, and punishments were to fall heavily upon his family and members of his
household.[7]

Meanwhile Alexis continued to shower Nikon with gifts, respectful messages and requests for blessings. It was not only a matter
of trying to maintain an old personal friendship despite the obstacles
public policy put in its way, but of assuaging his sense of guilt.
Alexis knew very well that Nikon's condemnation had been
obtained largely because of the stratagems of Paisios Ligarides and
that Paisios had resorted to lies and forgeries. He cannot but have
known, too, that Paisios had been trained in Rome and he may well
have suspected that he was an agent of the papacy.[8] Yet Paisios
could still be useful and he continued to enjoy the Tsar's protection.

Within days of signing the warrant for Avvakum's imprisonment, the bells of Moscow (the greatest in all the world, the sounds
of which gave Alexis delight) pealed out in celebration for the
declaration of his eldest son, the thirteen-year-old Tsarevich Alexis,
as heir apparent to the throne. It was a joyous public as well as

family occasion, made all the happier by the fact that the Church had only just been purged of the likes of Nikon and Avvakum. The formal ceremony, based on the old Roman precedent by which an Emperor would associate his heir with him in government in order to facilitate the peaceful transfer of power to his successor when he died, was carried out with great pomp in the Hall of Facets and was followed by a series of banquets. Henceforth the Tsarevich, hitherto secluded from the public eye, was to make regular appearances with his father, and that autumn, at a reception for a Polish embassy (and to his father's great pride), young Alexis was actually to give a speech in Polish and in Latin on the theme of union between the Slavonic peoples.[9] Nor did Alexis neglect the education of his other children. His daughters were supplied with teaching aids including sumptuously illustrated 'amusement books'; even his negro slave Savelii was taught to read and write, and learned the Psalter and the Book of Hours. But particular care had been lavished on the education of his eldest son. For the last three years his chief tutor had been the Belorussian scholar Simeon Polotskii and it was thanks to him that the Tsarevich, an apt and eager pupil, became so proficient in Latin and in Polish.[10] It was a reflection of Alexis's own advanced views and care for learning (he himself always regretted his lack of foreign languages). But it was also a measure of his political ambition.

When the apple of his eye made that famous address to the embassy in Polish and Latin, Alexis made a point of suggesting to the Polish ambassadors that, whatever his own qualifications, his son might make an acceptable King of Poland. But although the Greek Patriarchs in Moscow gave their blessing to the idea the Polish ambassadors (though they were flattering about the Tsarevich's accomplishments) evaded the issue, and when King Casimir abdicated and retired to France early in 1668 a native Pole, Michael Wiśniowiecki (who had a Habsburg wife), was elected to succeed him. Even so, Alexis (egged on in his ambition by Paisios Ligarides who was meanwhile ingratiating himself with his old friends in the *Propaganda Fide* in Rome by representing himself as working towards the return of the Muscovite Church to the Catholic fold) was not to abandon the idea of uniting the Polish and the Muscovite crowns.[11] And the idea accorded well with his continuing attempts to promote his standing and prestige abroad as one of Europe's greatest, most civilized and most accomplished monarchs.

This much was evident from the embassy he sent in 1667 to Spain and France. Its purposes were to canvass approval for the Romanov candidature for the throne of Poland, to encourage the development of mutual trade, but not least to let it be known that Alexis was blessed with qualities that merited universal admiration – that he was not only intelligent, handsome and good-natured but 'addicted to many learned philosophical sciences and to the study of arms. . . [and that] thanks to his . . . wisdom, valour and goodness of heart, he . . . [was] qualified to rule not only his own state [of Muscovy] but many other lands as well'.

While a concerted effort was made to achieve recognition for him abroad not merely as a 'most illustrious' but as a 'most serene highness' (Serenissimus),[12] at home Alexis was trying to create an environment that would accord with his new image of himself. In 1667 he ordered the Hall of Facets to be repainted 'with the very best murals, better than the old' under the direction of a brilliant and innovative Russian painter called Simon Ushakov. He had wanted the work completed in time for the Tsarevich Alexis's coming of age. This could not be done, however (it had to be explained to him that if the weather should turn cool too soon the paint would 'not be firm and permanent'), and so the work was delayed until the spring of 1668. Nevertheless 1667 saw other massive redecoration programmes carried out. The Tsarevich's apartments were refurbished in blue and yellow silk and velvet, a new dining hall was built for him, and a spate of new paintings were commissioned for Alexis himself. The topmost rooms in the Kremlin apartments were redecorated with floral motifs; the Dutch artist, Daniel Vuchters, began a whole series of large-scale works for the state apartments – 'The Capture of Jerusalem', 'The City of Jericho', and, continuing the theme of conquest, a number of scenes depicting the life and achievements of Alexander the Great, while Alexis's Armenian painter, Saltanov, began work on a canvas which reflected his autocratic views: Dionisios, Tyrant of Syracuse.[13] But the most ambitious of all his artistic undertakings was the construction of a new palace at Kolomenskoe.

Alexis had laid the foundation stone of his extraordinary project on 2nd May 1667 but he had conceived of the idea some time before, and foresters, working under the direction of Colonel Kravkov, had begun felling trees the previous autumn (in forests as far away as Briansk and Riazan). The structure was to be built largely of timber. Stone, presumably, would have made for too much damp. Besides, timber was cheaper; it involved no difficulties in obtaining a skilled labour force of sufficient size to work it, and it allowed construction to proceed at a much faster rate. Even so the scale was to be huge. The chief designers were both Muscovites – Ivan Mikhailov, a guardsman, and a master carpenter called Simon Petrov. Yet the real creator was Alexis himself. Kolomenskoe was to be an expression of his tastes, his mind, his sense of poetry.

At first glance the new palace was to give the impression of a Muscovite fairyland with its bulbous, shingled domes and its clusters of steep-pitched towers soaring up towards the skies. The metal pennants that turned together in the wind and the stockade-like construction of the outworks vaguely suggested a fantastic military encampment, and only the glinting double-headed eagle that seemed to hover in the air above the dome of the great dining hall reminded one that the Tsar of Muscovy, and not a fairy prince, sometimes resided there. Yet if the massing reflected Muscovite traditionalism, there were western features in the architecture too. The windows of the state apartments, with their broken pediments and decorations, were palpably Baroque; elsewhere there was some swirling gabling that might have been Dutch or Hanseatic; and approaching from some angles one would have been struck by a most elegant, Italianate *piano nobile*.

The palace was to contain well over two hundred rooms, some cramped, some immense, ranged in higgledy-piggledy manner round two quadrangles that were not square, with a wing sprawling out untidily towards the east; and the parts were connected by a glorious profusion of corridors and stairways. In short the plan seemed confused and labyrinthine. Yet the design was rational even if its logic did not reveal itself at once. The layout of the principal suites was to be much like those of palaces in the West (one would walk through a series of interconnecting rooms, each grander than the last); the whole was appropriate both for occasions of state and for leisured privacy and, besides, it was to be marvellously comfortable. The ceilings of the grander rooms were to be a lofty twenty feet above the floor; there were to be capacious bath-houses, an amplitude of closets, and a play-room for the children that was more than a hundred and twenty feet long. The Tsarevich Alexis, of course, was to have his own set of apartments with its own games room. There would be suitable accommodation for visiting dignitaries, ample space below stairs for an armoury and guard rooms, coach-houses and kitchens; and the gardens, tended by guardsmen too old for active service and supervised by the imperial horticulturalists Gregory Hood and Valentine David, were to provide a delightful setting for the whole grandiose architectural scheme.

It was to take three years and more before the Palace of Kolomenskoe could be considered finished in its every detail, with all its elaborate carving (carried out for the most part by Belorussian craftsmen) chiselled into shape, painted and gilded; and with all its other decorations, furniture and follies installed. But the structure itself was completed the same autumn. Between June and November Alexis went there several times to survey progress and during Christmas he was able to entertain the Prince of Georgia to dinner there.[14] If, of all his properties outside Moscow, the Izmailovo estate represented Alexis the progressive agriculturalist, and others his love of nature and the hunt, the Palace of Kolomenskoe represented the lover of exuberance and fantasy.

His exuberance, and his taste for merry-making, found expression more frequently now that the years of war and of incessant troubles seemed to be over. It was seen in the huge tree made out of sugar which was trundled out to astonish boyars attending a reception; in his staging a display of Samoyeds riding reindeer; in his slipping a dose of evil-smelling mercury into someone's glass at a feast and watching for the reaction; and in the rude spectacle he was to stage in the winter of 1668–9 which featured not only a fight between an old bear and a wolf, but a mass battle between wolves and hounds which was to leave many of the latter dead or maimed.[15] Such scenes of conflict between beasts afforded him amusement; they also seem to have helped him in assessing and manipulating men and hence in plotting strategies.

His recent promotion of Afanasy Ordyn-Nashchokin was the culmination of one such strategy, the aim of which was to establish personal control of the entire state apparatus. Hence the growth of the Private Office and its ramifications; hence also the gradual emasculation of the Council, which until now had played a significant role in foreign affairs. But Afanasy was not only made overlord of foreign relations; he was given control of the Ukrainian Office and three other departments too. No one could remember anyone of such humble, albeit gentle, origins, rising so high without a close connection to the Tsar through marriage. This, together with his promotion to boyar rank, showed decisively that Alexis favoured the combination of ability, industry and absolute loyalty and obedience to himself above heredity and tradition.

There was little overt resistance – but resentment did flash out in

October 1667 when an aristocratic career diplomatist, Matvei Pushkin, was designated marshal to the Polish embassy visiting Moscow. He at once protested at the humiliation of being allotted a function so inferior to that of Afanasy, and refused to carry it out. By way of explanation he pointed to 'Afanasy's ancestry', and asserted that the great offices he now held had hitherto always been the preserve of 'honourable men and not those of Afanasy's sort'. Afanasy duly protested at the 'dishonour' Pushkin had done him, and the verdict was delivered by the faithful Bashmakov (who was now a Councillor himself). Ancestral precedents in such cases, he stated, 'had not counted, do not count now, and will not count in the future'. Pushkin must apologize, and carry out his duties. When he refused he was arrested and warned that if he persisted his estates would be confiscated. He retorted proudly that he would rather die first, but this availed him nothing, and he did not die.

In fact Afanasy's rise was no more than the most brilliant of many. Councillors stemming from the gentry now presided over five departments, including two of the important financial ones. Moreover, five commoners (an unheard-of number) now held Councillor rank, and three of them held substantial ministerial appointments. In short, high office was no longer the preserve of the aristocracy as it had been twenty years before. Great clans like the noble Sheremetevs and Cherkasskiis, the Repnins, Saltykovs and Sheins, seemed to have lost their political clout. No doubt the huge extension of the Council (to about four times the size it had been in the earlier years of Alexis's father's reign) had helped to disguise the process; and the disgrace accruing to old aristocrats like Sheremetev from military defeats had made their exclusion from high office easier. Even so a few aristocrats still figured prominently in the government. When the impotent Il'ia Miloslavskii died in May 1668, having been paralysed by a stroke for months, the Great Treasury, the Cavalry Department and the Foreigners Office were all transferred to Boyar Prince Nikita Odoevskii. A Dolgorukii, a Romodanovskii and a Khovanskii were all scions of princely stock who held both boyar rank and a ministerial portfolio. So did Prince Khilkov who, as Armourer, supervised the artistic side of court life. But it seemed clear that Alexis judged it more convenient on the whole to employ aristocrats as military commanders, provincial governors, ambassadors and court functionaries, rather than in key positions in Moscow. There was no doubt that in social terms power in Muscovy had been redistributed.[16]

But though Alexis had hoisted his own men up the ladders of advancement he had to protect them – and not only from aristocrats like Pushkin, but in some cases from their ministerial colleagues and bureaucratic subordinates. Afanasy in particular needed his support. He was too conscientious, too much of a stickler for most of those with whom he had to deal. He was soon embroiled – perhaps too embroiled – in struggles over the routing of departmental business, and matters were not helped by his absence in Courland for many months from May 1668 conducting diplomatic business. His memoranda of complaint to Alexis show him to have been high-minded in his approach to business, and intolerant of those who mixed public affairs with private dealings or whose actions fudged clear-cut decisions. They also show that his views accorded ill with those who displayed the ingrained Muscovite habits of doing favours and taking bribes.[17] Afanasy, as Alexis well knew, was incorruptible and a zealous upholder of the integrity and honour of the state's affairs, as well as being ingenious and clever. On the other hand, there were times when he seemed to seek unnecessary confrontations and to make mountains out of molehills. The price to pay for Afanasy's brilliance was his excess of temperament. Yet Alexis defended him consistently, for he relied on Afanasy not only to serve as his 'eye' abroad and to restructure Muscovy's foreign policy to meet the new situation, but to exploit the peace economically.

A major step towards economic recovery had already been taken with the promulgation in the spring of 1667 of the Trade Statute which Afanasy had masterminded. The principles upon which it was based were set out clearly in the preamble: that the encouragement of trade was one of the most important concerns of government, since it increased taxation income and raised the general level of the country's prosperity. It must therefore be protected – both from foreign competition and from venal and obstructive officialdom. To this end, foreign merchants were forbidden to deal anywhere except at ports and frontier towns unless they paid swingeing additional taxes; nor were they to deal between themselves without paying duty; and they were to be excluded from the retail sector altogether. This gave Russian merchants some elbow-room; and they were given still more by the abolition of internal duties on goods in transit and by a ban placed on local officials, including provincial governors, from hindering or detaining them when they passed through their territory. Henceforth protection for the Russian man of enterprise was to come from the centre.

In order to promote a faster commercial tempo, taxation rates on all but luxury goods were reduced; attempts were made to encourage the saving ethic by barring the lower orders from buying 'useless' luxuries (such as expensive cloth), and ordering their confiscation in default, to prevent them 'falling into poverty'; and steps were taken to foster the creation of Russian merchant companies by making credit facilities more easily available and encouraging collectives of urban dwellers to form banks. A major aim of the new economic strategy, then, was to facilitate the formation of venture capital and induce the birth of a healthy, indigenous 'bourgeoisie'. But at the same time the economy of the state itself had to be protected. To this end foreign merchants were subjected to much more stringent customs controls, and the increased import duties were henceforth to be collected in gold or hard currency at artificially fixed rates of exchange. Exports of precious metal were banned and imported goods were to be marked for quality and those found to be below standard banned from sale.[18]

The Trade Statute was not to overcome Muscovy's chronic economic backwardness; nor was it to enable her merchants to compete effectively with the English, Dutch or Germans. To judge from the experience of the rest of eastern Europe probably nothing could have been done to achieve these things – not even the wholesale immigration of enterprising people like the Jews. But it diagnosed at least some of the major problems correctly, and set precedents which future generations were to draw on.

Yet until such time as private initiative generated the yearned-for prosperity (and it was a very tender plant) the state had to secure some income of its own from trade. This consideration prompted Alexis within a month of issuing the Trade Statute to break its spirit, if not its letter, by concluding a five-year deal with an Armenian company based in Persia, allowing it to bring silk through Russia for sale in the West in return for a fat commission (estimated to produce a total of about a quarter of a million rubles for the crown). Alexis, of course, had long been active in the Persian trade,[19] and he put a high priority on protecting and extending it. Hence the arrangements he also put in hand in the late spring of 1667 for the construction of a naval flotilla to operate in the Caspian Sea.

This was another of his half-practical, half-romantic visions. The ships would be invaluable, of course, in protecting the Persian route (there had recently been losses due to piracy); but the project was also inspired by a belief that it might be possible to find a navigable route from the Caspian to southern Asia and the East Indies. The idea was not ridiculous. Pliny, Strabo and most other ancient authorities described the Caspian as a gulf of a much larger ocean, and though the Holstein ambassador, who had sailed across it some few decades before, declared it to be landlocked, learned doctors of Leipzig University had since produced a scholarly refutation of this view.[20] Having decided to build a flotilla, Alexis determined that it should be built on western lines. His old dream of a seagoing fleet operating from the Baltic was to be fulfilled in the south – and with a great burst of Russian energy. Thirty carpenters experienced in building boats, blacksmiths capable of forging chains and anchors, and in due course barge-loads of sailcloth, ropes and armaments were sent downstream from Moscow to Deznovo, upriver from Kazan. There the work was started under the direction of Colonel van Boeckhoven and with the help of half a dozen Dutch experts led by a sailing master, Lambert Helt.

There were to be four vessels: two sloops, a yacht, and a handsome, three-masted man-of-war, eighty feet long, twenty-one in the beam, which was to carry an armament of twelve guns as well as a contingent of soldiers. This was to be the flagship. It would bear the imperial arms and standard – and the proud name of *The Eagle*. By the autumn of 1668 the ships were all but ready and another contingent of Dutchmen were on their way to Muscovy to help sail them once they were commissioned. They included experienced mates, a boatswain, ships' carpenters, sailmakers (one of whom, Jan Struys, was to write a graphic account of his adventures in Russia), a master gunner and a ship's surgeon. Their leader was David Butler who had been engaged at a salary of twenty rubles (or a hundred guilders) a month. He was to be *The Eagle*'s captain, and very well qualified for the enterprise he was – for besides knowing how to sail a ship and navigate by the stars he had been to the Indies and knew many of the local languages.[21]

It was at this late stage that Andrei Vinnius, a registered Moscow merchant and a Dutch translator at the Foreign Office, presented a memorandum recommending the building of a galley fleet for the Caspian, which, he claimed, would prove very useful if a route to India were found. Sailing ships, he argued, were less useful than galleys on the Caspian, which was not as deep, nor as stormy, as other oceans. Besides, ships could encounter contrary winds against which they could not sail and days when they would be becalmed, whereas if an appropriate wind blew up a galley could hoist sail and run as fast as any ship. A ship, moreover, could not sail upriver, nor manoeuvre as easily as a galley could if it encountered pirates; and galleys could be crewed by prisoners, which would make the fleet much cheaper to run.[22] This belated wisdom (if wisdom it was) must have been unwelcome. Much less welcome still, however, was the succession of reverses which drew Alexis's attention away from the work of reconstruction, from his little navy, from his new palace, from the new glass factory he planned, and from a dozen other fascinating and delightful projects.

The period of tranquillity ushered in by Andrusovo and the conclusion of the great synod was to prove all too brief. Fires and rebellions soon darkened the horizon. Within days of the promulgation of the Trade Statute a fire had ravaged Archangel, consuming a large proportion of the goods in store there. During the following winter Alexis gave attention to the problem of countering the chronic fire problem in Moscow itself, and drew up a plan by which the city's bells would ring out alarms in different ways to indicate the precise part of the city in which the outbreak had occurred. Nonetheless on 22nd August 1668 another conflagration erupted on the south side of the river which burned until dawn. Hours later the Kitaigorod and then the Belgorod districts went up in flames causing considerable damage and loss of life. This prompted Alexis to send another order to Elizarov, head of the Land Office, which was responsible for administering Moscow. It concerned salvage operations and the maintenance of street-lines, and called for the guards to provide fire-watch pickets in every sector of the city to provide an immediate response to any future outbreak. The public's response, however, tended to be much less rational. Rumours began to spread that the unusual number of fires since Nikon's deposition must be due to his summoning up lightning in revenge. Indeed, it was soon reported in Warsaw and in Rome that the fires had caused such an outcry against the Tsar that Alexis had sent men to fetch Nikon back to Moscow.[23]

Nikon himself began to entertain hopes that he might be asked to return, no doubt encouraged by the presents Alexis continued to send him – not only food, but a fine copy of the Gospels, silver dishes and chasubles – and his requests for blessing. Nikon replied (still signing himself Patriarch) that he would only give it face to face, but meanwhile he did begin to attend feasts in the refectory and to enjoy some of the food which Alexis had sent – while claiming to do so only in imitation of Christ's humility, saying 'Bless those who curse you and do good to those that despitefully use you'. The expected call to return was never to come, however, and in due course Nikon began to take a more active part in the monastery's life. He raised a cross by the little lake in the grounds which bore the inscription: 'Nikon, by the grace of God Patriarch, set up this cross of the Lord, being imprisoned . . . in the Ferapontov Monastery for God's word and for the Holy Church.' And he had the same device inscribed on all his plate.[24] Nikon was promoting a cult of himself as a martyr. But it was not to gain much immediate popularity nor prove as dangerous as the rebellion against the church reforms which now burst out into the open.

It was heralded by a long petition from the Solovka Monastery which reached Alexis's desk in the autumn of 1667. This contained a long critique of the new church books (a burden, they claimed, too heavy for human strength to bear) and a reminder that their faith, the old faith, was also the faith of the Tsar's own forefathers. The changes which had been ordained, it continued, had been inspired by Greeks who did not even know how to cross themselves properly, and they were causing confusion among the people. The petition implored Alexis to protect them from the new teachers and the foreign patriarchs who were trying to deprive them of their 'true Christian faith'. But their plea was also a threat. They were afraid 'lest we anger our Lord Jesus Christ'; they would rather die than 'be condemned to torments everlasting'. They were to honour that promise. Within a year they had expelled their conformist Archimandrite and were defending themselves with guns against the troops sent by Alexis to subdue them. Nor was this an isolated instance of rebellion. As the dissident Lazar warned Alexis, 'Do not think that we are few. There are a hundred thousand men in Russia ready to die for the faith of their fathers.'

He did not exaggerate. What Alexis had long feared and striven to avoid had at last come about. Spiritual rebellion was turning into armed rebellion and on a country-wide scale. Preaching monks from Solovka were encouraging people to resist the state – and not only in the distant north. There were connections between the Solovka rebels and the Don Cossacks in the far south; there were alarming cases of sedition in the west – in May 1668, for example, a monastery official and an artilleryman were arraigned in Pskov for calling the Tsar and his new Patriarch 'villains . . . [who] believe in Antichrist' (the artilleryman, who recanted, was imprisoned; the monk was burned to death); and troops had to be sent to deal with aggressive dissenters who had formed communities in the forests and marshes of the central provinces as well.[25]

These circumstances put paid to any chance there may have been of Alexis countenancing a reconciliation between the churches of Russia and Rome for the sake of adding Poland to his dominions.[26] And with conformity already having to be procured to an increasing extent by force of arms, a fresh and considerable demand was suddenly placed upon his army. Trouble had long been expected from the Don Cossacks. Elements from their ranks had been responsible for piratical activities on the lower Volga the year before (which required the dispatch of reinforcements to the local garrisons). Furthermore, there was reason to suspect that the Don Cossacks were in touch not only with Solovka but with Nikon too. But the military crisis of 1668 was precipitated by events not on the Don but in Ukraine.

On 16th February news arrived that Hetman Ivan Briukhovetsky had broken his oath of loyalty. His Cossacks had attacked the local Muscovite garrisons and the Tatars were streaming into the area and cooperating with him and with Cossacks from western Ukraine under their leader Doroshenko. In a matter of days the garrison at Hadiach was overwhelmed and the commanders of several other towns had been slaughtered or carried off into captivity by the Tatars. The news was received with consternation in the Kremlin. It was subsequently rumoured abroad that Alexis fell ill of a depression for over a week. But, ill or not, the Private Office papers show that he took personal charge of the campaign that ensued.[27]

He planned a two-pronged approach to regain the lost ground and to relieve those garrisons still holding out in Ukraine. The first force, under Yuri Dolgorukii (who was to be replaced a few weeks later by G. S. Kurakin), was to approach directly from the north; the second, under G. G. Romodanovskii, would sweep round into Ukraine from the east (guarding against any possibility of the rebellious Ukrainians being joined by the Don Cossacks). The two armies, which had a combined strength of about 60,000 men, would come to form a pincer, which would ultimately close in the vicinity of the beleaguered garrisons in Nezhin and Chernigov, and then make Kiev secure. It was to take three months and more before these forces were to make contact with the enemy – by which time Briukhovetsky had been lynched by his own people, and his rival Doroshenko had been proclaimed Hetman of all Ukraine. This complicated the task, but despite the distance (which made for an interval of several days between the sending of an order and its execution), Alexis retained personal charge of operations.

By the middle of June both forces had engaged the enemy. At first things went well. Reports came in of a hard-fought but inconclusive battle between Romodanovskii's corps and Doroshenko's Ukrainians and over 20,000 Tatars; and of Kurakin repelling an attack and taking over eighty Tatars prisoner. Alexis responded by sending both commanders messages of encouragement and pay for their troops. Then, on 19th July, he instructed them both to proceed at once to the relief of Nezhin and thus complete the pincer movement. But Kurakin stopped on the way to besiege Glukhov and then retired to Putivl where Romodanovskii joined him. Alexis was not pleased and Kurakin soon received another of those famous blasts that indicated the Tsar's displeasure: Why had he not marched to the relief of Nezhin and Chernigov as he had been ordered? Had he no pity for the garrisons at the end of their tether there? How would he answer for it on the Day of Judgement? Why had he forgotten the Saviour and the miraculous powers that he could wield? Why had he allowed himself to be swayed by others ('rogues and small-minded chatterers who think first of themselves and only afterwards about what is right')? Why had he stayed so long at Glukhov? 'It would have been better to have stormed Glukhov and shed much blood than that the suffering unfortunates at Nezhin and Chernigov . . . should be abandoned to no good purpose'. As it was, Kurakin had angered God and the Tsar by shedding blood for nothing. He had lowered the morale of his troops, merited the Tsar's anger, and earned himself shame and ignominy in the eyes of his fellow men.

In the event Kurakin fell ill and the advance continued under Romodanovskii's command. Doroshenko withdrew, leaving his lieutenant Demian Mnohohreshny in charge, but given the return of Muscovite troops in strength, the mood in eastern Ukraine changed again, and Mnohohreshny came to terms with (and was subsequently installed as Hetman by) Moscow.[28] Alexis barely had time to congratulate himself, however, before he was overtaken by a series of personal calamities.

On 26th February 1669 the Tsaritsa Maria gave birth to her thirteenth child, another girl. The baby survived no more than forty-eight hours. Four days after that Maria herself died. A stunned Alexis followed the coffin to the grave. The funeral was an occasion for solemn grandeur. The coffin was borne up by eight young noblemen and canopied with a cloth of gold; the two older Tsareviches, Alexis and Fedor, both clothed in black, figured prominently in the cortège and they were followed by ministers, court pensioners, foreign envoys and crowds of dignitaries and representatives of various classes. The grief erupted afterwards. Maria had been his partner, his support and consolation for the past twenty-one years, and Alexis was reported to be ill and swollen up with tears for many days. His children gave him some comfort, of course, but in June another of them died, the four-year-old Tsarevich Simeon. The heavens seemed to weep in sympathy, for there were tremendous rain and hail storms that summer. Crops were flattened, bridges and animals swept away in the resultant floods. The harvest that year was dangerously thin and special payments had to be made to some of Alexis's own peasants, who had lost their crops, to keep them alive over the winter.[29]

A malevolent fortune had dealt Alexis several blows in quick succession and he did not recover from them quickly. Yet those around him urged him to set about choosing a second wife, and in November 1669 the traditional review of possible candidates got under way. On 21st November and on 7th and 11th December Alexis looked over groups of girls, each of them wearing a silk dress. He rejected all of them – albeit politely, for several of them were the daughters of his guard commanders. The review continued into the new year, four or five candidates being presented at a time.[30] But he seemed to have little taste for any of them. And then, in January 1670, the Tsarevich Alexis, the apple of his eye, was suddenly taken very seriously ill, and with an ailment that left the palace doctors entirely at a loss.

In desperation, and afraid it must be due to witchcraft, Alexis apparently sought the remedy in witchcraft too. In any event an under-secretary was rushed off to a remote village two-thirds of the way to Archangel and told to report to Dementii Bashmakov immediately on his return. The man had been instructed to seek out the daughter of an old sorceress called Ulita Shchipakova, who had died, and to search her house 'for roots, herbs, stones and written spells which she used to help guard sick people from bewitchments . . . and question her to find out what ailments each of them is good for . . . and whether she had taught her skills to anyone else . . .'.[31]

But if the mission succeeded the help came too late. The Tsarevich Alexis died on 17th January. It was said that there was great sobbing and wailing at the funeral, but that the Tsar himself showed barely a flicker of emotion. Onlookers attributed this to his strength of character and bravery of soul.[32] Perhaps he had simply become inured to sorrow.

The death of the Tsarevich Alexis cast a shadow over the future of the dynasty again. Two younger sons still survived, but Fedor, though he was an intelligent boy, was anything but robust, and the four-year-old Ivan seemed to be mentally retarded. This made another marriage and the siring of more sons all the more urgent. So the review of potential brides was soon resumed – and, suddenly, one girl did succeed in attracting the Tsar's fancy. She was a lively, dark-haired girl of eighteen called Natalia Naryshkina. She was the daughter of an officer in one of the new-formation cavalry regiments and related to Fedor Naryshkin, Lieutenant-Colonel in Artamon Matveev's regiment of guards.[33] Indeed, Natalia was the ward of Artamon Matveev. Furthermore, Artamon had persuaded the Tsar to make several secret visits to his house recently. (It eased his spirit to escape from the palace for a few hours and relax informally with his old friend.) It seems highly probable, then, that Artamon was the matchmaker; but the proprieties had to be observed. Hence, in February 1670, Natalia, the sight and sound of whom lightened Alexis's gloom and added sweetness to a life turned sour, was called to the palace along with two other girls – to be examined by the master of the household, Bogdan Khitrovo, and by one of the palace physicians. In due course she was called back a second time. She was not the only one, but despite the care taken to ensure that the proper formalities in the choice of a bride for the Tsar were followed, the selection (which seems to have been pre-arranged) did not pass off without a challenge.

On 22nd April Bogdan Khitrovo brought Alexis two sealed letters which had been found about the palace. They concerned another candidate (a girl called Beliaeva), and contained allegations that Artamon had used sorcery in order to gain undue influence over the Tsar. The letters were, of course, anonymous. The same day Dr Stefan von Haden, one of Alexis's physicians who was involved in the review, reported that he had just been approached in the street by one Ivan Shikhirev, the uncle of one of the bridal candidates. Bogdan had rejected the girl, he said, because her arms were too scraggy. This was not true, he claimed, and he asked von Haden (who claimed not to know the girl) to intercede on her behalf. Shikhirev was immediately arrested and interrogated. At the

same time a thoroughgoing enquiry was launched into the author-
ship of the anonymous denunciations. Alexis directed it personally.
Extracts from each of the letters were copied out and circulated to
every bureaucrat in Moscow in an attempt to identify the handwriting. Hundreds of samples were collected and compared with
the originals, and Alexis himself doodled one of the extracts over
and over again in a notebook. It read: 'Save me, O Lord, from the
sly one; save me from the iniquitous man.'[34]

He was deeply troubled by the whole affair. The attempt to
suborn his doctor and the anonymous denunciations were obviously
connected in something more than the coincidence of their timing;
they were directed at his chosen bride, and against the dearest and
most faithful of his friends. The charges were abominable. They
sought to undermine his trust; they challenged his judgement. He
would not believe these canards. But although Natalia was duly
declared to be his prospective bride that April, the wedding was
postponed to the following January – perhaps to allow a full year of
mourning for the Tsarevich; perhaps because of a great storm of
rebellion which was blowing up in the south-east of the country, a
rebellion led by the Don Cossack Sten'ka Razin.

Razin had long been a thorn in Alexis's side. He had been responsible for the pirate actions on the river Volga three years before; he
had subsequently taken over the fortress of Iaitsk and in 1668 had set
out from there on a huge plundering expedition of Persian towns on
the Caspian, which endangered good relations with the Shah on
which Alexis depended for the realization of his great plans for trade
development. In 1669 Razin had arrived in Astrakhan, volunteering
his loyalty, and had been pardoned, since when he had returned to
the Don. But he still had an armed gang of ruffians about him –
Cossacks, fugitive peasants, the flotsam of society – and that winter
his gang grew into an army. In the spring of 1670 Razin led it out
along the main road of rebellion.

He soon captured the important Volga town of Tsaritsyn (later
Stalingrad); he defeated a small force of guardsmen sent downstream against him; and, another, larger, force sent up from Astrakhan simply deserted to his side. In June Astrakhan itself fell into his
hands, betrayed by elements of its garrison (which included servicemen sent there under a cloud for their behaviour in the copper riots
years before). And in July 1670 Razin turned back up the Volga with
a very formidable army behind him and headed towards Moscow. Before he left, he set fire to *The Eagle*, flagship of Alexis's

nascent fleet. Like so many revolutionaries, he hated novelties.

The Razin rebellion, although avowedly aimed against the Tsar's advisers rather than against Alexis himself, was more dangerous than any of the many previous challenges to his rule, and it exploited every stream of discontent. It attracted peasants yearning to be free of serfdom and townsmen resentful of taxation and the price of liquor; it appealed to those who hated, or were confused by, the new order in the Church, to Nikonites and Old Believers, and to all those who saw familiar ways of life threatened by innovation (whether soldiers subjected to the cruel discipline of foreign officers, or civilians who sensed the oppressive net of central government tightening around them). And Razin also touched the pagan hearts hidden under so many Russian skins. As the rebels pressed on up the Volga towards Simbirsk the flames of rebellion were lit in all the eastern and south-eastern provinces; and even in Moscow men were overheard whispering approvingly of Sten'ka Razin.

Alexis despised the rebels. This *canaille* embodied all those forces of confusion against which he had struggled all his life. They rejected rank and hierarchy; they spurned their duty towards God and their sovereign; they tortured and murdered his loyal officers and agents; they looted; they destroyed things beautiful and useful; they turned everything upside-down. Sten'ka himself was a pagan. He observed none of the religious fasts; he did not go to church, and, worse, he took part in 'sacrilegious and satanic rites'.[35] Yet he had the effrontery to pass off one of his cronies as the Patriarch of Moscow, and the cruelty to dress up another in finery and declare him to be his poor dead son, the late Tsarevich.

Alexis showed no outward sign of fear; but he took no chances. He ordered all who deserted Razin and came over to his side to be rewarded with money and presents of red caps and boots;[36] he ordered local levies to be raised to fight the rebels and by August he had mustered a strong force to send against them. It was commanded by Boyar Prince Yuri Dolgorukii and well equipped with spiritual as well as military armaments – a cross from the Miracle Monastery, service books, and twenty-seven pounds of incense. The force left Moscow, their forty-eight rose-red banners flying, at the end of the month.[37] Within a few weeks the core of the rebel army had been broken at Simbirsk and Razin had become a fugitive.

It took longer to dowse all the embers of rebellion. In the weeks that followed, Dolgorukii, based on the town of Arzamus, dispensed justice to the captured rebels. Some were impaled alive; many were beheaded, and giant gallows drooped as if in hideous submission, each borne down by the weight of forty or fifty hanging men. The day of judgement had not yet come for all the insurgents, however; Razin was still at liberty; Astrakhan still held out in rebel hands; and Alexis himself continued to feel somehow vulnerable. At the end of October he was at Semenovskoe reviewing army units. At dawn on the 29th he wrote to his sister Tatiana and the rest of his family, apologizing for his unusually long absence. So many troops could not be inspected so quickly, he explained, but he hoped to return that evening 'God willing and if we are still alive'.[38]

However, by the end of 1670 the state of Muscovy was once again secure. Alexis had survived the greatest of his trials, and by January 1671 snow-covered Moscow was bustling with excitement over the forthcoming marriage of their relieved but care-worn Tsar to his bright, youthful Natalia.

Chapter IX

Renaissance

The wedding took place on 22nd January 1671, but the celebrations were muted and by no means everyone present wished the bride well. Indeed Alexis's own daughters could scarcely mask their dislike of her. Evdokia, after all, was actually older than her step-mother, Martha was of an age with her, and all of them were a good deal uglier. Not unnaturally they regarded Natalia as an intruder on their father's affections, but family fortunes were also at stake. The Naryshkins might be expected to be showered with honours and preferments; the Miloslavskiis to be overshadowed and sink in fortune. On these accounts they resented her – and the thirteen-year-old Sophia, who was more intelligent than the others, resented her most of all.

Sensitive to their feelings, Alexis tried to soften the blow. The circular he issued ordering special prayers to be said for himself and his bride stressed that the marriage was one of duty rather than of love; Artamon Matveev who had brought the couple together was given only a minor role in the ceremony (Nikita Odoevskii was best man), and no Naryshkin was promoted at the investiture which followed the wedding, although a Miloslavskii was raised to boyar rank that day.[1] And Alexis went out of his way to demonstrate that he loved his daughters especially no less than before. Yet there was no disguising the fact that he doted on his new wife, this girl of less than half his age.

Natalia helped him rediscover his joy in life. Whenever possible he dined alone with her (often retiring with her afterwards for his customary afternoon nap). He took an almost avuncular delight in introducing her to all the grand, pleasurable and interesting pursuits that he himself enjoyed. He took her hawking; he strolled with her through the delightful and exotic gardens he had made; he showed her his zoo at Izmailovo with its lions and tigers, its polar bears and porcupines and those curious creatures called moose that had been brought from North America. He enjoyed indulging her; and when, that autumn, it became clear that she was pregnant, he indulged her even more. Having discovered that she found dwarfs amusing, he obtained no fewer than fourteen for her, and he soon added another eight to her collection.[2]

Natalia brought lightness and brightness into his life – much as its many windows brought sunlight streaming into the new palace at Kolomenskoe. They stayed there several times that year, and Alexis began to use it for formal audiences too. He had received a Polish embassy there within a month of the wedding, expecting them to be astonished by it. Its roofs glistened with gold; its lavish carvings, freshly painted, were alive with colour, and the main apartments, at least, were sumptuously fitted out. There were splendid hangings, exquisite furniture, pictures representing nature in all its moods, others of classical heroes, while one vast expanse of ceiling was painted to resemble the vault of heaven with all the signs of the zodiac. But in the throne room was a wonder to surpass all the other wonders, a wonder inspired by such extraordinary devices as had amazed the Western Emperor's envoy, Bishop Liutprand of Cremona, when he had been ushered into the presence of the Byzantine Emperor Constantine VII more than seven centuries before – for Alexis's throne was flanked by two fierce-looking lions (made of copper and sheepskins) which, at the touch of hidden levers, rolled their eyes and roared.

As Simeon Polotskii expressed it in a poem he composed to celebrate its completion:

In one word this palace is perfection,
A great construction worthy of the Tsar;
Magnificent, like the Tsar's own honour,
There is none better, except in heaven.
The ancient world had but seven wonders;
Our own age has an eighth – this splendid house![3]

Yet Kolomenskoe was only one expression of the ideas which had been gusting through Alexis's mind of late. Some of them were drawn from conversations with learned men; some from reading – for Alexis had never lost his thirst for knowledge and despite his deteriorating eyesight (he now wore spectacles) he still devoured books. Since his library was subsequently destroyed in a fire it is not possible to establish precisely what he read, but it is clear from what is known about the books of those who were closest to him, of the libraries of the Foreign Office and the Apothecary Department (on which we know he drew), and of the materials in his private archive, that he was familiar with many classical works, especially history; and that (as a foreign visitor of the time remarked) he 'had gained a basic understanding' of natural as well as of political science.[4] Such alien learning was anathema to traditionalists like Avvakum, who dismissed Plato, Pythagoras, Aristotle, Hippocrates and Galen as 'pigs feeding off their own excrement'.[5] But this was a view to which Alexis could not subscribe. He was far too curious a man, and there is reason to suppose that his curiosity may have led him to flirt with 'the higher learning' of arcane science, with hermetic philosophy, the supposedly 'original wisdom' of the ancient Egyptians.

Both fashion and ambition might have been expected to incline him in this direction. Occult science was still regarded as respectable in the Habsburg Empire at that time;[6] and hermetic wisdom promised, ultimately, to offer the initiate the means to become 'Ter Maximus', the most powerful as well as the wisest of all princes. It was a philosophy that accorded well with his belief in a holistic universal order, and one which was not necessarily inconsistent with religious faith. Moreover its terms of discourse would have been familiar to him. He understood all too well the contrast between divine harmony and earthly disharmony; he understood the concept of perpetual motion from his interests in mechanics and hydraulics, and from observing the water-wheels that he had installed on his estates; and there is reason to suppose that he was familiar with the notion of a universal cure if not of a universal language. In all, then, Alexis's interests might well have rendered him vulnerable to the promises of hermeticism, the philosophy of the elite and the elect, a science which promised to relate all his interests from astronomy to alchemy and from music to ballistics, and to produce a comprehensive and all-illuminating explanation of the world.

A predisposition does not imply actual acquaintance, still less involvement, of course, but we do know that some of Alexis's closest associates had some knowledge of hermetic lore. Simeon Polotskii, for example, owned copies of such important hermetic works as John Dee's *Monas Hieroglyphica* and Caussin's *Symbolica Aegiptiana Sapientia*; and Paisios Ligarides (who, though now distanced from the Tsar, had spent much time in his company in recent years) also dabbled in the occult. He had survived a charge of 'vain astrological calculations' five years before, and in a letter he had written to a Catholic associate abroad in 1668 he had not only referred to 'the prophetic sphinx', but mentioned the Egyptian priest himself – '[Hermes] Trismegistus Mercurius'.[7] Furthermore, one piece of direct evidence survives which links Alexis to 'the ancient wisdom of the Egyptians': secreted among his private papers was a picture of an Egyptian obelisk complete with hiero-glyphs[8] – hieroglyphs which, once deciphered (or so many scholars of the time believed), might provide the missing key to the uni-versal mystery.

Yet, though intrigued by the occult, Alexis never became wholly absorbed by it. He was too much of a pragmatist, too much involved with the immediate, and with a host of practical schemes. He was currently mounting yet another campaign to find and exploit deposits of precious metals; attempting to step up arms production;[9] and he had many commercial schemes on hand both abroad and at home. He invested the vast sum of 23,000 rubles on five thousand mirrors, over two million needles, pins and brooches, and quantities of Russian leather and iron for expert to Persia – and hoped thereby to double his investment. Among the complex commercial deals he set in train at home in August 1671 was one involving a thousand tons of salt to be sold at Nizhnii Novgorod as prices rose. The proceeds were to be used to purchase grain, stur-geon and caviare for shipment to Moscow. And, as always, he demanded a strict account of every kopek spent and every price at which a bargain was struck. He was equally meticulous in con-trolling household expenditure. He personally annotated lists of comestibles to be consumed in the dining rooms of his wife and sons; monitored expenditure on construction projects on his estates, on the purchase of dogs for his kennels, horses for his stables, food for his workmen, charity for the poor and for the ransoming of Christian prisoners in Istanbul.[10]

His passion for detail was allied to his continuing campaign to discipline his subjects. When the behaviour of a prominent servitor displeased him (as I. S. Khitrovo was to do when sent to the Don in 1675) he would not scruple to have an inventory of the man's estates drawn up, thereby intimating that unless there was a radical improvement in the man's performance, they would be confiscated. But the digests of reports and the lists of petitions that he regularly ploughed through often drew his attention to quite low-ranking servicemen, and if it appeared that they had failed in their duty his reaction would be severe indeed. When two junior officers appealed against a posting to the province of Kaluga Alexis responded with fury and in writing. Not only was their petition reproachful and disrespectful, he informed them, but they deserved no consideration whatsoever. So far from having 'covered themselves with blood for the Sovereign' as others had done; so far from having served truly and reliably and suffered in his service, they were cunning, conscienceless, complaining intriguers, and greedy to boot. He rejected their petitions and reduced one of them to the ranks.[11]

It is hardly surprising, therefore, that when, in the spring of 1671, the great rebel Sten'ka Razin was at last apprehended, Alexis was ready with a list of questions to be put to the villain at his interrogation. He wanted to know about Razin's relations with the son of the Kabardinian chieftain who had posed as the Tsarevich Alexis; why Razin had praised Nikon and yet now dishonoured him; why he wanted to kill the visiting Greek hierarchs, and a variety of other matters.[12] In June the rebel was duly executed before a great throng of Muscovites. But even when dead Razin was to present a challenge to order. Popular legends soon grew up about his name. People began to talk of him as of a secular Christ, as of another Charlemagne or Barbarossa who would rise from the dead one day and bring deliverance to the oppressed. There were also more immediate reverberations of the great rebellion. That autumn some of Razin's erstwhile followers who had sought refuge in the north broke through to Solovka and stiffened the resistance of its rebel monks; and there was a revival of the pretender craze as well. The same year a young man was arrested on suspicion while trying to cross the frontier into Poland. It transpired that his name was Ivan Kleopin and that he was about to proclaim himself to be the Tsarevich Alexis. Kleopin was evidently unbalanced mentally; nevertheless he was hanged.[13]

Foreign affairs claimed the larger part of Alexis's attentions at this juncture however. In May 1671 Afanasy Ordyn-Nashchokin had led the Muscovite delegation to Andrusovo for another negotiating session with the Poles. Yet he was no longer head of the Foreign Office by that time; nor altogether in his master's favour. By the end of the year he had retired, ostensibly on grounds of ill-health. His departure has been variously ascribed to differences over policy and to his position having been made impossible by uncooperative colleagues and insubordinate inferiors; but there were other reasons. Afanasy was the sort of man who insisted on having things done his way; and when he was thwarted he would demand the Tsar's support, on occasion peremptorily: 'You promoted me,' he wrote, 'so it is shameful of you not to support me, to act contrary [to my advice] and so give joy to my enemies who in acting against me, act against you too.'[14]

This was not the sort of language in which Alexis expected to be addressed even by a servant of proven loyalty whose skills and expertise he rated highly. Besides, able and subtle as he was, Afanasy tended to be angular in his vision, whereas Alexis saw everything. And so it was that when Afanasy petitioned to be relieved of office lest his continued presence should result as he put it in 'the ruination of the state's affairs', his request was granted, and he retired to become a monk in a monastery near his native Pskov.

He had suggested that Alexis should appoint a man 'of great lineage with many friends in high places' as his successor. Only such a personage, he opined, could command the necessary respect to be effective in so high an office.[15] This advice could be regarded as a considered recommendation to return to the old system of government by aristocratic Council; the abandonment of Alexis's method of direct rule through his Private Office and the associated inner 'cabinet' of trusted agents – or else as the fractious jibe of an old, tired and disenchanted man. In either event his advice was ignored. Alexis replaced him as Foreign Minister not with an aristocrat but with a commoner – first by a stop-gap, Dementii Bashmakov, and then with Artamon Matveev (who had been promoted Gentleman-Councillor and made Minister for Ukraine the previous October). The inner 'cabinet' continued to function, and it was soon immersed in the complicated business of securing Muscovy's defences in the south.

The primary aim, of course, was to protect the state's existing frontiers; but it was no longer Poland that constituted the major threat to them. Indeed, Poland was already perceived as a comparatively weak power that might have to be shored up. The threat came rather from the south – from the Ottoman Empire, its satellites and friends, not least within Ukraine itself. Rebel Astrakhan, the great strong-point in the south-east, had been re-taken from the rebels in November 1671, and the year before a peace agreement had been concluded with the Crimean Khan, who had undertaken to put a stop to Tatar raids into eastern Ukraine. Even so it was recognized that the Crimean economy might not be able to dispense with the plunder and ransoms on which it had been so long dependent, and besides the Khan was a vassal of the Sultan. Furthermore, Hetman Doroshenko of western Ukraine had become another of the Sultan's vassals, and by March 1672 it appeared that Hetman Mnohohreshny of eastern Ukraine might defect to him. In order to forestall this, Mnohohreshny was taken to Moscow. Poland's agreement in April to leave Kiev in Muscovite hands lent further stability to the situation. However, the mood of the eastern Ukrainians remained as uncertain as ever; Doroshenko was already engaged in sporadic warfare with the Poles, and the struggle threatened to develop into a general war, drawing in a resurgent Turkey, its vassal the Crimean Khan and hence Muscovy herself.

Preparations were put in hand to meet such a contingency. An invitation from Doroshenko to cooperate against Poland was rejected; the Sultan was warned not to intervene; Dementii Bashmakov and the Private Office staff were set to work organizing military preparations, stock-piling grain at key points, inspecting and repairing defences; and Artamon Matveev, while doing all he could to stabilize the political situation in eastern Ukraine, began to plan a diplomatic offensive in central and western Europe in order to drum up support for Poland. It was not a moment too soon. In May the Sultan launched a major offensive against the Poles.

At this juncture Natalia went into labour and, on 30th May, gave birth to a baby. It was a boy, and its delighted father immediately attended a round of thanksgiving services and gave a series of receptions and dinners at which the guests were regaled with vodka, imported wines, exotic fruits and fantastic confections. He also chose the occasion to raise both his father-in-law and Matveev to the rank of sub-boyar. A month later the child was christened Peter. The Tsarevich Fedor and Alexis's eldest sister Irina stood as godparents; the court painter Simeon Ushakov painted the child's portrait; and Simeon Polotskii wrote a celebratory ode for the occasion which represented the infant Peter as a future conqueror who would win back Constantinople from the Turks.[16]

Then news came that the Turks had captured the key Polish citadel of Kamieniec-Podolski, had laid siege to Lwów, and forced King Michael to conclude a humiliating peace – he recognized Turkish suzerainty over western Ukraine and, indeed, became a Turkish vassal himself, paying a heavy annual tribute to the Sultan. Thanks partly to a revival of Polish patriotism, and partly to Muscovite pressure, the treaty was never to be ratified. Nonetheless Alexis had to be ready to back diplomatic pressure with military support. Orders were sent out to provincial governors ordering the mobilization of everyone with a service obligation – if necessary at the expense of postponing all administrative and judicial business (for which they were responsible at a local level) except that involving banditry.[17] And meanwhile, envoys were sent to the Emperor Leopold, the Doge of Venice, the Electors of Saxony and Brandenburg; to Sweden, Holland and Denmark; to England, Spain and Louis XIV of France; and to Pope Clement X who was asked to sanction a 'crusading' alliance of all Christian powers against the Turks and to urge the Emperor and the King of France in particular to join it.[18]

As usual, the envoys received instructions about matters not connected with their main diplomatic purposes. One of them, the Scotsman Menzies, was commissioned to seek out and engage 'trumpeters of the very best sort who can play dances on the high trumpet', while Colonel Nicholas van Staden who had been sent to Courland, Sweden and Prussia just two weeks before Peter's birth was instructed to engage not only trumpeters, but 'experts capable of staging any sort of comedy'.[19] Alexis had it in mind to create a theatre at his court. Indeed, the idea had been long in mind. Twelve years before, his envoy to the Duke of Tuscany had reported on the magic of the Florentine theatre. He had been struck by one scene in particular. It depicted

> the sea, with waves and fish, on which people were sailing, and the sky with moving clouds on which people were sitting. They descended to take hold of a man by the arms and carry him up and away with them. . . . And an old man came down from the sky in a carriage; and opposite him in another carriage was a most beautiful maiden; and the 'horses' harnessed to the carriages moved their legs as if they were alive.

And if this was astonishing, so were other scenes, not least a stage battle, in which the actors had 'fought' with sabres and swords, and fired guns, as the result of which three of the actors had 'died'; besides which there had been dancing and 'many other wondrous things'.

This account had prompted Alexis to write to John Hebdon asking him to engage 'masters to make a comedy'.[20] But, perhaps because he feared creating a scandal at a time when the Church was in a crisis, nothing more had come of the project. Now, however, the mood of the country was less threatening and, encouraged by Natalia and by Artamon Matveev (who had evidently seen some amateur theatricals in the Foreign Suburb), Alexis proceeded – and without waiting for the foreign experts to arrive. The first play was staged at his mansion at Preobrazhenskoe on 17th October 1672 under the direction of a Lutheran pastor, Jan-Gottfried Gregory, a resident of the Foreign Suburb who had been educated at German universities where theatricals were popular. The cast, over sixty strong, was made up of immigrants and the sons of civil servants; and the lead was played by the son of the court physician Dr Blumentrost. The play (which had taken five months to prepare) was *Ahasuerus and Esther*, though it was far removed from a simple miracle play. It has been called 'one of the clearest signs of a new spirit replacing the old Russian stagnation and Byzantine exclusivity'.[21] But in fact it was a highly exclusive occasion.

Alexis watched it in solitary splendour, sitting in an armchair in the centre of the auditorium. Natalia and the older children also watched, but through the chinks of a box which was wholly enclosed; and a handful of selected courtiers saw the performance too, though from the slips at the side of the stage. But despite the lack of virtuoso trumpeters and a full orchestra (an organ or a harpsichord had to substitute for these); and although the performance lasted the best part of ten hours, Alexis was spellbound, entranced by the illusion of it all. Afterwards he commanded a theatre to be constructed over the Apothecary Office in Moscow, and two dozen carpenters under the direction of a guards centurion, Danilo Kobylin, were soon working day and night to get it finished in time for a re-staging of *Esther*, which was to be given with a full orchestra in 1673.[22]

Meanwhile Alexis spend a good deal of time playing the leading role in another form of theatre – ceremoniously receiving icons which had accompanied military commanders and ambassadors on their missions; inspecting troops on their departure for Kiev; attending a series of artillery trials. War was looming, and the outcome of events in the theatre of life was not as predictable as the outcome of the play *Esther*. Nonetheless attempts were made to predict them. On 13th December 1672 a rare meeting of the Council had been held. Grand strategy was almost certainly the purpose of its deliberations, but it probably also considered an astrological forecast which had been brought post-haste to Moscow at this time. It was a colourful representation of the path of a comet which had been sighted over Košice in north-eastern Hungary in late October and early November. The comet's movement had been plotted in relation to the positions of the sun and moon, and the various sightings, including its final disintegration in a mass of flames, had been superimposed upon one another. The suggestive shapes that resulted had been developed into lively representations of lances and scimitars, cannon and exploding grenades, crosses, an Ottoman banner, and a picture of God's eye. These auguries had been construed by Varlaam Iasinskii, Rector of the Kiev Brotherhood, who had coordinated the opinions of 'several skilled interpreters'. They were encouraging.

It forecast an alliance between Muscovy, Poland, and the Habsburg Emperor, and a war between them and the Sultan which would only last six months. The Christian monarchs, under God's all-seeing eye, would put up a formidable defence, and the Tsar's cannon would smash the Turkish scimitar.[23] It seemed credible, but then the astrologers had an inkling of what Alexis's hopes were; and in fact the worldly, as opposed to the heavenly signs, looked less encouraging. The Sultan, Mehmet IV, had visited Kamieniec and prayed in its cathedral which had been converted into a mosque. There were reasons to fear that he planned another major offensive for the spring of 1673; and that Poland and Muscovy would have to stand alone against it, for the project to form a grand crusading alliance received no positive response. Vienna was satisfied with the strength of its defences; the Doge was cool towards the idea; Brandenburg was preoccupied with the threat from France; Anglo-Dutch hostilities ruled out their participation; Spain showed no interest either. The experienced Romodanovskii was in command at Kiev; reinforcements were on the way to him, and Cossack scouts were already testing out the enemy's defences across the Dnieper. But in the circumstances prudence dictated a defensive stance.

Yet Muscovy's diplomatic offensive on behalf of Poland seemed to stand Alexis in good stead when, in the autumn of 1673, it was reported that King Michael of Poland was seriously ill and likely to die. For a third time the prospect arose of uniting the crowns of Poland and Muscovy. The Pope (anxious to bring Russia within the Catholic fold) had commended Polish–Muscovite cooperation; and when the King did die, support for a Romanov candidate emerged within Poland itself. At this point, as if to emphasize Muscovy's virility, Alexis mounted a winter campaign. Romodanovskii advanced across the Dnieper to carry the war into Doroshenko's camp. He captured Kaniew and advanced on Pereiaslav, and before long the Hetman of the Muscovite Ukraine, Samoilovych, was proclaimed Hetman of all Ukraine (though to ensure the continuance of his loyalty his sons were held hostage in Moscow), and most of the Cossack notables of western Ukraine swore loyalty to the Tsar.[24]

Meanwhile a proposal had arrived from Poland suggesting that the twelve-year-old Tsarevich Fedor stand for election as Poland's next king. It stressed the similarities of 'language, temperament and organisation' between Russians and Poles; the fact that there was no natural frontier dividing the two states, and the benefits that such a union would bring in providing an unsurmountable wall defending Christendom and making for 'the ruin of Islam'. But there were conditions attached. Muscovy would have to provide financial and military aid and return the gains made in the war; and Fedor would have to become a Catholic and marry the late King's widow. This was difficult to accept, and in any case Alexis did not favour the idea of his son standing for election. Instead he made counter-proposals. He himself would be prepared to receive an invitation to be King. If he were crowned, and if all the Polish notables, clerical and lay, were to swear loyalty to him, then he would guarantee that their estates would be immune from interference by the state (for he understood what they really meant by 'golden liberty'). Furthermore, provided Poland furnished conscript soldiers he would organize her defences. If Poland needed 'a wise, devout sovereign, skilled in military affairs', the reply concluded, the crown should be formally offered to him, whereupon negotiations could take place about the other details.[25]

There was no lack of other candidates, however (including a strong challenge from the Habsburgs), and in the end a Pole, Jan Sobieski, was elected King. No doubt Alexis was disappointed, but at least Sobieski was not pro-Swedish, and although his wife was French (and France was the Sultan's friend) he was soon taking a belligerent stand against the Turks. A more disagreeable choice might have been made. Besides, it would not have done for Alexis or Fedor to have become King at too high a price; and in any case Alexis had concerns enough without those of Poland being added to them. One was the appearance in the Cossack centre of Zaporozh'e of yet another pretender claiming to be the Tsarevich Simeon. He was said to have birth-marks which proved his legitimacy and dared to issue letters bearing what purported to be an official seal. The claim was ridiculous. They said that the pretender was fifteen years old whereas the real Simeon, had he lived, would only have been nine. Yet the man was dangerous. His pretence might rouse the Cossacks, destabilize Ukraine, raise the spectre of another great rebellion, and gain the support of foreign powers. Hence foreign governments were informed of the baselessness of the pretence and the Zaporozhians were ordered to surrender him.

They prevaricated for months, but threats to cut off their pay and supplies and the Muscovite victories in western Ukraine eventually persuaded them where their duty lay. In September 1674 the pretender was brought to Moscow together with his chief associate (who turned out to be one of Razin's followers, a deserter from the guards). It transpired that 'Simeon', a sharp-nosed young man with a mass of black, curly hair, was twenty-two years old and a Pole. He was brought to the Kremlin on a cart containing a gallows, axe and block, interrogated under torture by senior ministers, and then taken to Red Square where his limbs were lopped off one by one. The quivering trunk was then impaled upon a spike – and left there for three days to serve as a general warning.[26]

The very same month Alexis's eldest surviving son, Fedor, had been presented to the people with awesome pomp. Indeed this ceremony represented the summation of Alexis's work over many years to elevate the monarchy by surrounding it with a mystic aura, and to impress foreigners as well as his own subjects with its majesty. Hence his importation some years earlier of vastly expensive copies of Byzantine regalia; his efforts to collect the orders of ceremony for the old Byzantine rituals and for the coronations of contemporary monarchs such as the Emperor and the Polish King. Hence also the compilation under his direction of the magnificent *Titulary*, completed in 1672, which contained the full titles and formalized portraits of every Russian ruler since Riurik, besides those of many foreign monarchs, and heraldic devices representing all the territories that they ruled.[27] The purposes of the ceremony (as Alexis explained the matter in a speech to the Council) were to commit Fedor 'to the service of Almighty God', to induct him into the holy ecumenical and apostolic Church, and to present him to the Patriarch and 'all ranks of people in the entire state of Muscovy'. But Fedor's debut was in fact as much a political statement as a series of symbolic rites to mark his attainment of adult status and his entry into full communion with the Church.

It was a long and formidable ordeal for so delicate a boy. First Alexis took him to receive the congratulations and prostrations of the Councillors who were waiting in the ante-chamber. Then they went in procession to the Church of the Saviour Untouched by Hand where the Archimandrite of the Trinity–St Sergius monastic centre was waiting for them. Led by the Archimandrite, who bore the famous icon aloft before them, the procession set off again along the wooden walk-ways overhung with canopies which had been set up between the major buildings in the Kremlin. They moved at an awesomely slow pace, the clatter of their footsteps muffled by the thick carpets that had been laid down, so that they seemed to glide along.

Near the head of the procession came the Tsar's own choir singing ancient Byzantine chants. Alexis followed, supported by a retinue of Councillors and Gentlemen of the Bedchamber. Behind him came Fedor and his entourage. The route was lined by guardsmen, some with long muskets, some with drawn sabres. When the procession reached the Cathedral of the Annunciation priests sprinkled the Tsar and the Tsarevich with holy water; and as they moved on towards the Cathedral of the Archangel a great crowd, including representatives of foreign powers, watched, as if at a pageant on a stage. The crescendo built up steadily. When Alexis and Fedor entered the Cathedral the Patriarchal choir struck up with the prayer for long life (the *Mnogoletie*); then, having made obeisance to the icons and the relics there and received the Patriarch's blessing, the procession emerged into the open, augmented now by the Patriarch and a forest of crosses and icons held aloft by the assembled clergy. The participants moved off according to the prearranged order, forming a series of gorgeous patterns as they made their way towards stands which had been set up to receive them on Red Square. The highest, covered with an extraordinarily fine Persian carpet that glittered with gold, was occupied by the Tsar and Tsarevich; there was another for the Patriarch. The reading stands were swathed in precious silks; choirs stationed themselves on the flanks. The climax of the ceremony approached and when it came it was mesmeric.

The prelates bowed twice, twice again, then three times to Alexis. They made the same mystic greeting to his son. After this Alexis led Fedor down the steps to meet the Patriarch, who swung his censer, smoking with burning incense, at them three times, and then over the regalia borne up by courtiers stationed nearby. Then all the bishops swung their censers at the main actors, twice to one side, twice to the other, while the choirs intoned Psalms. A prophetic passage from *Isaiah* was read out; the imperial pair were blessed and sanctified again with holy water; there were readings from the Gospels and a sung Hallelujah; yet more clouds of incense rose; a prayer for the aggrandizement of the Tsar and his family was intoned; and the Icon of the Saviour was taken to the Patriarch, who made the sign of the cross to all four sides and made a three-fold prayer.

Then the speeches began, each one followed by the prayer for longevity sung in the Byzantine mode. First the Patriarch made an address; then Alexis; then Fedor himself, who, when he had finished, prostrated himself before his father. Fondly, Alexis kissed him on the head – yet even this was done ritually, in the form of a cross. More speeches followed, more singing, more blessings. Finally the clergy departed for the Cathedral while the procession of the Tsar and Tsarevich returned at measured pace to the dining hall of the palace. There it was announced that a bonus would be paid to all ranks of servicemen in honour of the occasion, and word was sent to the representatives from Ukraine, to the Polish Resident and other foreigners reminding them that they had seen 'the Sovereign Tsarevich's most bright eyes and observed how tall he is'.[28] Soon afterwards Fedor was crippled in a riding accident and henceforth had to hobble about on sticks.

Meanwhile Natalia had given birth to a second child, a girl. Alexis had her christened Fedora after her eldest step-brother in order to create another bond (if only a symbolic one) between the two branches of his family. The more links the better. They might encourage the growth of affection if only for his sake. The same motive informed a letter he wrote to his family while on his annual pilgrimage to Zagorsk. He addressed it first to his daughters (listing all their titles), and only then to their stepmother and aunts, and to his sons 'your brothers Fedor, Ivan and Peter'. He informed them that he had arrived in good health; gave them his fond blessing, and assured them, too, that the grace of the Trinity, the intercession of the Virgin Mary, and the prayers of the miracle-workers Sergius and Nikon would be with them.[29] This reference to Nikon and the attribution of saintly qualities to him may seem surprising, but it accorded with Alexis's complex and ambiguous attitude towards the ex-Patriarch.

He had sent him several presents since the trial. At first Nikon had refused them, but in 1671, when Alexis had begged his forgiveness, he had relented, since when they had kept up a correspondence and

Nikon had responded to his requests for prayers. On the occasion of his marriage Alexis had sent Nikon seven hundred rubles in cash besides furs, cloths and towels, and in November 1673 he had sent him a further two hundred rubles to celebrate the birth of another daughter, Natalia, and to pray for the soul of the Tsarevich Alexis. For his own part Nikon tried to consolidate his reputation for holiness not through asceticism (for he gladly accepted the magnificent sturgeons, salmon and gingerbreads that the Tsar sent him; indeed, on more than one occasion he complained about the lack of fruit), but as a healer. As his regime was lightened (from 1672 he was allowed to move freely about the monastery and even to take walks outside it), sick people, mainly simple peasants, began to visit him, and he would treat them with prayers, with ointments and with medicines. Several were cured, mostly epileptics and the mentally ill, though one girl subsequently died (of her disease, said Nikon, not from his treatment). As his reputation as a healer grew the number who came to seek his help increased to forty or more a day, at which the monastery authorities began to restrict visitors, though he was allowed to continue his curing on a more modest scale. But if Alexis retained a special regard for Nikon as a holy man, he remained suspicious of him. In 1671, the very year of their reconciliation, he had launched an enquiry into his activities, and he took a personal interest in its progress until it was eventually wound up in 1675. In the meantime an armed guard accompanied Nikon wherever he went.[30]

Alexis's treatment of Nikon may have softened. Not so his attitude towards prominent Old Believers still at liberty. In November 1671 he had ordered the arrest of Boiarina Morozova and her sister. They had been interrogated, and when they remained obstinate he had had them chained up in a Kremlin dungeon. Sensing that, like Avvakum, she felt a call to martyrdom, he wrote Morozova a letter, addressing her as a 'second St Catherine' and begging her to conform for the sake of the country, for the sake of her own honour. Later he had gone to the gallery above her dungeon and peered down at her. Glancing up she saw him – and in an immediate gesture of defiance crossed herself in the old way and ostentatiously kissed her chains. The Patriarch himself pleaded for her release, but Alexis refused. The woman had too much charisma; she might provide the dissenters with the leadership they lacked. Yet he dared not make a martyr of her either. So the word was put about that she was mentally ill.

Even so, Morozova and her sister, and their friend Maria Dani-lova, were flogged and tortured in an attempt to reduce them to submission. When this failed to break their spirit, in April 1673 Alexis had them incarcerated in the monastery of Borovsk in Kaluga province. Two years later he was to have their case reopened. As a result Maria was removed to a compound for common criminals; the others were placed under strict regime (their books, their icons, and most of their clothing were removed, and their diet reduced to the barest minimum). Before the end of 1675 all three women were dead. Yet they were the willing victims of their faith, and Alexis had used violence against them only as a last resort. Indeed, he had been prepared to compromise. If only Morozova would cross herself with three fingers, he had once told her, if only she would keep her objections to herself, then she could remain at liberty. He preferred persuasion to force. On the other hand his considerable armoury of persuasive weapons included the spear of moral blackmail, and he had not shrunk from using it. Years before Morozova had been told that her obstinacy would bring ruin to her son. When he had fallen ill Alexis had sent him medicine; when he died his mother was told that her bereavement was God's punish-ment for her disobedience. And a year before she died Alexis (having long since warned her that her behaviour put them at risk) confiscated all the family estates to the crown.[31]

Dissenters still blessed the Tsar; but they detected signs of God's disfavour towards the reformed Church. Its Patriarchs, for example, were being struck down with amazing rapidity. Ioasaf II had died in February 1672. His successor Pitirim, who was appointed five months later (the electoral synod had openly declared that they would elect whomever the Tsar wished them to elect), survived no more than nine months, whereupon the position remained vacant for almost a year. The man eventually chosen this time (he took the name of Joachim) was a former army officer, a man noted for his administrative abilities rather than for any remarkable spiritual gifts.[32] Contrary to his own Law Code, Alexis transferred some of the Monastery Office functions to the Patriarch. But it was administrative convenience, not deference to the Church, that prompted him to do so. Alexis was by now firmly established as the spiritual as well as the secular master of his realm. He was an icon for Russians to revere; a superior being who seemed to be in closer communion with God than anyone else. Yet his own body reminded him that he was mortal.

Now in his mid-forties, he looked older than his age. His face was lined; his body flabby – indeed it bordered on the gross. But this was only due in part to over-indulgence. He had developed a tendency to dropsy. As yet it did not seriously impede his activities, but he knew that his kidneys were prone to malfunction. That is why he had taken to wearing a little dish made out of nephrite around his neck, for learned men regarded nephrite as a powerful counter to kidney disorders, an antidote to depression, a restorer of a failing appetite. And whenever he left Moscow on an expedition, trunk-loads of medicaments would go with him. There were bottles of oil of cloves and cinnamon essence, strawberry spirit and tincture cordialis, a variety of balsams and remedies for indigestion, sugared nuts, basilicons and plasters. There were aphrodisiacs and perfumes too, preparations made from blood stone and quantities of 'apo-pleptic vodka', besides a dozen bottles of 'elixir proprietatis'. This had been prescribed for him in 1673 as an antidote and prophylactic for all diseases. Convinced of its merits, Alexis made sure that all his family took it regularly as well,[33] and indeed the medicines seemed to be effective enough. At least his appetite for work seemed undi-minished and he still hungered for diversion.

There were frequent hunts, of course, on which, when possible, he took Natalia and his children; there were spectacular fights between animals of different species, sometimes staged on ice; even occasional displays of fireworks; and informal parties too. In October 1674, for example, he gave one for some members of the Council at which musicians performed on organs and trumpets, pipes and drums, and unspecified games were played. The guests did not depart until dawn, having consumed considerable quantities of alcohol.[34] But Alexis had come to regard the theatre as the emperor of entertainments. What amounted to a drama school had been set up in the Foreign Suburb with Gregory as its director; competent string players as well as trumpeters, percussionists and players of keyboard instruments were now available for the pit, and masters of perspective to paint the scenery – so that the new pro-ductions were much grander and more polished than the first.

That autumn *Judith and Holofernes* was presented at Preobraz-henskoe. It had been written by Simeon Polotskii who had evidently used a mediaeval Jewish play as a model, but it opened with a prologue addressed directly to the Tsar in which he was extolled as a conqueror, bidden to watch the action unfold, and promised to be shown how God changes grief to joy. There followed no fewer than twenty-nine scenes, divided into seven acts. The theme, as in *Esther*, was the trials and ultimate triumph of the Jews. 'Judith' herself did not appear until the fourth act. Yet, long as the play was, it was calculated not to pall. The humour of rustic characters provided a counterpoint to the high drama; a scene portraying mock punishments gave rise to some hilarity, and one character (no doubt poking fun at the Tsaritsa) declared that though she was a goddess she preferred the domesticity of the stove. *Judith* aimed to engage all the emotions,[35] and it seems to have succeeded. Here was a mirror held up to life, a world of illusion that reflected so many of the feelings experienced by its august audience.

. *Judith* was followed by a re-staging of *Esther*, *The Woeful Comedy of Adam and Eve*, *The Refreshing Comedy of Joseph*, *The Little Comedy of Bayazet and Tamerlane*, and others. *Adam and Eve* in particular contained many of the same baroque features that figured in the allegorical plays given at the court of the Habsburg Emperor Leopold I. The action took place on two stages. The upper stage, representing heaven, was inhabited by singing angels, archangels and personifications of Truth, Right, Compassion and Peace; the lower stage was for the earthly creatures including the snake and his wife. Love (expressed in what nowadays might be regarded as a rather sentimental way) was a major theme of the play. But to judge from the surviving texts, *Joseph* was more successful as emotive drama, dealing as it did with the themes of betrayal, and of paternal (and filial) affection – besides which it contained a quite passionate love-scene in which Joseph was very hard put to it to resist the blandishments of Potiphar's shameless wife. *Bayazet*, by contrast, set in the reign of Michael Palaeologus who had recaptured Constantinople from the crusaders, was all blood and thunder, enlivened by battle scenes, the appearance of a horse on stage, and all sorts of loud and exciting effects. But even *Bayazet* had a moral content, castigating pride and unjust punishment, and it proclaimed a message exhorting everyone to be loyal to the Emperor even unto death.[36]

Each of the plays was also calculated to hold Alexis's attention by reflecting back to him one or another of his interests and ambitions. *Joseph*, for example, mirrored his concern to raise agricultural production and guard against the contingency of famine; *Bayazet* his ambition of winning ground against the Turks, and ultimately capturing Constantinople. The plays were also satisfying in that they portrayed resolution after conflict. Evil plots were invariably uncovered; malicious characters unmasked; right always triumphed. Yet in life, unhappily, resolutions were more elusive; it was more difficult to scotch malicious plots and to unmask people who intended evil. The court was rarely free from the pervasive odour of suspicion. What resentments might not be harboured behind respectful faces and unctuous manners? What grudges might not people bear – against men who had been promoted 'out of turn', against Natalia and the Naryshkin clan, against the Tsar himself? Denunciations were not, of course, uncommon, and not a few of them were baseless and malicious. But when a hint of suspicion fell on anyone the investigation would be immediate and thorough, sometimes cruelly so.

In 1675 it fell on Prince F. F. Kurakin for harbouring a witch, a blind woman called Fen'ka. Kurakin was at once placed under arrest, while a commission made up of some of Alexis's closest aides (Nikita Odoevskii, Artamon Matveev, the trusty Larion Ivanov, and Danilo Polianskii of the Private Office) interrogated Fen'ka. Little if anything was discovered about a plot (if plot there was), though Fen'ka admitted that she was a witch and she eventually died under torture.[37] But another case, investigated the same year by the same commission under Alexis's personal direction, was probably more disturbing still. It involved a number of people including some tailors and a court falconer, Zot' Polozov. The chief suspect, however, was the wife of another nobleman, Arina Musin-Pushkin. The truth of the affair is still shrouded in secrecy, but the punishments were harsh, and the case was subsequently to give rise to rumours picked up by visiting foreigners which touched Alexis's personal life to the quick.

Arina, so the tale went, had been Alexis's mistress; she had borne him a son called Ivan, and he had subsequently arranged for her to marry Musin-Pushkin in order to cover his traces.[38] The available evidence is insufficient to confirm the story or to dismiss it. It is not impossible that Alexis might have sought solace in a sexual escapade after Maria's death. On the other hand, the story might have been the invention of an over-imaginative or hysterical young woman encouraged by resentful people of the sort who were so ready to support pretenders. What is certain, however, is that had such a rumour gained wide currency it would have done serious damage to Alexis's image and caused distress to his family.

Alexis seems to have been indisposed more frequently than usual that year. In February he had at the last moment to cancel a grand hunt involving bears, wolves and foxes, borzois and mastiffs that he had arranged; and although he had recovered sufficiently to attend divine service next day in the Cathedral of the Assumption the troubles recurred. In the autumn more medicine than usual was being sent to his apartments.[39] But he was too heavily drugged by the exercise of power ever to stop working. Even when unwell he would still go compulsively through all the papers that were sent up to him, though, as his scrawly handwriting of this period indicates, he was working faster than in earlier days.

The matters he was supervising through his fifteen Private Office secretaries ranged from cases involving security to church affairs, and from the army to every aspect of the court economy. His estates now comprised nearly half a million acres of ploughland alone; and he was still acquiring more. He launched a survey with a view to achieving a vast expansion in tar and potash production; and he was heavily involved in the fish trade, in building works, stock-raising and a host of other projects. Sometimes he would produce an idea that might help solve a technical problem that had arisen (as when he suggested that layers of schist, dung and flax waste might serve to reinforce a dam); and he remained as thorough as ever he had been. That winter he annotated a detailed report on the Izmailovo estate; he dealt personally with endless petitions; and when half-a-dozen glasses belonging to the Tsarevich Fedor were found to be missing he took the trouble to hold a full inquiry and had a number of suspect noblemen searched and put in irons (though he never recovered the glasses).[40]

Such care might seem obsessive, even morbid – a reflection, perhaps, of some deep anxiety, of a universal and terrible mistrust. Yet his concern for the minutiae made him a more effective ruler. It exemplified his old principle of thoroughness; and his acquaintance with thousands of trivia helped him to perceive the canvas as a whole, to form appropriate policies and to re-shape existing laws. Details did not restrict his vision; they served to broaden it. Besides, he dealt with matters great as well as small. He might concern himself with minor trading operations, but he also mounted pioneering embassies to India and China, and these small- and large-scale operations were connected. His envoy to China, a Moldavian Greek called Spafarius, was instructed to persuade its ruler to enter into commercial as well as diplomatic dealings with Moscow, and the mission to India was charged with establishing direct trade in gems in return for furs. Both envoys were to report back on the most efficient routes and to engage craftsmen capable of building bridges out of stone. Shorter routes and stone bridges improved communications, a matter on which Alexis had come to place a high priority. Quicker receipt of intelligence could double its value; faster turnover in trade implied bigger profits; speedier movement of troops allowed greater economy of force.

Banditry, on the other hand, impeded communication. That year Alexis ordered a great drive against robbers lurking in the forests around Moscow, and had the trees cut down on either side of the main roads in order to reduce the cover they provided. He also issued an edict banning anyone below the rank of Moscow gentry and their servants from wearing hats and coats of foreign design or having their hair cut in the foreign fashion.[41] In part this was a sumptuary law intended to emphasize social distinctions and to discourage profligate spending by the lower orders. But it also demonstrated that, unlike so many modernizers, Alexis had come to understand that over-hasty cultural change would bring considerable political risks in train. Yet though foreign cultural influences were curbed in the country as a whole, Alexis himself continued to embrace them.

This was evident from the proliferation of imported musical instruments at court. His palaces were full of organs, the king of instruments. Even his three-year-old son Peter now had his own clavichord and cembalum. And it was evident in the music played at court – the ballet *Orpheus* given at about this time was evidently danced to the music of Heinrich Schütz who was to be so much admired by the young Johann Sebastian Bach.[42] Furthermore, the plays, which contained so many secular features, also reflected foreign influence, as did the objects adorning his palaces, and much of their decoration. So far from being an isolationist, Alexis often seemed to be as closely attuned to the West as to his own country. It was partly a matter of taste, partly a matter of diplomatic wisdom, for Alexis had long been anxious to impress foreigners not only with the military might at his disposal but with the civilization of his court. It helped foster respect; it helped nourish the impression that Muscovy belonged to the family of European, Christian nations, and so helped smooth the process of negotiation.

He was still trying to build up a front against the Turks; he was also trying to fob off (as politely as he could) attempts by the Emperor, Holland and Denmark to inveigle him into war against Sweden – for though he still hoped to gain a port in the Baltic, that was for the long term; at this juncture he knew that his military resources were insufficient. Nevertheless, when a new ambassador arrived in Moscow, he would have him escorted into the city by as many as nine troops of cavalry with pennants flying, drums beating and trumpets blasting out so loudly that it was all an inexperienced rider could do to keep his seat upon his horse. Entire regiments of infantry, each handsomely uniformed in a different colour, would be drawn up as guards of honour, and often Alexis would show off some of his new iron cannon and boast that no monarch in Christendom possessed the like.

A reception of such pompous formality was accorded to the Emperor's ambassador, Bottoni, when he arrived in August 1675. Yet, as he subsequently realized, Alexis had already taken a sight of him – for on his way into the city Bottoni had noticed packs of hounds and huntsmen. It transpired that Alexis and Natalia were with them. Indeed, she was sometimes to be seen sitting beside the Tsar in his English coach with its glass windows (a thing unheard-of for a Tsaritsa hitherto). The time-honoured segregation of the sexes at court was beginning to break down. Two days after Bottoni's arrival, Alexis threw a party for Natalia at Vorob'evo to celebrate her name-day. And, albeit unofficially, she was in evidence again at the second audience which Alexis accorded to Bottoni. This took place at Kolomenskoe with appropriate pomp (the ambassador's procession was led by thirty falconers riding greys and dressed in their splendid uniforms with great wings attached to their arms and shoulders which they would lift and spread out in salute). Alexis wore a red shirt made of watered silk with a great deal of silver lace and a silver moire caftan. Beside him stood poor, crippled Fedor, making his first public appearance since his debut, looking rather wan but holding a sceptre in his hand like his father. Four handsome young noblemen stood before them shouldering their ceremonial axes. The protocol was tediously formal, the atmosphere stuffy. . . .

Then, suddenly, Alexis burst out laughing. He was amused by a mistranslation that the embassy's interpreter had made. And he had hardly managed to bring himself under control when there was a strange scuffling sound. A door to the great hall swung open. It revealed Natalia (who had been watching everything with the door ajar) and the four-year-old Tsarevich Peter, who had become over-excited and kicked it wide open.[43]

There was much merry-making that autumn. Aside from the hunting there were dinners followed by musical performances, parties at which the vodka, hock and sweet wine flowed. Often the guests would not stagger home until well into the early hours, for, as the official record put it, Alexis would 'drink them all drunk'. In November another comedy was staged, and there were also two command performances by a conjuror who had been discovered among the staff of the imperial embassy. The man had extra-ordinary talents. He could not only dance on a rope, but do all sorts of amusing and amazing tricks. He could juggle with knives; and possessed such sleight of hand that he could make coins and even garlands of flowers move about, apparently of their own accord.[44] Alexis was spellbound. He was always intrigued by those myster-ious grey areas which divided the possible from the impossible.

On the 17th and again on the 19th of January 1676 Alexis gave audiences to the Dutch Ambassador Konrad van Klenk, and learn-ing that Klenk had a boy in his entourage who was a fine musician, persuaded him to let him play in the presence of Natalia and the court. The performance delighted him, and he gave those present the impression that he was in good spirits and excellent health. But within a few days he was ill. He seemed to have caught cold; the dropsy returned, and his condition soon deteriorated alarmingly. He became very swollen; he was unable to take medicine, and he was running a high fever. His doctors, the learned Michael Grahmann, Johann von Rosenburg, Laurence Blumentrost and the rest, examined him and consulted one another. They concluded that he had a 'scurvy' connected with the dropsy he had had some years before, and they gave him ice to hold on his stomach to reduce the inflammation and the fever. From what we know of the symptoms Alexis may well have been suffering from glomerulonephritis, a disease which is rarely fatal and from which most victims recover spontaneously, without any treatment. But his latent, or chronic, renal trouble coupled with his tendency to high blood pressure seems to have created a crisis involving the heart as well.[45] Certainly by 28th January Alexis understood that he was about to die. Accordingly he gave orders for the release of many prisoners, and dictated a will and a prayer.

In doing so he was momentarily overcome by emotion – by love of Natalia who maintained a vigil at his bedside, and by fears. He feared for Natalia and what might become of her; he feared for his country which would face rule by a Tsar even younger than he himself had been at his accession and with a much weaker constitu-tion. But not least he feared for himself and for the state of his soul.

He recalled the words of Psalm 49 – that the humble and the mighty, the rich and the poor, the wise, the foolish and the brutish, all share a common fate. He recalled the Book of Ecclesiastes, that all things were but vanity. And it came very hard to him, a man so well endowed with power and riches and so much love of life, to have to surrender everything so suddenly and so soon. One imagines him weeping as he spoke:

> When I ruled the empire I was so exalted that I believe the whole world knew of my glorious imperial reputation and millions served me as slaves with fear and reverence. They thought of me as if I were immortal. But now I taste no refreshing sweetness, nor do I smell sweet odours. I am overcome by great bitterness and by a sorrow that cannot be consoled – for I am nailed to my bed by the spear of a cruel disease, and the sword of death is looking for the moment at which to take away my life. Then I shall have to be buried, just like the poor. Hungry worms are ready to devour me indiscriminately, to reduce me to nothing. Alas! Alas! I am a great emperor; yet I hold the smallest worms in dread. Alas! Human life is wretched; there is no happiness; all my joy is turned to mourning.

He may well have recalled that awful picture of corruption seen decades earlier when he had stood vigil by the fast-putrefying corpse of the Patriarch Joseph. But if he did he may also have remembered the words of the Patriarch's address at his coronation: if you are to be sovereign, first be master of yourself. Somehow he recovered himself, and continued to dictate his testament in an ordered way.

He affirmed his faith in the Trinity, committed his soul to God and gave orders that he be buried near his father and the martyred Tsarevich Dmitrii in the Archangel Cathedral. He named Fedor as his successor, bade him follow in his footsteps and asked his brothers to serve and obey him. Then he turned to Natalia and was all but overcome with grief again. She faced great adversity. Had he ever imagined that he would die so soon, he would never have married her. The sight of her, her face, usually so beautiful, now swollen and a sea of tears, her eyes bloodshot, her hair dishevelled, distressed him. So did her groaning as if she were in childbirth. Parting from Maria had been bitter enough, he sighed, but this parting was unbearably cruel. He tried to stop her weeping. Tears would do no good, he told her. Then his fears returned. He recalled his actions as Tsar and wondered how he could account to God for them: 'I do not know what answer my Creator will give me. I am weighed down by despondency, for I do not know what to say or how to escape eternal torments.'

Then, once again, he returned to practicalities. Natalia, he said, while wearing black for the rest of her life, should live an independent life after he died and Fedor was to have no power over her, but show her the same obedience and duty as if she were his natural mother. Natalia was not to remarry, of course, but Alexis warned her against taking the vows of a nun too soon, before being sure that she had strength enough to obey the rules. Nor was she to mourn him for too long. It would be unfitting, and besides grief and lamentation did not suit her. He then performed the customary farewells, asking forgiveness and absolution of the Church and from its ministers – first of the 'blessed pastor Nikon', then of the incumbent Patriarch and of the bishops, the hierarchs and all monks. He addressed the boyars and people of all ranks, asking them, too, for forgiveness.

The agony returned. He seemed to see 'the terrible angel of death threatening me, and my mind is all dissolved'. Then, rallying, he asked Natalia ('thou most dear to me above all this creation') to lift his failing body in her arms while he prayed his last prayer to his Redeemer:

> O God, great and wonderful, O God strong and immortal, high and ineffable, look down on thy sinful servant. Do not bar me for ever from the sight of thy glory; do not destroy me for my sins. Show me thy grace at the gates of death. Receive me, penitent as I am; include me in the fellowship of the good. Do not cut me off from the choir of thy elect, but let me laud thee forever in the company of thy angels and saints. Do not let the prince of darkness snatch me away. . . . Into thy hands I commend my spirit. Thine is the kingdom and the glory, now and forever, world without end. Amen.[46]

On the night of 29th January 1676 Alexis sank into everlasting sleep, cradled in Natalia's arms. Early in the morning of 30th January he took part in his last procession, to the grave. His coffin, covered with cloth-of-silver, was accompanied by priests and deacons bearing smoking censers and flickering candles, by the Patriarch and prelates, and by the palace and the patriarchal choirs. The mourners were led by the crippled Fedor who was carried on a chair. They buried him, as he had ordered, in the Cathedral of the Archangel.

There were many who showed grief, not least among the soldiery. Only a few days earlier Bottoni, who had been present at the Blessing of the Waters ceremony, had noticed the fervency with which the officers had prostrated themselves before Alexis: 'The sight [he reported] was quite touching and fond; the general devotion and love of the Russians towards their monarch moved the hearts of all who were present to tears.'[47]

Simeon Polotskii composed 'A Lament of Russians' to mark the occasion; orders were issued to ensure that the Tsar would be properly commemorated, and interceded for, in every church in the land. Even the Old Believers continued to pray for his soul. And when news of Alexis's death reached Nikon, he sighed deeply, then burst into tears. Yet he refused to grant the written pardon which his old friend had requested from him on his death-bed. Pointing to a painting of the Day of Judgement he said: 'He and I will be judged together there, at the terrible advent of our Lord. We fulfil the Lord's will: Forsake and ye will be forsaken.'

God might forgive Alexis, but Nikon intended to continue his battle with the Tsar into the world to come.[48]

Chapter X

Legacies and Reputations

Alexis was born into an age of tumult. No century since has been quite so plague-ridden, tempestuous and disorderly. All Europe was in ferment – a crucible seething with conflicts both between states and within societies. Long-accepted truths were questioned; authority everywhere was subjected to repeated challenge; lawlessness had become endemic. Spain, Italy, France and England were all shaken by rebellions and revolutions; central Europe was wracked by the Thirty Years War, and eastern Europe, too, was caught up in the turmoil. The once magnificent Ottoman governmental machine had fallen out of kilter; the deep frontier zone between states extending through the Balkans and the steppes was ravaged by marauding armies and anarchic strife; Poland-Lithuania, the largest state in Europe, had begun its irreversible slide towards ruin, and, early in the century, the state of Muscovy itself had dissolved into a terrible slough of chaos. The Tsardom was eventually re-established, but it remained a fragile entity, continually menaced by enemies within and without. Such were the circumstances that moulded Alexis's outlook. They also set the mark against which he must be judged.

His reign, like those of so many other monarchs of the period, amounted to a struggle for stability,[1] a war against anarchy; and in conducting this war Alexis drew on the ideological models available to him to build up a vision of an ideal order that would reflect the divine order that prevailed in heaven. This vision became all-pervasive, and as it did so his quest for order came to inform his every activity. As he wrote in his falconry rules, 'Everything must be done with good order, discipline and exact arrangement [for]. . . without order nothing can be made secure or strengthened.'[2]

He perceived good order to be the necessary condition of the good life and for success in anything; disorder in anything to be the

229

recipe for disaster. This simple principle lay at the very centre of his philosophy, side by side with his religious faith. It also encapsulated his primary political objectives: to command obedience; to impose conformity; to counter provincialism and promote centralization; to achieve harmony.

For this he had to be an effective autocrat. Yet the autocratic tradition had been broken with the extinction of the old dynasty, and the new, Romanov, dynasty had great difficulty in establishing its legitimacy. Alexis's father, though an autocrat in name, had not been an autocrat in practice; and Alexis himself was repeatedly challenged by a succession of pretenders. Somehow he had to entrench the dynasty, and re-establish the autocracy in reality as well as name. In pursuing these aims Alexis was served by the fact that his own yearning for stability was shared by substantial segments of the elite, and by a mood of popular xenophobia, both of them bred by the Time of Troubles. But by 1645 these were declining assets; the obstacles, by contrast, were growing.

Alexis's initial response to the challenge was that of an intelligent young man who placed a high value on ideas. He provided philosophical justifications for autocracy – drawing mainly on the Byzantine example and, not least, on that of the Byzantine Church, from which the Muscovite Church was descended. Precisely how much Byzantine literature was available in Moscow at that time is questionable; but Alexis clearly understood, or came to understand, the essentials of the Byzantine political tradition. Prelates and scholars from the Orthodox East, men steeped in Byzantine lore and literature, visited Moscow, and what they offered was eagerly seized upon to reinforce his understandings. These understandings were reflected in his theocratic philosophy. Alexis was to assert that his personal exercise of power was an expression of God's will, and that, in secular matters at least, God's will and the Tsar's were to be equated.[3] They also inspired him to launch Muscovy's parallel to the Counter-Reformation – the attempt to enforce religious discipline on the population through a reorganized and revitalized Church, whose practices were to be aligned with the Greek.

His determination to restore the autocracy helped to account for Alexis's passion for history, too. His was not merely a bookish antiquarianism; nor was it a critical interest in the past. Apart from seeking to record his own achievements by writing a history of his own wars (a task begun but not pursued), his purpose was to find historical precedents that might serve to legitimize his objectives.[4]

And it did not preclude invention. Alexis claimed to be a 'divinely-crowned wearer of the [imperial] purple' and to be descended from the Roman Emperor Augustus (a claim ridiculed by the immigrant Croatian scholar Krizhanich who might otherwise have retained the Tsar's favour). He also spent immense sums on regalia, including a copy of the Emperor Constantine's diadem encrusted with gems;[5] and in order to suggest a continuity between the Riurikid and Romanov dynasties he referred to Ivan the Terrible as his forefather or predecessor (the word *praded* can mean either). Of all the young Tsar's heroes – David and Solomon, Alexander and Constantine the Great – Ivan was the nearest and the chief. It may seem odd that so staunch a Christian and so doting a father should profess admiration for so cruel a figure – for he knew very well that Ivan had killed his own son and had probably ordered the murder of the head of the Church, with whom, according to the Byzantine ideal, he should have worked in symphony. But Ivan had also been the last effective upholder of autocracy. His reign of terror had cowed the old nobility and crushed localism under foot. He had overcome the very challenges which Alexis himself feared he might have to face. It made political sense in the circumstances to admire Ivan.

But the possession of clear objectives resting on a coherent philosophy is no guarantee of political success. The question asked at the beginning of this book still requires an answer. Is the conventional view of Alexis as a passive figure manipulated by his favourites correct? Or was he an effective autocrat? And if the latter is true, how did the image of him as the pious, passive Tsar come to be created? The two problems are intertwined, but let us start with the image.

His reputation can be traced back to contemporary rumours. These fall into two main categories: the first consists of disparaging comments originating primarily from those parties adversely affected economically by the measures of 1648–9 and from objectors to Alexis's policies towards the Church (though Avvakum, the leader of the main stream of religious opposition, seems never to have spoken of him in such terms). Korepin, a mortgagor of Prince Cherkasskii, who was brought within the tax-paying net in 1648 (and who may have been used as a stalking-horse by his patron), reacted with these words: 'The Tsar sees everything in the way that Boyars Morozov and Miloslavskii tell him to. They control everything, and the Tsar knows all but is silent. The devil has taken his mind away.'[6] In the 1660s a bishop enraged by the government's failure to act as he deemed necessary asserted that Alexis was 'possessed' by those around him and, hence, incapable of action. 'The boyars are of Haman's race. The Tsar does not know what to do.'[7]

The interesting feature of such remarks is that they represent a variation on a popular myth about government current at that time – that a Tsar was incapable of acting unjustly; that when injustice occurred as the result of governmental action it could only be a consequence of the Tsar's agents, 'the boyars', perverting the Tsar's good intentions. The behaviour of the crowds in the urban riots of 1648 and 1662 and in the Razin rebellion of 1670–71 in attacking the government while hesitating to attack the Tsar himself, attests to this belief. So does the fact that the many pretenders to the throne during Alexis's reign all claimed to be *tsarevichi*, legitimate heirs rather than alternative Tsars. It has been suggested that this myth of the Tsar's essential goodness and the dangers of 'boyar power' had been inspired by none other than Ivan the Terrible.[8] It was certainly a myth supportive of autocracy; but it was a short step from promoting respect for the Tsar by dissociating him from unpopular governmental actions to representing him as the creature of his boyars. It is ironic that a myth originally intended to support one Tsar should have served to denigrate another. But it is even more ironic that disrespectful comments of this kind should have served ultimately to promote so much loose talk about 'boyar power' in historical writing that deals with Alexis's reign, and to build up an historiographical image of Alexis himself as a cipher in the hands of his advisers.

For while there are grounds to believe that Alexis, however precocious he may have been, was indeed heavily dependent on Morozov's judgement until 1648, there are no sufficient grounds to suppose that he depended so heavily on anyone thereafter. Indeed, for all Nikon's resentful outburst in 1658, as we shall see, the balance of the evidence supports the contrary view. Contemporary allegations of the kind that have been cited were, after all, made by interested parties most of whom had no direct knowledge of how and why particular decisions had been reached or evaded. They do not constitute the sort of evidence which should be accepted without question. Yet they have been accepted by historians as eminent as Kliuchevskii and Platonov. And it is curious indeed that the latter's characterization of the Tsar as weak-willed, cowardly, and unable to prevent stronger personalities taking advantage of him (while it bears no resemblance to Alexis) should fit his contemporary Nicholas II with such uncanny accuracy.

There was another category of contemporary observation which places Alexis in quite a different light. Paul of Aleppo, the Swedish and Venetian ambassadors, and other visiting foreigners, all report that Alexis was cruel, and they give instances of his severity. Paul of Aleppo (not without Arabic hyperbole) writes of his 'massacring' the boyars and ducking courtiers; the Swede compares Alexis's cruelty to Ivan's, and the Venetian reports his impatience with anyone who disagreed with him or who protested about the difficulty of carrying out an order. He also describes Alexis pulling Prince L'vov's beard and throwing the son of his Swedish interpreter to ferocious dogs and pigs.[9] In short, their picture is of a tyrant. The similarities between so many of these stories (the truth of only some of which is corroborated by other sources) suggests a common origin – court gossip. But the fact that the Venetian Ambassador, held in quarantine throughout his stay in Muscovy, was almost wholly reliant on information provided by the chief of Alexis's Private Office suggests very strongly that such gossip had been inspired – that it reflected a deliberate exercise in image-building mounted by Alexis himself. If so, his purpose is not difficult to fathom – to arouse fear of, and hence obedience to, his person by resurrecting the spectre of Ivan, the terror of the boyars.

These reports of his harshness and brutality have been discounted by historians – and rightly so, for although he lost his temper with members of his Council on occasion, uttered many terrible threats and resorted to torture, Alexis confined exemplary executions to the lower orders, and he did not live up to Paul of Aleppo's characterization of him as a great slaughterer of boyars. He did not because he had no need to. The threats themselves were usually an effective substitute for violence in bringing the prominent to heel, and dismissal from office or confiscation of estates served to discipline the obstinate among them. Alexis applied his principle (expressed in his falconry rules) of 'measure and proportion' to his punishments as well. Nevertheless he found a reputation for cruelty a useful aid in establishing his order.

However, Alexis used another means of image-building which has served probably more than anything else to promote the posthumous myth that he was only a symbolic Tsar who hovered over events and allowed 'favourites' (Morozov, Miloslavskii, Nikon, Odoevskii, Ordyn-Nashchokin, Matveev) to govern for him. This means was ceremony. The high value which Alexis placed on ceremonial is not to be explained simply by his piety or his taste for the theatrical, but by his need to reinforce his legitimacy and to re-establish effective autocratic power. Just as extravagant professions of his own humility and piety legitimized his rule in terms consistent with traditional Russian assumptions about the sin of exercising authority, so ceremony was a means of his emphasizing his divine right to rule by creating an impression of himself among the public as a superior, almost ethereal, creature. Both his public magnificence and his public piety were intended to inspire awe, and hence obedience. The extravagant protocol with which he surrounded himself, even when hawking, was comparable to that devised by his contemporary, Louis XIV of France. And both had a common inspiration. Louis might have been echoing Alexis's own thought when he wrote that 'In exercising a totally divine function here on earth, we must appear incapable of turmoils which could debase it.'[10] Hence Alexis's reputation as *tishaisheishii*, the quietest, but the most immovable, the most serene, as well as the most pious, of Russians monarchs – a term which had its parallel in his claim to be recognized by foreign governments as 'Serenissimus', not merely 'Illustrissimus'.[11]

Yet though he spent long hours in church he never allowed worship to interrupt business (he even wrote, or dictated, letters during mass), and though he gave the impression of sitting in godlike majesty high above the earthly fray he was in fact constantly involved in it. In order to preserve the illusion of distance, however, he often preferred to act through intermediaries. Thus, for example, he furnished Fedor Rtishchev with the funds, the authority and, perhaps, with the inspiration to set up a school staffed with Ukrainian scholars (and indeed Rtishchev's reputation for charitable works was largely founded upon the Tsar's largesse); he used Nikon to bring order to the Church, and employed trusted personal agents like Artamon Matveev on a host of delicate missions. But above all, the Private Office was his instrument for action.

Staffed by the ablest young bureaucrats and directed by Alexis personally, his Private Office not only managed his complex personal economy, administered certain elite regiments and launched a variety of enterprises and projects; it also intervened in all sorts of routine government business. When it was wound up, papers were redistributed to no fewer than twenty-nine departments,[12] and even now it is impossible to trace all its ramifications. The operations of the Private Office were secret, and many historians have followed Solov'ev in taking this as evidence of Alexis's 'inability to act directly and openly. . . . Like all people of his character, Alexis . . . hid himself [and] arranged [matters] on the sly in order to avoid opposition and discontent.'[13]

In fact Alexis acted both directly and indirectly. He personally instructed and debriefed ambassadors and personally interrogated suspects;[14] and when he acted through intermediaries it was not because of some failing in 'character' but out of political wisdom, for reasons of state. Solov'ev failed to grasp what both Alexis and Louis XIV had grasped – that in order to support his claim to divine right a monarch must sustain an impression of aloofness and distance. Most historians since have also failed to consider whether Alexis might not have possessed political skill; whether from time to time there might not have been political advantage to be derived from a pretence of non-involvement, or in behaving ambiguously – the more so in such unstable times when dangerous passions were so easily aroused. Since a great part of the Office's work concerned high policy and security its operations were necessarily secret; nor could soundings on delicate issues be taken openly. And what advantage would there have been in attracting opposition and generating discontent gratuitously by always showing one's hand?

When Alexis acted openly he acted decisively to resolve some problem large or small. But by no means all problems were susceptible of decisive resolution, and these had to be handled with discretion, not precipitately, by force. There can be no question that the 'inspired' image of Alexis as a godlike figurehead and the secrecy with which he surrounded the court and his political activities were to have a damaging effect on his historical reputation. Nonetheless his success as a Tsar should be gauged, not by unwarranted assumptions about his character, nor on misunderstandings about his role and image as Tsar, nor yet on misinterpretations of contemporary comment – but by the extent to which he achieved his objectives.

Alexis wanted to become an effective autocrat, and this he certainly became. In doing so he had to deal with three institutions which impinged on his monopoly of power or which had the potential to impinge upon it – the Assembly of the Land (*zemskii sobor*), the Council of State (*boiarskaia duma*), and the Patriarchate. The Assembly of the Land, the only institution that might conceivably have evolved into a parliament, had been in almost continuous

session for ten years under Tsar Michael, and almost every important decision had been made in its name. It was called several times
in the first few years of Alexis's reign, but after 1653 he was never to
summon it again. As for the Council and the Patriarchate, Alexis
succeeded in drawing their political teeth as well.

According to Kotoshikhin, Alexis's father had been able to 'do
nothing' without the Council, whereas Alexis himself 'governs the
state as he wishes'.[15] This was not achieved all at once, however. He
moved gradually from government by conference to personal rule.
Alexis began by enlarging the Council. In the first half of his reign
(before 1660) he raised no fewer than ninety-two men to the first
two Council ranks (*boiar* and *okol'nichii*), most of them in the first
seven years. In the second half of his reign he made only thirty-six
such promotions. The proliferation of honours in his early years as
Tsar served not so much to placate powerful nobles by bringing
them into the political process, as to balance the 'old guard', which
he had inherited, with men of his own choice. Indeed the doubling
of the Council by 1652 had the effect of diminishing the honour
attaching to membership. But the most significant changes came
later, with radical shifts in both the social balance and the function of
the Council.

At the beginning of his reign it had been overwhelmingly aristocratic in composition (about 70 per cent); only a quarter of the
membership had risen from the gentry; and only one bureaucrat
had attained membership. In the last years of the reign (1667–75), by
contrast, barely a quarter of the Council were aristocrats; members
of gentry origins accounted for over 50 per cent; and no fewer than
five bureaucrats were raised to membership.[16] By the end of his
reign, then, indeed for some time before that, the aristocratic
element on the Council had shrunk to insignificance, and it had
become nonsense to talk of 'boyar power' in the sense that had been
justified in 1645. But, more significantly, the Council was emascu-
lated as an independent political force. Although Alexis held frequent meetings with his Councillors, as time went on he consulted
them as ministers and generals (in cabinet committees, as it were)
rather than collectively. He also discouraged Councillors from discussing policy with one another behind his back. The Council
retained a ceremonial role; but in the latter part of his reign Alexis
called full meetings very rarely. So far from allowing it to control
him, he had made the Council his instrument.

The third potential threat to autocracy, the Patriarchate, only emerged during the reign in the person of Nikon. The Patriarchate itself was of no great longevity. The metropolitan see of Moscow had only been raised to patriarchal status in 1589 and it was the most junior of the five patriarchates of the Orthodox world. Tsar and Patriarch were supposed in the Byzantine tradition to work in symphony together, but the balance of the relationship had always favoured the Emperor (Photius, the Patriarch of Constantinople, whose contrary views Nikon came to embrace, had himself been deposed from office). Indeed, the Moscow Patriarchate had only recently been afforded the potential to challenge the Tsar. Its prestige had risen with the extinction of the Riurikids and during the Time of Troubles, and it was further enhanced by the Patriarch Filaret, Alexis's grandfather, who had borne the title 'Great Sovereign'. Filaret, rather than his son, Tsar Michael, had been the effective ruler of Muscovy until his death in 1633.

In retrospect Alexis himself may be seen to have encouraged Nikon's ambitions by swearing to obey him when Nikon was elected Patriarch in 1652, and by bestowing the title 'Great Sovereign' on him two years later. However, if these seemed to have been mistakes in retrospect they had not seemed so at the time. It must be remembered that Nikon did not develop the case for the superiority of the Patriarchate until after he had relinquished the patriarchal throne; there is no reason to suppose that in swearing obedience to Nikon Alexis had anything but spiritual obedience in mind; and the title 'Great Sovereign' only indicated Nikon's status as Regent-elect while Alexis was absent on campaign and hence placing not only his own life, but the good order of the state, at risk. In any case Nikon was still a close friend as late as 1655, and he had needed extra clout in order to push through the reforms which Alexis required of him and to act as an effective counterweight to the governmental machine in Moscow at a time when Alexis was away campaigning and had yet to assert himself fully as autocrat. By 1658, however, circumstances had changed. The Private Office had been established; Alexis had returned to Moscow and was exerting personal authority. Nikon had served his purpose.

Several years were to pass, however, before Nikon was deposed, and this has often been taken as further 'proof' of Alexis's weakness. Yet circumstances restrict even an autocrat's room for manoeuvre. It is a truism that opportunities for decisive political action arise only occasionally; that otherwise a statesman can only prepare, have patience, and repeatedly test the condition of the political waters until the circumstances are found to be propitious for action. The Nikon problem was fraught with such dangers that only a fool would have rushed in to resolve it. It was not immediately apparent that Nikon would refuse to abdicate or to install his successor without taking any part in determining who his successor might be. The arrangements eventually put in hand to depose Nikon canonically involved complex dealings with the four senior Orthodox Patriarchs; and measures had to be taken to ensure that Nikon would have no significant support within the hierarchy or among the public when he was put on trial. All this took time to arrange.

But another factor also counted. It is clear from the cat-and-mouse game Alexis played with Nikon that he found it useful to keep him in limbo. So long as he remained there the ex-Patriarch continued to serve as a lightning-conductor, attracting dissident resentment. So long as he remained there Alexis could use him as a lever against the Old Believers, allowing them to believe that he might restore him to office if they remained obstinate and that he might sacrifice him as a reward for their compliance. Once Nikon had been deposed it would be apparent to all that the Tsar himself was responsible for the church reforms. It was hardly a coincidence, then, that when the time came for resolution it was comprehensive. Nikon was deposed, the reforms were confirmed, and both the 'right' and 'left' oppositions (the Old Believers and those who opposed state supremacy) condemned virtually simultaneously at the Council of 1666–7. It is also evident that Nikon's fall was not due simply to 'boyar hostility', though Alexis no doubt encouraged that view, but threatening to impinge on the Tsar's authority. And in playing the leading role at the trial Alexis relied, not on 'the boyars' (who in fact gave him precious little support), but on Ligarides, Bashmakov and Matveev and on the cooperation of the two Eastern Patriarchs whom he had persuaded to attend – representatives of the old Orthodox world called in to counter a dangerous development in the new.

Alexis's handling of the Nikon affair may lay him open to charges of Byzantine manipulation and even of deceit, but not of weakness. And once the point of resolution had been reached Alexis's command of the Church was virtually secured. Synods met his wishes in everything. He had made the Church to all intents and purposes an arm of the State – and, thanks to Nikon, it was a more efficient arm than it would otherwise have been. Nevertheless although a compliant Church was useful it did not suffice. Imposing order on Muscovites was analogous to taming a wild beast (a process to which Alexis had been introduced in childhood and in which he retained an interest all his life) and other instruments were also needed.

One, of course, was the army. Troops, more particularly *strel'tsy*, were required to suppress revolts, guard commercial routes against bandits, and back up the authority of provincial governors. They were also deployed to protect missionary priests sent into the rural outback to bring its inhabitants to obedience to God and the Tsar (as Avvakum himself had to be protected on such missions early in his career). The gentry constituted a more important instrument than the soldiery, however. They maintained day-to-day order over large parts of the countryside (where, given the low rate of urbanization, the vast majority of Russians lived) and acted as agents for central government in such matters as dispensing local justice and tax collection.[17] Alexis's dependence on the gentry to carry out such functions, as much as the need (pending the remodelling of the army) for gentry levies to fight his wars, accounts for the imposition of serfdom. Perhaps mindful again of Byzantine precedents, Alexis made no serious attempt to impede the conversion of service estates to hereditary ownership; but he insisted that possession carried with it an obligation to serve the state. Ultimately, however, the gentry were more useful at home, acting as agents of the centralizing state and keeping the peasants in their place, than they were on campaign.

The bureaucracy, however, was Alexis's favourite instrument for imposing order. This was predictable, perhaps, for bureaucracy was the concomitant of absolutism. The Muscovite bureaucracy saw a significant growth during his reign; it also became much more highly stratified than it had been before (it has been calculated that there had been seven different pay categories in 1654; as many as twenty-two by 1676[18]); and the prestige of its members rose considerably. It had its limitations as an instrument, however. The service may have been no more corrupt (at least after 1648) than its counterparts abroad; nor was it particularly difficult to find suitable recruits (though it was the practice to farm out specialist financial tasks to merchants, who sometimes found it difficult to distinguish between the state's business and their own). The main problems (apart from funding) were to create, or extend, a suitable ethos of service, and, naturally, to foster understanding and acceptance of the laws and edicts to be administered, especially outside the major cities, where illiteracy was rife, and custom or the wishes of local notables tended to prevail. An appreciation of the problems involved in enforcing obedience to the rules throughout the realm may well account for Alexis's expenditure of so much of his time in ensuring that his writ would at least run on his own extensive estates. And even the bureaucracy in Moscow needed a watch-dog and a gadfly. These Alexis provided through the medium of his Private Office.

The influence of the Private Office on the service as a whole was stronger than the number of officials working in it at any one time might suggest. His secretaries were evidently extremely industrious; since they acted in the Tsar's name they had more authority than those with whom they had to deal; and since they might suddenly call a department to account or descend on it without warning to carry out an audit, they helped to keep the bureaucrats generally on their toes. Furthermore, a high proportion of those who served as under-secretaries in the Office were moved, on promotion to full secretaries, to other departments, and at least three of them reached Councillor rank and ministerial responsibility. So did the three secretaries – Dementii Bashmakov, Fedor Mikhailov and Danilo Polianskii.[19] Hence the Private Office provided an increasing number of functionaries, trained[20] and tested by the Tsar in person and inculcated with his standards, who could carry these standards into the bureaucracy at large.

But Alexis used other trusties too – men of proven ability, implicit loyalty, and discretion. They included officers, falconers, courtiers, priests, even a few aristocrats (a class which he tended to confine to military commands and provincial governorships). Members of this cadre of personal agents were sent on diplomatic and military missions, to carry out delicate tasks concerning the Church, to set up new industries, to run commercial ventures, to convey personal expressions of the Tsar's pleasure or displeasure, to investigate matters that had aroused his interest or suspicion, and generally to speed up the machinery of state and keep those who operated it on their mettle. By the latter part of the reign they constituted a very effective instrument of power, a means to help Alexis establish his own order.

Yet if good order was an end in itself it was also a means to other ends, not least aggrandizement and, above all, conquest. It cannot be without significance that the only specific role that Alexis commended to his heir, Fedor, in his testament was to wage war.[21] But how effective was Alexis in his chosen role as conqueror? How able was he as a strategist? The record is mixed. The recapture of Smolensk and Seversk served to avenge his father's failure in the war of 1632–4, and although he was eventually forced to disgorge most of his subsequent gains in Belorussia, Livonia and Lithuania, by the time he died he was in possession of the greater part of Ukraine. His ability as commander-in-chief has probably been underestimated, however. It is true that the notes he made during his first campaigns demonstrate no more than that he understood what was happening, that he was much concerned with logistics and morale, and that he knew that war and diplomacy formed a continuum. Even if he did not direct operations personally, however, he had a sufficient grasp of grand strategy and of technical matters, as well as enough sound advice at his disposal, to carry out the task. It could be claimed that until he reached Riga luck had favoured him and that his early military successes were due as much to Polish weakness as to Muscovite strength and generalship; but the real test came later.

Alexis was obviously sensible to make peace with Sweden when he did – though he was to continue to the very end his efforts to gain access to the Baltic (as late as 1673 he was pressing for free trading rights at Riga and Reval). And his dogged determination in the face of successive disasters to fight on for Ukraine had its rationale, despite the appalling costs. But his talents showed best in maturity, during the later stages of that struggle, when he repeatedly contrived to restore positions in Ukraine that seemed lost; in his attempts to incorporate it into the Russian state (gradually colonizing it with bureaucrats, forcing its Church to recognize the authority of Moscow instead of Constantinople, trying to integrate its elites and to win their loyalty); and finally in resuming the advance in the 1670s when he directed campaigns with skill from Moscow. His appreciation of the political dimensions of war, the importance he attached to sound staff work, his care in timing and pacing operations, and his understanding of the concept of economy of force give the impression that Clausewitz might have had as little to teach him about the essentials of war as Machiavelli about the art of statesmanship.

Much more significant, however, was his achievement in rebuilding the army. In the words of an eighteenth-century military historian, 'Tsar Alexei Mikhailovich laid the foundation not only of a standing army but of its organization according to the principles of military science.'[22] The importance of modernizing the army had been recognized before his time. Previous regimes had imported armaments and engaged foreign mercenaries. It was the scale and thoroughness of his army reforms that was significant. He modernized the army's equipment and its training. He also changed its organization and its composition, introducing a measure of conscription. The effects were most marked on the infantry and artillery, but they affected the cavalry too. In 1651 only 7 per cent of the army had consisted of new-formation regiments; by 1663 80 per cent of the army did so. In 1645 the cavalry had consisted almost exclusively of gentry and members of the lowest provincial service class (*deti boairskie*); by 1674, 60 per cent of the cavalry concentrated in Ukraine consisted of new-formation troops.[23] The reforms required the engagement of foreigners on a massive scale. It has been estimated that three thousand Scots alone entered Alexis's service,[24] and there were Englishmen, Irishmen, Danes, Germans, Frenchmen, and others too, including Poles. It has been claimed that eventually over a quarter of the army consisted of foreigners, and while this may seem exaggerated, it could not have been so in respect of the officer corps.[25]

The cost was immense and had a considerable impact on Russian institutions, on the economy and society, not all of them foreseen. Part of the cost was met at the expense of the magnates and the Church, whose urban dependants were subjected to state taxation. More was afforded by the setting-up of the Monastery Office to administer church estates. Alexis made exceptions to this rule (like Henry VIII he believed that 'of our absolute power we be above the law'), but despite this and despite the fact that the hereditary holdings of the monasteries and the Patriarch increased by about 10 per cent by the end of his reign,[26] the wealth of the Church was henceforth at the mercy of the state – and the state exploited it using a variety of devices including the raising of forced loans which were never to be repaid. This was no crude and total act of expropriation, however, as had taken place in England; nor were the proceeds squandered as Henry had dissipated the wealth of the sequestered English monasteries.[27] Nevertheless the yield was insufficient. War plunder helped to an extent, though it was not enough to close the gap between income and expenditure. One consequence of the shortfall was the inflation crisis of the late 1650s and early 1660s. Another was the growth of Alexis's attention to the economy, industry and trade.

He founded new industries, encouraged existing ones, and tried to develop agriculture.[28] He sponsored prospectors exploring for useful or marketable minerals and plants, not least in Siberia, and though he was himself the most substantial merchant in the realm he strove to help native Muscovite merchants towards prosperity as well. The growth of the merchant elite (*gosti*) by 1675 to almost three times the number they had been in 1649 was hardly an accurate measure of his success (for the *gosti* were saddled with extra obligations to the state), but the Trade Statute had a beneficial effect, encouraging what Soviet scholars term 'the formation of the all-Russian market' – a largely spontaneous development which was conducive to the centralization programme by which Alexis set such store. Otherwise, however, he was forced to resort to taxation and to state monopolies, which were hardly conducive to general prosperity. For all his good intentions and his receptiveness to fresh ideas, Alexis could find no better solutions to the problem of expenditure outrunning income than those employed by other European monarchs of the time. However, the economy was to be helped, albeit indirectly, by Alexis's attempts to improve communications.

The conquest of distance was always a challenge to him, and no monarch of the time made greater use of maps.[29] These helped him to direct campaigns from afar and to visualize parts of his dominions that he had never seen. They also gave him a knowledge of trade routes that passed over seas and deserts to emporia as difficult of access as Bokhara, Isfahan and Venice. He was intent, however, on breaking the hold which the English and the Dutch had taken on world trade by finding a direct route to the Indies, India and China and on claiming a share of their commerce free from intermediaries. The supposed sea-route to these countries via the Caspian proved non-existent, of course, but Alexis also sought a north-east passage to the ocean we now know as the Pacific. He sent expeditions to farthest Siberia (a useful source of sables, walrus tusks and native tribute); he commissioned maps of these vast regions, and a report on the possibility of finding a passage to the Orient through the White Sea via Novaia Zemlia.[30] It was the uncertainty, as much as the distance, involved that ruled this out as a viable alternative to the tedious overland routes. On the other hand, the quest for speedier, direct, reliable communications both internally and abroad led to the improvement of the old courier service and to the establishment of regular posts on the routes not only to Archangel and Siberia, but to Kiev, to Riga and the West.[31]

Such activity shows Alexis to have been intelligent as well as cunning, obstinate and persevering. But it is primarily as a manager of men that he stands out as a monarch above the ordinary. He understood the limits of his power as autocrat and the need to play the politician. The blessed state of harmony that he yearned to establish demanded conciliation, yet order was the foundation of harmony and had to be maintained with rigour. His most difficult task was to steer a steady course between the Scylla of concession and the Charybdis of repression. Fine judgement was required, and the difficulties and reverses he experienced honed Alexis's powers of judgement to a very fine point indeed. Furthermore, he had the wit to recognize that the loyalty of his servitors was the key to success.

That loyalty had to be won, however – and no Russian Tsar was better at winning it than Alexis. His qualities of human warmth and sympathy, so evident in his letters consoling Odoevskii on the death of his son and supporting Afanasy Ordyn-Nashchokin when his son Voin defected, served him well in this. They even earned him the love of the arch-dissenter Avvakum, who would never, even when despairing of him, regard the Tsar as other than a fine soul led astray. But Alexis took good care not to confine his exercise of these charismatic gifts to the prominent. On Sunday, 28th March 1668 (to take a random example) he held a reception for the staff of the Apothecary Court and for under-secretaries serving in a variety of ministries. Next day he held a levée for craftsmen of the Armoury's precious metals workshops.[32] Soldiers, functionaries of all kinds and, not least, foreigners in his service were also rewarded by the sight of the Tsar's bright eyes and sometimes by a kindly word from his gracious lips. Such small acts, more than material reward, perhaps, inspired love, and the effect was noticed by the Swedish envoy shortly before his death when he remarked the affection in which the guards so obviously held their Tsar. Moreover, Alexis knew how to exploit such love, sometimes by withholding tokens of his affection (though often intimating how it might be regained). His style of managing men may well have derived from his handling of falcons, but it frequently succeeded.

The career of Prince G. G. Romodanovskii provides an illustration. As early as 1652 he was punished for protesting against what he considered to be an inappropriately lowly appointment on grounds of precedence, and he was to receive more than one of the Tsar's notorious tongue-lashings in later years for failing in some aspect of his duty. But in berating him Alexis also hinted at the way Romodanovskii might restore himself to favour. The man responded, and lived to receive commendations and senior commands.[33] The judicious use of sticks and carrots had helped to make a reliable servant out of a hot-headed young aristocrat.

This pyschological handling of men was employed far down the hierarchy. A significant proportion of Alexis's time was spent scrutinizing lists which his Private Office secretaries had compiled of proposed promotions, rewards, and answers to petitions. And his decisions were made with a view to their exemplary effects. Not only rewards and punishments but their scale were carefully graded to rank and measured in proportion to service or disservice – whether by a land grant, a present, or an enquiry after someone's health; whether by an expropriation order or the threat of one, the withholding of an expected favour, a public disgrace or an admonitory message. Alexis knew the value of instilling fear as well as of arousing affection. As Dr Collins remarked with truth, Alexis was 'severe in his chastisements, but very careful of his Subjects' love'.[34]

His training, notably the influence of *The Secret of Secrets*, had instilled such care into him. As he remarked to Nikita Odoevskii in 1658, 'Aristotle writes that all sovereigns should choose the sort of man [for a post of high responsibility] who will reconcile the Sovereign with the people and not aggravate relations with them.'[35] Once, in choosing Nikon to be Patriarch, he failed to observe this principle (though Nikon had earned a reputation as a conciliator in the provincial riots of 1650). He may also have miscalculated Nikon's obduracy and placed too much reliance on the man's personal loyalty to him. On the other hand, Alexis himself made a valiant attempt at reconciliation in his dealings with the Old Believers. Without ever conceding a substantial point of principle, he summoned up all his persuasive powers, all his charm, and a fine sense of timing, while searching all the while for some chink in the adversary's armour, whether a fear or an ambition, which he might exploit. In Avvakum and Morozova, however, he could find none. They were irreconcilable.

The dissent which they represented was bred of conservatism and fed on xenophobia, values which Alexis understood but which he could not share. Taking a wider view, one perceives him to have been trapped by circumstances. There was no way of reconciling the modernization necessary to Muscovy's survival with the popular yearning for exclusiveness and isolation that stemmed from the country's essentially peasant nature. Attempts were made to assuage the sense of outrage. Foreigners (officially if not in practice) were confined to the Foreign Suburb; they were pressed to convert to Orthodoxy; foreign styles of icon-painting were condemned, and foreign dress was banned. But, as Alexis well knew, these were mere anodynes. The massive scale of his recruitments abroad, the difficulties placed in the way of these recruits leaving his service;[36] the inflow of Ukrainians, Belorussians, Lithuanians and Balts from the conquered territories; the subjection of servicemen and peasant conscripts to Western military discipline; the training of Russians in new techniques; the encouragement of foreign learning – all these carried with them the seeds of inevitable and unpredictable cultural change.

There were limits, after all, to the ability of one man, however able, however charismatic, however skilled in managing and manipulating men, to foresee all the consequences of his actions, still less to control them. Nevertheless, once he recognized that some developments might hold dangers (and he was always as close and perceptive an observer of affairs as he was of nature) he tried to ward off the adverse effects. His ability to learn both from his own mistakes and from mistakes made in other countries served him well in this. Two examples must suffice.

In the early years of his reign he had exploited the popularity of saintly cults in order to foster patriotism and respect for ecclesiastical authority, and to strengthen his centralization programme. Relics were gathered in from the provinces with great pomp and the Kremlin was made into a veritable pantheon of saintly heroes. The policy reached its climax in 1653 with the re-entombments of Job, Hermogen and Philip. But having recognized that problems might arise in controlling a proliferation of cults, Alexis lost his enthusiasm for new saints and set out successfully to discourage the creation of new ones.[37]

The other example instances his learning from the experience of foreigners. An unexpressed assumption runs through his thinking: that Russia must never be allowed to follow the example of Poland. It was not a matter of contempt for *liakhi* (the old Russian term for Poles) which was expressed; nor fear of Catholicism; and it was certainly not contempt for Polish culture, of which Alexis was a fervent admirer. Rather it stemmed from his perception that the state of Poland was sliding towards collapse and disintegration, and, more particularly, from an understanding of the reasons for its doom – an elective and limited monarchy, the growth of magnate power, the proliferation of noble status, the glorification of noble liberty, and contempt for the authority of central government (a trait noticeable in Poland even today). The Polish example spurred Alexis to follow policies which were almost precisely opposite. As we have seen, Alexis reinforced autocracy, strengthened central government, stamped on localism, strove to monopolize liberty, and, although for other reasons he followed the Polish example in sanctioning serfdom, he also took steps to prevent the proliferation of noble status by closing off the gentry class to new entrants.[38] Many factors fuelled Russia's progress towards absolutism, but an appreciation of what the emasculation of the Polish monarchy entailed was one of them; and whatever view one takes of the merits of Russian absolutism, which Alexis did so much to entrench, and however one estimates the possibility and the desirability of alternative governmental traditions establishing themselves, it was arguably Alexis's crowning achievement to have ensured that Russia would not follow Poland's road to ruin.

Yet if Alexis became one of the wisest of monarchs, he was also one of the unluckiest. In 1655, at a most critical juncture, his tsardom was struck by the plague, and with devastating force; abrupt changes in the balance of power thwarted his attempts to seize an outlet to the Baltic; reforms intended to promote unity resulted in schism; and he was never able to realize his dream of administering justice equally for all. Yet he was unluckiest of all in dying when he did. Had he but lived another twenty years it is difficult to imagine his country suffering quite so many of the lurches and reverses which followed his death, and his work would scarcely have been so diluted. If only he had lived into his sixties he might have been able to bequeath the state directly to an adult and carefully educated Peter.

As it was, the continuity was broken. It is true that his successor Fedor burned the books of precedence, thus destroying any possibility that the notion of lineage determining promotion might be resurrected. It is also true that the struggle against the Turks was continued and that, in 1686, the city of Kiev was permanently annexed. But too much was allowed to slip. The Private Office was wound up immediately on Alexis's death; the Monastery Office disappeared in 1677, and the court theatre ceased to function. What mattered more, however, was that the impetus behind the military reforms slackened; that the aristocracy was allowed to gain ground at the expense of the bureaucracy despite the burning of the books of precedence, and that the Council regained some of its former authority. Worse still, as Alexis had foreseen on his death-bed, the inexperience of his successor and the rivalry between Miloslavskiis and Naryshkins and their adherents promoted discord within the Kremlin which tended to weaken the authority of government. When Fedor died in 1682 and the heirs of both clans, Ivan and Peter, were proclaimed joint Tsars, the discontented *strel'tsy* took control of Moscow for five months, giving encouragement both to religious dissidents and to aristocratic power-seekers, notably 'the braggart' Boyar Prince Khovanskii. In reaction, Khovanskii was executed and Avvakum met his quietus at the stake. Eventually, towards the end of the century, Peter took power into his own hands.

The story of what followed has often been told – but usually in the light of panegyrics and sycophantic anecdotes rather than in historical perspective. Peter (let there be no question about it) accomplished much. He was successful in war; he built St Petersburg; he made Russia a maritime power. Yet to cut away the Petrine myth and to consider all his reforms critically and in their long-term contexts is to find that most of his successes were built upon foundations laid, or on precedents provided, by his father; and that most of his achievements which were not so based were to prove, over the course of time, to be inconsequential or disastrous. Alexis, after all, had begun the modernization of the army; he had grasped the importance of naval power, of industrial development and of encouraging commercial enterprise. If Peter broke down the dam of Russian isolationism it was Alexis who had first breached that dam. He had helped to reduce the force of patriarchalism by introducing a public element into legal relationships, and had made virtually all his subjects feel the power of the state. And if Peter's abolition of the Patriarchate and his 'bureaucratization' of the Church was, indeed, his 'most decisive break with the past',[39] Alexis had already destroyed its latent power to challenge the state and had already harnessed its economic resources.

Peter's introduction of a poll-tax did serve to overcome a long-standing problem, for the household basis of direct taxation had never worked satisfactorily; and his establishment of an Academy of Sciences was of some importance (though the Apothecary Office under Alexis had been a considerable scientific centre); but Peter's much-vaunted 'rationalization' of government was perhaps rather less significant than is commonly assumed. The creation of 'the governing Senate' and the replacement of the *prikazy* by Colleges (whose principle of hierarchical yet collective authority mirrored traditional Muscovite practice as well as Swedish models) did not necessarily serve to promote efficiency, and his *Heraldmeister* merely took over certain functions of the old *Razriad*. Peter poured a great deal of old wine into new bottles. Even his Table of Ranks formalized an existing system of precedence (the *generalitet*, for example, replicated the four Council ranks). Alexis had already established the principle that ability and service, not lineage, qualified a man for office; and it was Alexis, not Peter, who was the true father of the bureaucratic state.

Peter, of course, was a much more programmatic reformer than Alexis had been, even though he was driven by events more often than he pretended to be. Both of them worked towards the creation of a police state, but whereas Alexis's instincts led him in that direction, Peter was guided rather by his enthusiasm for foreign, and particularly for German, models. Furthermore, whereas Alexis understood that no people can escape its past and that force alone could not overcome it, Peter imagined that he could graft Western institutions and Western manners onto Russians successfully – indeed, that he could accomplish almost anything by force. As crude and precipitate as Alexis had been subtle and circumspect, Peter plunged his country into a maelstrom of change. The result was dissonance. Alexis's vision of a harmony reflecting the order of heaven upon earth was destroyed. In importing not merely Western technology but Western manners, fashions, and institutions, and forcing them upon his subjects, Peter disrupted Russia's organic development, fractured the cohesiveness of society and the homogeneity of its culture. And yet in the long run Alexis's legacy can be considered to have been more enduring than Peter's.

If Peter wrenched Russia out of 'mediaeval backwardness' and forcibly changed the direction of its historical development, his success was only temporary. Eventually it was to spring back onto its former course.[40] Soviet Russia today reflects the pre–Petrine rather than the Petrine era. Its culture is homogeneous; there is the same stress on ideological purity and conformity as in Alexis's time. The same lip-service is paid to internationalism as once it was to ecumenism, and Moscow is still assumed to be the Third Rome, the messianic centre of the world. Nor is that all. There is the same collectivism, the same difficulty in distinguishing judicial from administrative action; the same desperate drive to obtain Western technology, the same suspicion of Western ideas, the same high value on secrecy. Even dissent tends to follow the old pattern – vehemently confronting the totality of the state with innocent idealism; and the methods and the style of countering it do not differ in essence from Alexis's. But above all the centralist tradition which Alexis consolidated, and the bureaucracy which he nurtured, have endured. In these respects at least one imagines that, were Alexis to return to the Kremlin today, he would not feel altogether out of place.

Abbreviations

AI	Akty istoricheskie		Fedorovicha i Alekseia
AAE	Akty arkheograficheskoi ekspeditsii		Mikhailovicha zapisok
ASBAR	Akty sobrannye v	PRG	Pis'ma russkikh gosudar'ei
	bibliotekakh i arkhivakh	PSZ	Polnoe sobranie zakonov
	rossiiskoi imperii	RBS	Russkii biograficheskii slovar'
ChOIDR	Chteniia obshchestva istorii i	RIB	Russkaia istoricheskaia biblioteka
	drevnostei rossiiskikh	RS	Rod Sheremetevykh (Barsukov)
DAI	Dopolneniia k aktam	SEER	Slavonic & East European Review
	istoricheskim	SGGD	Sobranie gosudarstvennykh gramot
DB	Domashnyi byt' russkikh tsarei		i dogovorov
	(Zabelin)	SN	Starina i novizna
Dneval'nye	Dneval'nye zapiski prikaza	Sob. Ul.	Sobornoe ulozhenie
	tainyth del	SP	Sobranie pisem
DR	Dvortsovye razriady	TsGADA	Tsentral'nyi gosudarstvennyi
DRV	Drevniaia rossiiskaia		arkhiv drevnykh aktov
	vivliofika	VI	Voprosy istorii
DTP	Dela tainogo prikaza	VT	Vykhody tsarei
OSP	Oxford Slavonic Papers	ZhMNP	Zhurnal ministerstva narodnago
PDS	Pamiatniki diplomaticheskikh		prosveshcheniia
	snoshenii	ZORI	Zapiski otdeleniia russkoi i
Povs	Povsiadnevnykh dvortsovykh		slav'ianskoi arkheologii
	vremeni . . . tsarei Mikhaila		

251

Notes

Introduction

1. The register was printed in V. Lamanskii (ed.), 'Prikaz Tainykh Del', *ZORI*, II, St Petersburg, 1861. It lists those papers of Alexis's Private Office which had not been dispersed upon his death. See also I. Ya Gurliand, *Prikaz velikogo gosudaria tainykh del*, Yaroslavi 1902, pp. 382–6. The collection, minus some documents which have been lost since the catalogue was compiled, now forms Fond 27 of the Central State Archive in Moscow (of which the Petrine register is No. 11), and, directly or indirectly, this book is largely based upon it.

2. The servitor concerned was Prince Iakov Dolgorukii. He answered that Alexis had done more than Peter to improve the administration of the law, but less in other respects. The judgement may be questioned; the reader must decide. – S. F. Platonov in V. Kallash (ed.), *Tri veka*, Moscow, 1912, I, pp. 85–114.

3. V. N. Berkh's work (*Tsarstvovanie Tsaria Alekseia Mikhailovicha*, 1831) is little more than a catalogue of events with patriotic glosses and hopelessly outdated; for the shortcomings of the latest attempt (J. Fuhrman, *Tsar Alexis: His Reign and His Russia*, 1981) see the review in *SEER*, pp. 112–13. For other attempts, mostly ephemera, see the Bibliography.

4. P. Medovnikov, *Istoriia znacheniia tsarstvovaniia Alekseia Mikhailovicha*, Moscow, 1854.

5. Notably Lamanskii, *loc. cit.*, and P. Bartenev, *Sobranie pisem Tsaria Alekseia Mikhailovicha*, Moscow, 1856 (some of which had been published in Mukhanov, *Sbornik*, 1836).

6. E.g. *Iz arkhiva tainykh del* (*SN*, Book 15), etc.; S. A. Belokurov, *Dela tainogo prikaza* (*RIB*, Vols 21–23 and 38) and *Dneval'nye zapiski prikaza tainykh del 7165–7183gg.* (*ChOIDR*, Vols 224–5) Books 1–2, Moscow, 1908; I. Ya. Gurliand (ed.), *Dela tainogo prikaza* (*RIB*, Vol. 23), 1904, and *Prikaz relikago gosudaria tainykh del*, Yaroslavl, 1902 (appendices).

7. Gurliand, *Prikaz velikogo gosudaria tainykh del*, Yaroslavl, 1902; A. I Zaozerskii, *Tsar' Aleksei Mikhailovich v svoem khoziaistve*, Petrograd, 1917 (a second edition appeared in 1937 under a different title – see Bibliography).

8. G. Fedotov, *Sviatoi Filipp*, Paris, 1928.

9. S. M. Solov'ev, *Istoriia Rossii s drevneishikh vremen*, II, St Petersburg, 1894, xii, col. 606 and x, col. 1491; V. Kliuchevskii (trans. L. Archibald), *The Rise of the Romanovs*, p. 158; S. F. Platonov, 'Tsar' Aleksei Mikhailovich: opyt' kharakteristiki' in V. Kallash, *loc. cit.* also his *Lektsii po russkoi istorii*, St Petersburg, 1910, pp. 384–91.

10. E.g. E. lo Gatto (*Storia della Russia*, Firenze, 1946, p. 218) concludes that he 'lacked energy and personal tenacity'; N. Riazonovsky (*A History of Russia*, Oxford, 1972, p. 196) calls him 'a weak ruler'; J. D. Clarkson (*A History of Russia*, London, 1962, p. 167) tells us that he was 'a man of great piety and no force o. character', and too devoted to his comforts to give consistent guidance to state affairs.

11. E.g. N. Pavlenko, *Petr Pervyi*, Moscow, 1975 (in the series 'Lives of Remarkable People'); P. G. Skrynnikov, *Ivan Groznyi*, Moscow, 1980, and his *Boris Godunov*, Moscow, 1979.

12. Robert Lyall, *The Character of the Russians*, London, 1823, pp. 541–2.

Chapter I The Education of a Prince

1. The account of Alexis's childhood environment and upbringing is based principally on Ivan Zabelin, *DB* (4th, enlarged, edition), 2 parts, Moscow, 1915–18, especially I, pp. 91, 107, 110–11, 151, 159–64, 170ff., 235, 240–49, 270ff., 296; and II, pp. 4–7, 11, 21–7, 30, 39–42, 45–51, 55, 58–61, 66, 71–5, 79–84, 87–9, 96, 100–111, 146–50, 158–63, 235, 242–4, 248–50, 256, 259–60, 265, 283ff., 297, 301–8, 311, 317, 322, 510–16, 560–62, 592–3, 622–3, 686–701 and 815. Other sources are cited below.

2. The commemorations of St Alexis the Miracle-Worker fall on 12th February and 20th May.

3. So far Morozov had only managed to double his modest fortune and now owned estates containing 200 peasant households. Subsequently, however, he was to accumulate immense wealth – see D. I. Petrikeev, *Krupnoe krepostnoe khoziaistvo xvii v.*, Leningrad, 1967, pp. 20–21 and *passim*.

4. Attributed by V. Burtsov.

5. I. Zabelin, *Opyty izucheniia russkoi drevnosti i istorii*, part I, Moscow, 1872, p. 107.

6. S. F. Platonov, 'Tsar' Alexis Mikhailovich: opyt kharakteristiki' in V. V. Kallash (ed.) *Tri veka: Rossiia ot smutnogo vremeni do nashego*, II (1912), pp. 94–125; also Platonov, *Stat'i po russkoi istorii*, St Petersburg, 1903, pp. 32–49. Others have copied this erroneous conclusion, most recently J. Fuhrmann, *Tsar Alexis: His Reign and His Russia*, Gulf Breeze, 1981, p. 4. His tutor Grigory L'vov was still attached to his entourage when Alexis was in his eighteenth year – see Bartenev, *Soebranie pisem*, p. 112.

7. See, for example, C. Mango, *Byzantium: The Empire of New Rome*, London, 1980, pp. 127 and 144.

8. See L. Shchepotev, *Blizhnii boiarin Artamon Matveev*, St Petersburg, 1906.

9. See T. Rainov, *Nauka v Rossii xi–xvii vekov*, Moscow–Leningrad, 1940, pp. 353–4.

10. K. I. Serbina (ed.), *Kniga bol'shomu chertezhu*, Moscow–Leningrad, 1950. See also D. M. Lebedev, *Geografiia v Rossii xvii veka*, Moscow–Leningrad, 1949, pp. 19ff.

11. See W. Ryan's articles in *OSP*, 12 (1965) and *SEER*, Vol. 56, No. 2 (1978); also his 'The *Secreta Secretorum* and the Muscovite Autocracy' (forthcoming). I am grateful to Dr Ryan for sight of this paper.

12. See Zabelin, *Opyty*, I, p. 114 (commenting on Solov'ev).

13. Arkheograficheskaia kommissia, *VT*, p. 106. At the age of ten, however, he had appeared before some prominent clerics (*vlasti*) to recite the holy credo and a little discourse on the destruction of heretics and schismatics – *ZORI*, II, p. 23.

14. *VT*, p. 109.

15. *ChOIDR*, Vol. 174 (1893), Book 1, pp. 1–38.

16. *AI*, III, pp. 387–8.

17. *VT*, p. 117.

18. Berkh, I, pp. 22 and 25–8.

19. Barsukov, *RS*, III, pp. 276–7.

20. On the Valdemar affair see *ChOIDR*, Book 2, 1892, No. 1, pp. 1–22; also G. Vernadsky, *A History of Russia*, Vol. 5 (*The Tsardom of Muscovy*), Part 2, pp. 381–6.

21. Zabelin, *DB*, II (1915 ed.), p. 317.

22. E.g. *VT*, pp. 125–6.

23. *AI*, III, pp. 404–7.

24. See note 20 above, p. 10.

25. *Povs*, Part I, Moscow, 1769, p. 269: *DR*, Vol. 3, p. 1.

26. Alexis to Nikon, May 1652, Bartenev, *SP*, p. 164.

27. *Povs*, I, p. 270.

28. *SGGD*, III, pp. 417–21 (pp. 412–13 for the text of the oath quoted).

29. On this question see L. V. Cherepnin, *Zemskie sobory russkogo gosudarstva v xvi–xvii vv*, Moscow, 1978, pp. 272–4.

30. N. Novombergskii, *Gosudarevo slovo i delo*, I, Tomsk, 1911, Nos 57, 60, 61, 135 and 157; see also V. Marin, 'Slovo i delo gosudarevo', VI, 41, No. 3 (March 1966), pp. 215–18, and A. Zaozerskii, *Tsarskaia votchina*.

31. P. Pascal, *Avvakum et les debuts du raskol*, Paris, 1938, p. 64; Novombergskii, *op. cit.*, I, pp. 369–70. R. Hellie (*Enserfment and Military Change in Muscovy*, Chicago, 1971, p. 135) claims that Alexis's legiti-

macy was questioned 'largely [*sic*] because he had not been installed by an Assembly of the Land'. This is not so. Most Russians, including rebels, had no such fine sense of constitutional precedent.

32. Solov'ev, II, x, col. 1492; Vernadsky, *op. cit.*, I, pp. 383 and 385 suggests that Valdemar appealed to certain members of the Council, and to sections of the gentry and other groups, as a suitable alternative candidate as Tsar, and that Morozov and his friends feared that Valdemar might seize the throne. There is insufficient evidence to support such a view, however. Although it took three weeks to answer Valdemar's petition it seems more probable that this was due to deliberations on the diplomatic consequences and financial terms of his departure rather than to attempts to keep his 'candidature' alive. See also Berkh, I, p. 24.

33. Solov'ev, II, x, col. 1495; *Povs*, I, pp. 273–4.

34. Berkh, I, pp. 29–30; Zabelin *DB*, II, pp. 478–9.

35. A. M. Sakharov, *Ocherki istorii SSSR xvii veka*, Moscow, 1958, pp. 114–15.

36. Artsybashev, *Povestovanie o Rossii*, III, Moscow, 1846, Book 6, p. 86.

37. For the text of Alexis's speech see Archimandrite Leonid, *Chin postavleniia na tsarstvo Tsaria . . . Alekseia Mikhailovicha* (Pamiatniki drevnei pis'mennosti, No. 16), 1881, pp. 11–14: for the Patriarch's, *Ibid.*, pp. 14–19, and *passim* for the ceremony in general. Also W. Palmer, *The Patriarch and the Tsar*, II, 1873, pp. 390–95. Cf. the speech with those delivered at previous coronations (e.g. *SGGD*, III, pp. 81–3) and see D. J. Bennet, Jr., 'The Idea of Kingship in 17th Century Russia', unpublished Harvard doctoral dissertation, 1967, especially pp. 91–2.

Chapter II In the Shadow of Morozov

1. E.g. the petitions of Morozov and other councillors dated 1646 in *ZORI*, II, pp. 711–13.

2. *Povs*, II, p. 8; Berkh, I, pp. 47 and 42.

3. The Abbot of the Prilutskii Monastery (see Zaozerskii, pp. 268–9); Zabelin, *DB*, II, pp. 478–9.

4. Alexis to Matiushkin, 3rd, 9th and 30th April 1646 in Bartenev, *SP*, pp. 11, 1 and 18. For evidence of his addressing Irina as 'Mother', see *PRG*, V, pp. 1–2

5. On Alexis as a pigeon-fancier see th remarks of Muscovy merchant Franci Pargiter – Pepys, *Diary*, V, p. 272.

6. For an interesting analysis of class, kin ship and other factors as determinants o Council membership, see R. Crummey 'The Origins of the Noble Official: Th boyar elite 1613–1689' in W. Pintner an D. Rowney (eds), *Russian Officialdom* London, 1980, pp. 47–75. For evidenc of Grigorii L'vov's promotion, see V. Veretennikov, *Istoriia tainoi kantseliarii* Khar'kov, 1910, pp. 8–9.

7. The most frequently cited source on th administrative machine is Kotoshikhin *O Rossii v tsarstvovanie Alekseia Mikhail ovicha* (various editions), Chapter 7, bu see also N. V. Ustiugov ('Evoliutsii prikaznogo stroia') and S. M. Troitski ('Finansovaia politika') in N. M. Druz hinin *et al.* (eds), *Absoliutizm v Rossi (xvii–xviii vv)*, Moscow, 1964, pp. 134– 67 and 281–319 respectively; N. V Ustiugov in *Ocherki istorii SSSR. Perioc feodalizma xvii v*, Moscow, 1955, pp 366–84 and N. F. Demidova, 'Prikazy in *Sovetskaia istoricheskaia entsiklopediia* XI, cols 560–66. Individual studie include S. Belokurov, *O posol'skon prikaze*, Moscow, 1906; Iakovlev, *Prika sbora ratnykh liudei*; I. P. Kozlovskii *Pervye pochty i pervye pochtmeistery Moskovskom gosudarstve*, 2 vols, Warsaw 1913, I, pp. 25–33.

8. The system has often been derided a 'haphazard' and 'casual' (e.g. A. M Sakharov, *Ocherki istorii SSSR xvii v* Moscow, 1958, p. 54 and R. Nisbet Bain *The First Romanovs*, London, 1905, p. 16 but perhaps unjustly. It is not th machinery but its operation whicl determines the efficiency of govern ment.

9. For a perceptive, if occasionally conten tious, study of the 17th-century Musco vite bureaucrat, see B. Plavsic in Pintne and Rowney, *op. cit.*, pp. 19–45.

10. S. P. Mel'gunov, *Religiozno-obshchest vennye dvizheniia xvii–xviii vv v Rossii* Moscow, 1922, pp. 42–51; see alsc

Iakovlev, *op. cit.*, pp. 452–8.

1. See *Khrestomatiia*, note 1, pp. 390–3; Petrikeev, *op. cit.*, pp. 23–4.

2. *SGGD*, III, 422; K. V. Bazilevich, *Denezhnaia reforma*, Moscow–Leningrad, 1936, p. 5; Troitskii, *loc. cit.*; Kotoshikhin (Uroff edition), note 193, p. 503; Sakharov, *op. cit.*, pp. 78–9.

3. Zabelin, *DB*, II, pp. 437 and 445; Samuel Collins (*The Present State of Russia*, London, 1671, pp. 102–3) subsequently reported that Morozov 'diminished the number of household servants, [and] brought the rest to half wages'. Some of Tsar Michael's clothes were subsequently sold off.

4. Hellie, *op. cit.*, pp. 183 and 188–9.

5. N. N. Ardashov, *Raskhodnye knigy i stolpy pomestnago prikaza (1626–1659)*, I, Moscow, 1910, pp. 67ff.

6. See for example the petition from trading people in various districts of 1646 – *ASBAR*, IV, pp. 14–23.

7. *Povs*, II, pp. 11–13; Hellie *op. cit.*, pp. 178–9 and note 101, p. 354; Iakovlev, *op. cit.*, pp. 67 and 257; Hellie, pp. 127, 68–9 and 133–4. Also Berkh, *op. cit.*, I, p. 40. While it is true that some mercenaries and new-formation troops were used on the southern frontier after 1645, Hellie's view that the service levies had relatively little to do after that date seems questionable.

8. N. Novombergskii, *Slovo i delo gosudarevy*, I, Moscow, 1911, pp. 188–91, Iakovlev, *op. cit.*, p. 78, Veretennikov, *loc. cit.*; Zaozerskii, pp. 290–91, P. P. Smirnov, 'Chelobitnye dvorian i detei boiarskikh', *ChOIDR*, 254, No. 3 (1915), pp. 20, 67–70; P. P. Smirnov, *Posadskie liudi*, II, p. 8; Solov'ev, II, x, cols 1495–6.

9. Zabelin, *DB*, I, p. 389; Kotoshikhin (Uroff), II, pp. 5, 7, 12–13.

20. On *mestnichestvo* see A. I. Markevich, *Istoriia mestnichestva*, Odessa, 1883; also S. O. Shmidt, 'Mestnichestvo i absoliutizm' in Druzhinin, *op. cit.*, pp. 168–205. For examples concerning military appointments at the time, see *Povs*, II, pp. 10–11, 13–17, 23–4 and 29–30; for a typical case of a row over who should serve at which table at a dinner given for the Patriarch, *Ibid.*, pp. 35–6, and *passim*: also Zabelin, *DB*, I, pp. 343–6.

21. Paul of Aleppo. *The Travels of Macarius*, II, p. 34.

22. Zabelin, *DB*, I, pp. 384–5; N. F. Kapterev, *Patriarkh Nikon i Tsar' Aleksei Mikhailovich*, I (1909), p. 16 and II (1912), p. 1; Ustiugov and Chaev in N. V. Ustiugov *et al.* (eds), *Russkoe gosudarstvo v xvii veke*, Moscow, 1961, pp. 295–329. See also V.S. Rumiantseva, 'Kruzhok Stefana Vnifant'eva', *Obshchestvo i gosudarstvo feodal'noi Rossii*, Moscow, 1975, pp. 178–88.

23. Berkh, I, pp. 76–7; A. V. Kartashev, *Ocherki po istorii russkoi tserkvi*, II, Paris, 1959, p. 134; Solov'ev, II, x, col. 1518.

24. Kapterev, *op. cit.*, II, p. 82. Text in *ASBAR*, IV, pp. 481–2. It was subsequently repeated – see *Ibid.*, pp. 489–91 and *AI*, IV, pp. 28–9; Zabelin, *DB*, II, p. 297; *Tsarstvovanie*, pp. 17 and 20; 'Fedor (Bol'shoi) Rtishchev' in *RBS*.

25. Berkh, I, pp. 45–7; Kotoshikhin, I, 6; Solov'ev, II, x, col. 1514; also Collins, *op. cit.*, p. 103. An order of ceremony (*chinovnik*) was actually drawn up for the marriage – *TsGADA*, F. 135, No. 311.

26. *TsGADA*, F. 27, No. 527, Oct.–Nov. 1647. See also *ZORI*, II, pp. 707–9; Gurliand, pp. 210–11. Zaozerskii (pp. 81–2) associates this with Alexis's remembrance for Prince Michael Odoevskii, but he was not to die until the early 1650s (see infra, Chapter IV). The name Michael occurs five times in the text but we cannot identify the Michael concerned and there is no mention of any specific occasion for the charity.

27. *TsGADA*, F. 27, No. 57. For another example of the young Tsar's desk work, see *Ibid.*, No. 51.

28. *AI*, IV, pp. 52–3.

29. Bartenev, *SP*, pp. 222ff; Barsukov, *RS*, II, p. 365.

30. Berkh, I, pp. 37–8 and 42–3; Collins, p. 103; *Vremennik Moskovskogo obshchestva istorii*, VI, 1850.

31. *Povs*, II, pp. 54–9; *DRV*, xiii, pp. 189–211; Barsukov, *RS*, iii, pp. 366–7; Zabelin, *DB*, II, p. 461; 'Fedor (Bol'shoi) Rtishchev' in *RBS*. On the dress for Alexis's wedding, *TsGADA*, F. 396 (Oruzheinaia palata), opis' 1/4, Nos 321/3932 and 360.

32. *Materialy dlia istorii raskola*, cited by Kap-

terev, I, pp. 16–17; *DRV*, XIII, p. 214.

33. Paul of Aleppo, II, p. 158; also G. P. Fedotov, *The Russian Religious Mind*, I, pp. 189–92.

34. Berkh, I, p. 45. A few days later Ivan Andreevech Miloslavskii was made a sub-boyar.

35. Collins, p. 140. One of her suspected lovers was allegedly William Barnsly of Barnsly Hall in Worcestershire.

36. A Vogt, ed., Constantine Porphyrogenitus, *Le livre des cérémonies*, I, Paris 1935, p. 2 (the translation used here is by R. Witt and A. Bryer).

37. Zabelin, *DB*, II, p. 316.

38. Zaozerskii, p. 82.

39. Kapterev, I, pp. 19–21; Vernadsky, I, pp. 424–5. The compiler, however, was Abbot Nathaniel of the Michael Monastery in Kiev, not Stefan who only supplied the introduction and a postscript – see V. S. Rumiantseva in *Obshchestvo i gosudarstvo feodal'noi Rossii*, Moscow, 1975, pp. 186–7.

40. For Alexis's audiences to foreign envoys see *Povs*, II, pp. 44, 46–7, 51–2, etc. For the background on relations with the Crimea, Solov'ev, II, x, cols 124–5; with Poland, *Ibid.*, II, x, cols 1493–4; with Sweden, Attman *et al.*, pp. 89–95. Also Sakharov, pp. 116f.; with England, Solov'ev, II, x, cols 1649–52. Alexis's envoy G. S. Dokhturov who had been in England over the winter of 1645–6 provided first-hand information on the English Revolution – See Z. I. Roginskii, *Poezdka Gerasima Semeonovicha Dokhturova v Anglii v 1645–1646* (cited by Cherepnin in Druzhinin *et al.*, *op. cit.*). The aid took the form of grain, which was easily convertible into money.

41. Hellie, p. 55; Iakovlev, pp. 73, 85 and 553; Smirnov, *Posadskie, op. cit.*, II, p. 69.

42. The following account of the Moscow uprising of 1648 is based on a variety of sources, including eye-witness accounts, which diverge from each other over the chronology of events, and sometimes over events themselves. I have done my best to reconcile them. The more important sources include A. Zertsalov, 'K istorii Moskovskogo miatezha 1648g', *ChOIDR*, III, 1893, *smes'*, pp. iii–iv and 1–12; *Idem*. 'Novyi istochnik dlia istorii

Moskovskoi vosstanii 1648g', *ChOIDR* I, 1893 (a contemporary Dutch account), *ChOIDR*, I, 1896; P. P. Smirnov 'Neskol'ko dokumentov k istori Sobornogo Ulozheniia i zemskog sobora 1648–9 godov', *ChOIDR*, 1913 *smes'*, No. 1; *Vremennik imperatorskog Moskovskogo obshchestva istorii i drevnoste rossiiskikh*, Vol. 17, col. 1934; *Letopis' mnogikh miatezhakh*, Moscow, 1788; L Loewenson, 'The Moscow Rising o 1648', *SEER*, 1948–9, Vol. 27, pp. 146– 56; S. Baron (ed.), Adam Olearius, *Th Voyages and Travells of the Ambassadors* and Smirnov, 'Chelobitnye' *loc. cit.* Se also S. V. Bakhrushin, *Nauchnye Trudy* II, Moscow, 1954, pp. 46–91.

43. *AAE*, IV, No. 29; Bartenev, *SP* (1856) pp. 243–4. Boris himself had written t his bailiffs on the eve of his exile, warnin them that the change in his status shoul not be allowed to affect the running o his estates. If they could not maintai order they were to report the matter an the Tsar would see to it that any rebe lious peasants were suppressed (*Khres tomatiia*, p. 393). However, he also mad some concessions, allowing forest right to his neighbours and surrendering pea sant runaways – Iakovlev, p. 79 and A. I Iakovlev (ed.), *Akty khoziaistva boiarin B. I. Morozova*, Moscow–Leningrad 1940–45, I.

44. *DAI*, III, No. 45; Bartenev, *SP*, pp. 245–6

45. Zaozerskii, pp. 295–6, citing Pommer ing and Iakubov.

Chapter III The Pursuit of Good Orde

1. *ChOIDR* 1913, Book 4, pp. 6–7; Zertsa lov, 'Novye dannye', *ChOIDR* 1887 Book 3, pp. 5, 10 and *passim; Ocherki*, p 247. See also V. Latkin, *Materialy dli istorii zemskikh soborov xvii stoletiia*, S Petersburg, 1884; L. V. Cherepnin *Zemskie sobory russkogo gosudarstva c xvi– xvii vv*, Moscow, 1978, pp. 275–30! (esp. p. 292).

2. Report of the Swedish envoy Pommer ingen, 4th October 1648, quoted by A G. Man'kov, *Ulozhenie 1649 goda* Leningrad, 1980, p. 51.

3. E.g. in his correspondence wit! Odoevskii – see *infra*, Chapter IV, not 29.

4. The Emperor was Nicephorus Phocas – see G. Ostrogorsky, *History of the Byzantine State*, Oxford, 1980, p. 286.
5. *Sob. Ul.* (many editions), Cap. X, clauses 1–6.
6. Zabelin, *DB*, II, (1915), p. 514; *Povs*, pp. 77–8.
7. *Sob. Ul.*, Cap. XVII, clause 42.
8. See Jerome Blum, 'The Rise of Serfdom in Eastern Europe', *American Historical Review*, 72, 4 (1957), pp. 807–36.
9. *Sob. Ul.*, Cap. XIX, *Strel'tsy* and certain other classes of semi-professional soldiers constituted an exception, paying quit-rent and excise duties rather than the *tiaglo* (clause 11). The order ascribing *posady* to the crown was issued on 25th November 1648 (*AAE*, Vol. 4, No. 32).
10. *Sob. Ul.*, Cap. XVI. In Moscow province the holdings varied from 200 *desiatiny* for a boyar to ten *chetverti* for the lowest-ranking serviceman. These were not standard measures but depended on the type and condition of the land involved. However, they approximated to 540 acres per boyar and 13½ acres for the lowest service rank.
11. *Sob. Ul.*, Cap. XIV. There are specific references here (clause 10) to the legislation of the Byzantine Emperors Basil I and Leo VI.
12. *Sob. Ul.*, Cap. XX.
13. *Sob. Ul.*, Cap. XXV.
14. *Sob. Ul.*, Cap. XXII.
15. *Sob. Ul.*, Cap. XXI, clauses 4, 94 and 97.
16. See L. V. Cherepnin, 'Zemskie sobory i utverzhdenie absoliutizma v Rossii' in Ustiugov *et al.* (eds), *Absoliutizm v Rossii (xvii–xviii vv)*, Moscow, 1964, pp. 92–133. More generally see the discussion in Cherepnin, *Zemskie Sobory, loc. cit.*
17. Kotoshikhin, 4th ed., St Petersburg, 1906, p. 118.
18. Chistiakov in Ustiugov *et al., op. cit.*, pp. 254ff. A. M. Sontsev-Zasekin, Governor of Seversk and Ryl'sk, was dismissed in March 1649 – Zertsalov, 'Novyye dannye', *loc. cit.*
19. Evidence was subsequently uncovered of an uprising planned to take place on 6th January 1649 – see Solov'ev, II, x, cols 1523–5. Two *strel'tsy* involved were beheaded and two more had their tongues torn out, evidently for trying to

implicate Prince Cherkasskii. Another conspirator was Savinka Korepin, a lessee of Nikita Romanov's who resented being transferred as a tax-payer to the Moscow *posad*. The trial, involving torture, was attended by the entire Council on Alexis's order. Korepin's seditious remarks about the Tsar have been repeated uncritically by a number of historians as if they were the evidence of an impartial observer rather than someone seething with resentment.
20. Pommeringen in K. Iakubov, 'Rossiia i Shvetsiia v pervoi polovine xvii v', *ChOIDR* 1898, No. 1; also Zaozerskii, pp. 295–6, Hellie, p. 207, Zabelin, *DB*, I, pp. 300–302.
21. *AI*, IV, pp. 124–6; *AAE*, IV, No. 321; Zabelin, *DB*, II, p. 294; P. Pascal, *Avvakum et les débuts du raskol*, Paris, 1938, pp. 163–5; V. P. Adrianova-Perets (ed.), *Russkaia demokraticheskaia satira xvii v*, Moscow–Leningrad, 1954, p. 165; N. Findeisen, *Ocherki po istorii muzyki v Rossii*, I, Moscow–Leningrad, 1928, pp. 144–60.
22. See R. J. W. Evans, *The Habsburg Monarchy 1550–1700*, Oxford, 1979.
23. *The Life of Avvakum written by Himself*. Ordained a priest in 1644, Avvakum had arrived in Moscow towards the end of 1647. He returned to his parish to find his house destroyed. Appointed archpriest at Yur'evits on the Volga, he was beaten up and driven out within weeks; he had the same experience at Kostroma. On his return to Moscow he recounted his experiences to the Tsar and was berated by Stefan Vnifant'ev for abandoning his flock.
24. Kapterev, I, p. 44.
25. *Ibid.*, II, pp. 98–9.
26. S. A. Belokurov, *Materialy dlia russkoi istorii*, Moscow, 1888, pp. 455–6.
27. The order enforcing *edinoglasie* was duly promulgated – *ASBAR*, IV, pp. 487–8. See also Kapterev, I, pp. 98–102, and Pascal, *op. cit.*, p. 156.
28. Kapterev, II, pp. 134–6; Solov'ev, II, x, cols 1529–33.
29. Kapterev, I, p. 44; A. V. Kartashev, *Ocherki po istorii russkoi tserkvi*, II, pp. 122–3.
30. See Solov'ev, X, ii, cols 1559ff. For the

text of Alexis's letter to Bodgan, see *Akty otnosiashchiesia k iuzhnoi i zapadnoi Rossiei*, III, p. 488.

31. D. Obolensky (*The Byzantine Commonwealth*, London, 1971, pp. 467–72) argues that the ideology of the 'Third Rome' had no significant impact on Muscovite policy. This may be correct in respect of the 15th and 16th centuries but not of the 17th. See also W.-K. Medlin, *Moscow and East Rome*, Neuchâtel, 1952, esp. p. 228.

32. Vernadsky, II, pp. 568–9; N. K. Gudzii *et al.* (eds), *Zhizn' Protopopa Avvakuma im samim napisannoe*, Moscow, 1960, p. 378. When Paisios left for Jerusalem Alexis sent another Arsenyi who knew Greek, Arsenyi Sukhanov, to accompany him, giving him a commission to describe the Holy Places and report in detail on the ceremonies of the Greek Church when he returned.

33. They also included sections of the *Epanogoge* dealing with the respective duties of Tsar and Patriarch (see Vernadsky, II, p. 561) which were to influence Nikon in his bid to increase the authority of the Patriarchate (see *infra*, esp. Chapters VI and VIII). See also L. R. Lewitter, 'Poland, the Ukraine and Russia in the 17th century', *SEER*, XXVII (1948–9), pp. 157–71 and 414–29.

34. Alexis's instructions to P. Khomiakov are described and analysed by Zaozerskii, pp. 80–82. The original is in *TsGADA*, F.27, No. 532, ff. 143–5 among a mass of other correspondence concerning the farming of his estates and construction works upon them, including much correspondence with Peter Stepanich and Daniel Leont'evich about the Khoroshevo estate.

35. *TsGADA* F. 396, opis' 1/4. He was employed in the *Oruzheinaia palata*. Soon afterwards one Alexander Crawford, apparently an expert in market gardening, was granted a monopoly of the importation of selected seeds – an indication that there was interest in encouraging the introduction of new cash crops (reference lost).

36. K. V. Bazilevich, *Denezhnaia reforma Alekseia Mikhailovicha i vosstanie v Moskve v 1662g*, Moscow–Leningrad, 1936.

37. Zabelin, *DB*, I, p. 466.

38. Berkh, II, pp. 129–30.

39. *Povs*, II, pp. 109–10; Berkh, I, pp. 67–8.

40. See note 19 above. The fact that the person sentenced under an article of the Code, in a famous case reported by Kotoshikhin, for firing into the Tsar's apartments while allegedly aiming at jackdaws perching on the Miracle Monastery was one of Boris Morozov's retainers, called Sumarokov, must also have aroused suspicions – *TsGADA*, F. 27, No. 22.

41. Zabelin, *DB*, I, pp. 373–83. The charge was levelled by Efrem Bakhmetev; his grudge was that Khitrovo was allegedly misusing his office to obtain a service estate at his family's expense. Alexis sentenced Bakhmetev to be strapped to a 'goat' (a contraption designed to hold the body in a fixed position) and flogged for 'dishonouring' Trubetskoi and Khitrovo.

42. *ZORI*, II, pp. 711–13. Gurliand (p. 41) attributes this undated document to 1646, but it refers to Mikhail Rtishchev as *okol'nichii* and since he only reached that rank in 1650 it was probably written *c*.1650–51.

43. *DAI*, III, p. 252; Bartenev, *SP*, pp. 23–4.

44. Collins, p. 65.

45. Bartenev, *SP*, pp. 27–33.

46. See M. N. Tikhomirov, *Pskovskoe vosstanie 1650g*, Moscow–Leningrad, 1935. The disturbances had begun in February and March.

47. See the discussion in Cherepnin, *Zemskie sobory, op. cit.*, pp. 312–18.

48. Kapterev, II, pp. 135–6; Berkh, I, pp. 51–4 gives another, idiosyncratic account; see also *DAI*, III, pp. 265–76; *Tsarstvovanie*, pp. 4–5; Medovnikov, pp. 58–60; Sakharov, p. 85.

49. Collins, p. 4.

50. Hellie, p. 188.

Chapter IV Spiritual Rearmament

1. L. V. Cherepnin, *Zemskie sobory*, Moscow, 1978, pp. 324–7.

2. For a useful analysis of the eastern European situation that gave rise to the war, see L. V. Zaborovskii, *Rossia, Rech' Pospolita i Shvetsiia v seredine xvii v.*, Moscow, 1981, pp. 16–29.

3. Ya. S. Lur'e and Yu. D. Rykov, *Perepiska Ivana Groznogo s Andreem Kurbskim*, Moscow, 1981, p. 30; also J. L. I. Fennel (ed.), *The Correspondence between Prince Kurbsky and Tsar Ivan IV of Russia 1564–1579*, Cambridge, 1955, pp. 84–5.

4. Fedor Shilovtsov of the Miracle Monastery – see I. Zabelin, *Opyty*, I, pp. 117–18.

5. P. Pascal, *Avvàkum et les débuts du Raskol*, Paris, 1938, p. 341.

6. The order was confirmed by the Council in May, N. F. Kapterev, *Patriarkh Nikon i Tsar' Aleksei Mikhailovich*, II (1912), p. 101.

7. Alexis's surviving papers include sheets of musical notation (neums) as well as prayers which he may have composed himself and transcripts of liturgical matter with his corrections – *TsGADA*, Fond 27, No. 337. Here again Alexis was following in the footsteps of Ivan, who is said to have composed music; Alexis's son Fedor was also to do so, though Alexis's own contribution to the development of Russian music remains to be assessed. See N. D. Uspenskii, *Obraztsi drevnerusskogo pevcheskogo iskusstva*, Leningrad, 1968.

8. See Paul of Aleppo, quoted by Gurliand, p. 205.

9. On the second occasion Alexis's retinue was particularly grand, including over twenty Councillors. A dinner he gave there cost the immense sum of 3,000 rubles – *DR*, III, St Petersburg, 1852, cols 290–9; *Povs*, II, p. 146; Berkh, I, p. 73.

10. Gurliand, pp. 205–9.

11. Paul of Aleppo, *Travels*, II, pp. 240–42.

12. F. C. Conybeare, *Russian Dissenters*, Cambridge (Mass.), 1921, pp. 53 and 45.

13. See G. P. Fedotov, *Sviatoi Filipp*, Paris, 1928, pp. 192–6.

14. Bartenev, *SP* pp. 87–116; Zaozerskii, pp. 241–2.

15. Alexis to Nikon, May 1652 – see *infra*, note 22.

16. Report of the Swedish agent in Moscow, *ZhMNP*, May 1898, p. 341. Paul of Aleppo (*Travels*, II, p. 34) and the Venetian ambassador (See Chapter V *infra*) report in markedly similar terms on Alexis's (spurious) reputation for cruelty.

17. *Povs*, II, p. 133; Alexis to L. Grigoro, 3rd July 1652 – *ZORI*, II, p. 351.

18. Gurliand, pp. 205–9.

19. *ZORI*, II, pp. 669ff.; also Solov'ev, II, xii, cols 608–10. For a partial translation and commentary, see M. Cherniavsky, *Tsar and People*, pp. 67–8. Alexis devised a special ceremony to take place in the Monastery refectory at which the letter was to be read out loudly and clearly. Having heard it the offending Nikita was to be relegated to the stables, scene of one of his offences – see Alexis to A. B. Musin-Pushkin, 25th June 1652, *ZORI*, II, pp. 786–8.

20. Maria gave birth to another daughter, Margarita or Martha, on 27th August 1652.

21. Alexis to Nikon, 25th May 1652, *ASBAR*, IV, pp. 149–50; Bartenev, *SP*, pp. 210–12.

22. It is dated simply 'May 1652'. Joseph had died early in April (see *infra*).

23. Solov'ev, II, x, col. 1558.

24. Bartenev, *SP* pp. 156–85.

25. In this, too, Alexis was following Byzantine precedent – see *infra*, Alexis to Odoevskii, 3rd September 1652. The Emperor Theodosius was reputed to have written a prayer letter to the remains of St John Chrysostom who had been ill-treated by the Emperor's mother – Solov'ev, II, x, col. 1551. On the details of Philip's life, see Fedotov, *op. cit.*; on Philip's clash with Ivan, see A. A. Zimin, 'Mitropolit Filipp i oprichnina', *Voprosy istorii religii i ateizma*, XII (1963); for Agapetus as an ideological source for the confrontation, see I. Sevchenko, 'A Byzantine Source of Muscovite Ideology', *Harvard Slavic Studies*, II (1954), pp. 141–79; for other interpretations of the letter see W.–K. Medlin, *Moscow and East Rome*, Neuchâtel, 1952, p. 167 (who, like Solov'ev and others, sees it as reflecting Alexis's weakness and representing a victory for the Church) and Cherniavskii, *op. cit.*, p. 49.

26. The text is printed in *SGGD*, III, pp. 471–2 and Berkh, II, pp. 148–51. Solov'ev's version (II, x, col. 1552) is incomplete and rendered into modern

Russian. Partial English translations are to be found in R. Nisbet Bain, *The First Romanovs*, London, 1905, p. 129 and G. V. Vernadsky, *The Tsardom of Moscow 1547–1682*, New Haven, 1969, I, pp. 419–20. Curiously enough, although Alexis claimed Ivan as his 'forefather' (*praded*) there was no blood relationship between them, though Alexis and Philip did share a common ancestry.

27. This was reported in the first of six letters from Nikon informing Alexis of the expedition's progress – *SGGD*, III, pp. 474–8.

28. *TsGADA*, Fond 142, No. 382. This is not included in *SGGD* (see note 27 above).

29. Alexis to Odoevskii, 3rd September 1652, Bartenev, *SP*, pp. 222–5. The letter ends with an exhortation to stand united in the cause of truth and to render justice equally to all.

30. Vernadsky, *op. cit.*, II, 562–3; *The Life of Avvakum written by Himself*, trans. J. Harrison and H. Mirrless, London, 1929, p. 52.

31. 6th February 1651, *ASBAR*, IV, p. 70.

32. Vernadsky suggests that Alexis posted Odoevskii to Kazan for this reason.

33. *Life of Avvakum, op. cit.*, pp. 52–3.

34. Kapterev, *op. cit.*, pp. 122–3.

35. It is extremely doubtful, however, if Alexis ever intended to cede (rather than delegate) any of his powers to the Church as is often suggested. The source most quoted for the oath to Nikon (Palmer, I, pp. 582–3, citing Mikhailovsky, pp. 29ff., and IV, pp. 10–12; also Sipovskii, *Rodnaia starina*, III, pp. 211–12) is derived from an account written several years later by Nikon himself (the text is printed in *ZORI*, II, 1861, p. 153) and in view of what transpired in the interim (see *infra*, Chapters VI and VII) its accuracy cannot be taken for granted. Although the earliest extant account in print (Paul, *Macarius*, I, pp. 409–10) states that Nikon's 'sentence' (presumably his jurisdiction in canonical matters) was to be absolute, not subject to appeal, Alexis was shortly afterwards to commute Nikon's sentence on Avvakum. Furthermore, Alexis's file on Nikon's election contains a description of his installation

and of the blessings used in which the term 'Autocrat' is included in his own title and Alexis added the word himself at another point in the text (*TsGADA*, Fond 27, No. 75, ff. 15 and 26), though it is, of course, uncertain when he did so. All in all, I am inclined to accept the opinion of D.J. Bennet Jr. ('The Idea of Kingship in Seventeenth Century Russia', Harvard Ph.D. dissertation, 1967, p. 136) that 'at the time of Nikon's accession . . . the Church was an organ of state and the Patriarch an agent of the Tsar'. See also note 53 *infra*.

36. Kapterev, *op. cit.*, I, pp. 44–5. By 'world' he meant the Orthodox world.

37. Ustiugov and Chaev in N. V. Ustiugov *et al.* (eds), *Russkoe gosudarstvo v xvii veke*, Moscow, 1961, pp. 295–329; Vernadsky, *op. cit.*, pp. 573–4.

38. The Donation of Constantine was an 8th-century forgery designed to establish papal supremacy. The forgery was not exposed until the 18th century.

39. Some sources have it as Margarita.

40. His factor Andrei Vinnius was commissioned to buy orange trees and rare birds for the palace, along with various purchases for the state, from Holland in 1652 – I. P. Kozlovskii, *Perviia pochty i pervye pochtmeistery v Moskovskom gosudarstve*, 2 vols, Warsaw, 1913, I, p. 174. Alexis had given orders to investigate the possibility of transplanting vines from the Terek and the training of Russians in the techniques of wine-making since August 1651 – See *AI*, I, pp. 177–9.

41. Lamanskii, *ZORI*, II, 1861, pp. 702–6.

42. The provision of flintlock muskets and carbines was much stepped up between 1647 and 1653, by which time more than 26,000 had been supplied (in addition to 10,000 matchlocks), and a further 10,000 plus a quantity of gun-barrels had been stockpiled. The manufacturing techniques of the state workshops, however, left much to be desired. According to the Swedish agent de Rodes, reporting in 1652, over half the Russian-made muskets exploded on testing (B. G. Kurts, 'Sostoianie Rossii v 1650–1655 po doneseniiam Rodesa', *ChOIDR*, 253, No. 2 (1915), p. 100). This may account both for the application to Sweden in

October 1653 for 20,000 muskets and for Queen Christina's government ignoring the request. The application was renewed on 13th February 1654 (A. Attman *et al.* (eds), *Ekonomicheskie sviazi mezhdu Rossiei i Shvetsiei v xvii v*, Moscow–Stockholm, 1978, pp. 99–100). Similar requests were sent in 1653 to Frederick III of Denmark (*Ibid.* p. 193) and Holland (N. A. Baklanova, 'Privoznye tovary' in *Ocherki po istoriei promyshlennosti v Rossii v 17 i v nachale 18 stoletii*, Moscow, 1928, pp. 5–118), from which several hundred tons of powder and lead were also ordered. In general on the course of military reform at this juncture, see Hellie, p. 193.

43. *TsGADA*, Fond 27, No. 85. The document is undated but was probably drafted in 1653. The quoted passages occur on ff. 2′–3′. At the subsequent manoeuvres and review he also dressed extremely opulently and changed his apparel several times a day – I. Zabelin, *DB*, II, pp. 483–4.

44. Barsukov, *RS*, IV, pp. 23–5.

45. *PSZ*, I, No. 114. See also *DRV*, VIII, pp. 83–107, especially p. 87.

46. Barsukov, *RS*, IV, p. 13.

47. The best treatment of the background to the decision of 1652 to set up the Foreign Suburb is by S. H. Baron, 'Origins of Moscow's Nemeckaja Sloboda', *California Slavic Studies*, V (1970), pp. 1–17.

48. K. V. Bazilevich, *Denezhnaia reforma Alekseia Mikhailovicha i vosstanie v Moskve v 1662g*, Moscow–Leningrad, 1936, pp. 6–7. In a parallel measure the Russian government was to ban liquor sales on the outbreak of war in 1914.

49. For an analysis of these assemblies, see Cherepnin, *op. cit.*, pp. 331–7. Alexis's final terms, taken to Poland in April, had, in effect, insisted that Poland relinquish sovereignty over Ukraine and dismantle the Uniat Church there in addition to previous demands.

50. Among many accounts of these developments see Pascal, *op. cit.*, Kapterev, I, pp. 120–29 and 227–34, Ustiugov and Chaev, *loc. cit.*, and Avvakum himself (Gusev *et al.* (eds), *Zhizn' Protopopa Avvakuma im samim napisannoe*, Moscow, 1960, for the text and for notes and discussion).

51. He was first addressed as such in November 1652, but the first official use occurs in the official record of the Assembly of 1st October 1653 – *SGGD*, III, p. 481. See also Medlin, *op. cit.*, pp. 189–91.

52. Much of Nikon's correspondence with Alexis during the latter's absence from Moscow was to concern the provision of military supplies and logistical support for the army – see *infra*, Chapter V.

53. See *ZORI*, II, p. 728. As Kapterev (II, p. 178) rightly points out, in granting Nikon the title Great Sovereign, Alexis 'had no notion of surrendering to the Patriarch any of his power in the church, still less the state. Nor did he intend Nikon to be on a par with him. He was merely delegating trust.'

54. *Povs*, II, pp. 197–8.

55. *ZORI*, II, pp. 1–2. These modern army units were mainly officered by foreigners, who were not only needed as instructors but for active service duty since so many of the Russian gentry considered service in such units socially degrading – Hellie, p. 192.

Chapter V Alexis Goes to War

1. Mobilization order issued in March 1654 – *PSZ*, I, St Petersburg, 1830, No. 96.

2. See e.g. the orders issued by Alexis and Nikon in 1654 and 1655 – *ASBAR*, III, pp. 121–6. Nikon claimed to have provided and equipped 10,000 men from the patriarchal estates alone, and that the rest of the Church provided a thousand – Paul of Aleppo, *Travels*, II, pp. 60–62.

3. Kotoshikhin, X, 8–10. The troops had to buy their food out of their pay though the state did issue rations on credit when necessary. The nobility mostly supplied themselves and their retainers.

4. See L. V. Zaborovskii, *Rossiia, Rech' Pospolitaia i Shvetsiia v seredine xvii v.*, Moscow, 1981, p. 36. These missions were successful, although intervention by the Crimea remained a possibility.

5. A good account of the Muscovite war plan and its implementation is provided by A. N. Mal'tsev, *Rossiia i Belorussiia v seredine xvii v.*, Moscow, 1974, pp. 29ff.

6. Not only Kolomna but Stefan Vnifant'ev and the Bishop of Tobol'sk failed to sign

the final document. Nikon proceeded to apply to the Patriarch of Constantinople for answers to questions designed to demonstrate that the opposition was heretical. He was soon to have the Bishop of Kolomna removed from his see and imprisoned for his opposition to the reforms – see Kapterev, I, 1909, pp. 150–52; A. V. Kartashev, *Ocherki po istorii russkoi tserkvi*, 2 vols, Paris, 1959, I, pp. 153–4; F. C. Conybeare, *Russian Dissenters*, Cambridge (Mass.), 1921, p. 49; Ustiugov and Chaev in Ustiugov *et al.*, *Russkoe gosudarstvo v xvii v.*, Moscow, 1961, pp. 295–329.

7. Nikon had written to Alexis on 27th February 1654 informing him of provisions being made for the new foundation and telling him of an apparition – *TsGADA*, Fond 142, No. 384. The terms of the endowment are set out in Alexis's letter to Nikon of 6th March 1654 – Palmer, I, pp. 261–70; see also III, pp. 508–10 and 512.

8. Solov'ev, II, x, cols 1659–62. The original account of these scenes is printed in *DR*, III.

9. *ZORI*, II, pp. 762–3.

10. A register of the icons Alexis took on campaign and the damage suffered by them was retained in his Private Office – *ZORI*, II, p. 39.

11. *Povs*, II, pp. 219ff; Berkh, I, pp. 87–90 (quoting a contemporary account). On the banners see A. M. Sakharov, *Ocherki istorii SSSR xvii vek*, Moscow, 1958, p. 62; Paul, *Travels*, I, pp. 366–7; Berkh, I, pp. 107–8; A. Danielsson, 'Ryska Fanor från 1600– talets mitt', *Föreningen Armémusei Vänner* (Meddelande xxvii från Kungl. Armémuseum), ed. Heribert Seitz, Stockholm, 1966.

12. As it was, even small amounts of coin had to be rushed from Moscow as soon as they were collected in order to pay expenses at the front – K. V. Bazilevich, *Denezhnaia reforma Alekseia Mikhailovicha i vosstaniia v Moskve v 1662 g.*, Moscow–Leningrad, 1936, p. 8.

13. *PRG*, V, pp. 1–2.

14. Bartenev (ed.), *SP*, p. 229.

15. *ZORI*, II, p. 716.

16. Zaozerskii, pp. 234 and 241–2. Perfil'ev had worked in the Kazan' Court Office

and had been on the staff of Buturlin's mission to Ukraine. Abroad he was referred to as Vice-Chancellor, which reflected his involvement in foreign affairs (e.g. Alexis to Doge Francesco Molino, 23rd November 1655, Archivio di Stato, Venice, Lettere Principi: Russia (1655–1796), No. 1, f. 2^v). Papers marked 'secret' had to be taken to Alexis unsealed (*ZORI*, II, p. 684). This development was accompanied by a decision to extend his autocratic title. On 1st July he made a note in his diary to include the term 'Autocrat of Great and Little Russia in all [*sic*] matters' (Zaozerskii, *op. cit.*, pp. 240–41). Hitherto the title had only been used occasionally. And with this went a determination to stop Councillors discussing business privately, behind his back (Paul, *Travels*, I, pp. 398–9). For a list of his entourage on campaign, see *Povs*, II, p. 215.

17. Alexis to his sisters, 3rd June 1654, *PRG*, V, pp. 2–3.

18. Alexis to his sisters, 4th, 10th and 30th June 1654, *Ibid.*, pp. 4–5 and 7; *Povs*, II, p. 233; Mal'tsev, *op. cit.*, p. 35.

19. See I. I. Orlovskii, *Smolenskii pokhod tsaria Alekseia Mikhailovicha v 1654 godu*, Smolensk, 1905, pp. 14–19 and ff. for the details of the siege from the defenders' point of view. For a Polish view of the war, see L. Kubala, *Wojna moskiewska r. 1654–1655*, Warsaw, 1911.

20. *ZORI*, II, p. 740.

21. Mal'tsev, *op. cit.*, p. 41.

22. E.g. *TsGADA* Fond 27, No. 82, ff.14ff. He filled at least 39 notebooks on his 1654 campaign and associated military matters alone, aside from the war diary (Fond 27, No. 86) evidently kept by the campaign chancery under Councillor-Secretary Lopukhin. There was another bundle of notebooks on Trubetskoi's operations – 1713 register of Secret Office papers, *ZORI*, II, pp. 2–3.

23. Alexis to his family, 23rd August 1654, *PRG*, V, pp. 11–12. Orlovskii (*op. cit.*, pp. 29–34) claims the Muscovites lost 7,000 dead and 15,000 wounded, but this seems exaggerated. One *strelets* colonel was among those killed, but Artamon Matveev survived the storm.

24. Mal'tsev, *op. cit.*, p. 43.

25. Pronskii to Alexis, September 1654, quoted by Barsukov, *RS*, IV, pp. 99–100; also Berkh, I, pp. 93–4.
26. Paul, *Travels*, I, p. 328.
27. *ASBAR*, IV, p. 111.
28. Gibbenet, II, Appendix, p. 474.
29. Solov'ev, II, x, cols 1667–9.
30. See the succession of orders printed in *DAI*, III, pp. 442–8, 453, 463, 475–6, 488–90 and 493–9.
31. *PRG*, V., pp. 14–15.
32. *DAI*, III, pp. 508–11. For Alexis's letter to I. V. Morozov of 15th January 1655, calling for a report on losses from the plague and his subsequent correspondence enquiring about the fate of individuals, see *ZORI*, II, pp. 719ff.
33. *DAI*, III, pp. 511–13; Solov'ev, II, x, cols 1670–71.
34. *Life of the Archpriest Avvakum*, p. 37.
35. Quoted by Barsukov, *RS*, IV, p. 14.
36. *SGGD*, III, pp. 538–40; Paul (*Travels*, I, pp. 366–9) also gives an account.
37. Bazilevich, *op. cit.*, pp. 22–3; *DAI*, IV, p. 3.
38. And for that matter Jews and Muslims – see A. G. Man'kov, *Razvitie krepostnogo prava v Rossii vo vtoroi polovine xvii veka*, Moscow–Leningrad, 1962, p. 222.
39. Barsukov, *RS*, IV, p. 132.
40. Zaozerskii, *op. cit.*, p. 294, note 1.
41. Paul, *Travels*, I, pp. 389–93.
42. *Ibid.*, I, pp. 373–6.
43. *Ibid.*, II, pp. 49–50; Kapterev, *op. cit.*, I, pp. 152–5.
44. For an inventory of the movables, see *ChOIDR*, 1887, Book 3, *otdel* 1, pp. 1–128.
45. *DAI*, IV, p. 31. The more important decisions were referred to him. Hence, in April and May 1654, on the advice of Dr Hartmann Grahmann, he sanctioned the purchase of 'unicorns' horns' (probably narwhal tusks) which, when powdered, were thought valuable as a cure for bubonic plague, and vast quantities of herbs (*DAI*, IV, pp. 31–2). The medical school accommodated thirty students on a course which lasted four years. Of the first intake seventeen were posted to the army in the field on completing the course; the rest were assigned to the Guards Office – see *Ocherki russkoi istorii xvii v*, II, p. 65.
46. Zaborovskii, *op. cit.*, p. 129.
47. Alexis to Matveev, 23rd January 1655, *ZORI*, II, 1861, pp. 726–7.
48. Alexis to his sisters, 14th March 1655, Bartenev, *SP*, pp. 44–5; *Povs*, II, pp. 262 and 267.
49. Letters of 5th and 15th May 1654, *PRG*, V, pp. 28–30.
50. Alexis to Buturlin, 25th April 1654, *ZORI*, p. 733.
51. Alexis to Tobolin (about Ivan Sharapov), *Ibid., loc. cit.*
52. Alexis to his sisters, *PRG*, V, pp. 34–6. For subsequent amendments to the plan, see Mal'tsev, *op. cit.* p. 45.
53. Berkh I, pp. 101–3. On Vilna at that time see M. Lowmiańska, *Wilno przed najazdem Moskiewskim 1655 roku*, Wilno, 1929.
54. See P. N. Batiushkov, *Pamiatniki russkoi stariny v zapadnykh guberniakh imperii*, vyp. 6, 'Vil'na', St Petersburg, 1874, pp. 55ff. There had been similar scenes, though on a smaller scale, in Polotsk – see *Vitebskaia starina* IV, Part 2, p. 77 (I am grateful to Gershon Hundert for drawing this to my attention). By contrast, cities which surrendered, such as Mogilev in 1654, were generally granted charters protecting their rights and freedoms, though even then Jews were generally excluded and Catholic churches dismantled or reconsecrated – See I. Grigorovich (ed.), *Belorusskii arkhiv drevnykh gramot*, I, Moscow, 1824, pp. 103–9.
55. *AI*, IV, pp. 267–8.
56. See L. S. Abetsedarskii, *Belorusy v Moskve xvii v.*, Minsk, 1957. In February 1656 agents were sent to Shklov and Mogilev to recruit goldsmiths and silversmiths for the court (p. 13); armourers were also sought (p. 27). Nikon employed printers and woodcarvers from Orsha at the Iveria Monastery and other Belorussian craftsmen at the 'New Jerusalem' Monastery (pp. 8 and 12). Boris Morozov was to settle over a thousand Belorussians on his Moscow estates, and other notables, not least Alexis himself, looked to Belorussia as a source of labour (p. 7). In September 1654 Alexis ordered Trubetskoi to send him Belorussian physicians and medicines from Kopys and Shklov –

L. S. Abetsedarskii and M. Ya. Volkov (eds), *Russko-Belorusskie sviazi*, Minsk, 1963, pp. 301 and 307–8. However, Alexis still looked farther afield for expertise. Thus in May 1655 Jan van Sweden was commissioned to recruit Western craftsmen and to obtain newssheets (*Flugschriften*) published in the West – I. P. Kozlovskii, *Pervye pochty i pervye pochtmeistery v Moskovskom gosudarstve*, 2 vols, Warsaw, 1913, I, p. 61. See also *infra*, Chapter VII.

57. Collins, pp. 64–5.

58. I. Ya. Gurliand, 'Ivan Gebdon, komissariat i rezident'.

59. *Akty iuzhnoi i zapadnoi Rossii*, XIV, St Petersburg, 1889, pp. 817–19. But see also L. S. Abetsedarskii, *Belorussia i Rossiia*, Minsk, 1978, p. 170; and V. K. Shcharbakoi, *et al.* (eds), *Gistoryia Belarusy ȳ dokumentakh i materialakh,* I, Mensk, 1936, p. 495.

60. Paul, *Travels*, II, pp. 209–10.

61. I. S. Sharkova, *Rossiia i Italia: torgovye otnosheniia xv – pervoi chetverti xviii v.*, Leningrad, 1981, p. 54. (I am indebted to the author for kindly sending me a copy of her book.) Alexis did not receive the ambassador personally (the Secretary of his Private Office dealt with him) but responded by sending an embassy, led by Chemodanov, to Venice.

62. See, *inter alia*, Mal'tsev, *op. cit.*, p. 95; C. B. O'Brien, *Muscovy and the Ukraine*, 1963, pp. 38–9.

63. Zaborovskii, *op. cit.*, pp. 132–3. The offer, dated 22nd June 1655, promised to guarantee the city's rights and did not envisage permanent subjection. The Swedes were preparing to blockade Gdansk at that point. Gdansk was a city of German, rather than Polish, traditions and had a history of struggle against the Polish gentry and the state (King Stefan Bathory had had to lay siege to it less than a century before).

64. See Ye. S. Iarantseva in J. M. Letiche (ed.), *A History of Russian Economic Thought: Ninth through Eighteenth Centuries*, Berkeley, 1964, p. 207.

65. Bazilevich, *op. cit.*, pp. 21–2; *ASBAR*, IV (1836), pp. 130–31.

66. Zaozerskii, *op. cit.*, pp. 296–7.

67. *Ibid.*, p. 27; Kapterev, *op. cit.*, II, p. 190.

For Alexis's continuing patronage, see his endorsement of Nikon's request to found a new monastery at the mouth of the river Onega, *AI*, IV, pp. 244–5; for lists of endowments and some complicated property exchanges see Palmer, III, pp. 510 and 512–13.

68. Kapterev, *op. cit.*, I, pp. 201–2 and 462. See also D. Stremoukhov in *Speculum*, January 1953, pp. 84–101, esp. note 46.

69. Conybeare, *op. cit.*, pp. 56–8; Palmer, II, pp. 424–5; Kapterev, *op. cit.*, I, pp. 248ff.

70. Kapterev, *op. cit.*, II, p. 3.

71. *Ibid.*, II, pp. 286 and 290–91; Palmer, II, pp. lvi–lviii. See also Kapterev, I, pp. 198–9. This was by no means the only case of Alexis cursing in church. He once interrupted divine service in the Patriarch's presence to upbraid the officiant, calling him 'son of a heretic', for making a small mistake – *Ibid.*, I, p. 199 note 1.

72. Zaozerskii, *op. cit.*, pp. 242–4. Part of his Private Office remained in Moscow, however.

73. *PRG*, V, p. 56.

74. *Vremennik Moskovskogo obshchestva istorii i drevnostei rossiiskikh*, Book 6, 1850, pp. 41–4.

75. Paul, *Travels*, II, pp. 33–4.

76. *Ibid.*, p. 35.

77. *TsGADA*, Fond 27, No. 101, ff. 1–2.

78. Bartenev, *SP*, pp. 77–8. He refers here to *stolniki*, the court rank immediately below Councillor rank (though the names of Councillors occur in the lists – see note 77 above). The letter is undated. It has been attributed to 1662 (S. G. Barkhudarov *et al.*, *Slovar' russkogo iazyka xi–xvii vv.*, vyp. 2, Moscow, 1975, p. 38, col. 2). If so, Alexis made a practice of ducking courtiers over several years and was rather slow to explain the circumstances to someone so close to him as Matiushkin. In view of Paul's references I am inclined to date it no later than 1660, and probably earlier (see notes 76 and 77 above).

79. *Povs*, II, p. 277 (the case of Michael Naumov, June 1655); Alexis to Khomiakov, 22nd June 1656, P. Barten'ev, *Pis'ma tsaria Alekseia Mikhailovicha k P. S. Khomiakovu 1656–7*, Moscow, 1861, pp. 2–3.

80. On Alexis's stay in Polotsk see Barsukov, *RS*, IV, pp. 265–73.
81. *DAI*, IV, pp. 58–63. The wounded were evacuated to Polotsk where those who recovered were released home – Alexis to Boyar Vasily Sheremet'ev, Governor of Smolensk, Barsukov, *RS*, IV, pp. 287–8.
82. *PRG*, V, pp. 61–3.
83. *TsGADA*, Oruzheinaia palata, opis' 1659–61, Nos 416 and 488; *strel'tsy* were also employed for this purpose, but their discipline proved poor and they had to be replaced – Hellie, *Enserfment* p. 206. In general on the siege see Barsukov, *RS*, IV, pp. 296–308; also Berkh, I, pp. 104–8.
84. O. B. Alekseeva *et al.* (eds), *Istoricheskie pesni xvii veka*, Moscow–Leningrad, 1966, pp. 127–8.
85. For the papers of Odoevskii's mission see Mukhanov, *Sbornik*, 1836, pp. 483–542; some texts are also printed in *SGGD*, IV, pp. 1–12.

Chapter VI The Autocrat Asserts Himself

1. See Vimina, *Historia*, p. 323, and the discussion in Gurliand, pp. 326–8.
2. For the text of Alexis's falconry rulebook, see Bartenev, *SP*, pp. 87–116; for a partial translation into English, see *SEER*, 1924; see also Bartenev, *SP*, pp. 116–23 and 247–8. The pomp and secrecy surrounding Alexis's falcons almost caused the Emperor Leopold's ambassadors to burst out laughing when, as a special favour, they were shown some of them in February 1662 – but, seeing the imposing look on the faces of the Tsar's messengers, they restrained themselves – Mayerberg, pp. 283–4.
3. E.g. the detailed accounts in his letter to Matiushkin of 11th April and 27th May 1657 – Bartenev, *SP*, pp. 60–61 and 69–71 (on the dating, see Zabelin, *Opyty*, p. 285). For the frequency of his hunting excursions, see *Dneval'nye*, I (*ChOIDR*, vol. 225), pp. 13 *et seq.*
4. *TsGADA*, Fond 27, No. 118, Part vi, ff. 31 and 37 (Baklanova, 'Privoznye tovary'). I am grateful to Dr W. Ryan for identifying what Alexis describes in his convoluted way as 'little observation

tubes . : . through which to look out from a trench and squeeze in one's hand so that it should not be visible' as polemoscopia. Alexis also wanted 'a glass through which . . . one can see everything upside-down'. See also Rainov, *Nauka*, p. 354.
5. *TsGADA*, Fond 27, No. 118, Part iv. ff. 38–9, 42–4 and 47–9, and Part vi, ff. 29–30 and 35–6 (Baklanova, pp. 58ff.). In 1660 Hebdon imported three sets of eight tapestries, one depicting the Emperor Constantine, one Philip of Macedon, and the other plants. He fulfilled most of Alexis's other requests, too, and somewhat more speedily.
6. Zabelin, *DB*, I, pp. 137, 162 and 92.
7. Belokurov, 'O zapisnom prikaze', *Iz dukhovnoi zhizni moskovskago obshchestva xvii v.*, Moscow, 1903, p. 55.
8. *PDS*, X, cols 932–1150.
9. 'Fedor (Bol'shoi) Rtishchev' in *RBS*.
10. See Barsukov, *RS*, IV, pp. 388–9.
11. Kapterev, I, p. 430; Paul, *Travels*, II, pp. 248–9; D. J. Bennet, Jr., 'The Idea of Kingship', pp. 149ff. See also note 38, Chapter IV.
12. *Dneval'nye*, I (*ChOIDR*, 225), pp. 20–27 *passim*; W–K. Medlin, *Moscow and East Rome*, Neuchâtel, 1952, p. 186; Kapterev, II, pp. 167–9.
13. Barsukov, *RS*, IV, pp. 385–6; Bartenev, *SP*, p. 214. The Monastery's design followed the description of the Holy Sepulchre obtained by Arsenyi Sukhanov (See Chapter III, note 32). It was destroyed by enemy action in the Second World War.
14. *AI*, IV, pp. 251–4.
15. O'Brien, *Muscovy and the Ukraine*, pp. 45–50; Vernadsky, II, pp. 510–19; Zyzykin, II, p. 366.
16. Palmer, IV, pp. 117–19.
17. *Ibid.*, IV, pp. 120–39.
18. *Ibid.*, IV, pp. 145–8 and 142–3.
19. I. Shusherin, *Zhitie Sviateishago Patriarkha Nikona*, St Petersburg, 1817, quoted by Palmer, IV, pp. 142–3 (Shusherin, one of Nikon's favourites, wrote the life in about 1680); Kapterev, II, pp. 155ff.
20. Nikon to Alexis, July 1658, Palmer, IV, pp. 149–56.
21. Palmer, IV, pp. 158–61 (citing Shusherin),

and pp. 156–7 (citing N. I. Subbotin).
22. Paul, *Travels*, II, pp. 253–5; Zaozerskii, pp. 196 and 194; Kapterev, II, pp. 93–4.
23. Theiner, pp. 35–6. Alexis's remarks about Odoevskii were made to Yuri Dolgorukii (Barsukov, *RS*, IV, pp. 431–2). For a convenient account of Vyhovsky's manoeuvrings, see O'Brien, *Muscovy*, pp. 53ff.; also Vernadsky, II, pp. 521–2.
24. The *Prikaz sbora soldatskogo stroia* was specifically intended to draft infantrymen; Hellie, p. 195; Kotoshikhin (Uroff), note 35, pp. 571–2.
25. Zaozerskii, p. 299.
26. E.g. on 2nd June 1657 Alexis received Col. Zmeev and 32 officers of his regiment, Col. Junkmann of the dragoons, Lt-Cols Trauernich, van Strobel, Serwin and Skyger, and many other officers on their departure for Borisov in Belorussia and many other stations, including Astrakhan where they were to train *strel'tsy – Dneval'nye*, I (*ChOIDR*, 225), pp. 18–20. This was by no means an isolated occasion. For other examples, see *Ibid.*, pp. 93–4 and *infra*. The 26-year-old Patrick Gordon was among those who met Alexis at Kolomenskoe in 1661 (Gordon, *Passages*, pp. 44–5). On the Trafert and Hebdon missions, see *DAI*, IV, p. 134; Miliukin, *Priezd*, pp. 128–9. See also *infra*, note 55.
27. E.g. Alexis's order of 27th February 1659 cancelled Il'ia's transfer of a captain from one of the new-formation regiments – Gurliand, pp. 233–4 (Gurliand mistakenly attributes it to 1658). On Alexis's personal administration of regiments, see the schedule of his papers in *ZORI*, II, p. 10. For an example of his instructions on training, see his letter to Yuri Dolgorukii, Zaozerskii, pp. 248–9.
28. Alexis's list passed to Ordyn-Nashchokin on 22nd February 1659, *TsGADA*, Fond 27, No. 118, ff.119–20 (Gurliand, pp. 108–9). Dr 'Belyi' has been identified as Dr Balau (or Blau?) of Rostock – M. A. Alpatov, *Russkii istoricheskii mysl' i zapadnaia Evropa*, p. 100.
29. Miliukin, p. 7; for the text of the oath taken by van Horn on his appointment as a *gost'* in 1656 see *Ibid.*, pp. 275–6; on his stock-piling tools as well as experts,

ibid., pp. 128 note, 129 and 140; and Baklanova, p. 162 (*TsGADA*, Fond 27, No. 118, Part iv, ff. 229–32).
30. Richter, *Medicin*, II, pp. 265ff. On 19th March 1657 Alexis had personally ordered a trunkful of medicine from Governor Ordyn-Nashchokin at Tsarevich Dmitrii town – *TsGADA*, Fond 143, opis 2, No. 215, f. 1; also Miliukin, p. 150. Binyon was soon sent abroad on a book-buying mission for the Apothecary Office.
31. On the collection of herbs, see Alexis's autograph order of 14th April 1657 – Bartenev, *SP*, p. 50 and *DAI*, III, p. 253. See also A. V. Balov, 'O kharaktere i znachenii drevnykh kupal'skikh obriadov i igrishch', *Russkii arkhiv*, Moscow, 1911, III, pp. 5–52; and J. G. Frazer, *Balder the Beautiful*, II, pp. 45–75. On his measures to promote fertility, see his letter to the Archimandrite of the St Sergius Monastery, *TsGADA*, Fond 27, No. 347 (printed in *ZORI*, II, p. 698); also Zaozerskii, pp. 83–4.
32. Solov'ev, xii, cols 605–6. Alexis subsequently apologized to Streshnev. A similar story is told of Alexis's son, Peter the Great.
33. Vimina, p. 302; Forsten, *ZhMNP*, May 1898, p. 74. Again, the same was to be said of Peter the Great.
34. Ye. Likhach on Ordyn-Nashchokin in *RBS*. See what amounts to a citation in Alexis's letter to Ordyn-Nashchokin confirming his promotion – *AI*, IV, pp. 262–3.
35. Alexis to Sheremet'ev, Barsukov, *RS*, V, pp. 13–15. See the analysis in R. Crummey, 'The Origin of the Noble Official: The Boyar Elite 1613–1689' in Pintner and Rowney, *Russian Officialdom*, especially Table III–1, p. 53.
36. Gurliand, p. 130. On Odoevskii's uncertainty about addressing his reports, see Alexis's letter to him of 13th July 1658, Barsukov, *RS*, IV, pp. 420–23. On Alexis and Khovanskii, see Solov'ev, xii, col. 615.
37. Solov'ev, xi, cols 45–7.
38. *Ibid.*, cols 43–4; Zaozerskii, p. 253 (Dalyell had entered Alexis's service in 1656).
39. Solov'ev, xi, cols 66–9.

40. Alexis to Matiushkin, Bartenev, *SP*, pp. 64–5. The crisis caused Alexis to abandon his summer hunt for eleven days.
41. See Kapterev, I, Chapter xi.
42. *Ibid.*, II, pp. 12–15 (this according to the hostile Deacon Fedor).
43. Palmer, IV, pp. 210–16, 218–22 and 234; Kapterev, II, pp. 93–4.
44. Palmer, IV, pp. 235–9; Ustiugov and Chaev in *Russkoe gosudarstvo xvii v*, pp. 295–329.
45. Palmer, IV, pp. 164ff.; Man'kov, *Sobornoe Ulozhenie*, p. 203, citing N. M. Nikol'skii, *Istoriia russkoi tserkvi*, Moscow–Leningrad, 1931; Kapterev, I, pp. 432ff.
46. Palmer, IV, pp. 242–5, 257–60 and 269–83.
47. Even Palmer, a fierce protagonist for Nikon, concedes this – IV, p. 293.
48. Palmer, IV, pp. 286–7; O'Brien, pp. 72ff.
49. Hellie, pp. 271 and 218.
50. *SGGD*, IV, pp. 69–72; Bazilevich, pp. 46–8.
51. Alexis to Ordyn-Nashchokin, after 5th October 1660 – Gurliand, p. 289.
52. *Dneval'nye*, I (*ChOIDR*, 225), pp. 58–60; Gurliand, p. 107; Zaozerskii, p. 250.
53. Alexis accused Prince I. I. Lobanov-Rostovskii of 'lying' to him on this account – Zaozerskii, p. 251; also *ZORI*, II, pp. 746–7.
54. *ZORI*, II, p. 32.
55. Miliukin, pp. 135–7, citing *TsGADA*, Fond 27, No. 118, Parts i and iii (items dated 30th November 1660 and 25th February 1661) and No. 539, ff. 76ff. Miliukin adds that a 'General Lord William Keletrav' (?Killigrew) and over 3,000 officers and men were engaged with the permission of the King and Parliament, and that Alexis made arrangements for their reception at Archangel. But, as Miège confirms (p. 224), they never arrived. The 'regiments' referred to were obviously skeleton formations of officers and NCOs. Russians were to constitute the rank and file.
56. Baklanova, 'Privoznye tovary'.
57. Hellie, p. 195 and note 121, pp. 359–60. Over 5,000 men were raised from Alexis's own estates in 1660 (though not all of them entered his military service).

The rate was one man from every twelve households; the norm for the rest of the country was one in twenty (or one in thirty from the estates of serving gentry, widows, etc.).
58. Palmer, IV, pp. 307–13; *ZORI*, II, pp. 622–4. In December Alexis ordered the wealth of all monasteries to be assessed, presumably in order that they should make their full contribution to the war effort – *Ibid.*, pp. 401–2.
59. Hellie, pp. 196–8 and 216–17.
60. *TsGADA*, Fond 27, No. 151 (for 1659); Miliukin, p. 162.
61. *Dneval'nye*, I (*ChOIDR*, 225), p. 108. See also Hellie, pp. 190–91. Another reception for foreign officers was held on 15th November 1661, *Dneval'nye*, I, pp. 114–15; Gordon, pp. 35–45.
62. Kotoshikhin estimates the state's income at this time at approximately 1.4 million rubles (VII, 48, and Uroff's note 378, p. 547). According to A. M. Sakharov (*Ocherki*, 1958, p. 62), a colonel received 30–40 rubles a month plus food; Hellie (pp. 190–91) puts it at 20–35 a month. A provincial gentleman on active service received up to 15 a month (in addition to his land grant).
63. E.g. the order of May 1661 to prospect for silver in the upper Dvina and river Mezen areas – *SGGD*, IV, pp. 72–3. Attempts to raise loans in Amsterdam failed, as they had done in Venice, though hemp worth 180,000 Joachimthalers was sold – Bazilevich, p. 50.
64. Collins, p. 110. On 23rd November 1660, for example, an order instituting a search for deserters in the Olonets region was issued – *DAI*, IV, pp. 229–31.
65. Collins, p. 45.
66. Gordon, pp. 43–4.
67. *ZORI*, II, pp. 682–4.
68. Bazilevich, pp. 23–4, 39–40 and 49. Alexis had been aware of the danger – see his secret message to Ordyn-Nashchokin (c. 1660–61) in Gurliand, pp. 351–3.
69. *TsGADA*, Fond 27, No. 162. Mayerberg, no doubt reporting another inspired rumour, reports that 400 coiners were condemned in 1661.
70. Bazilevich, pp. 35–6; Solov'ev, xi, cols

72–4; Berkh, I, pp. 144–7. On payments to the Cossack shipwrights see *TsGADA*, Oruzheinaia palata, 1659–61, No. 416. On the Courland project, see the report of Alexis's envoy, Zhelia-buzhskii, of February 1661 in Bantysh-Kamenskii, III, p. 8. He had also requested the Duke's help in recruiting shipwrights and mining experts. Courland was no mean mercantile power at the time, maintaining its own fort and factory on the Gambian coast. On the composition of the army on the western front, see Hellie, p. 195.

71. Mayerberg, pp. 297–8. The mode of assault had a precedent. Some years earlier, according to the Venetian Ambassador, Alexis had taken 'the Chancellor', Prince L'vov, by the beard – Vimina, p. 322.

72. The territorial losses were due to Muscovite weaknesses rather than Polish strengths. An important factor was popular resentment of Muscovite occupation which had been allowed to build up in the conquered provinces. Vyhovsky had resisted acceptance of copper coins in Ukraine and there had long been complaints about the irregularity in paying Ukrainian Cossacks (Bazilevich, pp. 33 and 36; O'Brien, *Muscovy*, pp. 45ff.; Vernadsky, II, pp. 510ff.). Complaints about Muscovite troops illtreating the local populations of Belorussia and Lithuania as well as Ukraine had also been arriving for years, e.g. from the 'loyal gentry' of Vilna in 1658 (*Akty otnosiashchiesia k istoriei zapadnoi Rossii*, V, p. 104); and there had been a rising tide of peasant unrest in the Muscovite war zones (Man'kov, *Razvitie krepostnogo prava*, p. 161).

73. *Dneval'nye*, I (*ChOIDR*, 225), pp. 112ff.; Collins, p. 105.

Chapter VII Tempests and Turning Points

1. See *Dneval'nye*, I (*ChOIDR*, Vol. 224, 1908), pp. 118ff.

2. Collins, pp. 111 and 116. 'Sentinels and Guards placed around his Court', writes Collins, 'stand like silent and immovable Statues. No noise is heard in his Pallace, no more than if uninhabited.

. . . In the night season the Czar will go about and visit his Chancellors Desks. . . He has his spyes in every corner, and nothing is done at any Feast, publick Meeting, Burial or Wedding but he knows it. He has spyes also attending his Armies to . . . give a true account of their action.'

3. For the reports of these missions see the relevant sections of *PDS*. Also Bantysh-Kamenskii, II, Part 2. For Pepys's description (November 1662) see R. Latham and W. Matthews (eds), *The Diary of Samuel Pepys*, III, London, 1970, pp. 267–8. Evelyn thought they made 'a glorious show' (*The Diary of John Evelyn*, London, 1959, p. 449). For Venetian reactions, Archivio di Stato, Venice, Collegio: Commemmoriali, Registro III, ff. 151ᵛ–152ʳ| (May 1663).

4. Specifically from Courland – see Gurliand, pp. 107 and 136; also Zaozerskii, p. 250. Nikiforov's instructions should be found in *TsGADA*, Fond 27, No. 216.

5. On the maps, see Zabelin, *DB*, I, p. 231; on the Courland shipbuilding project, see Solov'ev, xii, col. 526; on the state export monopolies, Bazilevich, pp. 51–3.

6. See Bazilevich, pp. 39–44, 55–6 and 61–2. According to Mayerberg, 400 counterfeiters were imprisoned in Moscow (See Chapter VI, note 69, above); other offenders, including the powerful government factor Marselis, suffered confiscation of property, although Alexis's corrupt father-in-law, who was reputed to have minted over 100,000 rubles for himself, suffered only the Tsar's displeasure and contempt. On corruption see also *PSZ*, No. 344.

7. Mayerberg, p. 319.

8. See *Dneval'nye*, I, p. 147.

9. Kotoshikhin (VII, 9), Mayerberg and Patrick Gordon (*Tagebuch*, I) all provide contemporary, but not eye-witness, accounts of the rising. V. I. Buganov has edited the most convenient collection of documentary evidence about it (*Vosstanie 1662g v Moskve: Sbornik dokumentov*, Moscow, 1964). The best modern analyses of the events and their background are Buganov's *Moskovskoe vosstanie*

1662g (Moscow, 1964) and Bazilevich (esp. pp. 85–111). It is on these that the following account has been based.

10. Collins, pp. 11 and 119–21.

11. For Collins's advice on bleeding, 30th April 1664, *TsGADA*, Fond 142, opis' 2, No. 738; his rules for health, 20th January 1665, *loc. cit.*, No. 740; for other reports and prescriptions both for Alexis and the Tsarevich Alexis, *loc. cit.*, No. 741. For Engelhardt's prescriptions dated July 1662 (immediately before the riots), *TsGADA*, Fond 143, opis' 2, No. 580, ff. 1–7. Sample prescriptions for 1663 are provided by Richter, *Geschichte der Medicin*, pp. 239–40 (I am grateful to Professor Maurice Lessof for his comments on these). For a full account of the banquet at which Alexis suffered a nose-bleed, see G. Miège, *A Relation of Three Embassies*, London, 1669, pp. 290–5. The available evidence suggests the onset of a heart malfunction which may have subsequently affected the kidneys (see *infra*, Chapter IX). Alexis's illness may have reinforced his interest in training Russians to become physicians – see the report made to him in 1662 on the training of medical students, *TsGADA*, Fond 143, opis' 2, No. 64.

12. Collins, p. 45.

13. An indication of this was the interest Alexis took in the resources of the conquered provinces. That year he ordered a book about yields of the Mogilev district in Belorussia to be translated so that he could read it – Gurliand, p. 108. Two other translations he ordered at the same time were of a Polish chronicle and the Law Code of Lithuania.

14. Bazilevich, pp. 73–4, *PSZ*, Nos 338 and 339; *SGGD*, IV, No. 29.

15. Zaozerskii, p. 303. Even three years after the rising Alexis made a point of issuing the men of Kravkov's regiment (which had come to his rescue) with a ruble and a fustian coat apiece because they had not joined 'the criminal rebels' at Kolomenskoe (*Ibid.*, pp. 303–4). In April 1665 he had given the regiment (over 1,100 men strong) another ruble per man to celebrate the birth of his son Simeon (*Ibid.*, p. 196). Account books recording payments and special rewards made by

the Private Office to *strelets* and other regiments (including the Viatka infantry and the Danish Lieutenant-General Baumann's regiments), but principally Kravkov's, for the years 1664 and 1665 (*ZORI*, II, p. 30) seem to indicate Alexis's continuing concern for the model units in the army as well as for his security.

16. See *ZhMNP*, June 1898, pp. 317 and 340.

17. E.g. of a townsman of Smolensk who had declared that a gallows hovered over the Tsar – Zaozerskii, p. 289.

18. V. I. Veretennikov, *Istoriia tainoi kantseliarii petrovskogo vremeni*, Khar'kov, 1910, pp. 17–18; Gurliand, p. 26; V. S. Rumiantseva, 'Sysknoe delo tainogo prikaza o Vologodskikh Kapitonov', *Istoriia SSSR*, No. 2 (1978), pp. 170–80. See also her study, based on Private Office papers, of the confluence of religious and economic discontent, and the flight into the forests (a mass phenomenon from the end of the 1650s), in L. V. Cherepnin *et al.* (eds), *Krest'ianskie voiny v Rossii xvii–xviii vekov*, Moscow, 1974, pp. 270–86.

19. E.g. on 23rd April 1663 when Alexis visited the Novodevichii Monastery 500 extra *strel'tsy* were called out – *Dneval'nye*, I, pp. 176–7. The Moscow garrison was by then double the size it had been before the war.

20. Collins, p. 115.

21. E.g. through Dementii Bashmakov who was transferred from the Private Office on promotion to the Razriad in May 1664. In 1665 Bashmakov was instructed not only to send daily abstracts of the activities of his Department to the Private Office but to take over a number of military and financial responsibilities previously discharged by Il'ia Miloslavskii – Zaozerskii, pp. 275–8.

22. Zaozerskii, pp. 6–8, 17 and 124–5; Zabelin, *DB*, pp. 503–6; *ZORI*, II, p. 75. The latter source also notes the considerable sum of 1,500 rubles spent on hiring ploughmen for Izmailovo.

23. Report by Prince Ivan Dashkov, 8th June 1664, with Alexis's comments *TsGADA*, Fond 27, No. 233 (7ff.), reproduced in Gurliand, pp. 353–6. For some of Alexis's personal files on his estates, *TsGADA*, Fond 27, No. 526

(37ff.); see also Zaozerskii, pp. 21–3.

24. Zaozerskii, pp. 17, 29–31, 126, 130 and 33–6.

25. Alexis's undated order to Fedor Elizarov, containing 21 points, in *ZORI*, II, pp. 780–85. See also Zaozerskii, p. 125.

26. Zaozerskii, pp. 17, 98–105, 118–21, 189, 219–20. In his concern for economy Alexis even set his mind to inventing experimental recipes which might provide cheap, easily transportable and storable nourishment for his soldiers and peasants. Such at least seems to have been his motive in ordering quantities of fish (some filleted, some not) to be dried, pounded, sieved, mixed with rye flour in ratios of three parts fish to four of flour, and the resulting mixtures baked and the dried crumbs used to make gruel which was then to be tested to determine 'what kind of preserve results'. The order was secret. – Zaozerskii, p. 84.

27. For records concerning the leather (*safian*) factory set up in 1660, see *DTP*, III (*RIB*, Vol. 23), pp. 1583–1643; on the glass factory at Izmailovo (which produced mainly for the court), see Baklanova, 'Steklannye zavody' in *Ocherki po istoriei torgovli i promyshelennosti*, pp. 132–41; for the Private Office records of income and expenditure from 1663 onwards, see *DTP*, III, pp. 393ff.

28. Collins, p. 112; Zaozerskii, pp. 66–7 and 219–20; *ZORI*, II, pp. 387–90 and Gurliand, pp. 170–72.

29. Zabelin, *DB*, p. 506; Zaozerskii, pp. 151–2 and 171; *ZORI*, II, pp. 387–90, and Gurliand, pp. 170–72.

30. Zaozerskii, pp. 57ff.; *ZORI*, II, *loc. cit.*

31. Ten thousand rubles were invested within a period of only eight months during 1665–6 – Gurliand, p. 173. For Private Office papers concerning the expedition to Persia, which returned in 1666, *DTP*, III (*RIB*, Vol. 23), pp. 1413ff.

32. For a discussion of this still unsolved problem of the merchant class, and cognate ones, see S. Baron, *Muscovite Russia*, London, 1980; also P. Bushkevich, *The Merchants of Muscovy*, Cambridge, 1980. On the Domodedovo experiment, see Zaozerskii, pp. 151–2; on the Pskov experiment (the brainchild of Ordyn-Nashchokin), see Solov'ev, xiii, cols

716–18; also Likhach, 'Ordyn-Nashchokin' in *RBS*. One of the stumblingblocks here was the vested interests of the richer merchants, who resented competition from the smaller fry.

33. For documentary sources on these troubles see *DAI*, IV, pp. 297ff. and 318ff., and V, pp. 39ff., 68–73.

34. Alexis to Romodanovskii (undated but from internal evidence attributable to 1662–3), *ZORI*, II, pp. 770–71. Alexis subsequently attempted to turn this letter into verse – Solov'ev, xii, cols 612–13.

35. For accounts of the chaotic developments in Ukraine from 1663 to the Peace of Andrusovo in 1667 (see Chapter VIII *infra*), see Vernadsky, *Tsardom*, II, pp. 533–40; O'Brien, *Muscovy*, pp. 88–114 ff.; also W. E. D. Allen, *The Ukraine* (Cambridge, 1940). For Alexis's account of differences of opinion among his advisers, see Zaozerskii, pp. 284–5.

36. Solov'ev, *Istoriia*, xi, cols 160–2.

37. On the establishment of this postal service see Kozlovskii, *Pervyia pochty i pervye pochtmeistery v moskovskom gosudarstve*, 2 vols, Warsaw, 1913; also Gurliand, p. 299. Some at least of the foreign news digests are to be found in *TsGADA*, Fond 155 – see D. C. Waugh, 'News of the False Messiah: Reports on Shabbetai Zevi in Ukraine and Muscovy', *Jewish Social Studies*, xli, Nos 3–4 (Summer–Fall 1979), pp. 301–22 (I am grateful to Gershon Hundert for drawing this article to my attention).

38. *ZORI*, II, pp. 771–5. An incomplete English version is Palmer, appendix, pp. 210–11.

39. Material confirming Alexis's concern about countering such manifestations, and about suppressing the Kapitons in particular, can be found in *TsGADA*, Fond 27, No. 258 – see Rumiantseva, 'Sysknoe delo', *loc. cit.* On Archbishop Joseph of Kolomenskoe's critical remarks about the Tsar, see Solov'ev, III, 745–6.

40. Nikon had spoken out publicly at a service at 'New Jerusalem' in February 1662. The text is in Palmer, IV, Chapter 5, esp. pp. 366–7.

41. See *Dneval 'nye*, I, p. 121 (10th January);

Kapterev, II, p. 80.

42. On Nikon's overture to Ligarides, Palmer, IV, p. 383; for Streshnev's questions and digests of Ligarides's answers, *Ibid.*, I, pp. xxvii–xxxix; for Nikon's rebuttals, *Ibid.*, I, pp. 1–615. For the Council of 26th November 1662, see *Dneval 'nye*, I, p. 162.

43. Kapterev, II, pp. 289–97; Palmer, IV, pp. 381–430.

44. See *SGGD*, IV, pp. 84–117; for the background, Kapterev, II, pp. 307–17.

45. Kapterev, II, pp. 307–17; *SGGD*, IV, pp. 126–31; Palmer, III, pp. 78–80 and IV, pp. 471–94.

46. *The Life of Avvakum Written by Himself* (trans. Harrison and Mirrlees) in S. Zenkovsky (ed)., *Medieval Russia's Epics, Chronicles and Tales*, New York, 1974, p. 434.

47. N. K. Gudzii, V.E. Gusev *et al.* (eds), *Zhizn' Avvakuma im samim napisannoe i drugie ego sochineniia*, Moscow, 1960, pp. 185–90 and notes, pp. 410–13.

48. For the Patriarch of Jerusalem's letter to Alexis, 20th March 1664, Palmer, III, pp. 350–56. *SGGD*, IV, pp. 134–43 provides the Greek text and Russian translation. As Palmer points out, the Russian text stresses the Tsar's general supremacy whereas the original limited this to political matters alone – Palmer, *loc. cit.*, esp. note 9, p. 322. Alexis could not read Greek and was therefore dependent on the translator, but there can be little doubt that the alterations coincided with his wishes. See also Kapterev, II, pp. 297–304.

49. Palmer, V, Appendices, pp. 155–6, translating Roll IX, No. 11 of the Synodal Archive. See Cap. VIII.

50. See the evidence of the clergy at the subsequent enquiry, *Ibid.*, V, Appendix xv, pp, 152–6.

51. See the materials in Palmer, IV, pp. 514–75 (Shusherin's life of Nikon and documents from the Synodal Archive) and V, appendix xiv (depositions of the Ziuzin enquiry). Another victim was the Metropolitan Jonah of Rostov who had accepted Nikon's blessing – but though he was replaced as administrator of the Patriarchate he nevertheless retained his see.

52. The text of Ziuzin's letter to Nikon is in Palmer, IV, pp. 526–35.

53. The text of Nikon's message to Alexis on his return to Moscow is in Palmer, IV, pp. 539–41. For Ziuzin's remark, see Subbotin, *Delo Nikona*, p. 108, translated by Palmer (IV, p. 536); also the transcript of Ziuzin's own evidence at the enquiry – Palmer, V, appendix xvi, esp. p. 176.

54. Palmer, III, pp. 372–9.

55. Text in Richter, p. 270; see also Zaozerskii, pp. 292–3 (citing A. Prozorovskii (ed.), *Sozertsanie kratkoe*, pp. 38–9).

56. The proposal brought from Vienna by two Jesuits ostensibly foundered over the question of the Tsar's titles – Archivio Segreto Vaticano, Misc. Arm., VI, 39, ff. 39–41.

57. Belokurov, *Dneval 'nye*, p. 204; on urban rights, *SGGD*, IV, pp. 163–5. The policy of integrating the Ukrainian elite into Muscovite society was to be applied subsequently to other Cossack communities, where it also served as a major factor in achieving political control – see my article 'Transformations in Cossackdom' in B. Kiraly and G. Rothenberg (eds), *War and Society in East Central Europe*, I, New York, 1979, pp. 393–407.

58. Kapterev, II, pp. 30–5.

59. *Ibid.*, II, pp. 21–2. More specifically, the questions invited their acceptance of the Orthodoxy of the four Greek Patriarchs, of their Greek books and manuscripts, and of the conclusions of the 1654 synod in Moscow.

60. Avvakum (Harrison and Mirrlees) in Zenkovsky, p. 435; *DAI*, I, 448.

61. Kapterev, II, pp. 25–8. Yet Morozova was to remain firm in her beliefs – see Chapter IX *infra*.

62. *Ibid.*, II, pp. 323ff. In January 1666 Alexis had sent a secret emissary to the Patriarch Dionysios, whose denial that Afanasy Ikonskii was his exarch was to destroy the credibility of Paisios Ligarides – *Ibid.*, II, pp. 318–21.

63. *Dneval 'nye*, I, pp. 230–31; Kapterev, II, pp. 322 and 333 ff.

64. Gurliand, pp. 46–7.

65. Alexis's subsidies to Liubomirskii were channelled through his agents Benjamin Helmfeldt and Peter and Leonhardt

Marselis – Kozlovskii, I, pp. 86–7.

66. The text of Alexis's personal note to Ordyn-Nashchokin (providing a gloss on his instructions, which were to concede the ultimate transfer of Kiev to the Poles while insisting on its continued occupation by Muscovy for a period) is printed in *ZORI*, II, pp. 766–7.

Chapter VIII Trials

1. Palmer, III, pp. 437–41 and V, pp. 675–81; Kapterev, II., pp. 337–8. The mass of papers pertaining to the affair in the Secret Office archive includes minutes of the trial (*ZORI*, II, pp. 8–14; Palmer, V, appendix xxxii). Alexis's opening speech has been reconstructed from the versions in Solov'ev and in Shusherin's life of Nikon.

2. Palmer, V. pp. 675–721, III, 168–90 and 420–34; Kapterev, II, pp. 339–50. I have conflated various accounts here.

3. For the act of deposition, *SGGD*, IV, pp. 182–6 and *PSZ*, I, pp. 629–31. See also Palmer, III, pp. 436–49 and V, pp. 722–34; Kapterev, II, pp. 350–52, and S. A. Belokurov, *Materialy dlia russkoi istorii*, Moscow, 1888, pp. 81–111.

4. For the terms of the Andrusovo settlement see *PSZ*, I, pp. 632 ff. (also Solov'ev, xi, cols 172–87; and O'Brien, *Muscovy*, pp. 110–18).

5. Palmer, III, pp. 207–57; Kapterev, II, pp. 228–52.

6. For digests of the synod's conclusions see Palmer, III, pp. 480–518; for the condemnation of schism (13th May 1667), *DAI*, V. pp. 483–8 (selections from which are translated into English in G. Vernadsky *et al.* (eds), *A Source Book for Russian History*, I, New Haven, 1972, pp. 258–9); on the question of jurisdiction over clerics, *ASBAR*, IV, pp. 212–14; also Kapterev, II, pp. 36–49 and 366 ff. The synod deferred to Alexis's wishes even when they involved breaching the canons. Thus his grants to Nikon's three monasteries, though admitted to be irregular, were allowed to stand. Alexis subsequently granted the Patriarch jurisdiction over lay servants of the Patriarchate as well as clerics (*AI*, IV, pp. 461–4), a reversion from earlier norms which was probably due to the difficulty

the state was experiencing in administering efficient justice, because of the shortage of competent judges, and the expense. What the Tsar granted he could take back, of course.

7. I have modified the translation from Avvakum's autobiography in S. A. Zenkovsky's *Medieval Russia's Epics, Chronicles and Tales* (New York, 1974), pp. 441–6. Also N. K. Gudzii *et al.* (eds), *Zhizn' protopopa Avvakuma*, notes, pp. 376–7 and Kapterev, II, pp. 36–7. The sentences were to be carried out during Easter week 1670 – Vernadsky, *op. cit.*, I, p. 260.

8. See Palmer, III, pp. lix ff. and the references therein.

9. *Dneval 'nye* (*ChOIDR*, Vol. 225), pp. 252–3. Collins (pp. 12–13) is mistaken (or misprinted) in referring to the customary age of declaring a Tsarevich as fifteen. Alexis himself had been declared at thirteen (see Chapter I). Albeit unconsciously, this accorded with Jewish practice as did so much else in the Russian tradition (not least sexual and dietary laws: the 1667 synod went so far as to ban the stunning of animals before they were killed for food). See also *Iz arkhiva tainykh del*, pp. 42–7 and 'Fedor (Bo 'shoi) Rtischev' in *RBS*. At the time of the Tsarevich Alexis's coming of age his brother Fedor was six.

10. On the negro Savelii, see Zabelin, *DB* II, p. 305. Polotskii (his real name was Samuel Emel'ianovich Petrovskii-Sitianovich, but he was called Polotski because he came from Polotsk) was a polymath, a poet and a political philosopher as well as a theologian. Unlike Yuri Krizhanich, the Croatian scholar who had come to Moscow in 1659, his political ideas commended themselves to Alexis. Krizhanich is said to have championed the idea of a *Rechtsstaat*, or 'natural rights' based on reason and upheld by laws. He also thought unrestricted monarchical power to be contrary to the laws of God and nature. Polotskii on the other hand, though also influenced by 'enlightened' western-European ideas, was much firmer in his support of absolutism (see L. N. Pushkarev, 'Gosu darstvo i vlast' v obshchestvenno

politicheskoi mysli kontsa xvii v',
Obshchestvo i gosudarstvo feodal'noi Rossii,
Moscow, 1975, pp. 189–97). Krizhanich
had been exiled to Tobol'sk in Siberia in
1661 – See S. A. Belokurov, 'Iurii Kriz-
hanich v Rossii', *ChOIDR*, II–III (1903),
II (1907), II (1909), and I. Tatarskii,
Simeon Polotskii, ego zhizn' i deiatel'nost',
Moscow, 1886.

11. Paisios Ligarides to P. Scierecki, O. P.,
25th September 1668, Theiner, pp. 61–2.
The prospect of religious reunion created a buzz of activity in Rome – see A.
Šeptycky (ed.), *Monumenta Ucrainae His-
torii*, III, pp. 292 ff. and IV. For a Polish
view of Alexis's attempts to obtain the
crown of Poland, see Z. Wójcik, 'Russian Endeavors for the Polish crown in
the 17th century', *Slavic Review*, Spring
1982, pp. 59–72.

12. *ZORI* II, p. 28 lists the report of
Ambassador P. I. Potemkin's mission.
The extract from his testimonial given
to the Duke of Liria is taken from Bcrkh,
I, pp. 233–6. On the question of the title
Serenissimus being claimed of England,
see Miège, p. 195 and Gordon, pp. 79–
90. Alexis was later to demand the additional title 'Most Potent' (see the papers
relating to Menzies's mission to Venice
in 1673 *infra*).

13. Zabelin, *DB*, I, pp. 178 ff., 151, 63, 193
and 223–4.

14. *Dneval'nye*, pp. 235–6; Zabelin, *DB*, I,
pp. 446–8, 477–503 and 785–9; Zaozer-
skii, pp. 66–7; V. M. Meshcherina, *Kolo-
menskoe*, Moscow, 1958, and G. H.
Hamilton, *The Art and Architecture of
Russia*, Harmondsworth, 1954. On
Alexis' visits there, *Dneval'nye*, p. 270.
The palace was to be demolished by
Catherine II.

15. *Dneval'nye*, p. 226; Zabelin, *DB*, II, p.
316; Collins, p. 63; *The Voiages and
Travels of John Struys*, London, 1684, p.
129.

16. Ordyn-Nashchokin's other departments
were the Novgorod, Galats and Vladi-
mir *cheti* (*Iz arkhiva*, p. 143). For
the Pushkin case, *Ibid.*, pp. 48–52 and
Dneval'nye, pp. 263–4. Gentlemen
Councillors I. Pronchshichev and G.
Anichkov ran the Great Income and
New Quarter Offices respectively, P.

Elizarov and S. Larionov presided over
the Land Office (which administered
Moscow) and Elizarov and Zaborovskii
ran the Kostroma Quarter and the
Monastery Office. Councillor-Secre-
taries (all of whom were commoners
and had risen through the bureaucracy)
who held ministerial portfolios at this
juncture were Dementii Bashmakov
(the *Razriad*), Grigory Karaulov (Office
of Service Estates), and Alexander
Durov (Guards Office); two more
(Dokhturov and Golosov) served under
Nashchokin at the Foreign Office. Of
the aristocrats Yuri Dolgorukii was in
charge of the Kazan Palace Office in
1667–8, Ivan Khovanskii of the new
Courier Service Office, and Yuri
Romodanovskii of the Gunnery
Department (*Iz arkhiva*, pp. 143–5).
Generally on the question of the 'demo-
cratization' of the Council see R.
Crummey, 'The Origins of the Noble
Official' in W. Pintner and D. Rowney,
(eds), *Russian Officialdom*, pp. 46–75,
especially pp. 54–7.

17. See Solov'ev, xii, cols 388–9 and 395–6.
His complaints seem to have prompted
a tightening-up of financial procedures.
E.g. on 30th July 1669 an order was
issued which improved accounting procedures in government departments and
stopped personal loans from official
funds – see *DAI*, V, pp. 413–15.

18. *SGGD*, IV, pp. 189–204; *DAI*, pp. 677–
91. Also Likhach's article on Nashchokin in *RBS*.

19. *SGGD*, IV, pp. 204–5. On Alexis's
current involvement in the Persian
trade, see *DTP*, III (*RIB*, Vol. 23), and
TsGADA, Fond 27, No. 355.

20. See Olearius (2nd English edition), pp.
141–2 and Alpatov, p. 100. The Private
Office papers contain descriptions of
two routes to India (with accounts of
towns and rivers along the way), as well
as an explanation of why it was not possible to reach China and the East Indies
by sea from Astrakhan (and a notebook
on what turned out to be the more practical idea of finding a North-East passage to the Orient) – *TsGADA*, Fond 27,
Nos 485 and 333. See also point 11 of A.
Vinnius's memorandum of 5th Decem-

ber 1668, *DAI*, V, pp. 404–5.

21. *DAI*, V., pp. 218–20, Struys, *op. cit.*, especially pp. 114–15 and 158–9. Butler's contract, signed in February 1667, contained provisions for cost-of-living allowance, medical care, the cost of bringing his wife to Muscovy and a year's salary for her if he should be drowned or killed 'which God forbid'. It is printed in *DAI*, V, pp. 211–12. *The Eagle* (*Orel* in Russian) is pictured opposite p. 177 of Struys's book.

22. Vinnius's memorandum (*loc. cit.*) was prompted by Butler's request for one galley to be built. According to Berkh (who claims to have found a model of it), it was.

23. On the fire at Archangel, 12th December 1667, Berkh, I, p. 237. For the draft fire regulations on 6th January 1668 (corrected in Alexis's own hand), Gurliand, pp. 361–2 (*TsGADA*, F. 27, No. 281). For the fires in Moscow of 22nd–23rd August 1668, and Alexis's orders, *Dneval'nye*, pp. 280–83, and Struys, p. 136 (however, his estimate of 35,000 houses destroyed seems exaggerated and the great fire occurred about six months, not six weeks, before his arrival in Moscow). On rumours that the fires were caused by Nikon's spells, see the report to Rome by the papal nuncio in Warsaw (based on accounts brought back from Moscow by the emissary of the Archbishop of Gniezno) – Theiner, *op. cit.*, pp. 62–3.

24. Berkh, I, pp. 305–8 (citing Shusherin).

25. The text of the Solovka petition (from S. Denisov's history of the schism) is translated in Palmer, II, pp. 449–59; Lazar's petition is quoted by Vernadsky, *The Tsardom of Moscow*, II, p. 704. For a Soviet account, which seeks to attribute the Solovka revolt to a downturn in its economic fortunes, and gives information on the community's connections with the outside world drawing on new archival material, see A. M. Borisov, *Khoziaistvo Solovetskogo Monastyria*, Petrozavodsk, 1966, pp. 210 ff. For the sedition case in Pskov, V.I. Veretennikov, *Istoriia tainoi kantseliarii*, Khar'kov, 1910, p. 14. For a study of rebellions in the central provinces based

partly on Private Office papers (Fond 27, Nos 258 and 259), V. S. Rumiantseva, 'O krest'ianakh-raskol'nikakh kanuna vosstaniia S. T. Razina' in Cherepnin, *Krest'ianskie voiny* (1974), pp. 270–86.

26. In 1667 Alexis had gone so far as to remark to the Polish ambassadors that since the Eastern and Western Churches had once been united it should not prove very difficult to reunite them, and he invited them to discuss the matter with the Greek Patriarchs then in Moscow. Paisios Ligarides was evidently very active in the cause, but some months later he declared it to be hopeless – Palmer, III, p. 541, Theiner, pp. 52–3 and 62–3. Alexis's complaisance on the question is also suggested by the fact that when (on 29th July 1668) he received a letter from the Patriarch of Jerusalem informing him that Paisios had been anathematized as a Catholic and a heretic (Kapterev, II, pp. 504–6), he responded by asking him to withdraw the ban and restore Paisios to his see as Metropolitan of Gaza. This he eventually succeeded in accomplishing (Palmer, V. pp. 742–4 and 746–7); also Kapterev, II, Appendix.

27. On Don Cossack contact with Nikon, Solov'ev, xi, cols 274–5; on rumours that Alexis took ill at the news of Briukhovetsky's betrayal, Theiner, *op. cit.*, pp. 62–3; on Alexis's military dispositions, *Iz arkhiva*, pp. 69–73.

28. On the numbers employed in the operation, Hellie, p. 271. For reports of the campaign, *Iz arkhiva*, pp. 120–21, 126–9, 134, 137–9 and 147. Alexis's draft orders and letters to Kurakin and Romodanovskii, *TsGADA*, F. 27, No. 278, ff. 1–7 (the letter berating Kurakin is on f. 3). A version is given in Solov'ev, III, xii cols 606–7. See also cols 373–96.

29. Berkh, I, pp. 248–50; Struys, pp. 129–30. On the crop failures, Novosel'skii, *Votchinnik*, p. 91; *DTP*, I (*RIB*, Vol. 21), p. 1477.

30. *TsGADA*, Fond 27, No. 287, ff. 1–7. Presumably this is the document reproduced in P.P. Pekar'skii's *Spisok devits iz kotorykh v 1670 i 1671 godakh vybral supruge Tsaria Alekseia Mikhailovicha*,

which I have not seen.

31. Zaozerskii, p. 279. Zaozerskii concludes that the mission was prompted by Alexis's fears of native sorcerers and curers, but the timing and the stress on Ulita's curative powers suggest otherwise.

32. Berkh, I, pp. 252–3.

33. Fedor Naryshkin had often been on guard duty at the palace, 1662–7 – *DTP*, III (*RIB*, Vol. 23), p. 487 and *Dneval'nye* (*ChOIDR*, Vol. 224, 1908), pp. 137 and *passim*.

34. *TsGADA*, Fond 27, No. 299. The file on the investigation (evidently incomplete) consists of three dossiers, the second and third of which (totalling 499 sheets) contain only samples of the handwritings of secretaries and under-secretaries. Alexis's own transcriptions of one of the sample passages appear in F. 27, No. 52. See also Gurliand, note 1, pp. 307–8.

35. The chief source of printed documents on the Razin rebellion is Ye. A. Shvetsova, *Krest'ianskaia voina pod predvoditel'-stvom Stepana Razina*, 4 vols, Moscow, 1954–76. For foreign eye-witness accounts, A. G. Man'kov, *Zapiski inostrantsev o vosstanii Stepana Razina*, Leningrad, 1968, and his *Inostrannye izvestiia o vosstanii Stepana Razina*, Leningrad, 1975. There are several convenient accounts in English, one in my *The Cossacks*, London, 1969, Chapter V.

36. *DTP*, III (*RIB*, Vol. 23), p. 1351; Shvetsova, *op. cit.*, IV, p. 15.

37. *DAI*, VI, pp. 56–9.

38. *PRG*, V, No. 68.

Chapter IX Renaissance

1. *ASBAR*, IV, pp. 232–3; *DRV*, xiii (1790), pp. 233–4. Also Berkh I, pp. 257–8. The rules of precedence were abandoned for the occasion.

2. *Ocherki russkoi kul'tury xvii veka*, II, p. 62; Zabelin, *DB*, II, p. 304.

3. Zabelin, *DB*, pp. 209–11 and 476; II, p. 305.

4. Luppov, pp. 111, 113, 135, 196 and 203; *ZORI*, II, p. 18; J. Reutenfels, *De Rebus Moschoviticus*, Padova, 1680 (for a Russian translation, see *ChOIDR*, Part 3, 1905).

5. See Avvakum's fifth *beseda*, Gudzii *et al.*

(eds), *Avvakum*, pp. 138–40.

6. See R. J. W. Evans, *The Making of the Habsburg Monarchy*, pp. 340 ff.

7. I am grateful to Dr A. Hippisley for sight of some of his material on Simeon Polotsky's library. See also Palmer, III, p. 100. For Ligarides's letter to P. Scierecki, 25th September 1668, see Theiner, *Monuments*, pp. 61–2. 'Hermes Trismegistus' had also figured in 16th-century Russian literature (Ryan, 'The *Secreta Secretorum* and the Muscovite Autocracy' in *Pseudo-Aristotle*, Warburg Institute, London, 1983, note 35). In May 1672 Alexis ordered Ligarides to return to Palestine, giving him 300 rubles as a parting gift, but the Greek lingered in Kiev, whence in August 1675 he was recalled to Moscow, but he was never to see Alexis again and eventually died in Kiev (Kapterev, II, pp. 512–18).

8. See D. C. Waugh, '*Azbuka znameni lits*: Egyptian hieroglyphs in the Private Chancery Archive', *OSP*, X (1977), pp. 46–50.

9. An expedition to prospect for silver led by Col. Riemann was on its way to Siberia (*DAI*, VI, pp. 156–8); Andrei Vinnius and Paul Menzies were both commissioned to engage skilled metallurgists in the course of diplomatic missions, on which see note 18 *infra* (*PDS*, IV, pp. 80–83). In 1671 the production of muskets at Tula was increased to 2,000 a year; the artillery foundry in Moscow cast sixty regimental cannon and received orders for a hundred more (Hellie, n. 22, p. 355 and p. 185). Arms imports were still required, however (Medovnikov, p. 166).

10. Zaozerskii, pp. 229–30; the Private Office income and expenditure books, *DTP*, III (*RIB*, Vol. 23), pp. 1–1413; *TsGADA*, Fond 27, No. 344, ff. 3 (not before 1672); relevant files covering the period 1661–73 are listed in *ZORI*, II, p. 29. See also *DTP*, I (*RIB*, Vol. 21), pp. 939–42.

11. Zaozerskii, p. 32. Alexis's undated letter to Tishka and Vaska (contemptuous diminutives of the two officers' christian names) are in *TsGADA*, Fond. 27, No. 338 (ff. 9) and printed in Gurliand, p. 51, note.

12. *ZORI*, II, pp. 733–5.
13. On the Razin legend, see my essay 'The Subversive Legend of Sten'ka Razin' in V. Strada (ed.), *Rossiia/Russia*, II, Torino, 1975, pp. 17–40. On Razin's followers reaching Solovka, Indova *et al.* in Druzhinin, *Absoliutizm*, pp. 50–91. On Kleopin, Zabelin, *Opyty*, I, pp. 116–17.
14. See Zaozerskii, p. 285; Likhach, 'Ordyn-Nashchokin' in *RBS*; Solov'ev, xii, cols. 387–8.
15. *ChOIDR*, VI, pp. 172–91 – translated in part by Palmer (V, p. 812, note 19).
16. Zabelin, *DB*, I, pp. 406–15 and II, pp. 5 and 559; Barsukov, *RS*, VIII, pp. 1–3. For Polotskii's ode, see S. Polotskii, *Izbrannye sochineniia*, Moscow, 1966, p. 503.
17. The text of the circular with Alexis's manuscript corrections is in *ZORI*, II, pp. 778–80. Compare this with his letter to Romodanovskii (*ibid.*, II, pp. 755–8).
18. The envoys were Paul Menzies, himself a Catholic, Under-Secretary Emel'ian Ukraintsev and Andrei Vinnius. For the Menzies mission see *PDS*, IV, pp. 753–851; for the letter to the Pope, Theiner, pp. 76–8; and Archivio Segreto Vaticano, Misc. Arm., VI, No. 39, ff. 84^r–91^r. Alexis's letter to Doge Domenico Contarini, dated October 1672, is in Archivio di Stato, Venice, Collegio: Lettere Principi: Russia. On the negotiations in Venice, Collegio, Esposizione Principi, No. 87 (ex-88) 6 ff.; Collegio: Cerimoniale, Registro III, ff. 171^r–2^v. Alexis also made an attempt to draw Sweden into the anti-Turkish struggle, but without success – Attmann, *Ekonomicheskie sviazi*, p. 197, note; Bantysh-Kamenskii, IV, p. 192.
19. Ye. Opochinin, *Russkii teatr*, St Petersburg, 1887, p. 22; N. Tikhonravov, *Russkii dramaticheskie proizvedeniia 1672–1725 godov*, I, St Petersburg, 1874, pp. vi–ix. The mission was only partially successful. Eight actors were engaged in Riga, but an attempt to hire the singer Anna Paulson and her troupe in Copenhagen failed, and when van Staden eventually returned to Moscow in December 1672 he was to bring only one trumpeter and four other musicians.
20. Ambassador Likhachev's report on the

Florentine theatre is in *DRV*, 2nd ed., IV (1788), pp. 348–54; O. A. Derzhavina, 'Teatr i dramaturgiia' in Artsikhovskii, *Ocherki russkoi kul'tury*, II, Moscow, 1979, pp. 130–31.
21. *Dneval'nye* (*ChOIDR*, Vol. 225), pp. 283–91; Zabelin, *DB*, II, pp. 335–7; Tikhonravov, I, pp. vi–xi and xx. For an account of the miracle play *Belshazzar* performed in Moscow in 1656, see Paul, *Travels*, II, pp. 130–31.
22. See Reutenfels's account (*op. cit.*); Zabelin, *DB*, I, p. 63 and II, pp. 328 ff.
23. *Dneval'nye, loc. cit.*; *TsGADA*, Fond 27, No. 312. The date of its receipt in Moscow is not known, but it is quite possible that it was composed and rushed to Moscow within four weeks of the last sighting of the comet on 15th November (see F. Braudel, *The Mediterranean and the Mediterranean World in the Age of Philip II*, I, London, 1972, p. 364). The explanatory text is printed in Guriland, pp. 380–82. More valuable, perhaps, than the astrological forecast was another curious item that reached Alexis at about the same time – depictions of monstrous insects (probably locusts) which had appeared in Hungary amid heavy snows, fed off one another and suddenly disappeared again. Perhaps this drew Alexis's attention because plagues of insects had devastated the harvest in the provinces of Moscow, Vologda and Iaroslav the year before (Novosel'skii, *Votchinnik*, p. 93 and Berkh I, p. 263). The document is in the same file as the preceding.
24. 'Iz arkhiva tainykh del', *SN*, XV (1911), pp. 165–7; Berkh, I, p. 281.
25. *SGGD*, IV, pp. 295–9; see also Solov'ev, xii, cols 501–18.
26. *SGGD*, IV, pp. 312–16 and 323–5; *AI*, VI, pp. 528–31.
27. *ZORI*, II, p. 21. For papers concerning the reproductions of the Byzantine crown, orb and sceptre (including their valuations) see *DAI*, VI, pp. 204–6. In January 1666 Alexis had sent for three learned Greeks who *inter alia* knew 'the printed ritual . . . of the former . . . Greek Emperors' – Kapterev, I, p. 43. The text of the *Titulary* is in *DRV*, xvi, pp. 86–251; the illustrations were repro-

duced in *Portrety, gerby i pechaty Bol'shoi Gosudarstvennoi Knigi 1672*g, St Petersburg (Arkheograficheskii Institut), 1903.

28. *SGGD*, IV, pp. 316–21; Solov'ev, xii, col. 604.

29. *PRG*, V, pp. 73–4. The letter (which bears a date but no year) might conceivably belong to 1675 when Alexis was also on pilgrimage to Zagorsk on the same date.

30. Solov'ev, xi, col. 275; Berkh, I, p. 368; *DTP*, III (*RIB*, Vol. 23), p. 156; Belokurov, *Materialy*, pp. 81–114; *ChOIDR*, p. 12; Solov'ev, xi, cols 280–82.

31. Bain, pp. 156–8; Vernadsky, II, pp. 706–8; Gudzii (ed.), *Avvakum*, notes, pp. 371–2; Zaozerskii, pp. 29–30.

32. Kapterev, II, pp. 61–2; Solov'ev, xiii, col. 746.

33. Zabelin, *DB*, I, p. 256; *DAI*, VI, pp. 323–4; Richter, p. 244.

34. *DR*, III, cols 108f.; Reutenfels, *loc. cit.*; Zabelin, *DB*, II, p. 323.

35. Solov'ev, xii, col. 760; *DR*, III, col. 1131; Zabelin, *DB*, II, pp. 336–42; Tikhonravov, I, pp. 106–203. A manuscript of *Judith* was in Peter the Great's library (Academy of Sciences Library, Peter collection, no. 114).

36. *DR*, III, cols 1131 and 1501; Tikhonravov, I, pp. xliii–iv; *Ibid.*, pp. 243–69 (for *Adam and Eve*), pp. 270–95 (for *Joseph*) and pp. 204–42 for *Bayazet*. Also Zabelin, *DB*, II, p. 337; Derzhavina, *loc. cit.*, p. 131–5 (who differs, however, in her interpretation of *Bayazet*); Vernadsky (II, pp. 738–9) and others seem to be mistaken in their belief that *Bayazet* was based on Marlowe's *Tamerlane*. See also S. Bogoiavlenskii, *Moskovskii teatr pri tsariakh Aleksee i Petre*, Moscow, 1914.

37. *DR*, III, cols 1428–30, 1443–4 and 1452–3; Zaozerskii, p. 292; Gurliand, pp. 309–10.

38. *DR*, III, cols 1297, 1301, 1325, 1398–9, 1411–12, 1422–3 and 1443; Gurliand, p. 309. The story of Alexis's supposed affair is told in the later editions of Olearius (Palmer, V. Appendix, p. 207, note 17), and by P. J. von Strahlenberg (*An Historico-Geographical Description . . . of Russia*, London, 1738, p. 224).

39. Barsukov, *RS*, VIII, pp. 95–8; *TsGADA*, Fond 143, opis' 2, No. 23, f.2.

40. Zaozerskii, pp. 18, 19, 85 and 128; *TsGADA*, Fond 27, No. 357, ff. 47 (Gurliand, pp. 368–76); *TsGADA*, Fond 27, No. 568; Barsukov, *RS*, pp. 139–41; Gurliand, pp. 342–8. Documents annotated in his own hand in *TsGADA*, Fond 27, No. 524 (e.g. no. 6) show that Alexis was working within days of his death.

41. On these embassies see Vernadsky, II, pp. 684–93 and 660–1; Berkh I, pp. 285–8, and *PSZ*, I, No. 596. The embassy to India had to turn back at Kabul. On control of banditry, *PSZ*, I, No. 607, p. 967. Also *DR*, III, cols 1438, 1514 and 1522.

42. *Ocherki russkoi kul'tury*, II, p. 284.

43. Berkh, I, pp. 297–301; *DR*, III, cols 1501–2 and 1552–5; Barsukov, *RS*, VIII, pp. 139–41, 146–7 and 150–3. The winged falconers were also paraded for the Danish and Swedish ambassadors – *Ibid.*, VIII, pp. 72–3 and *SN*, pp. 160–3.

44. E.g. 1st October – *DR*, III, col. 1080; Adolf Lyseck's relation, translated from the Latin in *ZhMNP*, XVI (1837), No. 11, pp. 391–2.

45. Barsukov, *RS*, pp. 167–70. On Alexis's doctors at this time see Richter, pp. 289 ff. For accounts of the diseases that Alexis may have been suffering from see D. A. K. Black, 'Excretary System Diseases', *Encyclopaedia Britannica*, 1973, Macropaedia, VII, esp. pp. 56–8.

46. Platon, *Istoriia russkoi tserkvi*, Moscow, 1829, II, pp. 216–22; Palmer, V, pp. 912–16 (whose translation I have amended).

47. Barsukov, *RS*, VIII, pp. 174–5; Berkh, I, pp. 298–9.

48. Shusherin, *Izvestiia*, 1871, p. 91; Barsukov, *RS*, VIII, pp. 172–3; Kapterev, II, pp. 361–5. In accordance with Alexis's wishes, Nikon was eventually allowed to return to the 'New Jerusalem' Monastery and resume the building programme there which had been suspended in 1666.

Chapter X Legacies and Reputations

1. The expression is T. K. Rabb's – see his *The Struggle for Stability in Early Modern Europe*, New York, 1975.

2. Bartenev, *SP*, pp. 87 ff.

3. E.g. in his letter to Romodanovskii,

ZORI, II, pp. 771 ff., and, for that matter, in his diatribe against Nikita of the Sabbas Monastery, see pp. 72–3 above.

4. Alexis collected historical documents as well as chronicles – see *DTP*, I (*RIB*, Vol. 21). He is also reputed to have aspired to writing history, and some of his papers suggest that this was so, though his motive would have been self-aggrandizement, not the creation of a disinterested record.

5. The phrase 'divinely crowned wearer of the purple' occurs in the official acts of the election of the Patriarch Ioasaf in 1667 – Palmer, III, p. 449. On the regalia, *DAI*, VI, 204–6. Typically he had three expert valuations made (by a Greek, a German and a Russian) before deciding what to pay.

6. *ASBAR*, IV, pp. 83–5.

7. Solov'ev, III, 745–6.

8. M. Perrie, 'The Popular Image of Ivan the Terrible', *SEER*, Vol. 56, 2 (1978), pp. 275–86.

9. Vimina, p. 321. (The Swedish and Syrian references have already been cited.)

10. Louis XIV, *Mémoires*, English trans., 2 vols, London, 1806.

11. This term was used in the act deposing Nikon – *SGGD*, IV, pp. 182–6; *PSZ*, I pp. 629–31. On his insistence on the title abroad, see Gordon, p. 89.

12. Zaozerskii, pp. 12–13.

13. Solov'ev, III, p. 619.

14. Additional examples concern his instructions to Ordyn-Nashchokin in 1660 and the case of Mikhail Pleshcheev (Gurliand, pp. 289–90 and 303–4).

15. Kotoshikhin, VIII.

16. Berkh, II, pp. 132–9 and 147; R. Crummey, 'The Origins of the Noble Official' in Pintner and Rowney, pp. 46–75, especially Table III–1.

17. A. Iakovlev, *Prikaz sbora ratnykh liudei 1637–1653gg.*, Moscow, 1917, pp. 544–5. In other areas the peasant commune, overseen by the regional *prikaznaia izba*, fulfilled such functions.

18. Demidova in Druzhinin (Kafengauz *Festschrift*), and N. V. Ustiugov, 'Evoliutsiia prikaznoga stroia russkogo gosudarstva v xvii v' in the same work, pp. 134–67.

19. Gurliand, pp. 337–48.

20. Some of them were sent to take courses in grammar and Latin at the school set up in 1655 by Simeon Polotskii – Zabelin, 'Dliia biografii Sil'vestra Medved'eva', *Opyty*, I, pp. 194–202.

21. 'Let him reign following in the steps of . . . my father; and wage war against enemies, trusting in Christ the King of immortal glory' – Alexis's testament, Palmer, V, p. 913.

22. Major-General Rusinov, quoted by L. Beskrovnyi, *Russkaia armiia i flot xviii v*, Moscow, 1958, p. 7

23. Hellie, pp. 269 and 218; also pp. 196 and 198–201.

24. W. Tooke, *History of Russia*, II, London, 1800, p. 29.

25. See Billington, *The Icon and the Axe*, p. 673, note 134.

26. Ustiugov and Chaev in Druzhinin, pp. 295–329.

27. L. Stone, *The Causes of the English Revolution*, London, 1972.

28. One of the more interesting projects, suggested by van Sweden, involved the manufacture of woollen cloth with wool from imported 'Spanish, English and maritime sheep' tended by specially trained shepherds – *DTP* (*RIB*, 21), p. 1305.

29. *ZORI*, II, pp. 25–8.

30. *Ibid.*, II, p. 5; Lebedev, *Geografiia*, p. 99. In fact an illiterate Cossack seafarer, Simeon Dezhnev, had sailed from the River Kolyma to the mouth of the river Anadyr, through the Bering Straits, as early as 1648, but it is uncertain if or when Alexis learned of this, and in any case the route was not passable every year because of ice – see R. H. Fisher, *The Voyage of Semen Dezhnev in 1648: Bering's Precursor* (Hakluyt Society, second series, Vol. 159), London 1981, Chapter 10.

31. Kozlovskii, *Pochta*, I; A. N. Vigilev, *Istoriia otechestvennoi pochty*, I, Moscow, 1977. This last development is usually attributed to Ordyn-Nashchokin, but the fact that the Private Office supervised the initiation of the service points to Alexis's personal involvement – see Gurliand, p. 299.

32. *Dneval'nye*, p. 274.

33. *Povs*, II, pp. 153–4; Barsukov, *RS*, p. 485. (Alexis's letters of condemnation and praise to Romodanovskii have already been cited.)
34. Collins, p. 110.
35. Barsukov, *RS*, IV, pp. 421–3.
36. For a valuable account of the treatment accorded to foreigners in the Muscovite service, see G. M. Phipps, 'Britons in Russia: 1613–82', *Societas*, VII, 1 (1977), pp. 19–45.
37. See A. Ye Golobinskii, *Istoriia kanonizatsii sviatykh v russkoi tserkvi*, Moscow, 1894.
38. Sakharov, p. 31.
39. J. Cracraft, *The Church Reform of Peter the Great*, London, 1971, p. 306.
40. See V. Weidlé, *Russia Absent and Present*.

Select Bibliography

* Works containing Alexis's own writings
† Other primary sources
‡ Contemporary memoirs and travellers' accounts

Abetsedarskii, L. S. *Belorussiia i Rossiia*, Minsk, 1978
— *Belorusy v Moskve xvii v*, Minsk, 1957
— & Volkov, M. Ya. *Russko-Belorusskie sviazi*, Minsk, 1963
†*Akty Istoricheskie (AI)*, 5 vols, St Petersburg, 1841–2
†*Akty sobrannye v bibliotekakh i arkhivakh Rossiiskoi imperii Arkheograficheskoiu Ekspeditseiu Imperatorskoi Akademii Nauk (ASBAR)* 4 vols, St Petersburg, 1836
†*Akty zapadnoi i iugo-zapadnoi Rossii*, St Petersburg, 1853
Alpatov, M. A. *Russkaia istoricheskaia mysl' i zapadnaia Evrope xvii – pervaia chetvert' xviii veka*, Moscow, 1976
Andreyev, N. *Studies in Muscovy: Western Influence and Byzantine Inheritance*, London, 1970
Andreev, V. V. *Raskol i ego znachenie v narodnoi russkoi istorii*, St Petersburg, 1870
†Ardashev, N. N. *Raskhodnye knigi i stolpy pomestnago prikaza (1626–1659gg)*, I, Moscow, 1910
Arkhangel'skii, M. O. *Sobornom Ulozhenii Tsaria Alekseia Mikhailovicha 1649 (7158) g. v otnoshenii k pravoslavnoi russkoi tserkvi*, St Petersburg, 1881
Arsen'ev, Iu. V. 'K istorii Oruzheinago Prikaza v xvii veke: Oruzheinichestvo boiarina G. G. Pushkina (1647–1655)', *Vestnik arkheologii i istorii*, xvi (1904), pp. 131–98
Artsykhovskii, A. V. *et al.* (eds), *Ocherki russkoi kul'tury xvii veka*, 2 parts, Moscow, 1979
†Attmann, A. *et al.* (eds.), *Ekonomicheskie sviazi mezhdu Rossiei i Shvetsii v xvii v.*, Moscow–Stockholm, 1978

‡Avvakum *Life of the Archpriest Avvakum* (trans. J. Harrison and H. Mirrlees), London, 1924 (See also Gudzii)
Bain, R. Nisbet *The First Romanovs*, London, 1905
Bakhrushin, S. V. 'Moskovskoe vosstanie 1648g', *Nauchnye trudy*, II, Moscow, 1954, pp. 46–91
Baklanova, N. A. 'Postanovka moskovskikh prikazov v xvii v', *Trudy gosudarstvennogo istoricheskogo muzeia*, vyp. 3, Moscow, 1926, pp. 53–100
— 'Privoznye tovary', *Ocherki po istorii torgovli i promyshlennosti*, Moscow, 1928, pp. 5–118
Bantysh-Kamenskii, N. N. *Obzor vneshnykh snoshenii Rossii (po 1800 god)*, Part II, Moscow, 1896
Baron, S. H. *Muscovite Russia*, London, 1980
‡ — (ed.), *The Travels of Olearius in Seventeenth Century Russia*, Stanford, 1967
†Barskov, Ya. L. *Pamiatniki pervykh let russkogo staroobriadchestva*, St Petersburg, 1912
†Barsov, Ye. V., ed., 'Akty otnosiashchiesia k istorii Solovetskogo bunta', *ChOIDR*, Book 4, 1883, smes', pp. 1–92
*Barsukov, A. *Rod Sheremetevykh*, 8 vols, St Petersburg, 1881–1904
— *Spiski gorodovykh voevod*, St Petersburg, 1902
Barsukov, N. A. *Solovetskoe vosstanie (1668–1676gg.)*, Petrozavodsk, 1954
*Bartenev, P. (ed) *Pis'ma tsaria Alekseia Mikhailovicha k P. S. Khomiakovu 1656–7*, Moscow, 1861
* — (ed.) *Sobranie pisem Tsaria Alekseia Mikhailovicha s prilozheniem ulozheniia sokol'nich'ia puti*, Moscow, 1856
Bartenev, S. P. *Moskovskii Kreml' v starinu i*

teper', 2 vols, St Petersburg, 1912–18

Bazilevich, K. V. *Denezhnaia reforma Alekseia Mikhailovicha i vosstanie v Moskve v 1662g.*, Moscow–Leningrad, 1936

'Elementy merkantilizma v ekonomicheskoi politike pravitel'stva Alekseia Mikhailovicha', *Uchenye zapiski Moskovskogo gosudarstvennogo universiteta Istoriial*, xiii, 1940, pp. 3–34

† — & Piontkovskii, S. A. (eds) *Gorodskie vosstaniia v Moskovskom gosudarstve xvii v: Sbornik dokumentov*, Leningrad, 1936

†Beliavskii, M. T. (ed.) *Dvorianskaia imperiia xvii veka (osnovnye zakonodatel'nye akty)*. *Sbornik dokumentov*, Moscow, 1960

†Belokurov, S. A. (ed.) *Dela tainogo prikaza (RIB, xxi)*, St Petersburg, 1907

† — (ed.) *Dneval'nye zapiski prikaza tainykh del 7165–7183gg.*, ChOIDR, 1908, Book 1, otdel 1, pp. 1–224 and Book 2, otdel 1, pp. 225–314

— *Iz dukhovnoi zhnizni moskovskago obshchestva xvii v.*, Moscow, 1903

— *Materialy dlia russkoi istorii*, Moscow, 1888

— 'Moskovskii pechatnyi dvor v 1649', ChOIDR, 1887, IV, smes', pp. 1–32

* — (ed.) *Pis'ma Tsaria Alekseia Mikhailovicha (PRF, V)*, Moscow, 1896

— *Plany goroda Moskvy xvii veka*, Moscow, 1898

Bennet, D. J., Jr. 'The Idea of Kingship in 17th century Russia' – unpublished Harvard Ph.D dissertation, 1967

Berkh, V. N. *Tsarstvovanie Tsaria Alekseia Mikhailovicha*, St Petersburg, 1831

Billington, J. H. *The Icon and the Axe*, London, 1966.

Boboriev, G. 'Paisii Ligarid (1662–1666)', *Russkii Arkhiv*, 1, 1893, pp. 5–32

†Bogoiavlenskii, S. K. 'Moskovskii teatr pri Tsariakh Aleksee i Petre: Materialy', ChOIDR

— 'Prikaznye d'iaki xvii v', *Istoricheskie zapiski*, I

— *Prikaznye sud'i xvii v*, Moscow–Leningrad, 1946

Brückner, A. *Beiträge zur Kulturgeschichte Russlands im xvii Jahrhundert*, Leipzig, 1887

Buganov, V. I. 'Kto byl glavnym predvoditelem "mednogo bunta" 1662g v Moskvei?', *Voprosy Istorii*, 40, No. 3 (March 1965)

— *Moskovskoe vosstanie 1662g.*, Moscow, 1964

† — *Vosstanie 1662g. v Moskve: Sbornik Dokumentov*, Moscow, 1964

Bushkevich, P. *The Merchants of Muscovy*, Cambridge, 1980

Charykov, N.V. *Posol'stvo v Rime is sluzhba v Moskve Pavla Meneziia 1637–1694*, St Petersburg, 1906

Cherepnin, L. V. *Zemskie sobory russkogo gosudarstva v xvi–xvii vv.*, Moscow, 1978

Cherniavsky, M. 'The Old Believers and the New Religion', *Slavic Review*, XXV, 1 (1966), pp. 1–39

— *Tsar and People*, New Haven, 1961

Chicherin, B. *Oblastnye uchrezhdeniia Rossii v xvii–m veke*, Moscow, 1856

Chistozvanov, A. N. 'Nekotorye aspekty problemy genezisa absoliutizma', *Voprosy Istorii*, 43, No. 5 (1968), pp. 46–62

‡Collins, S. *The Present State of Russia*, London, 1671

Conybeare, F. C. *Russian Dissenters* (Harvard Theological Studies, X), Cambridge (Mass.), 1921

†*Dela tainago prikaza*, 4 vols (*RIB*, Vols 21, 22, 23 and 38), St Petersburg/Leningrad, 1904–1926

†*Delo o Patriarkhe Nikone*, St Petersburg, 1897

Dewey, H. W. 'Old Muscovite Concepts of Injured Honour', *SR*, xxvii, 4 (1969), pp. 594–603

†Dopolneniia k aktam istoricheskim (DAI), 6 vols, St Petersburg, 1846–75

Druzhinin, N. M. *et al.* (eds) *Absoliutizm v Rossii (xvii–xviiivv)*, Moscow, 1964

†*Dvortsovye razriady (DR)*, III, St Petersburg, 1852

Eikhgorn, V. 'Ostavka A.L. Ordyn-Nashchokin', *ZhMNP*, June 1877

Epifanov, P.P. ' "Uchenie i khitrost' ratnogo stroeniia pekhotnykh liudei". Iz istorii russkoi armii xvii v', *Uchenye zapiski Moskovskogo gosudarstvennogo universiteta (Istoriia)*, No. 167 (1954), pp. 77–98

Esper, T. 'Military Self-Sufficiency and Weapons Technology in Muscovite Russia', *SR*, 28, No. 2 (1969), pp. 185–208

Farmakovskii, V. 'O protivogosudarstvennom elemente v raskole', *Otechestvennye Zapiski*, 1866, Books 23, pp. 487–518, and 24, pp. 629–57

Fedotov, G.P. *The Russian Religious Mind*, 2 vols, Cambridge (Mass.), 1946 and Belmont (Mass.), 1975

— *Sviatoi Filipp, Mitropolit Moskovskii*, Paris, 1928

— *Sviatye drevnei Rusi: x–xvii st.*, Paris, 1931

Findeisen, N. *Ocherki po istorii musyki v Rossii*, I, Moscow–Leningrad, 1928

Galaktionov, I., & Chistiakova, E. *A. L. Ordyn-Nashchokin*, Moscow, 1961

Gibbenet, N. *Istoricheskoe izsledovanie dela Patriarkha Nikona*, 2 vols, St Petersburg, 1882–4

†Golubtsov, A. *Pamiatniki prenii o vere*, *ChOIDR*, 2 (1892)

‡Gordon, P. *Passages from the Diary of General Patrick Gordon of Auchleuchries A. D. 1635–1699*, Aberdeen, 1859. (A fuller, but still incomplete, version of the Diary is M.C. Posselt (ed.), *Tagebuch des Generals Patrick Gordon*, 3 vols, Moscow – St Petersburg 1849–53).

†‡Gudzii, N. K.; Gusev, V. E. *et al.* (eds) *Zhizn' Protopopa Avvakuma im samim napisannoe i drugie ego sochineniia*, Moscow, 1960

†Gurliand, I. Ya (ed.) *Dela tainago prikaza*, II and III (*RIB*, Vols 22 and 23), St Petersburg, 1908 and 1904

'Ivan Gebdon – Kommissarius i Rezident', *Materialy po istorii administratsii Moskovskogo gosudarstva vtoroi poloviny xvii v.* Iaroslavl', 1903, pp. 37–49

— **Prikaz velikogo gosudaria tainykh del*, Iaroslav', 1902

Hellie, R. *Enserfment and Military Change in Muscovy*, Chicago, 1971

Hübbenet, see Gibbenet

Iakovlev, A. *Prikaz sbora ratnykh liudei 1637–1653*, Moscow, 1917

Ikonnikov, V. S. 'Blizhnii boiarin A. L. Ordin-Nashchokin', *Russkaia starina*, xl (October–November 1883), pp. 17–66 and 273–308

— 'Syn blizhniago boiarina A. L. Ordina-Nashchokina', *Russkii Arkhiv*, 12 (1886), pp. 521–3

†*Iz arkhiva tainykh del (sobytiia pridvornoi zhizni Tsaria Alekseia Mikhailovicha)*, *SN*, Book 15, (ed. A. A. Popov) Leningrad, 1911

Kalash, V. V. (ed.) *Tri veka*, I, St Petersburg, 1912

Kapterev, N. F. *Patriarkh Nikon i Tsar' Aleksei Mikhailovich*, 2 vols, 1909–12

Kartashev, A. V. *Ocherki po istorii russkoi tserkvi*, 2 vols, Paris, 1959

Keep, J. H. L. 'The Decline of the Zemskii Sobor', *SEER*, Vol. 36 (1957), pp. 100–122

— 'The Regime of Filaret 1619–1633', *SEER*, Vol. 38, No. 91 (June 1969)

Kliuchevskii, V. *The Rise of the Romanovs* (trans. L. Archibald), London, 1970

— 'Zapadnoe vlianie i tserkovnyi raskol v Rossii v xvii v', *Ocherki i rechi*, Moscow, 1913

†*Knigi razriadnyia po offitsial'nym onykh spiskam*, St Petersburg, 1855

†Kologrivov, S. N. 'Zapisnye vznosnye knigi bol'shomu gosudarevu nariadu', *Vestnik arkheologii is istorii*, vyp. 17, St Petersburg, 1906, otdel 2, pp. 84–124

Korf, S. A. *Administrativnaia institutsiia v Rossii*, 3 vols, St Petersburg, 1910

Kostomarov, I. I. *Ocherk domashnei zhizni i nravov velikorusskago naroda v xvi i xvii stoletiakh*, St Petersburg, 1860

‡Kotoshikhin, G. *O Rossii v tsarstvovanii Alekseia Mikhailovicha*, St Petersburg-1906

‡Koyet, B. *Posol'stro Kunraada fan Klenka k tsariam Alekseiu Mikhailovichu i Fedoru Alekseevichu*, St Petersburg, 1900

Kozlovskii, I. P. *Fedor Mikhailovich Rtischev*, Kiev, 1906

— *Perviia pochty i pervye pochtmeistery v Moskovskom gosudarstve* 2 vols, Warsaw, 1913

‡Krizhanich, Iu. *Russkoe gosudarstvo v polovine xvii veka*, 2 vols, 1859

— *Politika* (ed. M. N. Tikhomirov), Moscow, 1965

Kubala, L. *Wojna moskiewska r. 1654–1655*, Warsaw, 1911

†Kudriavtsev, I. M. (ed.) *Artaksersovo deistvo. Pervaia p'iesa russkogo teatra xvii v.*, Moscow–Leningrad, 1957

Kurdiumov, M. 'Zapiski o tseremoniiakh proiskhodivshikh pri dvore tsaria Alekseia Mikhailovicha po sluchaiu ob''iavleniia pokhoda protiv pol'skogo Korolia Iana-Kazimira', in *S. F. Platonovu ucheniki druz'ia i pochitateli*, St Petersburg, 1911, pp. 311–34

‡Kurts, B. G. (ed.) 'Sostoianie Rossii v 1650–1655gg. po doneseniiam Rodesa', *ChOIDR*, 253, 2, 1915 (Moscow, 1914), pp. 1–268

Kutepov, N. I. *Tsarskaia okhota na Rusi Tsarei Mikhaila Fedorovicha i Alekseia Mikhailovicha xvii vek (Okhota na Rusi*, II),

St Petersburg, 1898

*†Lamanskii, V. (ed.), 'Prikaz tainykh del', *ZORI*, II, St Petersburg, 1861

†Latkin, V. *Materialy dlia istorii zemskikh soborov xvii stoletiia*, St Petersburg, 1884

Lebedev, D. M. *Geografiia v Rossii xvii veka*, Moscow–Leningrad, 1949

Lebedev, V. I., *et al.* (eds) *Khrestomatiia po istorii SSSR xvi–xvii vv.*, I, Moscow, 1949

Leitsch, W. 'Russische Geschichte von der wahl Michail Romanovs', *Jahr bücher für Osteuropas* (neue Folge), 9, 10, 11, 1961–3 [A guide to sources.]

Leonid, Archimandrite *Chin postavleniia na tsarstvo Tsaria Alekseia Mikhailovicha*, (Pamiatniki Drevnei Pis'mennosti, No. 16), 1881

Lewitter, L. R. 'Poland, the Ukraine and Russia in the 17th century', *SEER*, XXVII (1948–9), pp. 157–71 and 414–29

Likhachev, D. C. *Puteshestviia russkikh poslov xvi–xvii vv.*, Moscow–Leningrad, 1954

Liubavskii, M. K. *Russkaia istoriia 17v. i pervoi chetverti 18v. Lektsii chitannyia na vysshikh zhenskikh kursakh v 1913–1914* [Notes taken by a student], 2 vols, Moscow, 1913–14

Loewenson, L. 'The Moscow Rising of 1648', *SEER*, XXVII, 68 (December 1948), pp. 146–56

Luppov, S. P. *Kniga v Rossii v xvii v.*, Leningrad, 1970

Lyseck, A. *Relation*, Salzburg, 1676 (Russian translation in *ZhMNP*, XVI, 11, 1837)

Mal'tsev, A. N. *Rossiia i Belorussia v seredine xvii v.*, Moscow, 1974

Man'kov, A. G. (ed.) *Inostrannye izvestiia o vosstanii Stepana Razina*, Leningrad, 1975

— *Ulozhenie 1649 goda: kodeks feodal'noga prava Rossii*, Leningrad, 1980

— *Razvitie krepostnogo prava v Rossii vo vtoroi polivine xvii*, Moscow–Leningrad, 1962

— (ed.) *Zapiski inostrantsev o vosstanii Stepana Razina*, Leningrad, 1968

Markevich, A. I. *Istoriia mestnichestva v Moskovskom gosudarstve v xv–xvii veke*, Odessa, 1883

Mayerberg, A. *Voyage en Moscovie*, Leide, 1688 [First, Latin, edition, 1661; Russian translation, Moscow, 1874].

Medlin, W-K. *Moscow and East Rome*, Neuchâtel, 1952

Miège, G. *A Relation of Three Embassies from his Sacred Majestie Charles II to the Great Duke of Muscovie, the King of Sweden and the King of Denmark*, London, 1669

Miliukin, A. S. *Priezd inostrantsev v moskovskoe gosudarstvo*, St Petersburg, 1909

†Moskvitianin, No. 14, 1851

†Mukhanov Sbornik, 1836

Neubauer, H. *Car und Selbstherrscher: Beiträge zur Geschichte der Autokratie in Russland* (Veröffentheilungen der Osteuropa-Instituts, München, Vol. 22), Wiesbaden, 1964

*†Novikov, N. I. (ed.) *Drevniaia rossiiskaia vivliofika (DRV)*

†Novombergskii, N. *Materialy po istorii meditsyna v Rossii*, St Petersburg, 1906
Slovo i delo Gosudarevy, I, Moscow, 1911

Novosel'skii, A. A. *Votchinnik i ego khoziaistvo v xvii veke*, Moscow–Leningrad, 1929

† — (ed.) *Vosstanie 1662g v Moskve* & Ustiugov (eds) *Ocherki istorii SSSR. Period feodalizma. xvii v.*, Moscow, 1955

O'Brien, C. Bickford 'Agriculture in the Russian War Economy in the later seventeenth century', *American Slavic & East European Review*, Vol. 8 (1949), pp. 167–74

— *Muscovy and the Ukraine from the Pereiaslavl Agreement to the Truce of Andrusovo, 1654–1667* (University of California Publications in History, No. 74), 1963

Orlovskii, I. I. *Smolenskii pokhod Tsaria Alekseia Mikhailovicha v 1654 godu (Pamiatnaia khizhka Smolenskoi Gubernii na 1906 god)*, Smolensk, 1906, prilozhenie no. 6, Smolensk, 1905

†Palmer, W. *The Patriarch and the Tsar*, 6 vols, London, 1871–6

†*Pamiatniki diplomaticheskikh snoshenii drevnei Rossii s derzhavami inostrannymi (PDS)*, 10 vols, St Petersburg, 1851–71

Pascal, P. *Avvakum et les débuts du raskol. La crise religieuse au xvii siècle en Russie*, Paris, 1938

— 'La durée des voyages en Russie au xvii-eme siècle', *Revue des études slaves*, No. 27 (1951), pp. 209–19

‡Paul of Aleppo *The Travels of Macarius, Patriarch of Antioch* (trans. F. C. Belfour), 2 vols, London, 1836

Pervye p'iesy russkogo teatra, Moscow, 1972

Petrikeev, D. I. *Krupnoe krespostnoe khoziaistvo xvii v. Po materialam votchiny boiarina B. I. Morozova*, Leningrad, 1967

Pintner, W. & Rowney, D. (eds) *Russian*

Officialdom, London, 1980

†*Pis'ma russkikh gosudarei i drugikh osob tsarskago semeistva (PRG)*, I, Moscow, 1848 (for fragments of Nikon's letters to Alexis). See also Belokurov, *Pis'ma*

Platonov, S. F. 'Moskovskoe pravitel'stvo pri pervykh Romanovykh', *Sochineniia*, I, St Petersburg, 1919, pp. 339–406

— 'Tsar' Aleksei Mikhailovich: opyt kharakteristiki', V. Kallash (ed.), *Tri veka*, I. pp. 85–114

†*Polnoe sobranie zakonov rossiiskoi imperii (PSZ)*, 45 vols, St Petersburg, 1830–1916

†Popov, N. A. & Somokrasov, D. (eds) *Akty Moskovskago Gosudarstva*, 3 vols, St Petersburg, 1890–1901, III (for Razriadnyi Prikaz material to 1664)

†*Posviadnevnykh dvortsovykh vremeni Gosudarei Tsarei . . . Mikhaila Fedorovicha i Alekseia Mikhailovicha*, 2 parts, 1769

Raikov, B. E. *Ocherki po istorii geliotsentricheskogo mirovozreniia v Rossiei*, Moscow–Leningrad, 1937

Rainov T. *Nauka v Rossii xi–xvii vekov*, Moscow–Leningrad, 1940

Razumovskii, D. V. 'Gosudarevy pevchie d'iaki xvii v', *Sbornik obshchestva drevnerusskogo iskusstva*, Moscow, 1873, otel 1, pp. 153–81

‡Reutenfels, J. *De Rebus Moschoviticus*, Padova, 1680 (Russian translation in *ChOIDR*, iv (1895) and iii (1905))

†Richter, W. M. von *Geschichte der Medicin in Russland*, 2 vols, Moscow, 1815

Russkii biograficheskii slovar', 25 vols, St Petersburg, 1896–1918 *(RBS)*

Sakharov, A. M. *Ocherki istorii SSSR: xvii vek*, Moscow, 1958

†Semevskii, M. I. (ed.) *Arkhiv kniazia F. A. Kurakina*, 10 vols, St Petersburg, 1890–1902

Serbinina, K. N. (ed.) *Kniga bol'shomu chertezhu*, Moscow–Leningrad, 1950

†Šeptyckyj, A. (ed.) *Monumenta Ucrainae Historica*, Vols 1–12, Rome 19 –1975

Ševčenko, I. 'A Byzantine Source of Muscovite Ideology', *Harvard Slavic Studies*, 2 (1954), pp. 141–79

Shchepot'ev, L. *Blizhnii boiarin A. S. Matveev kak kul'turnyi i politicheskii deiatel' xvii veka*, St Petersburg, 1906

Shusherin, I. *Zhitie Sviateishago Patriarkha Nikona*, St Petersburg, 1817

†Shvetsova, Ye. A. *Krest'ianskaia voina pod predvoditel'stvom Stepana Razina*, 4 vols Moscow, 1954–76

†Smirnov, P. P. 'Chelobitnye dvorian i dete boiarskikh vsekh gorodov v pervoi polovine xvii', *ChOIDR*, 254, No. 3 (1915) Part 1, pp. 1–73

† — 'Neskol'ko dokumentov k istori sobornago ulozheniia i zemskago sobor 1648–9 godov', *ChOIDR* (1913) smes' 1

— 'O nachale Sobornogo Ulozheniia zemskago sobora 1648–1649gg', *ZhMNP* 47, No. 9 (September 1913), pp. 36–66

— *Posadskie liudi i ikh klassovaia bor'ba dc serediny xvii veka*, 2 vols, Moscow– Leningrad, 1947–8

Smirnov, P. S. *Istoriia russkago raskola staroobriadstva*, St Petersburg, 1895

— *Vnutrennie voprosy v raskole v xvii v.*, S Petersburg, 1898

†*Sobornoe Ulozhenie:* The edition used is *Ulozhenie, po kotoromu sud i rosprava vc vsiakikh delakh v rossiiskom gosudarstvon proizvoditsia*, St Petersburg, 1780

†*Sobranie gosudarstvennykh gramot i dogovorou khraniashchikhsi v gosudarstvennoi kollegi inostrannykh del (SGGD)*, 4 parts, Moscow, 1813–28

Solov'ev, S. M. *Istoriia Rossii s drevneishikh vremen*, 15 vols, St Petersburg, 1894 (an various other editions)

Spinka, M. 'Nikon and the Subjugation o the Russian Church to the State', *Church History*, X (1941), pp. 347–66

†Stroev, P. M. (ed.) *Vykhody Gosudare Tsarei i velikikh kniazei Mikhaila Fedoro vicha, Alekseia Mikhailovicha, Fedor Alekseevicha (VT)*, St Petersburg, 1844

‡Struys, J. *The Perillous and Most Unhapp Voyages of John Struys*, 2nd English edi tion, London, 1684

†Subbotin, N. I. (ed.) *Materialy dlia istori raskola*, 9 vols, Moscow, 1875–90

Szeftel, M. *Russian Institutions and Culture u to Peter the Great,*

Tatarskii, I. *Simeon Polotskii, ego zhizn' deiatel'nost'*, Moscow, 1886

†Theiner, A. (ed.) *Monuments historiques rela tifs aux reignes d'Alexis Michailowitch Feodor III et Pierre le Grand, Czars de Russie*, Rome, 1859

†Tikhomirov, M. N. & Yepifanov, P. P. *Sobornoe Ulozhenie 1649g*, Moscow, 1961

— 'Novgorodskoe vosstanie 1650g.', *Istoricheskie zapiski*, No. 7, (1940), pp. 91–114

— *Pskovskoe vosstanie 1650g*, Moscow–Leningrad, 1935

Tikhonravov, N. *Russkie dramaticheskie proizvedeniia 1672–1725*, I, St Petersburg, 1874

†Tomašivskyj, M. *Monumenta Vaticana res gestas Ukrainae illustrantia*, I (1648–57), Fontes Historiae Ucrainae, xvi, L'vov, 1919

Torke, H-J. *Die Staatsbedingte Gesellschaft im Moskauer Reich: Zar und Zemlia in der altrussischen Herrschaftsverfassung 1613–1689*, Studien zur Geschichte Osteuropas, xvii, Leiden, 1974

*'Tsar Alexis and his Rules of Falconry', *SEER*, 3 (1924–5), pp. 63–4

†Undol'skii, V. M. 'Otzyv Patriarkha Nikona ob Ulozhenii Tsaria Alekseia Mikhailovicha: Noviia materialy dlia istorii zakonodatel'stva v Rossii', *Russkii arkhiv*, No. 7 (1886), pp. 605–20

— 'Zamechaniia dlia istorii tserkovnogo peniia v Rossii', *ChOIDR*, No. 3 (1846), pp. 24 ff.

†Uroff, B. 'Grigorii Karpovich Kotoshikhin, "On Russia in the Reign of Alexis Mikhailovich": an Annotated Translation', Columbia University Ph.D. thesis, 1970

Ustiugov, N. V. (ed.) *Voprosy sotsial'no-ekonomicheskoi istorii i istochnikovedeniia perioda feodalizma v Rossii* (Festschrift for Novosel'skii), Moscow, 1961

— Tikhonov, Yu. A., & Iakovlev, P. T. (eds) *Russkoe gosudarstvo v xvii veke*, Moscow, 1961

Veretennikov, V. I. *Istoriia tainoi kantseliarii*, Khar'kov, 1911

Vernadsky, G. *The Tsardom of Moscow 1547–1682* (Vol. 5 of his History of Russia), 2 parts, New Haven–London, 1969

Veselovskii, S.B. *D'iaki i pod'iachie xv–xvii vv*, Moscow, 1975

— 'Smety voennykh sil Moskovskago gosudarstva 1661–1663gg', *ChOIDR*, 238, No. 3 (1911), pp. 1–60

Viktorov *Opisanie zapisnykh knig i bumag starinnogo dvortsogo prikaza*, Moscow, 1883

‡Vimina, A. *Historia delle Guerre civile di Polonia . . . Relazione della Moscovia e Svetia e loro governo*, Venezia, 1671

Volkov, M. Ya. 'O stanovlenii absoliutizma v Rossii', *Istoriia SSSR*, 15, No. 1 (Jan.-Feb. 1970), pp. 90–104

†Waugh, D. C. 'Azbuka znameni lits', *OSP* (new series), X (1977), pp. 46–50

† — News of the False Messiah', *Jewish Social Studies*, xli, 3–4 (1979), pp. 301–22

‡Wickhardt, C. L. *Moskowitische Reisebeschreibung*, Wien [1677]

Wolff, R. L. 'The Three Romes: The Migration of an Ideology and the Making of an Autocrat', *Daedalus*, Spring 1959

Zabelin, I. Ye. *Domashnyi byt" russkikh tsarei v xvi i xvii st.*, Part I (4th, enlarged, edition with supplement), Moscow, 1918; Part II (posthumous edition), Moscow, 1915

— *Opyty izucheniia russkoi drevnosti i istorii*, I, Moscow, 1872

Zaborovskii, L. V. *Rossiia, Rech' Pospolita i Shvetsiia v seredine xvii v*, Moscow, 1981

Zaozerskii, A. I. 'K voprosu o sostave i znachenii zemskikh soborov', *ZhMNP*, 21 (June 1909), pp. 299–352

— *Tsarskaia votchina xvii v. Iz istorii khoziaistvennoi i prikaznoi politiki Tsaria Alekseia Mikhailovicha*, Moscow, 1937 (The first edition is entitled *Tsar Aleksei Mikhailovich v svoem khoziaistve*, Petrograd, 1917)

*†*Zapiski otdeleniia russkoi slavianskoi arkheologii (ZORI)* – See Lamanskii, etc.

†*Zapisnye knigi Moskovskogo stola (1636–65)* (*RIB*, Vols 2, 10, 11, 13)

Zenkovsky, S. A. 'The Russian Church Schism: its Background and Repercussions', *Russian Review*, 16, No. 4 (1957), pp. 37–58

— *Russkoe staroobriadchestvo: dukhovnoe dvizhenie semnadtsago veka* (Forum Slavicum, 21), München, 1970

Zernova, A. S. *Knigi kirillovskoi pechati izdannye v Moskve v xvi–xvii vekakh svodnyi katalog*, Moscow, 1958 (Bibliography)

†Zertsalov, A. N. 'K istorii Moskovskogo miatezha 1648g.', *ChOIDR*, III (1893), smes'; and I, 1896, otdel 1, pp. 1–36

† — 'Novye dannye o zemskom sobore 1648–1649gg', *ChOIDR*, III (1887), otdel 4, pp. 1–80

† — 'Novyi istochnik dlia istorii Moskovskoi vosstanii 1648g.', *ChOIDR*, I (1893)

— 'O miatezhakh v gorode Moskve i v sele Kolomenskom 1648, 1662 i 1771gg.', *ChOIDR*, III (1890), otel 1, pp. 1–439

Zyzykin, M.V. *Patriarkh Nikon. Ego gosudarstvennye i kanonicheskie idei*, 3 vols, Warsaw, 1931–9

Index

absolutism, *see* autocracy

Academy of Sciences, Peter establishes, 248

Adam and Eve (play), 220

agriculture: use of magic in, 135; experiments in, 156–60, 242

Ahasuerus and Esther (play), 211, 220

alchemy, 134, 205

Alexander VII, Pope, 173

Alexander the Great, 13, 14, 187

Alexandria, Patriarch of: Nikon's trial, 166, 174–5,177, 178, 180; remains in Moscow, 182

Alexis, St, 5–6

Alexis, Tsar (1629–76)

character and interests: use of language, xii, 30, 111; love of falconry, 7, 25, 37, 64, 65; interest in music, 11, 205, 223; influence of Ivan the Terrible, 14, 69, 71, 231, 260 n.26; and sport, 24–5; religion, 30–2, Nikon's influence on, 31–2, 57, 73; concern for detail, 33–4, 206, 222; influence of Byzantium, 36, 49, 183, 230; love of ceremonial, 36–7, 55, 214, 233–4; widely read, 37, 204–5; campaign for moral regeneration, 54–5; conception of 'good order', 55, 67, 229–30; devotion to St Sabbas, 69–70; warmth and sympathy, 85–7, 131, 138–9, 244; obsession with the West, 108–9, 120–2, 223; rule-book on falconry, 118–20; image-building, pp.130–1, 142–3, 233–4; interest in

the occult, 134–5, 205–6; violent temper, 135; redecorates Kremlin, 187; new palace at Kolomenskoe, 187–9, 204; taste for merrymaking, 189, 219, 224–5; interest in the theatre, 210–11, 219–21; passion for history, 230–1; allegations of cruelty, 233

and the Church: liturgical reform, 55–61, 84, 89–90, 93–4, 104; pilgrimage to Uglich, 63–5; reintombment of first Patriarchs, 69–70, 74–5, 79–83; and the death of the Patriarch Joseph, 74–9; election of Patriarch of Moscow, 83–5, 245; relationships with Nikon deteriorates, 111–12, 122–31; as the 'angelic prince', 130–1; replacement of Nikon, 139–41; opposition to liturgical reform grows, 164; attempts to depose Nikon, 164–6, 237–8; tries to reconcile Old Believers, 166–7; reconciliation with Nikon urged, 167–8; and Nikon's return to Moscow, 168–72; treatment of Old Believers, 174, 217–18; Nikon's trial, 177–81; election of Nikon's successor, 183; reforms, 183–4; synod arraigns Avvakum, 185; sends gifts to Nikon, 185, 194–5, 216–17; Solovka rebellion, 195–6; as spiritual head of Muscovy, 218; relations with the Patriarchate, 236–8

286

Acknowledgements

Bodleian Library, Oxford: Fig. 8; British Library: Figs. 1, 2, 3, 4, 5, 6, 7, 9, 10; The Kirkham Studios: endpaper maps.

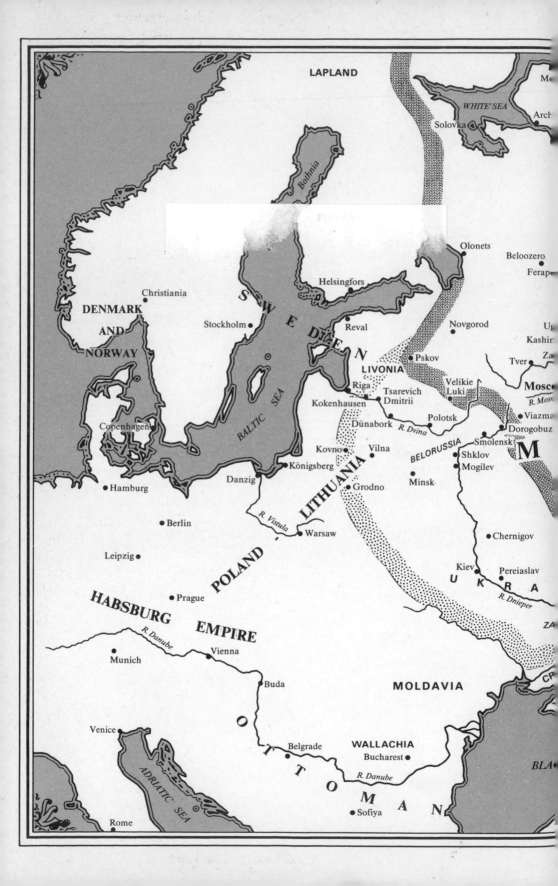